MARIO BOTTA
ARCHITECTURE AND MEMORY

MARIO BOTTA

ARCHITECTURE AND MEMORY

BOTTA

SilvanaEditoriale

MARIO BOTTA
ARCHITECTURE AND MEMORY

Bechtler Museum of Modern Art
January 30, 2014 – July 25, 2014

Board of Directors
Robert Bertges, Chair
Robert Lilien, Secretary
Lynn Good, Treasurer
John Boyer, President, Ex Officio

Exhibition concept
Mario Botta, Architect,
Mendrisio, Switzerland
John Boyer, President and CEO
Bechtler Museum of
Modern Art, Charlotte,
North Carolina

Exhibition coordination
Paola Pellandini
John Boyer
Shannon White
Ashley McCallister

Texts and documentation
Studio Mario Botta, Mendrisio

Photographs in the exhibition by
Robert Canfield
Enrico Cano
Alberto Flammer
Joël Lassiter
Pino Musi
Ralph Richter
Pietro Savorelli
Alo Zanetta
Fu Xing

B/W Prints
Digital elaboration and prints
with carbon black pigments
on acid free cotton paperboard
Hahnemühle 310g/m2
by Pino Musi, Photographer

Architecture models
Ivan Kunz, Andrea Biaggi
Stefano and Roberto Vismara
Simoné Salvadé

Technical installation
Shannon White
Allyson Burke
Dylan Chorneau
Christopher Gannon
Eric Olsen
Clayton Venhuisen

Press
Pam Davis

The exhibition at Bechtler
Museum of Modern Art was first
shown at Centre Dürrenmatt in
Neuchâtel (Switzerland) in
April 2, 2011 - July 31, 2011
and presents an extract of the
previous and major exhibition
held at the Mart Museum in
Rovereto (Italy) 2010 titled:
*Mario Botta.
Architetture 1960-2010*
MART Rovereto, Museo di Arte
Moderna e Contemporanea di
Trento e Rovereto
September 25, 2010 – January
23, 2011

ACKNOWLEDGMENTS
Mario Botta: Architecture and Memory at the Bechtler Museum of Modern Art is made possible by the generosity of Presenting Sponsor

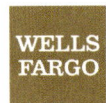

THE PRIVATE BANK

and these generous supporters:

Balfour Beatty Construction
Rodgers Builders

Wagner Murray Architects

This exhibition is also made possible with the support of the Swiss Arts Council Pro Helvetia

and in-kind support from WFAE

Catalogue

Editors
Paola Pellandini, Studio Mario Botta, Mendrisio
John Boyer, Bechtler Museum of Modern Art, Charlotte

Archive research
Maria Botta
With
Monica Grassi
Anna Meshale
Silvia Rossinelli

Documentation
Studio Mario Botta, Mendrisio
Andrea Albinolo
Elisiana di Bernardo
Emanuele Bressan
Juan Emanuel Campopiano
David De Prà
Francesa Molteni

Translation
Karen Ries for all essays
Elisiana di Bernardo
Paola Pellandini

Graphic Design
Studio Mario Botta, Mendrisio

Book cover
The Garnet Chapel
Photo by Enrico Cano

The renowned architect Mario Botta has designed some of the most striking cultural places in the world today. His public buildings – museums, libraries, theaters and sacred places – enhance the landscape throughout Europe, Asia and America. His work merges past and present in a contemporary language of architecture that goes beyond function to create places of transformational experiences.

Wells Fargo Private Bank is pleased to present this exhibition and catalogue, which together, showcase Botta's extraordinary works. The Private Bank serves our clients through a philosophy of continued innovation to arrive at a process that addresses their unique financial needs and aspirations.

We believe our goals are represented beautifully by this exhibition of exquisite architectural designs of originality and excellence, each uniquely serving its landscape and audience. Through this exhibition and catalogue, we invite you to experience the beauty of Botta's brilliant designs that are showcased so perfectly in the only building designed by him on the East Coast of the United States.

Madelyn L. Caple, CFP®
Regional Managing Director
Senior Vice President
Wells Fargo Private Bank

THE PRIVATE BANK

It is a great pleasure to present *Mario Botta: Architecture and Memory* at the Bechtler Museum of Modern Art. This project provides our visitors with a greater sense of context for Botta's remarkable achievement here in Charlotte. The exhibition gains additional power when designed for and shown in one of the buildings featured in the show. For the first time, the Bechtler can be seen among a variety of other museum commissions by Botta and, as a result, we gain a deeper appreciation for the evolution of his approach over the years. Moreover, we can sense more clearly his response to the cultural traditions and site-specific challenges of each location. Nuanced references to regional construction practices, the quiet celebration of local building materials and the dynamism and contrasts of the urban environment are revealed over a select group of building types. The choice of museums, libraries, theaters and places of worship was driven by their common objective as public realms that are intended to have a powerful and lasting effect on us as visitors. These are transformative spaces where we have the opportunity to enter as one kind of person and leave as another, as participants in an architectural experience that encourages in us a deeper appreciation of the buildings in our lives – the power of the built environment to inspire, mystify, comfort and educate.
Exhibitions of this scale and comprehensiveness require the support of many. We wish to thank our lead sponsor, Wells Fargo Private Bank, for the generosity they have shown not only in this instance but also for their early and frequent support of the museum and its efforts. This exhibition has received enthusiastic support from Swiss Ambassador Manuel Sager and we are very pleased to have received financial support from the Swiss Arts Council, Pro Helvetia. We are also grateful to these business leaders for their important support: Belk Inc., Childress Klein Properties, Electrolux, The Hartford, Balfour Beatty Construction, Rodgers and Wagner Murray Architects. We also wish to thank the museum's board of directors for their passion for and commitment to this exhibition.

None of these efforts would have been possible without the foresight, intelligence and supreme generosity of Andreas Bechtler and his family in the commitment of their collection to the city of Charlotte. It was Andreas who sensed that Botta would be the perfect designer for this new museum, and so we are doubly grateful for his many contributions to the success of this endeavor.

But in the end the most important thanks go to Mario Botta himself for giving our community a spectacular new architectural statement; one of profound presence and strength but also convincing intimacy and welcome. This exhibition and catalogue are meant to help us reflect on the central role that architecture plays in our lives. It forms the expectations of the young and it serves as reflections of our shared past to all. Its quality of design, the permanence of its materials and the skill of its execution all leave their imprint on us in ways that change us forever.

John Boyer
President and CEO
Bechtler Museum of Modern Art

Thank you!

Thanks to the Bechtler Museum of Modern Art in Charlotte for the organization of the exhibition "Architecture and memory," that introduces to the American public a significant part of the works shown in the retrospective "Mario Botta. Architetture 1960-2010" held at the MART museum in Rovereto, in 2010.
The possibility of showing my works of architecture within a space I myself designed allows them to acquire quite particular meanings.
Actually, visitors can immediately draw a parallelism between the museum spaces and the messages conveyed by the drawings, the photos and the models on display.
For this reason I thought it right to seize the opportunity of this exhibition to compare the projects with a completed work.
It is obvious that, for an architect, the presentation of his own work inside a building he himself designed becomes a challenge between the world of representation and that of built reality.
I, therefore, express my grateful thanks to the Bechtler and, in particular, to its founder Andreas Bechtler!

Mario Botta, December 2013

CONTENTS

12 ARRIVAL
John Boyer

22 FROM THE SPOON TO THE CITY
Gillo Dorfles, Aldo Colonetti, Mario Botta

36 **ENCOUNTERS**
Mario Botta

38 THE PRESENT PAST
Carlo Bertelli

86 GEOMETRIES OF LIGHT AND COLOR; IN TIME
Lionello Puppi

98 MARIO BOTTA AND SWITZERLAND
Roman Hollenstein

110 FROM THE VILLAGE TO THE CITY
Jacques Gubler

124 **LIBRARIES**

138 **MUSEUMS**

156 **THEATERS**

164 **SACRED SPACES**

194 AFTERWORD
Mario Botta

200 **APPENDIX**
202 BIOGRAPHY
204 LIST OF WORKS
222 PERSONAL EXHIBITIONS
226 GROUP EXHIBITIONS
233 MONOGRAPHIC BIBLIOGRAPHY
by Mercedes Daguerre

251 CRITICAL ANTHOLOGY
265 COLLABORATORS
268 BIOGRAPHIES OF THE AUTHORS
270 CREDITS

ARRIVAL
JOHN BOYER

> In the architectural opus, light generates space: without light, space does not exist. Natural light brings plastic forms to life, shapes the surface of materials, controls and balances geometric lines. The space generated by light is the soul of the act of architecture… Voids are what dictate spatial and functional relationships, controlling visual lines and generating potential emotions, expectations and interpretations… Light, for the architect, is the visible sign of the relationship that exists between the architectural work and the cosmic values of its surroundings: it is the element that shapes the work in its specific environmental context.[1] M.B.

The development of the Bechtler Museum of Modern Art was the outcome of the inspired vision of a dedicated and generous patron, as well as the expression of a gifted architect at his full power. But it is also the result of decades of strategic planning for a community's commitment to its cultural life. The museum represents the very best of private patronage and public cooperation. It is woven into a vibrant commercial and retail setting that enhances the success of performing and visual arts organizations – and vice versa. It is the product of complex public funding; of foundation, corporate and individual financial investment; and the arrival of a unique collection of modern art that served as the catalyst for the emergence of a new public institution. (1-3)

When Andreas Bechtler began to consider fully his receipt of his family's collection, especially in the context of his own long career as a collector and patron, it was clear that some significant accommodation would have to be considered to support all of the meaning and usefulness of the combined holdings. The first response was a most natural one in all ways. In the early 1990s Bechtler had begun to develop an artist colony on three hundred acres of land just northwest of Charlotte where pine-covered rolling hills meet more than one mile of shoreline of the Catawba River in an area known as Mt. Holly and Mountain Island Lake. This parcel of land, because of its peninsular shape when viewed from above, became known as Little Italy, and it was here that Bechtler began to erect a series of buildings dedicated to the arts. Over the course of a few years there was built a "main house" and several

 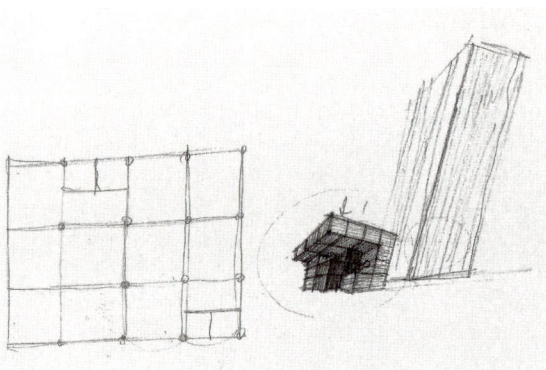

1./2. Preliminary studies of the Bechtler Museum of Modern Art in Charlotte
3. Front view of the Museum
4. Preliminary studies for the entrance court

art studios, the latter spread on either side of an open swath of land. The surrounding forest and meadows were left as pristine as possible, and this generally rustic aspect was underscored by the simple board and batten exterior construction of all of the buildings. Their interiors, though with an exceptionally fine finish, were also camp-like, with exposed wooden beams, tall ceilings and multiple views onto the generous vista with its year-round presentation of pines and hemlocks.

Over the years, this small community has welcomed painters, sculptors, photographers, composers and performers of no particular style and without any rigorous set of expectations. They are selected quietly, without a public or formal application process, and they stay at Little Italy for as short a period as six months to as many as several years. Without the pressures of required presentations, Bechtler has hoped to allow the best in these artists to emerge in the nurturing company of like-minded comrades in a setting of a great natural beauty and peace.

Into this context, then, Bechtler began to imagine a home for the newly combined collection with all of its strengths and diversity. The works were to provide an enduring inspiration for himself and his family, for the artists of Little Italy as well as for scholars, collectors and, periodically, the general public. To this end he had considered the possibility of an international search for an architect, and several were considered informally. But after much research and reflection, Mario Botta was chosen for a variety of convincing and prescient reasons.

Botta was already well known to Bechtler as the architect of the Tinguely Museum in Basel (1993-1996), an exuberant, light-filled building dedicated to the work of Bechtler's long-time friend, the Swiss sculptor Jean Tinguely. Niki de Saint Phalle, Tinguely's wife and celebrated artist with whom he often collaborated, was deeply involved with the Basel project, and she, too, was a good friend of the patron. In addition, Botta had collaborated with Niki on her Noah's Ark sculpture garden in Israel (1995-2001) and designed the entry gate for her Tarot Garden in Garavicchio, Italy (1995-1997). At about the same period, Botta had completed the San Francisco Museum of Modern Art (1989-1995), his first commission in the United States, and it had received an exceptionally strong reception. Bechtler and Botta also shared interests in other art and artists. Finally, while not a prerequisite, the architect's being Swiss was just another connection that would prove to foster a swift collegiality and common vision. All of these factors combined to encourage Bechtler to reach out to Botta, and he recalls that the decision was solidified for him in a dream. Late one night Bechtler was quite literally roused from his sleep by the clarity of this choice, and that was the conclusion of the process. (7)

The first stage of design was advanced in 2002 and was still based on the assumption that Botta would propose a

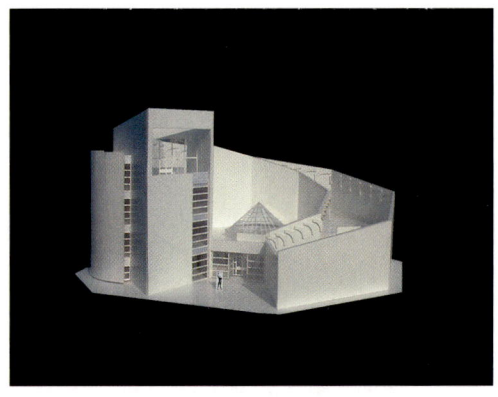

5. Sketch of the proposed museum for Little Italy, 2002
6. Model of the museum for Little Italy, 2002
7. Andreas Bechtler, Mario Botta and John Boyer, 2009
8. Andreas Bechtler and Mario Botta visualizing the the future Bechtler Museum of Modern Art, 2006

museum for Little Italy. (5) A site was selected on the northern half of the peninsula on a gentle rise with a long view over the Catawba River to the east. The gallery was placed near the shore about forty feet above the water. The general plan of the building was a spiral that embraced a central entrance vestibule which was covered by a glazed, circular pyramid. The ground floor held an auditorium, class rooms, a small store and other amenities. As the spiral turned, successive levels of gallery space would greet the visitor as they rose up over the course of three floors. Along the way were a library (second floor) and offices (third floor), and the sequence of exhibitions would terminate on the fourth floor at an outdoor balcony with spectacular views across the landscape. (6) The exterior was to be clad with a stone veneer laid horizontally and with a regular variation in height and width. Banks of windows were to be trimmed in black metal. The planning process had advanced quickly, bid documents were produced and construction was very near when a new possibility emerged.

On a parallel course, new ideas for a comprehensive cultural campus were being advanced by several entities in the center of Charlotte. The effort that was under way as Bechtler and Botta advanced their plans for Little Italy was the result of more than twenty years of strategic planning and careful study by various agencies and organizations in the city. In 2004 a new twenty-five-year plan for the community's cultural life was developed by the Arts & Science Council of Charlotte-Mecklenburg, in partnership with Foundation For The Carolinas and Charlotte Center City Partners. The planning process included a 130-member Blue Ribbon Committee of stakeholders to imagine a cultural vision for the community. The result was the Cultural Facilities Master Plan that included a $158 million capital investment in public funds to provide new and renovated facilities for several arts groups. Another $83 million was pledged by the private sector through the efforts of the Arts & Science Council for new and additional endowment support.

All of this effort was designed to coincide with the four-acre mixed-use development project advanced by Wachovia at the south end of Tryon Street. The initial desire was to develop a forty-eight- story office tower that would serve some of the needs of the corporation as well as other companies with which the bank had strong working relationships. Wachovia began to imagine a constellation of multiple cultural organizations in and around this new development at the southern end of center city. The objective was to ensure a vibrancy for this working and visiting community that could only be sustained through an interlocking engagement of commercial, retail, residential and cultural entities designed together from the start to ensure a single, consistent strategic vision. Were this combination to be successful, then the rewards would be felt clearly by all stakeholders. The project would amplify the

region's cultural life and educational opportunities, expand its tourism offerings and enhance businesses' ability to attract and retain talent. The political leadership of Charlotte and Mecklenburg County was also convinced of the significant benefits of this approach for the rest of the community and region as a whole. The cultural campus ultimately included a variety of visual and performing arts organizations each with its own independent architects, including the twelve-hundred-seat Knight Theater (Thompson, Ventulett, Stainback and Associates), new and greatly expanded facilities for the Harvey B. Gantt Center for African American Arts + Culture (The Freelon Group) and the Mint Museum, including its strong collection of craft and design (Machado, Silvetti and Clark Patterson). It was during the reconsideration of the cultural scope of the new development that conversations began with Bechtler and others about the possibility of bringing the new museum from Little Italy to uptown Charlotte. The new design for the Bechtler museum responded to the specifics of the site on South Tryon Street. (8) Although built to house the same collection and working with the same client, Botta arrived at a dramatically new approach that acknowledges the relationship with the urban setting. The museum would now be placed among a variety of building types of varying scales and defined by different materials. At the beginning, the museum was oriented toward the south resulting in a small urban garden or park between it and the new theater. But the orientation was amended to present the entry to the main street and the design took on a new clarity and presence. The museum's general composition, the exterior materials and the assumptions about plan were all changed in this new context. Botta has described the museum as "configured as a cube excavated on the inside… In a sense we can call it a molded space, where the visitors are 'enveloped' by the museum itself, not merely a building aligned on the street."[2] (11, 12)

One enters beneath a massive cantilevered gallery space which is supported by a swelling, multi-story column.(9) The entire exterior is covered with terra-cotta tiles or is glazed with black mullions. Botta had used terra cotta before very successfully in his Samsung Museum of Art in Seoul, South Korea (1995-2004), and the application here was equally demanding in the precision of both fabrication and installation. The use of terra cotta serves to amplify the idea of architecture as sculpture and the shaping of forms as part of the creation of space. The center of the museum is defined by its soaring four-story atrium which links all of the levels visually. A great strength of the design is its constant alignment with this central atrium, and the views to the entrance and the street thereby refresh the visitor's sense of place and orientation. (10) Botta has remarked that "architecture is a discipline that gives order to the space in our life, therefore it can give a structure to the organization of space." He further elaborated

9/10. View of the shaded court and entrance hall
11. Sketch of the final building for Bechtler, 2008
12. Studies of the building shape and entrance plaza

that "Heidegger once said that man can only live when he is able to orient himself in a space, that's why the buildings in our cities have to offer some reference points that enable man to know his own space. You feel more comfortable when you are able to control the space around you."⁴

The first floor has windows across its entire street front and offers a welcoming engagement to the visitor. (14) Once inside, we can also look directly into the lobby of the Knight Theater, beyond and this underscores the many visual and practical linkages between the buildings in the complex.⁵ The first floor contains the basics of visitor amenities, including a café and museum store. The second floor includes a video gallery, classrooms, an exhibition space and a sculpture terrace. The third floor serves primarily as administrative offices but also holds a small exhibition area. Finally, the fourth floor has more than ten thousand square feet of exhibition space that is defined by its vaulted ceilings and large windows that look across and through the atrium to the opposite exhibition spaces. These views also reach down to the lower floors and to the streetscape where the great Firebird by Niki de Saint Phalle stands in front of the museum. We are constantly reminded of where we are and what we have seen, even in a building that provides so many delightful spatial and visual surprises. (15)

The fourth-floor galleries also reinforce the supreme balance and calm of Botta's designs. The museum is based on a thirty foot square unit. This defining logic is not overbearing and often not even obvious. But it serves as a controlling force that brings a sense of unity and harmony to the various elements of the design. In this way Botta echoes one of the hallmarks of an early mentor, Le Corbusier, whose "regulating lines" were intended to inform architecture with an elegant internal system that brings order and still encourages variety. The fourth-floor galleries also employ dramatic vaults (13) as the architect has used earlier in works such as the Museum of Modern and Contemporary Art in Rovereto, Trento, Italy (design 1988-1992, built 2002). The gentle rhythm of their symmetrical placement may allude to the classical inspiration that can be seen in much of his work. But they also signal Botta's admiration for another early mentor, Louis Kahn, who was insistent in his exploration of natural light and history's sources of inspiration. "He was the one who understood the limits of technological development and the need for going back to origins… going back to origins is in fact the strongest cultural element in a society that constantly focuses on the future."⁶

Equally important is the role of the Bechtler Museum of Modern Art in the context of the larger site. Botta's profound sense of history and respect for the delicate balance of the urban fabric is well known and celebrated. He has written that the "city, as the supreme entity of the aggregation of life and hope, can become an instrument for

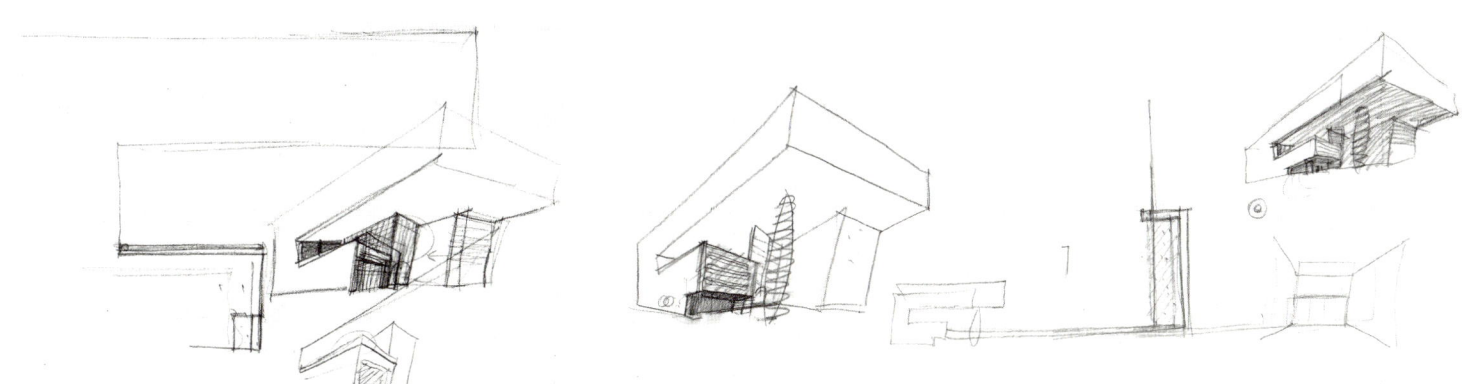

measuring the needs of its citizens and the values of this habitat, to arrive at a new understanding of the rapport that exists with our surroundings."⁷ The cultural complex presents buildings of many different sizes, materials and styles. They are set back from the street and each other in a convincing pattern of variety and purpose. They co-exist happily and serve to reinforce each other's best attributes.

While many of the buildings in the complex are quite different from each other, a few on South Tryon Street are linked by the use of brick and tile as the primary exterior building material. Across from the Bechtler stands St. Peter's Church begun in 1891. It was built in a rather demure Victorian Gothic Revival style with its surface animation coming more from a quality of pattern than color. The main material is a lightly weathered brick with occasional granite detailing. Its tower and steeple gently echo the height and general width of the museum's great column. In material and scale these two assertive vertical elements balance each other diagonally across South Tryon Street. Slightly to the north of St. Peters is a series of condominiums known as the Ratcliffe, designed by FMK and erected in 2002. The Ratcliffe is also in brick but in a contemporary model, precise in detail and cooler in tone. The three ceramic structures speak to each other around one of the great pleasures of the neighborhood, a narrow one and one halfacre public park known as The Green. This element stretches away from South Tryon Street and the museum to the opposite end of the block terminating on Church Street directly in front of a massive convention center. The park provides a generous spatial and visual release for this section of the urban core and psychologically extends the plaza in front of the museum for several hundred yards. In return, there are splendid views of the Bechtler, framed by trees and public art, from as far away as the convention center.

Therefore, even with its more intimate scale the museum serves as a crucial visual anchor for the cultural campus, providing the main welcoming element when viewed from the north, the arresting visual terminus when viewed from the convention center to the west, the principal framing device when viewed from the south and as a gracious partner for the Knight Theater to the east.

To be sure, the Bechtler is not the largest companion in this ensemble. But we are reminded that size often has little to do with scale or a sense of presence. The museum serves as a jewel box filled with remarkable offerings from a family of inspired patrons. Their sense of commitment to the community, their celebration of the value of art in our lives, and their generosity all reveal what Botta himself has assigned as the central role of architecture itself: "I think architecture is a civic duty that is related to mankind, a social duty that concerns society and an ethical duty, as architecture can represent values related to the way we live."⁸

---

1. *Mario Botta: Light and Gravity, Architecture 1993-2003*, (New York: Prestel, 2004), p. 8.
2. The "Bechtler Museum", CharlotteViewpoint.com, September 2007 (volume 4, issue 11).
3. As quoted in "Mario Botta – Philosopher Architect", Design Build Network (designbuildnetwork.com), January 18, 2008.
4. Ibidem.
5. The museum has an unusually high percentage of square footage that is dedicated to collections and program needs as a result of sharing a loading dock with the Knight Theater, a large chiller system shared with both the Knight and the Mint, and shared use of a three hundred-seat auditorium.
6. Ibidem.
7. *Mario Botta: Light and Gravity*, op. cit., p.11.
8. Ibidem.

13. Exhibition spaces on the fourth floor
14. The museum's entrance at night
15. Studies for the Museum's front view

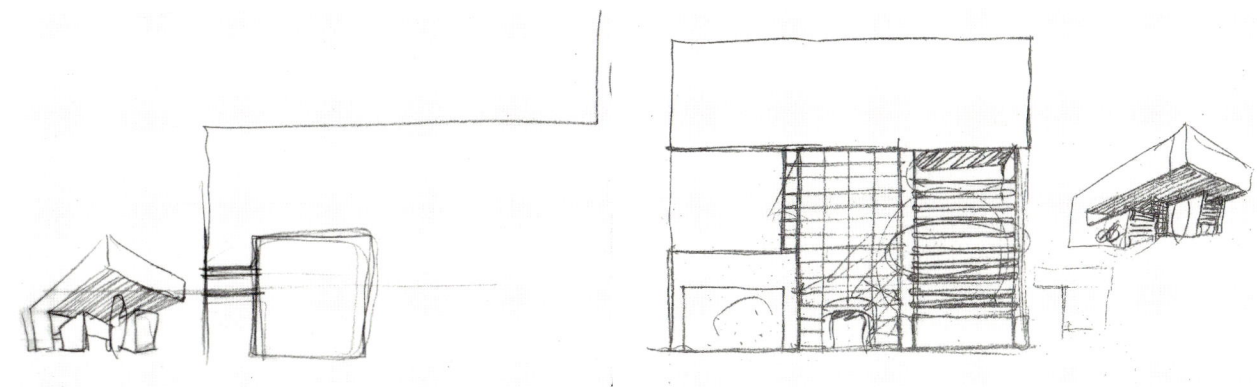

Mario Botta in Giancarlo Vitali's working studio (atelier) in Bellano, January 2008.

FROM THE SPOON TO THE CITY
GILLO DORFLES, ALDO COLONETTI, MARIO BOTTA

Gillo Dorfles welcomes us in his Milanese home in piazzale Lavater, a place which recalls some Parisian squares with deco buildings, immersed in green surroundings. Around a grand piano are paintings by his "friends" Fontana, Capogrossi, Mušič, indicating his wide variety of interests. Dorfles has always been an alert and ironic interpreter of the 20th-century "fluctuations of tastes"; he has always been able to inquire into novelty without nostalgia. With peaceful and open argumentations, yet not without a sharp and refined sense of irony, he leafs through and comments on the drafts of the Mart exhibition catalog with Mario Botta. Aldo Colonetti is also present, and the three of them

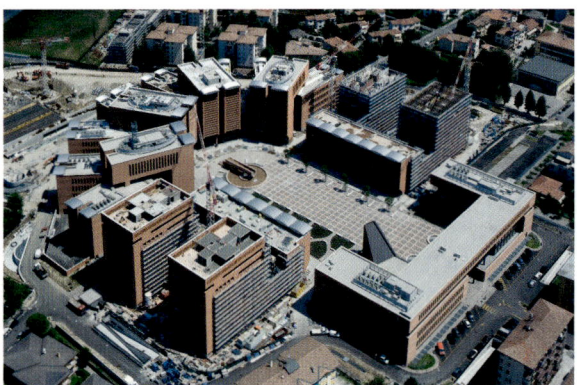

1. Mario Botta with Gillo Dorfles and Aldo Colonetti in Milan, July 25th, 2010
2. Aerial view of the new former Appiani area in Treviso, I, 2010
3. Friedrich Dürrenmatt Center in Neuchâtel, 2000
4. Jean Tinguely Museum in Basel, CH, 1996
5. Church of Santo Volto, Turin, 2006
6. Kyobo tower in Seoul, 2003

engage in a conversation, retracing Botta's fifty years in the "trade": a creative process under the banner of "doing" architecture in the furrow of the territory of memory, where stratification acquires an operative nature and establishes a new balance with the surrounding context.(1)

COLONETTI: The Mart in Rovereto, planned by Mario Botta, housed an exhibition of his works [in 2010]: architecture in the architecture; this is something that does not occur very frequently. Gillo, Mario has been working for fifty years. In this period he has realized works of very different dimensions: from the first one-family homes to a whole city area like Treviso (2), museums, banks and multi-purpose buildings, but also exhibition settings, design objects, theater set designs. It is almost as if Mario, following his own poetics, had interpreted Ernest Nathan Rogers' famous definition "from the spoon to the city".

DORFLES: Botta's figure differs from most other architects, not only for the outstanding quantity of accomplished works, but also because he departed from an "integral" vision of visual arts. In other words, his attention for painting and sculpture, the fact that he has dedicated museums to avant-garde artists like Friedrich Dürrenmatt (3) or Jean Tinguely (4), that he has realized many set designs; and above all that he started from a one-family home to later realize important works of architecture such as the great church in Turin (5), the museum and the skyscraper (6); all of this proves his ability to deal with a wide variety of issues with the same humility and, at the same time, with a high level of self-esteem.

COLONETTI: As Gillo has stressed, Botta's fifty years of activity are evidence of consistency, building skills, but also of humility in listening to the "others": from the grand masters of architecture like Le Corbusier, Louis Kahn, the poets, the artists like Guido Ceronetti. This proves his respect for other people's ways of thinking. However, he has never limited his listening to a self-referential fact. His

listening is aimed at acquiring the ideas, the poetic proposals, the paths, but also the provocations – not following a spirit of imitation, but in an attempt to give concreteness to his architectonic ideas, to transfer these experiences to his work. This is a major issue among architects, because we often speak of thought and planned architecture, but not of realized architecture. In this case, we are looking at designed and "realized" architecture. It is not a mere empirical fact, but a way of interpreting this profession.

BOTTA: Two remarks. The first is that I was obviously not born as an architect, but I became one by means of work, especially through other people's work. I feel as if I were a son of modern culture, and in particular of the considerations and the problems arising after the Bauhaus era. The planning hopes of the Avant-Gardes created the cultural territory that I inherited. It is undeniable that if I had been born in a different period, the cultural legacy would have been different. The second remark is that, over the years, the peculiarity of this profession has become clearer and clearer to me: it is not the architect who chooses what to build; it is chosen by a series of sometimes mysterious circumstances, which mold his walk of life. As a matter of fact, the client is indeed the history of the respective period, asking, from time to time, for a house, a church or a building to be designed. Within this condition the architect can, at best, decide whether to accept or refuse the commission. Architecture inevitably becomes the formal reflection of its own history, the image of the culture of its time, within the path of contemporaneity. From this point of view, all I can do, after fifty years of activity, is to ascertain that I have merely done what I was asked to do, starting from one-family houses, followed by museums, theaters and churches. The assignments have always arrived spontaneously, often unexpectedly, and I was not given a chance to "distinguish". It is obvious that all of this is conditioned by the motivation, the drive to "do", underlying the thought, the hopes, and even the illusions of our

7. Family house in Stabio, 1967
8. Church of San Giovanni Battista in Mogno, Maggia Valley, 1996
9. Church of San Giovanni Battista in Mogno, Maggia Valley, 1996
View of the apse

profession. The ambition to express our ideals by means of buildings is the true motor of our trade. I remember that one of the deepest emotions I ever felt in my career was seeing the carpentry of my first house being built. I observed the sun shining through that building for the very last time. A landscape condition that up to then had belonged only to nature was being transformed into an internal space. It was the evidence of a cultural condition overruling a natural condition. For me, this is, to this day, the true power of the architectonic fact.

DORFLES: I must say that one of the planning approaches that mainly strikes me in Botta's fifty years of activity is the fact that he has always been, first of all, from the very beginning, an attentive interpreter of the avant-garde architecture of the moment. I am thinking of the "lecorbuserian" houses (7) during his youth, proof of how a young man had already understood the importance of the Modern Movement. In the same way, I consider extremely interesting the fact that Botta, in his attempt to go beyond Le Corbusier's teaching, approached great masters like Kahn, without falling into the "mannerisms" of avant-garde architecture, immediately subsequent to the Modern Movement, which bore a hint of nostalgia of the Bauhaus teaching. In fact, in Mario Botta's works there is never that delight of the "voluptuous" and "pleasant", which is present in many contemporary architects, whom I nonetheless esteem, but who have let themselves be convinced and conditioned by certain sinuosities of architecture, which have only become possible with the use of modern digital technologies. Mario Botta has remained loyal to a vision of architecture which has its roots in the "Romanesque". Even though Botta has inserted some design modules that can be considered "Baroque" in his works (I am referring, for example, to the church in Mogno (8,9) with its elliptical plan), this is however not an example of Baroquism. As a matter of fact, when Mario, out of his love for Borromini, had a wood model of the church San Carlino di Roma (10) reproduced on the shores of Lake Lugano, hereby pay-

ing a magnificent tribute to Italian Baroque architecture, he was very careful not to be infected by it.

COLONETTI: Having the Masters close by, be it personally or only in the imagination, is always important and fundamental, but it is also difficult in the definition process of one's own planning autonomy. As Gillo has observed, your whole career is the evidence of attentive listening to "others", but at the same time it is a demonstration of the successful attempt to find your own expressive identity. You often refer to architecture as "gravity". In everyday building practice this attitude has led to the preferential use of certain materials; a use which is never merely aesthetic, it is connected to your way of interpreting architecture; by volumes, by voids, by the composition of contrasting shapes. Gillo has stressed your dominating character by using the term "Romanesque", not in its historical meaning, but on the level of architectural language.

BOTTA: Yes. What Gillo says is true, I feel a strong cultural obligation towards the Romanesque period. My teenage romances included Romanesque churches and baptisteries in Lombardy (Civate, Lenno, Giornico) (11). I have always been attracted by that period of art history for its ability to synthesize and describe, by means of elementary shapes, the complexity, the disputes and the hopes underlying the lives of the different communities. The charm of Romanesque architecture has influenced my approach to the shapes in space, to a global language which, at the same time, displays a richness of local variations (in France, Spain, Lombardy) which enable a sure historical and cultural recognizability. For these reasons, to this day, I am still more attracted by Romanesque culture than by smug Baroque shapes or more rational 19th-century structures, even though I am aware that architecture as a discipline is the direct consequence of comprehensive global history, and it is possible to find nourishment, at the same time, both in primitive ancestral shapes and in more recent culture. Ar-

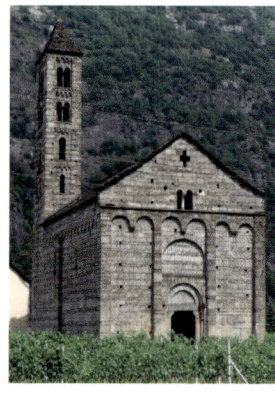

10. San Carlino in Lugano, 1999
11. Roman Church of San Nicolao in Giornico, Ticino, 12th century

chitecture, possibly even more than other arts, makes you feel part of humanity at large, not only of a historical period, as happened more than once during the 20th century with the creation of movements (neo-classical, neo-gothic, neo-liberty…). These are forms of architecture which thrived on inconsistent cultural trends. On the other hand, I recognize an iconic attention to and awareness of archaic and essential structures. There is an antiquity in innovation, with ancestral signs returning to feed the thinking of the various, more recent historical periods (as Henry Moore teaches us with his woman-mother, who has turned into an archetype for the whole history of mankind). Moreover, the Romanesque fascinates me for its absolute essentiality of contrasting large, full surfaces with openings of light, creating a relation between the man-made product and the cosmic context. Aldo Colonetti has also mentioned the issue of gravity. This term contrasts with the current cultural trends, which often misuse the term levity, relating to buildings. I think that architecture finds its deepest reason for being when it releases its static power to the ground; there is no architecture without gravity, the built work has to be taken in possession by Mother Earth, whom it constitutes an "all-in-one" with. I think that the beauty of cities lies in the way they root to the ground and in the way they form a single entity with the geological structure of the place. It is not possible to move a building, even just by a few meters, without radically altering the spatial relationships it defines with the surroundings. This is why I look with suspicion on many of the present slogans that consider levity an intrinsic value. In my work, I like to use the tool of geometry in a strong and structural way. Geometry establishes static balances as well as balances of space and light, which give peace to the building, like in a vegetable structure. Unlike current trends, I use geometry, sometimes even symmetry, to re-establish spatial balances. History has shown us that there can be very high-quality forms of architecture (simply consider Palladio) and other absolutely rhetoric and celebrative forms of architecture (like in Fascist architecture). Geometry offers a great potential, but it is up to the architect to make a positive or negative use of this tool.

DORFLES: I think it is very important highlight the fact that Mario has always taken the urban element in consideration, a sign of an essential sensitivity, which not all architects practice. An example of this is the extraordinary intervention in the former Appiani area in Treviso, with the insertion of a great square. Botta succeeded in building a real city area in this district, which was lacking a proper urban identity. Another excellent example of architecture is the insertion of a corner building (12) in Lugano, on the square of the former school area (Piazzale ex-scuole), in a context of a Hippodamian plan, misconceived as it is in Lugano. The same is true for a controversial building like the Casinò di Campione (13). I personally believe that this project is particularly interesting because it creates a real parenthesis on the lake shore, despite its grandiosity, which has been considered by many to be excessive. The large curve on the right and the empty space on the left, where the verticality of the structure is horizontalized by a square on the fifth floor, represent a very interesting architectural choice, which will be perfected with the extension towards the lake of a park, which was already envisaged in Botta's plan.

COLONETTI: Continuing from these considerations on Mario's architecture with regards to the city, I would like to draw your attention back to the exhibition venue in 2010, the Mart in Rovereto (14,15). Gillo and I believe that your project for Rovereto is one of your best works, apart from the architectonic composition and the language used to define the volumes, for the fact that the front of the museum does not exist, or better, it is concealed by the 18th-century architecture of Corso Bettini. I think that Botta's planning scheme, with regards to the relationship between the present architecture and the consolidated historic urban settlement, should become a common atti-

12. Ransila building in Lugano, 1985
13. Casinò in Campione d'Italia, 2006
14. Mart Museum in Rovereto, 2002
View of the central courtyard
15. Mart Museum in Rovereto, View from Corso Bettini

tude in contemporary architecture; expressive attention-seeking is important on the one hand, but on the other hand it is just as essential to maintain one's identity, creating a dialog with and paying respect to the pre-existing urban and architectonic texture, omitting any kind of historicism of post-modern origin.

BOTTA: I believe that the value of a work of architecture is not represented by the object itself, by the built volume, but rather by the spatial relationship it manages to establish with the reality surrounding it. In my opinion it is this dialog that characterizes the quality of the architectural product. If there were an instrument able to measure the quality of architecture, it would have to measure the intensity developing between the new building and the surrounding territory. Architecture alters the landscape and creates a better quality of life through the search for new balances. This is why Dorfles' consideration that the built work has to consider the context is extraordinarily relevant in our days. This consideration rings like a warning in a culture that interprets architecture as a self-referential icon. I think that every single building, even the smallest one, must contribute to the creation of a better quality of space. It cannot be interpreted as a sculpture to be used or moved at discretion. Its power lies in the fact that it rises from one single point to define unique and unrepeatable relations between space, light and horizon. I even like to think that architecture, in its structuring a vital space, aims at becoming city, at comparing itself and conversing with the urban settlement, as a space which gives an emotion, just like the artist who aims at exhibiting his works in a museum as a space of collective comparison. The city represents a territory of memory, a place of the past, where extinct generations confront themselves with the modernity of life by means of space configurations. The territory of memory is the real structure that supports our "work" and gives us the antibodies to contrast the uniformity induced by global culture. Compared to other disciplines architecture has

more resources because it has a deeper inertia, rooted in the territory, because it constantly builds a historical stratification, which is the real value of the European city.

COLONETTI: Gillo, Mario refers to the relationship between the city and architecture and to memory as the wider context. A context which is unique both in its corporeality and in its symbolic heritage, even only in the imagination, a reality which we live in, and we cannot and must not evade from. In your literary activity there is a very important work, "L'intervallo perduto" [*The lost interval*] (1980), which describes the absence of a physical or mental space between one fact and the other, between one thought and the other, basically a sort of "horror pleni", to quote another recent essay of yours (2009/2008). What particular attention should architecture have with regards to this contemporary trend of "filling everything up", of doing without intervals, as if our life were on a fast lane without breaks?

DORFLES: In this sense, architecture has an essential function. Today there is not only a redundancy of sounds, of visual and verbal communication, of objects. There is also a surplus of "ugly architectures". However, also a redundancy of "nice architectures" would be dangerous; in fact, it would be negative not to give enough space to a specific architecture as an expression of the present time, as inconsistent as it may be. In this regard, I cannot refrain from referring to the crucial point of our discussion. Could the Mart have been a museum at the center of the city, thus upsetting the living and symbolic level of the urban structure of a small town like Rovereto? It could have created an oasis of presumption, displaying a sort of "principle of performance", which would have been out of place. On the contrary, the fact that the museum has been erected behind two buildings and is accessible along Corso Bettini, prevented the town from being conditioned by an excessively imposing building. In my opinion this is an example worth imitating: speak in a low voice, but without denying your architectonic will.

BOTTA: The Mart is indicative of an attitude because it was the interpretation of the urban landscape that suggested the structure of the new project. Corso Bettini, with its 18th-century scenery, is indeed to be seen as the museum's foyer. The museum's set-back position, compared to the urban space, has created a backdrop, a proper scenic design, which can be perceived from the street. The relationships between the pre-existing and the new intervention are dictated by the spatial relations and not by volumes. Approaching the museum, on the street one discovers new spaces that in fact represent an introductory path to the museum itself, whereas the wide roofed square is the *pronaos*. I am interested in the direct comparison between the contemporary language in the backward part and the pre-existing buildings Palazzo Annone and Palazzo Alberti, which represent the gateway to the new presence. I think that this is a way of creating a dialog with the city and appreciating its structure, giving it an added value. For us Europeans, it is important to resort to attitudes that eventually clearly turn in favor of the city. It is always a question of moderation and of the ability to control the architectonic gesture. In fact, architecture can contribute to the consolidation, or to the violation, of a process of historic stratification. If this attitude is clear with regards to the context, at this point the architect can regain his freedom of expression, without having to give in to the winks or compromises of the language of the surroundings.

COLONETTI: Your consideration spurs us to speak of the Teatro alla Scala in Milan. After the initial and persistent polemic reactions, based on unjustified prejudices, your architecture was later on accepted and greeted by the city. The discussion on the past, the present and the future of the European City should be inspired by Mario Botta's project for the Scala (16). If we are to be respectful of the past, both in an archeological and academic way, perhaps we should not build any more; if, on the con-

16. Theater alla Scala in Milan, 2004

trary, we are transgressive, "creative", ignoring memory and history, we turn into a sort of "architects of a new world", which have never existed if not in science fiction, operating however, within a context which belongs nonetheless to the great European tradition. We have to find a balance between the respect for contemporary poetics and the reference context. Could Botta's Scala be taken as an architectural model, independently of the formal solutions which have been adopted?

DORFLES: Of course we cannot omit to mention the restoration of the Scala, an event of international significance, given the importance of this theater in Milan. As a matter of fact, it was practically impossible to give the Scala that urgently needed technological development without altering its structure. I consider Botta's solution an absolutely extraordinary intervention. Of course one could be irritated by discovering the profile of a modern and circular building behind the façade. But if we consider that all new needs have been met, one will soon realize that the "inconvenience" is minimal; also because the maximum height of the old Scala is at the same level as the new building.

BOTTA: The restoration of the Scala is important because, at the end of the planning phase and of all the controversies that characterized it, it shows that contemporary language can contribute to consolidating a historical stratification. A "conservative" restoration was carried out from the eaves level downwards, refurbishing the Piermarini structure and the neo-classic extensions on Piazza Scala and along via dei Filodrammatici. This made it possible to realize the two new volumes over the roofs – the first arising from the need, on the one hand, to create new spaces and the other to meet the new technological requirements for scenography – with their own static structure and with an appropriate language for our time. I used a soft language with the aim of designing an abstract wing, which had to be able to reinforce the neoclassic figurative architecture of the lower part, without clashing with a language which has established itself as an important part of the city.

COLONETTI: I would like to make a last consideration, since not only your architecture, but also your design is displayed in this exhibition. Your design, Mario, is characterized by a strong architectonic imprint; it is not a "drawing", inspired by the trends of contemporary languages. It has its own rigor and coherence, as if it belonged to another, "ancient" way of designing, very respectful of the expressive peculiarities of the different materials used.

BOTTA: As a matter of fact, I am an anomalous designer. I design my objects as if they were small pieces of architecture, and I am concerned with verifying their resistance, rather than considering them objects tied to an industrial process. In architecture, the timetable for a project has to be calculated over years, whereas the time span for the realization of design objects covers a few months. This is important for the work of an architect because it allows him to verify, within a reasonably short period, the technical and image experimentations underlying the projects.

COLONETTI: One last question, Gillo: the relationship between architecture and design is complex, sometimes hostile. It is infrequent to find an architect, like Mario, who has built a great deal and who dedicates himself to design, yet staying within his discipline. Is this a model that can be found in other architects, or is Botta an exception?

DORFLES: I would say that many have given in to the idea that design is nothing else but architecture in miniature, that design "stylistically" belongs to architecture. I think that there is no discrepancy between architecture and design; if anything at all, there should be complementarity. Not many architects or designers succeed in embracing both disciplines; Mario has managed to realize design objects with the same sensitivity he realizes his works of architecture because for him design is part of architecture. A chair, a vase, a table, up to the skyscraper in Seoul. One day Mario Botta could even design an airport!

17. Chair *Quarta*, 1984
18. Vase *Undici* from a serie of 13 vases in *pewter*
19. Table *Terzo*, 1983

Conversation in Milan, piazzale Lavater 3, Sunday, July 25, 2010. Transcription by Alessandra Coppa

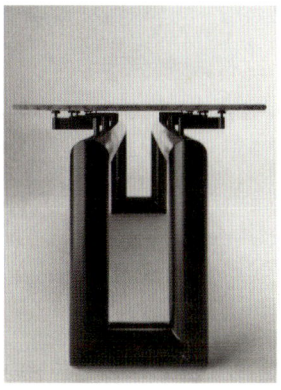

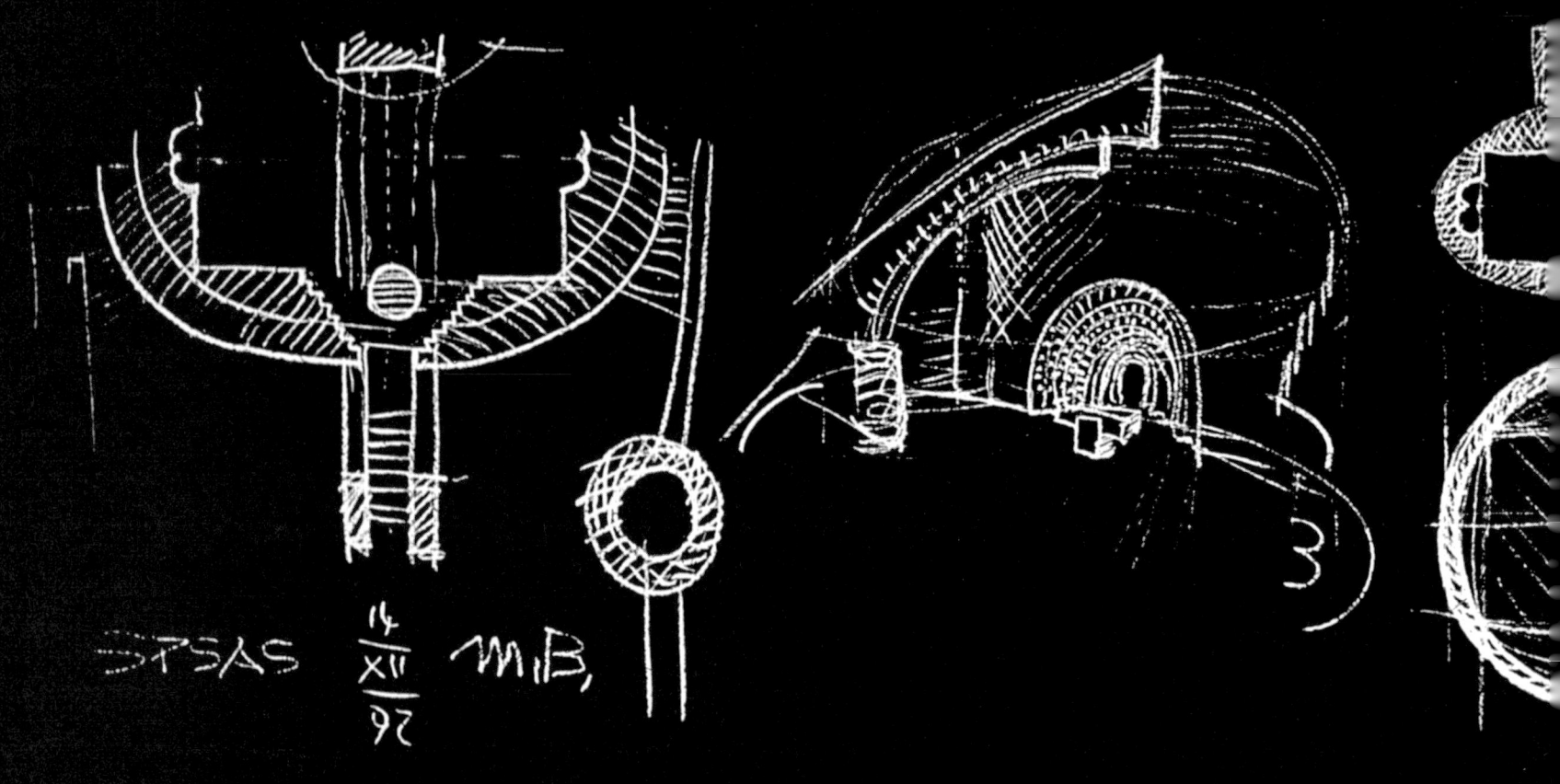

Sketches of the church in Mogno realised in situ for the exhibition at the SPSAS Gallery,
Palazzo Morettini, Locarno in 1993

ENCOUNTERS

CASA BALMELLI CAPPELLA ROVEREDO GERRIT T. RIETVELD FRANK LLOYD WRIGHT PABLO PICASSO PIER PAOLO PASOLINI HENRY MOORE LE CORBUSIER CARLO SCARPA LOUIS I. KAHN VENEZIA FRANCESCO BORROMINI GIOVANNI POZZI GIOVANNI XXIII GIORGIO MORANDI MARIO SIRONI ROBERT FRANK ROBERT DOISNEAU RUDOLF ARNHEIM IL ROMANICO ELADIO DIESTE GABRIEL GARCÍA MÁRQUEZ ARTURO BENEDETTI MICHELANGELI GIORGIO STREHLER MAX FRISCH FRIEDRICH DÜRRENMATT VARLIN CONSTANT PERMEKE NIKI DE SAINT PHALLE JEAN TINGUELY PAUL KLEE ALBERTO GIACOMETTI GIOTTO PIERO DELLA FRANCESCA ALEXANDER CALDER EDOARDO SANGUINETI PANTHEON PETRA-GIORDANIA MARCEL DUCHAMP PIET MONDRIAN KAZIMIR MALEVIČ GUIDO CERONETTI

Among the multitude of people, images and thoughts I have encountered during my walk of life I would like to remember some that have stricken my imagination more than others and given me feelings that have conditioned my view of the world. I feel a deep sense of gratitude towards these elective affinities and cultural legacies.

THE PRESENT PAST
CARLO BERTELLI

Harald Szeemann (1) would have been happy to read Mario Botta's words and see his choice of masters of the past, of things seen and done, of experiences and dreams; an enumeration with no distinction in time or space, projected into a present, where there is still room for poetry, contemplation, friendship. This catalog of memories is comparable to *Dappertutto,* the last Biennale, the unbiased exhibition which our common friend closed his circle of life with. It is splendid that Mario Botta has wanted to gratefully remember the works and the masters that have stirred and animated him, to some extent guided him. He still speaks of his training years with the same freshness of a little boy in exploration, evidence of a never-ending research. Over and above his enviable personal talent, his lively intellectual curiosity, and a personal history, presented with simplicity and intact amazement, his life is also the token of a generation. I am speaking of the generation approaching architecture at the end of the industrial era, when the myths that had nourished their fathers had just started creaking. At that time, the concern to find the right direction led young archi-

1. Harald Szeemann, Ingeborg Lüscher, Mario Botta, Zermatt 1991
2. Carlo Scarpa, Venice, 1972

tects to look at everything, but really everything the past had left at their disposal. The challenge was in the choice.

When Mario Botta graduated in Venice from the school of Carlo Scarpa (2), the decline of the "grand narratives" had begun. It is quite likely that no other teacher would have so happily prepared him to feel that it was time to embark on a new path within the complexity of post-industrial society. Carlo Scarpa liked to experiment with drawing and, even then, Mario Botta was a furious drawer. He liked to think with the pencil, to give shape to his imagination and put it to the test. He would roll a piece of paper into a ball and throw it in the bin. Then he would pick it out again to check if, by chance, he had let some idea slip away, maybe an idea worth following, and then he would start drawing again. The engineers would check the drawings later on.

The crisis of rational architecture, and on the other hand, the search for meaningful architecture, led to look at anything that could have stimulated an inner reflection. It was essential not to deny emotions, to be open to flexibility and to differences, a very different approach from the single notion of progress that had gone along with modernity. However, for me, belonging to a generation preceding that of Mario Botta, it is significant that the person who made me acquainted with this young architect long ago was Lodovico Belgioioso, who enthusiastically told me about the first houses built by Mario Botta. A master who had participated in the radical overhaul of rationalism was passing the baton.

It is touching, that, after leaving Venice (3) (4), young Botta's memories are inspired by Tita Carloni, and in particular by a building at the edge of a wood, made of wood and stone, but with a clear and confident design. Maybe Tita Carloni, the colleague and teacher, would have liked Botta to mention his Casa del Popolo in Lugano, with that daring cantilever that recalls avant-garde Russian architecture. But Botta's choice fell on a far more personal, I would even say intimate, building rising on the hill side. The building did not try to comply with the slope, it rather attempted to create a contrast with it. It is a way of living, is Mario Botta's comment, whose first project was a house.

After leaving the Venetian Lagoon, the young neo-architect set foot again in his homeland, like the Titans in the myth. And Mario Botta's land is very peculiar. From every window you can see a bit of Italy. Giovanni Pozzi once

3. Le Corbusier, Venice, 1965
4. Louis I. Kahn, Venice, 1969
5. Swiss 100 francs banknote with Alberto Giacometti's portrait and *L'homme qui marche*

wrote about the peculiar condition of being Italian and Swiss at the same time. Mario Botta's Switzerland is the genius of Max Bill, the irreverent subversion of Friedrich Dürrenmatt. The opposite of the idea of Switzerland that people have in the South. Italy is represented by another rebel, Francesco Borromini, the architect of an anti-classic Rome, who until some decades ago appeared on Swiss 100 franc notes. Now his place has been taken by another Swiss Italian, Alberto Giacometti with *Der Schreitende,* the Walking Man (5), the paradox of a *statue* that walks instead of *standing still*. Beat Wyss, in *Die Zeit,* compared it to the last act of *Waiting for Godot*.

The second memory, in this list proposed by Botta, is Frank Lloyd Wright's Fallingwater House. It is the debate on rationalism, the enthusiasm for organic architecture. But Botta does not invite anyone to side with one field or the other. He prefers to point to the fascination of the architecture-nature relationship. For the generation he represents it is not a question of siding with one front or the other anymore. It is more important to meet up with shape. Using a naïve look to recognize the beauty even in the shape of Duchamp's *pissoir*, once deprived of its *ready made* pre-condition. Even in this case, Botta proves that he belongs to the post-revolutionary generation. Solferino is a monument, not a battle.

Extraordinary, in this sense, is the description of how he discovered Gerrit Rietveld's chair. Mario Botta saw it first in black and white, he redrew it, built a scale model and then reacted with disappointment when he discovered that the original was painted in bright colors. The violence of provocation didn't exist anymore. We admire the perfection of Greek helms in the showcases and forget what they were used for.

The student has become a professor. He has founded an academy of architecture, right there, on the border between Italy and Switzerland, in his *Heimat*. The former hospital, a noble Neo Palladian piece of architecture by Luigi Fontana, 1860, lends itself perfectly as a venue for a university campus. And there, amidst the columns of the portico, the professor has wedged in a large, brightly colored sculpture by Niki de Saint-Phalle (6), representing Ganymede abducted by Zeus' eagle. It is a metaphor for students, who will be enraptured by the fascination of learning, even they will fly high and far. The classic structure of the triangular pediment and the columns is shattered by this irreverent insertion. But those who know Mario Botta also know that this is not a tribute to a personality of the international scene. The architect and the sculptress had a deep emotional bond,

6. Pronaos of the Turconi building – Academy of architecture Mendrisio with *L'Oiseau amoureux* [The bird in love] of Jean Tinguely and Niki de Saint Phalle
7. Carlo Bertelli and Mario Botta in Foligno at the exhibition of Piermarini, June 2010

and the artist's long agony was followed with real concern and affliction by her friend from Ticino. Mario Botta was seduced by Niki de Saint-Phalle's world, from the *Nanas* to the *Tarocchi* in Garavicchio, from the Stravinsky fountain to the Tel Aviv *Zoo*, which they realized together. The irony of the big dimensions, the reinterpretation of Gaudì's architecture, the spirit of adventure were bound to become part of Botta's legacy.

This pantheon inevitably also includes a bachelor machine, a creation by Jean Tinguely. The strong idea of the industrial society was the productiveness of machines, their perfection was taken as a role model for living. Tinguely's useless machines are not the parody of what once was – Botta was born in a land of hard work and emigration and he respects the generations who came before him. The machines are rather an elegy of the past, and their useless movements are sometimes nostalgic, other times, and more frequently, playful.

If progress is not an underlying myth anymore, if there are no more basic and global values justifying our actions, what should guide our behavior, how could we give a sense to human life and to society? Botta has more than once insisted on the power of memory. I went with him to that house, I stood exactly in that long corridor in Bondo, in Val Bregaglia, which was depicted by Varlin on a canvas that has been included in this catalog of memories. Varlin had settled in Val Bregaglia and had managed to understand its people like no other. To the point that the extension of that corridor in Varlin's painting seems to be the answer to the constant impulse the Bregagliotti live in, the uncertainty between staying or going. The door on the right leads to the cellar, into the depth of the house, whereas the open door at the end leads out, onto the street.

Shall we all be rich? Or shall we all live as if we were rich, with all-inclusive trips to the Bahamas, Maldives, Seychelles? So why did Botta choose exactly that *Repas frugal*, among the many possible Picassos?

Possibly as an expression of nostalgia of the probity in times of yore, on which we should establish, or re-establish, the new values.

I consider this to be Alpine morality, the great tension of Botta, the architect, whether he plans a bank in Athens or a museum in Tokyo. He is warning us: we cannot and must not reject history. He is telling us: we cannot plan architecture depriving ourselves and the future generations of the past. The anthology of "encounters" presented in this catalogue goes back in time, beyond the "short century".

HOUSE BALMELLI ROVIO

This house, built in the second half of the 50's near Lugano by architect Tita Carloni, whose studio I worked in during my apprenticeship as an architectural draughtsman (1959-1961), is the work of architecture that made it clear to me that the trade I was approaching could be experienced as a true passion. The contrast between the building's geometry and the territory's orographic profile conveyed an unknown beauty, which I interpreted as a possible new way of living.

Tita Carloni
Balmelli Residence, Ticino
1956

This chapel rises in the countryside, to the south of the village, not far away from the motorway Bellinzona – San Bernardino – Zurich. It is thought to date back to the 18th century, but has undergone various changes. Despite its reduced size, it evokes a powerful image which fascinates the observer for the essentiality, the intelligence and the size of the only opening (front, porch, shelter) hollowed out in the volume. Its iconic power has remained unaltered in spite of the sweeping changes which have occurred in the surrounding landscape.

ROVEREDO CHAPEL

Chapel in Roveredo,
Grisons, Switzerland
ca. 18th century

GERRIT THOMAS RIETVELD

1888-1964

Gerrit Thomas Rietveld
635 "red and blue chair", 1918
beech wood painted black with blue and red lacquered plywood,
13 in. x 34 ⅔ in. x 32 ⅔ in. x 25 ⅔ in.
Cassina/Maestri Collection

I saw an image of the "Red and Blue" chair (1918) in the late fifties in a publication on Dutch "neoplastic" architecture. I was stricken by its simplicity and expressive power. I first attempted to draw it, starting from a photograph, trying to reproduce, by constant approximations, the original proportions and sizes. Then I built a wooden prototype that stayed in my youth "atelier" for many years. The image I had used to reconstruct the model was black and white and my reproduction was in natural wood. My creative enthusiasm was (slightly) dampened when I discovered its vivid colors, although I knew the chromatic composition of Rietveld's Schröder House in Utrecht.

Fallingwater in Pennsylvania and the brand new Guggenheim Museum in New York became architectural landmarks in the United States in the late 50's. In both cases, the intensity of the relationship between the building and the surrounding context is evidence of the typical poetics of organic architecture, which believes in a possible new balance between the citizen-man and society. In the certainty of modern architecture mankind aspires to his own centrality, which remains a constant yardstick. The eclectic architecture of the early 20th century is overcome by new architectonic hopes.

FRANK LLOYD WRIGHT

1867-1959

Frank Lloyd Wright
The Edgar J. Kaufmann Residence (Fallingwater), 1934-1937
Bear Run, Pennsylvania, USA
© 2014 Frank Lloyd Wright Foundation, Scottsdale, AZ / Artists Rights Society

PABLO PICASSO

1881-1973

Le Repas frugal (The Frugal Repast), 1904
etching on paper, 18 ¼ in. x 14 ⅝ in.
Private Collection
© 2014 Estate of Pablo Picasso / Artists Rights Society (ARS), New York

Femme au chapeau (Woman with Hat), 1962
linocut on paper, 24 ⅜ in. x 17 ⅜ in.
Bechtler Museum of Modern Art
Charlotte, North Carolina, USA
© 2014 Estate of Pablo Picasso / Artists Rights Society (ARS), New York

Among the nicest and most poignant moments of my adolescence, I cannot omit to include the moments of contemplation in front of the reproductions of the paintings by the "masters of colors" that entered my house in mysterious ways. I remained bewitched for whole afternoons, far from the games and the playful atmosphere in the village, in front of the suggestion of those paintings and I dreamed up future lives. The figures of the blue and rose period, traced in Picasso's compelling style, were signs of the social commitment which nourished painting itself. Later the artist became a constant of trial and challenge vis-a-vis the time quickly flowing in the 20th century. Picasso embodied the power of art and it was clear to me that after him there would be no peace in painting.

This intellectual figure was present throughout my training period like a background canvas. Pasolini the poet, literary man and cultivated artist, had multifaceted forms of expression and also realized some extraordinary movie masterpieces. But it was a poetic image of his that fascinated me, a few months before his tragic death. In an article of February 1, 1975, he denounced the power vacuum in Italy. The ongoing change in civilization was leading to a replacement of the previous values of the rural and paleo-industrial culture by a new reality; this caused a real historic trauma which was accompanied by a value vacuum which Pasolini described by referring to an environmental condition: the "phase of fireflies", followed by the "phase in which fireflies disappeared".

PIER PAOLO PASOLINI

1922-1975

Pier Paolo Pasolini
Autoritratto (Selfportrait), 1965
ochre pencil on paper, 12 ⅝ in. x 9 ⅗ in.
© 2014 Artists Rights Society (ARS),
New York / SIAE, Rome

HENRY MOORE

1898-1986

Henry Moore
Recumbant Woman, 1935
ink and watercolor on paper, 12 ⅝ in. x 9. ⅛ in.
Private Collection
Reproduced by permission of The Henry Moore Foundation

Eight Reclining Figures from the Shelter Sketchbook Portfolio, 1967
lithograph on paper, 14 ⅜ in. x 12 ⅜ in.
Bechtler Museum of Modern Art
Charlotte, North Carolina, USA
Reproduced by permission of The Henry Moore Foundation

Moore's works throw up questions on the meaning of things, they inquire into matter, help to see. The encounter with Moore corresponds to the sweet and painful meeting with the woman-mother, a constant which inspires the artist's investigations and hopes. Woman, mother, stone: a painful return to the origins of life where the female figure bears a classic, timeless look, and we recognize her as a friend thanks to the peaceful acceptance of her breeding role, which reconciles us with everyday life.

One of the main figures of modern architecture, he is the one who managed to turn his lifetime events into architectural projects, in a half-century long "patient research". His ability to interpret and create new proposals within a changing environment, managing to seize the future and mold it into a new concept of beauty of living space, makes him into the central reference figure in the disputes undertaken by 20th-century architectural culture. He was among my "romances" in my early training period, and personally I had the privilege to be the "shop boy" in the atelier he had established in Venice for the new hospital project and later in Rue de Sèvres 35 in Paris.

LE CORBUSIER

1887-1965

Le Corbusier
*Study for the open hand:
"avion Karachi Le Caire - 27/2/54"*, 1954
pen and pencil on paper, 4 ¼ in. x 6 ⅔ in.
Private Collection
© 2014 Artists Rights Society (ARS), New York / ADAGP, Paris / F.L.C.

Spirales logarithmiques (Logarithmic Spirals), 1929-1931
oil on canvas, 39 ½ in. x 31 ¾ in.
Bechtler Museum of Modern Art
Charlotte, North Carolina, USA
© 2014 Artists Rights Society (ARS), New York / ADAGP, Paris / F.L.C.

CARLO SCARPA

1906-1978

Carlo Scarpa
Restauro e allestimento del Museo di Castelvecchio
(Restoration and Construction of the Castelvecchio Museum), 1961-1964
Graphite and pastel on paper, 16 ¼ in. x 13 ⅛ in.
inv. 31585 r
Castelvecchio Museum, Carlo Scarpa Archive
Verona, Italy

Together with art historian Giuseppe Mazzariol he supervised my graduation in Venice in 1969. Misunderstood in the academic world, at best considered by most of his inconsistent colleagues to be an architect "follower of D'Annunzio", he was a strong and free personality, a cultivated and insuperable teacher for the few students who managed to approach him. His talent was recognized as time went by, especially for his sublime set-ups in a continuous, coherent dialog with the displayed works. His works reveal that it is impossible to restore without creating; that the respect of the ancient necessarily goes through the assertion of a new modernity.

The ability to go to the origins of problems. "School: two men speaking under a tree!", the principle of communication and the tree as a protective microclimate. I met Louis Kahn in Venice on the occasion of the (never realized) project for the new congress center "Ai Giardini". I acted as a *trait d'union* between the client (Azienda Autonoma di Soggiorno) and the Philadelphia office (with Carles Vallhonrat). It was a messianic encounter, Kahn was aware both of the potential and the limits of technological development. Through architecture he explored a territory of memory – "the past as a friend" – which he considered to be a possible antidote to the flattening of internationalism, of electronic revolution, of consumer society... Every now and then the interpreter would get stuck on terms like "soul" or "spirituality", which Kahn used to describe architectural facts.

LOUIS I. KAHN
1901-1974

Louis I. Kahn
Studies for the Congress Hall in Venice, 1969
pencil on paper, 11 in. x 30 ⅞ in.
Private Collection

VENEZIA

The city of Venice guarded my university years in a high-quality athenaeum, which paid attention to the ongoing changes in the second half of the 20th century and on some occasions played a key role in the cultural debate. It is possible that the first signs of the urban crisis were perceived here more than in other contexts, as well as the violent ideological disputes and more in general, with regards to architecture, the bewilderment which followed the progressive demise of the Masters of the Modern Movement. An extraordinarily modern city in the separation of the goods-pedestrian routes, a city that describes a deep osmosis between history and contemporaneity, where it is possible to experience the fragile balance between the physical presence of architecture and the inevitable emotional interpretation.

Jacopo de' Barbari
Venetie-Veduta della città di Venezia (View of the City of Venice), ca. 1500
(partial view)
xylograph on six sheets, anastatic printing [facsimile], 53 in. x 111 in.
Private Collection

Francesco Castelli, called Borromini, was born in Bissone, on Lake Lugano, Canton Ticino, in 1599. I confronted myself with his juvenile masterpiece, the church San Carlo alle Quattro Fontane in Rome, on the four-hundredth anniversary of his birth. The wooden reconstruction of the church was erected in Lugano, on the lake shore. It was an intriguing operation for the ambiguity of the planning concept: on the one hand there was the out-of-context representation of a building (from Rome to Lugano), on the other the realization of a new reality (in real scale 1:1). The result had the power of a dream, offering different interpretations of Borromini's language and questioning the city of Lugano on the meaning of that flat water surface surrounded by mighty mountains. The San Carlino was later ingloriously destroyed on the decision of the Municipality of Lugano.

FRANCESCO BORROMINI

1599-1667

Model in 1/33 scale of San Carlino
Lakeside of Lugano, 1999
birch plywood, 36 in. x 26 ¼ in. x 26 ¼ in.

GIOVANNI POZZI

1923-2002

Book Cover
Giovanni Pozzi, *La parola dipinta*
(The Painted Word)
Adelphi Edition, Milan 1981

Every now and then he would visit my studio in Lugano. Punctual, discreet and initially shy, he preferred to listen to the brief explanations I improvised. He had a rare ability to interpret drawings, and his comments referred directly to built architecture. He was a fine philologist, who liked to go directly to the lecture of the details he considered important, comparing them with the ideas underlying the projects. Apart from the reasoning process, he appreciated the creative uncertainty, the intuitive click which can reset all previous achievements to zero; he knew the risks of interpretation and the solitude that torments the creative process.

"Cari figlioli, sento le vostre voci. La mia è una voce sola, ma riassume la voce del mondo intero. Qui tutto il mondo è rappresentato. Si direbbe che persino la luna si è affrettata stasera a guardare a questo spettacolo, che neppure la Basilica di San Pietro, che ha quattro secoli di storia, non ha mai potuto contemplare."

"La mia persona conta niente, è un fratello che parla a voi, diventato padre per volontà di Nostro Signore, ma tutti insieme paternità e fraternità e grazia di Dio, facciamo onore alle impressioni di questa sera, che siano sempre i nostri sentimenti, come ora li esprimiamo davanti al Cielo, e davanti alla Terra: Fede, Speranza, Carità, Amore di Dio, Amore dei Fratelli. E poi tutti insieme, aiutati così, nella santa pace del Signore, alle opere del Bene."

"Tornando a casa, troverete i bambini. Date una carezza ai vostri bambini e dite: questa è la carezza del Papa. Troverete qualche lacrima da asciugare, dite una parola buona: il Papa è con noi, specialmente nelle ore della tristezza e dell'amarezza […]."

On the evening of October 11, 1962, on the occasion of the opening of the Second Vatican Council, Pope Roncalli addressed Saint Peter's Square, improvising a brief speech. The unexpected "speech of the moon" echoed like a poetic, sweet and simple warning, managing to re-create a bond between a possible new course of history and the working reality I felt I belonged to.

JOHN XXIII
1881-1963

Pope John XXIII (called the "good pope"), born as Angelo Giuseppe Roncalli, speech held on the evening of October 11, 1962 at the end of the opening day of the second Vatican Council
Courtesy Corriere della Sera - RCS Quotidiani Spa

GIORGIO MORANDI

1890-1964

Giorgio Morandi
*Natura morta con sei oggetti
(Still Life with Six Objects)*, 1930
etching on paper, 7 ⅞ in. x 9 ⅖ in.
Private Collection
© 2014 Artists Rights Society (ARS),
New York / SIAE, Rome

I admired and researched his chalcographic works for years. The rarefaction of space in his compositions, the peace and silence that radiate from his paintings, are extremely rare values in painting. In Morandi the composure of the subjects and the drafting of figures are simply transformed into a form of pictorial expression. The observer perceives the complexity of the world within a room. His humility, in work and behavior, represents a wisdom, unknown by many, that every now and again emerges unexpectedly as a poetic fact.

Sironi analyses the industrial dimension of urban civilization at the beginning of the 20th century and announces the alienation and solitude of mankind. The painter perceives the desolation in the outskirts, compared to the frenzy in the factories. His paintings are metaphysical spaces full of anxieties, where the urban voids are highlighted by looming obscure shadows, the smokestacks emit poisons and the intense light of the sky turns black.

MARIO SIRONI
1885-1961

Mario Sironi
Il gasometro (The Gasometer), 1943
oil on canvas, 14 in. x 20 ¼ in.
Museum of Modern and Contemporary
Art of Trento and Rovereto
Francesca Giovanardi Collection
© 2014 Artists Rights Society (ARS),
New York / SIAE, Rome

ROBERT FRANK

1924

Robert Frank
For Mario Botta – merci pour la journée du mai 13 1995 – vive le souvenir (Thank you for day of May 13, 1955 - Long live the memory), 1995
black and white photograph, 11 in. x 14 in.
Private Collection

Photography as a sequence of motion pictures. I remember the helicopter trip with Robert Frank, an intrigued observer, when we went to visit two churches, built in the gorge of a valley and on the peak of a mountain in Canton Ticino. His gaze apparently directed the camera without clearly focusing on the surrounding spaces, he did not have that insisting look of a photographer. But Robert Frank could see without watching: the sequence of pictures he later sent me narrated the whole trip; a picture story that conveys the atmosphere of that day.

He took me by car to the storage houses for furniture and objects used in film sets; proper hangars crammed full of "everything and anything", sorted by function (tables, chairs, benches, chandeliers, sculpture casts...), just beyond the perimeter of the Parisian boulevards. He asked me to stand still among all the gimcrack; he shot pictures, but not in succession, one pose after the other, with relaxing breaks in-between. His gaze was always on me, ready to stop the fleeting moment. A fast and striking look, sweet, full of black and white poetry.

ROBERT DOISNEAU

1912-1994

Robert Doisneau
Mario Botta,
Paris, 1991
black and white photograph,
9 ⅓ in. x 6 ⅛ in.
Private Collection

RUDOLF ARNHEIM
1200 EARHART ROAD, #537
ANN ARBOR, MICHIGAN 48105
(313) 668-6483

30 dicembre 1992

Gentile Signor Botta

La professoressa Goldschmidt ha avuto la bontà di darmi il Suo indirizzo. Apprezzo molto l'occasione di dirLe quanto Lei ha detto sul disegno architettonico nelle citazioni date dalla Signora nei suoi articoli. Sono contento anche perché quel che dice Lei come risultato delle Sue lunghe esperienze corrisponde perfettamente a quel che ho chiamato "lo scheletro strutturale" nel mio libro Arte e Percezione Visiva; corrisponde anche a certe osservazioni che ho fatte nel mio libro sull'architettura, anch'esso tradotto in italiano. Fa piacere di veder la teoria confermata dalla pratica.

Mi fa piacere mandare queste righe alla bella città di Lugano, posto indimenticabile di un soggiorno sessanta anni fa. Mi saluti il Monte Brè e la chiesetta di Morcote!

Con auguri per il Nuovo Anno

Rudolf Arnheim

RUDOLF ARNHEIM

1904-2007

I never met him but we had some written correspondence on the project for the church in Mogno; he concluded one of his letters with "greet Monte Bré and the church in Morcote for me!". He left Germany for the United States in the 30's and never went back. In our correspondence I was struck by his insisting on the knowledge of details and the focusing on the meaning of words (in Italian). A true master of visual perception, he believed in semantic meaning and in symbolic values.

Letter from Rudolf Arnheim
to Mario Botta
December 30, 1992
Private Collection

The Romanesque buildings in Lombardy, with a particular attention for those in the lake region, have marked my approach to the world of architecture. The essentiality of volumes, the comparison with the surroundings, the ability to comply with local cultures and at the same time establish themselves as a recognizable language in the various regions of Europe stirred an interest and admiration that have always accompanied me in my work. Romanesque culture (architecture, sculpture and painting) has an ethical tension that has reached our days intact.

THE ROMANESQUE

Cruxification of Villars-les-Moines
(Crucifixion from Priory of Villars-les-Moines),
10th century
plaster cast of a stone slab,
23 ⅓ in. x 16 ½ in. x 7 ⅞ in.
Original conserved at the Art and History Museum
Fribourg, Switzerland

ELADIO DIESTE

1917-2000

Eladio Dieste, Engineer
Shopping Center in Montevideo,
Uruguay, 1985
Architects Guillermo Gómez
Platero and Rodolfo Lopez Rey

He worked mainly in Montevideo, Uruguay, as an architect-entrepreneur. I met him unexpectedly for the first time in Medellin, Colombia, in the 80's, at the Art Museum, where I had been invited to hold a conference. After the final questions and answers, while the room was emptying, a man advanced in years approached me, telling me that he was in transit and had heard of the event: "I also build with cotto tiles and I would like to show you some of my slides". The impact with those images was striking; that modest-looking man was a genius, a strong and cultured personality who had built true masterpieces, that were made known in the whole world by publications in the following decades.

An image, there is always an image behind literary narrative. "My stories originate from an experience, from a real scene that has caught my eye; I have never written a single line without an image". This was the explanation I got from Marquez during a conversation-meeting in Zermatt in 1991. The narration of the Latin-American universe through everyday life traces an epic world of a humanity that belongs to us.

GABRIEL GARCÍA MÁRQUEZ
1927

Herman Vieco, Mario Botta, Gabriel García Márquez
Zermatt, 1991

ARTURO BENEDETTI MICHELANGELI

1920-1995

Arturo Benedetti Michelangeli
London, June 1965
"Arturo Benedetti Michelangeli"
Documentation Center
Brescia, Italy

He wanted a project for the renovation of an old house in Mendrisio, a project which was never realized. He used to come to the studio accompanied by his secretary and gloomily repeated "I want a simple house, I am a farmer from Brescia (Italy)". He was concerned about materials, but not about the surrounding situation. I once objected that where he wanted the studio, it was difficult to get the piano in and the neighborhood noises might have disturbed him. "Those are the voices of life, whereas when I play at a concert I am disturbed by the buzz of a fly".

The performance "Galileo Galilei" in the early 60's at the Piccolo Teatro in Milan left a mark. The evocative power of the scene, the interpretation by Tino Buazzelli, the collective experience of the audience, the reality of a dream in the theater opened many new perspectives for me. From then on, the magic of imagination would have influenced my work.

GIORGIO STREHLER

1921-1997

Tino Buazzelli as Galileo
in *Vita di Galileo (Life of Galileo)* by
Bertold Brecht, Piccolo Teatro di Milano,
directed by Giorgio Strehler, 1962-63
Courtesy Archivio Piccolo Teatro
di Milano - Teatro d'Europa

MAX FRISCH

1911-1991

He began in Zurich as an architect, building within the rationalist culture of the Modern Movement, but his true vocation led him towards literature. Some of his intuitions "We asked for workers. We got people instead" set him apart as a critical conscience of his own country, which was increasingly closing itself within its own borders on the wave of the achievements of technological progress: "The walls that we erect day by day in order to defend our privileges could turn into the walls of our own prison".

Max Frisch in Berzona, Ticino, Switzerland, 1985
Courtesy Max Frisch Archive
Zurich, Switzerland

I had some brief encounters with the writer during his last years, and after his death I planned and realized the "Dürrenmatt Center" in Neuchâtel, where he lived. He was a lucid and fascinating personality, who mercilessly penetrated the precariousness of man, the isolation and solitude of whom he had denounced in a paradox and grotesque way in his literary creation. Beside his literary activity, I discovered his interest for painting and chalcography, two forms of art that he cultivated during his entire life as complementary forms of expression to his thinking. With critical awareness he stated: "I paint like a child, but I am not a child; I paint for the same reason I write, because I think".

FRIEDRICH DÜRRENMATT

1921-1990

Friedrich Dürrenmatt
Selbstbildnis ohne Spiegel
(Selfportrait without Mirror), 1978
pen on paper, 10 ¼ in. x 8 ¼ in.
Centre Dürrenmatt
Neuchâtel, Switzerland

VARLIN
1900-1977

Corridoio a Bondo
(Corridor in Bondo), 1964-1965
oil and carbon on jute, 67 in. x 85 in.
Matasci Foundation
Tenero, Switzerland

The humanity that fascinates the painter Varlin (Willy Leopold Guggenheim) lives on the fringes of the fringes. Only the working condition can save the world from the so-called technological progress, which fuels the consumer society with false and empty models. It is the world of the disinherited, tramps, pilferers, unemployed and prostitutes, who still have a gleam of dignity, still to be found among the losers. Varlin escapes from his native Zurich – "this sterile sanatorium for healthy people" – and lands in Val Bregaglia (curious fate for this spot of land with Segantini at the Maloja, Giacometti in Stampa and Varlin in Bondo).

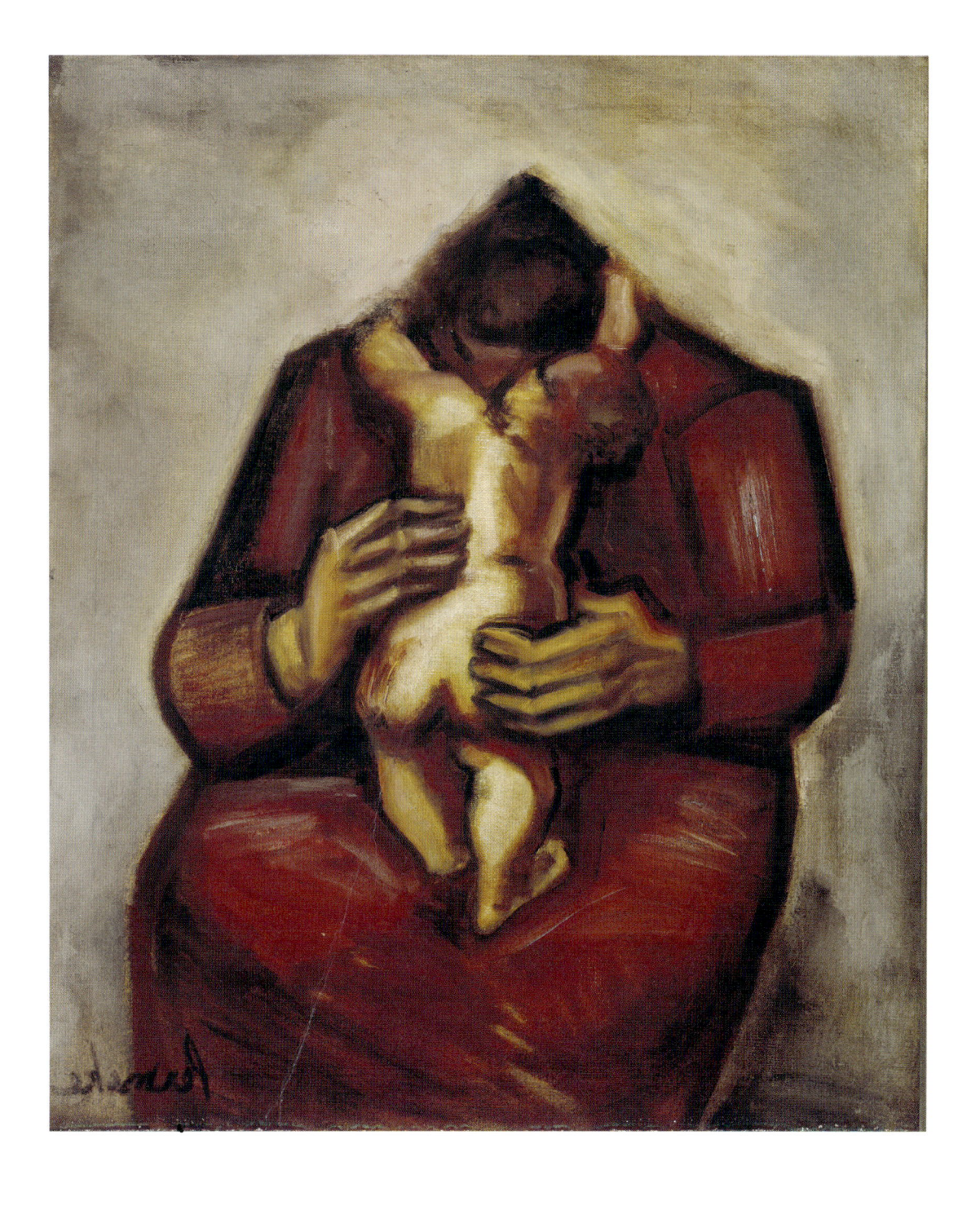

The Flemish declination of a strong and materic language finds its utmost expression through monumental celebration. With his figures of plebeians, laborers and fishers, Permeke confers new dignity to a forgotten humanity. The expressive power of his paintings communicates with the landscapes and the primeval elements of nature; painting that goes directly to the heart of the message.

CONSTANT PERMEKE

1886-1952

Constant Permeke
Maternità (Maternity), 1924-1925
oil on canvas, 47 ¼ in. x 39 ⅜ in.
© 2014 Artists Rights Society (ARS), New York / SABAM, Brussels

NIKI DE SAINT PHALLE

1930-2002

Niki de Saint Phalle
Le rhinocéros (The Rhinoceros), 1995
mixed media, 70 ⅛ in. x 93 ¼ in.
Private Collection
© 2014 Niki Charitable Art Foundation. All rights reserved / ARS, NY / ADAGP, Paris

Untitled, 1970
polyester, fiberglass and acrylic paint,
37 in. x 56 in. x 4 ½ in.
Bechtler Museum of Modern Art
Charlotte, North Carolina, USA
© 2014 Niki Charitable Art Foundation. All rights reserved / ARS, NY / ADAGP, Paris

We were united by the complementarity of our respective languages. Niki loved structured and geometrical spaces, in some cases even rigid and monumental ones, for her fantastic works to live in; she preferred austere "black and white" spaces for her colored creatures. "You build the (stone) ark, and I will mold the animals". This statement marked the beginning of a five-year long collaboration, leading to the realization of "Noah's Ark" in Jerusalem, designed with the hope of seeing Palestinian children play with their Israeli peers.

Normally works of art prefer silence; those of Jean Tinguely the thin and sharp sound produced by their own movements. Tinguely assembles objects, relics and waste which have survived industrial production and are doomed to end up in garbage dumps. His creativity begins at the end of the production cycle and interprets the worst of consumer society at best. The reassembled, inanimated waste objects find a new useless animation through an ironic and poetic look.

JEAN TINGUELY
1925-1991

Jean Tinguely
Va-et-vient (Coming and Going), 1991
mixed media, 59 in. x 27 ⅗ in. x 27 ⅗ in.
Private Collection
© 2014 Artists Rights Society (ARS), New York / ADAGP, Paris

Untitled, 1991
watercolor on pasteboard, 28 in. x 21 ⅞ in.
Bechtler Museum of Modern Art
Charlotte, North Carolina, USA
© 2014 Artists Rights Society (ARS), New York / ADAGP, Paris

PAUL KLEE

1879-1940

Paul Klee
Kleinstadt Idyll (Small Town Idyll), 1913
gouache and ink on paper and cardboard,
6 ⅓ in. x 4 ⅓ in.
Paul Prast Collection
© 2014 Artists Rights Society (ARS), New York

Ohne Titel [Tanzende Figuren]
(Untitled [Dancing figures]), ca. 1938
watercolor on primed burlap, 10 ⅖ in. x 8 ⅛ in.
Bechtler Museum of Modern Art
Charlotte, North Carolina, USA
© 2014 Artists Rights Society (ARS), New York

The lucidity of theoretical thinking in painting. His "Theory of Form and Figuration" accompanied me for years in the never-ending search for a logical connection between theory and pictorial practice. He was a great thinker and an even greater painter. I was surprised by his almost obsessive care in writing down the titles, the dates, the signature on the margins of his "papers", among parallel lines traced by pencil. How was it possible to have such an absolute expressive freedom and at the same time a systematic archival approach? His mind managed to foster the primordial magic signs in a cultured reality of expressive necessity.

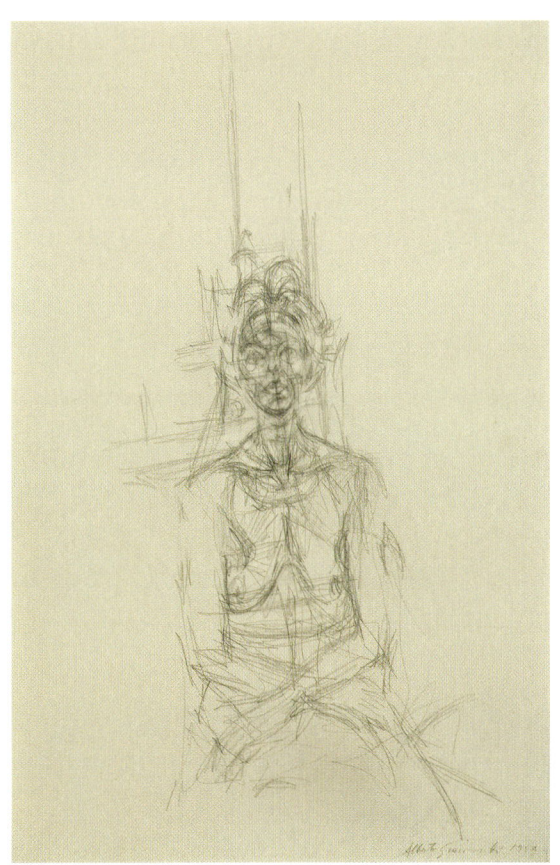

The looks, the figures, the women that Giacometti pursued as witnesses of his time belong to me; they are part of an identity I share, that goes beyond our common origin in the Italian part of Switzerland. The intensity of the look which the artist penetrates faces with recalls the severity and the posture of the women who protected my childhood. There is even some resemblance between the somatic traits of his tormented figures, almost burnt by life, and the memory I jealously retain of the persons I have loved most. Giacometti still is the cantor who, more than others, has endlessly, hopelessly dug into the mystery that lies in the folds of a face.

ALBERTO GIACOMETTI
1901-1966

Alberto Giacometti
Studi da maestri (Studies of the Masters), 1951
pencil on paper, 22 ¼ in. x 14 ⅛ in.
Private Collection
© 2014 Alberto Giacometti Estate/Licensed by VAGA and ARS, New York, NY

Annette, 1959
pencil on paper, 19 ¾ in. x 13 in.
Bechtler Museum of Modern Art
Charlotte, North Carolina, USA
© 2014 Alberto Giacometti Estate/Licensed by VAGA and ARS, New York, NY

GIOTTO

1267-1337

Giotto
Il bacio di Giuda (The kiss of Judas)
1303-1304 (partial image)
Scrovegni Chapel
Padova, Veneto, Italy
SCALA Photo Archive

His out-of-time, irresistible, captivating, absolute painting puts the observer in front of the charm of narrative. The constant references between the painted images and the surrounding landscape trace fairy-tale spaces that we identify as being real. His dry and essential language appears to be extremely modern, an expressive form that can be acknowledged in our everyday lives; his paintings prepare the ground for meditation and silence, they reconcile us with the expectations and hopes that dwell in the great past.

Painter of space; painter of geometry of space, which embraces the gravity of the gesture of the performers like in a scenic production. The architectural layout is omnipresent in his paintings, from the vast landscapes, where nature meets rarefied built spaces, to the portraits of single figures, where hieratic gravity and everyday signs coexist. Piero is the most architectural among figurative artists in the history of painting.

PIERO DELLA FRANCESCA
1416/1417-1492

Piero della Francesca
Madonna del Duca Federico (Pala di Brera)
1472-1474 (partial image)
Brera Art Gallery
Milan, Italy
Courtesy Italian Ministry of
Cultural Heritage and Activities

ALEXANDER CALDER

1898-1976

Alexander Calder
Untitled, 1969
gouache on paper, 29 ½ in. x 43 ⅛ in.
Private Collection
© 2014 Calder Foundation, New York / Artists
Rights Society (ARS), New York

Untitled, 1964
gouache on paper, 30 in. x 42 in.
Bechtler Museum of Modern Art
Charlotte, North Carolina, USA
© 2014 Calder Foundation, New York / Artists
Rights Society (ARS), New York

Calder's wire portraits prompt the observer to visually reconstruct the final image. It is a slightly hinted form of sculpture, which requires the direct complicity of the observer, who himself becomes an artist; a cunning idea that sustains the naïve game of the discovering child, whose imaginary world of dreams turns into reality. Calder's entire work is supported by a thin thread of magic.

Ab edendo

to B.

1

ero il cappello (del cappellaio cappellano, in amore) del prestigiatore prestidigitatore:
(ero la coppa (e anche la maschera) del maschio in coppia): ero la torre (la torta)
dei tarocchi: (la tana delle tortore: una trama tremante sopra un tetto): ero un perfetto
insetto: (una torma di tarme): ero il tuo trono (il tuo treno):

                                                                             (ero il tuo seno):

2

sono una testa della terra (abitabile abile): e ti guardo con questi miei occhi barocchi
che ti bruciano: ti vedo con la fronte che si spezza, con le labbra che si slabbrano
(con la lepre, la lebbra): (con la mia lisca e la mia cresta): sono una testa
antropomorfa, forma del fermo cerchio fatto circo (circa): ti cerco:

                                                                             (e sono il seno):

3

sarò la porta aperta che si perde (nel giro della bocca che si becca): (e che
ti tocca): faro di vena vera (e vera sfera che spera): e favo (e fiato soffiato
fragolato): la culla della colla della cellula (che dondola): tuo velo (e cielo):

sarò il tuo piatto catafratto (affatto contraffatto): (casa è cosa, nel caso, dove
si mangia): (utero d'uso): (corno d'ariete, lancia): (e plancia): (e pancia):
sarò il tuo dente incontinente (il tuo sogno, il tuo segno):

                                                                             (e sarò un seno)

Asked by Elvio Fachinelli (publisher of the magazine *L'Erba Voglio*) to write the preface of the book *La Casa Rotonda* (1982), Sanguineti sent a poem "Ab edendo". It was a surprise: what could a poet ever read behind the walls of a one-family home on the outskirts of a village?

EDOARDO SANGUINETI
1930-2010

Edoardo Sanguineti
"Ab edendo" ("Taste")
from: *Mario Botta.
La casa rotonda*, L'Erba Voglio,
Milan 1982

PANTHEON

Perfection built with zenithal light. Light, as a generator of space, finds its theoretical evidence in the Pantheon. But beyond the possible geometrical tests, it documents the highest expression of tectonic power, which has remained intact after two thousand years of history, with the magnificence of that single opening towards the sky, with its essential measures and intelligent conception.

Inside view of the Pantheon's cupola in Rome, 126 A.D.
Courtesy Italian Ministry of Cultural Heritage and Activities

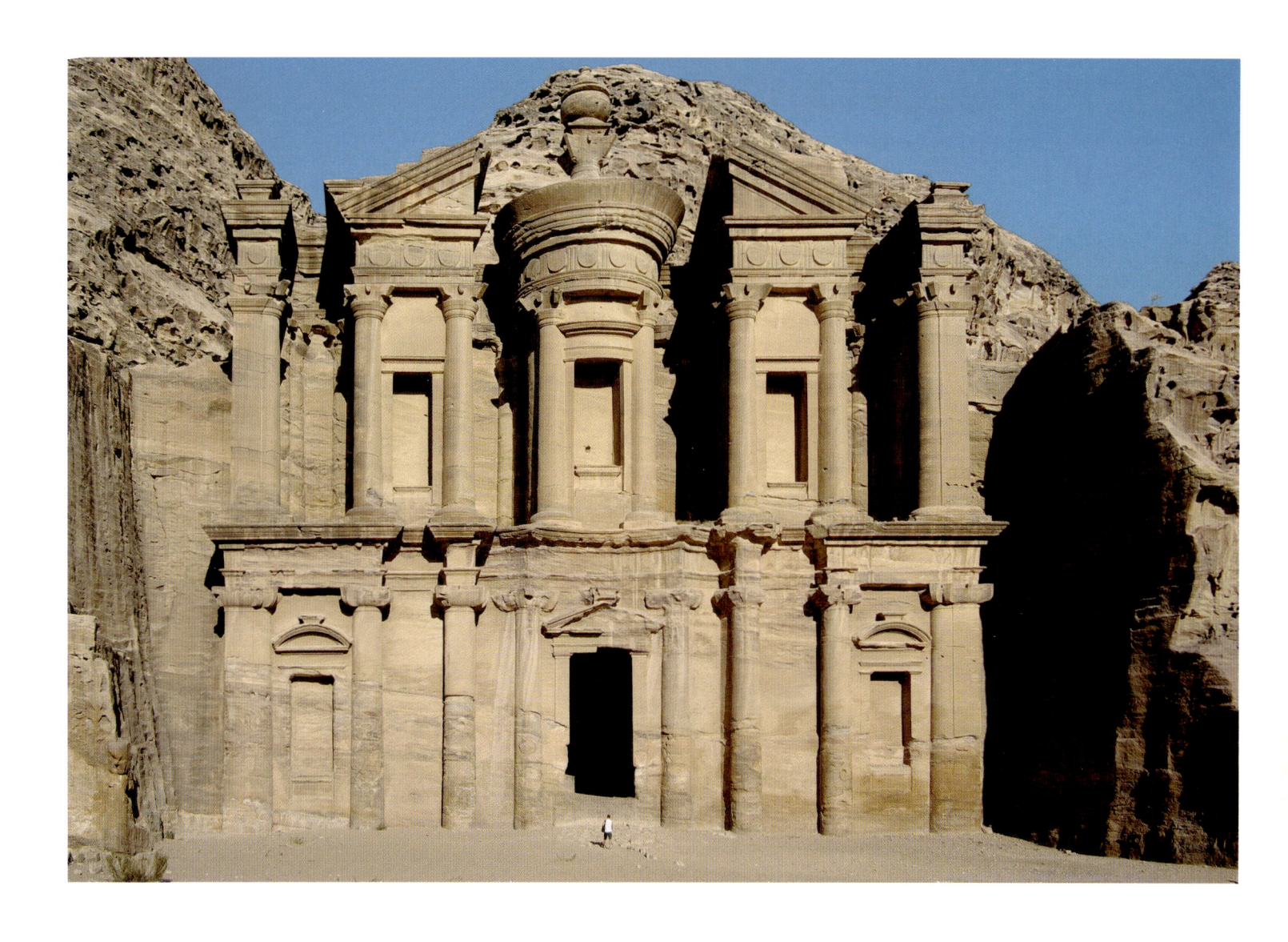

Beyond the narrow and enchanting gorge leading to Petra, the city speaks of the beauty of carved stone and of the power of spaces cut in rock. The eye of the beholder follows the light painted by the sun throughout the whole day. Turns are taken between the abundance of shadows and the sun-lit profiles. Natural light has never stood out as much in contrast with the deepness of the shadows.

PETRA

Petra, Jordan
Ed-Deir Monastery, 2nd century B.C.

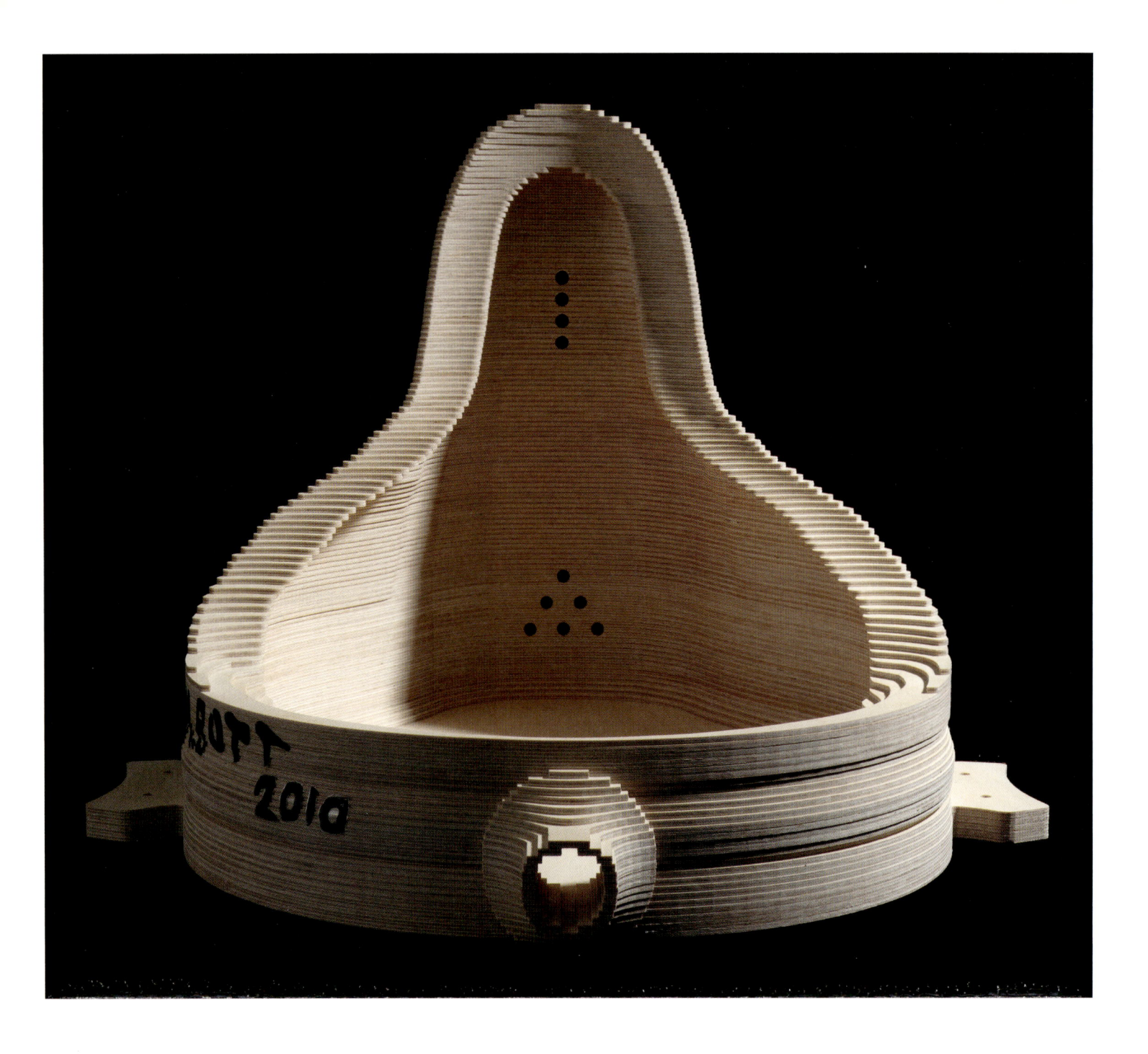

MARCEL DUCHAMP

1887-1968

Mario Botta
Tribute to Marcel Duchamp, 2010
birch plywood, 14 ¼ in. x 19 ¾ in. x 23 ¾ in.
Private Collection

The power of ideas in the work of art. Among the various movements of the post-war artistic Avantgardes, Marcel Duchamp practices, more than others, a radicalization, putting the idea at the center of artistic research. With his *ready made* he turns a reproducible, everyday object into a unique, absolute work of art; in a unique, signed artistic form, put on a pedestal, conferring it a new sacredness in the eyes of the beholder. What remains in life are ideas, and art is the absolute form of the need of infinite that underlies the very sense of being of mankind. Beyond the *ready made* we withhold the possibility to recover a poetic presence which is able to give a new centrality to mankind.

The prominence and the purity of the painting, the rigor of abstraction, the intuition of a new world tending to overhaul any form of naturalism. Once again critical intelligence underlies pictorial intuition. The final aims are not of this world: harmony, immortality, silence are evoked by black lines that meet orthogonally, tracing monochrome fields in pure primary colors.

PIET MONDRIAN

1872-1944

Piet Mondrian
Composition II with Red, Blue, Black and Yellow, 1929
oil on canvas, 17 ¾ in. x 17 ¾ in.
National Museum, Belgrade, Serbia
inv. no I. str. 43
Donation of the city of Amsterdam in 1931

KAZIMIR MALEVIČ

1878-1935

Another juvenile "romance". The fact that a black square on a white background could represent the existing tensions in the world was made clear to me by Malevič and the Russian Avantgardes of that time. I was stricken by the fact that the social tensions of that time naturally influenced the poetics of the artists, who reveal themselves to be real and true seismographs of the history and the hopes of their time.

Kazimir Malevič
Suprematiste composition - objects of 1916
(Suprematist Composition - objects of 1916),
ca. 1920-1921
pencil on paper, 8 ¼ in. x 7 ¼ in.
Paul Prast Collection

The last no-global? His critical mind certainly stood out in the crowd. Ceronetti asked me to plan a puppet theater. A small, fragile and wandering architecture, with a built-in stage, ready to tell stories and dreams. Nowadays, a small mobile theater is not a meaningless object. On the contrary, it can turn into a tool exuding a new beauty and emotion, creating a contrast with the flat, uniform surroundings. Then, at the end of the performance the theater is recomposed in its shell, silently and discreetly, waiting on hold, at the borders of a widening, to become once again the protagonist for new dreams the following day.

GUIDO CERONETTI
1927

Mario Botta
Theater of the Sensitives
Model, 2007

ature architect by the parish priest of the small town, which was designed by Botta, then only 15 years old, in 1961; later, in 1963, upon enrollment in the Liceo Artistico di Brera of the Art college of Beato Angelico in Milan (2), it would be built up to its completion in 1965.

GEOMETRIES OF LIGHT AND COLOR; IN TIME

LIONELLO PUPPI

Half a century of activity behind him, lavished with unconditional generosity, almost tending to prodigality, without ever eluding the confrontation with the typology issues, including the most difficult ones, of architectural space and *design*, with an undeterred, almost stubborn loyalty to his original vocation, but hostile to narcissistic repetitiveness and satisfied mannerism; this is how Mario Botta stands out, with the linguistic and formal originality of a true Master, in the scenario of architecture, in many ways frantic and contradictory – and, further, place of overbearing and false arrogances; and of deplorable downfalls -between the last decades of the 20th century and the first decade of the third millennium.

"I could have become a photographer or a painter – is what he told Antonio Gnoli in a long interview, published in the daily *La Repubblica* on November 23, 2009 –, but in the end I decided to draw and plan. At the age of 15 I discovered that building had some kind of magic. And I built my first house": which turned out to be the incredible surprise of the parish house in Genestrerio (1), a task commissioned to the aspir-

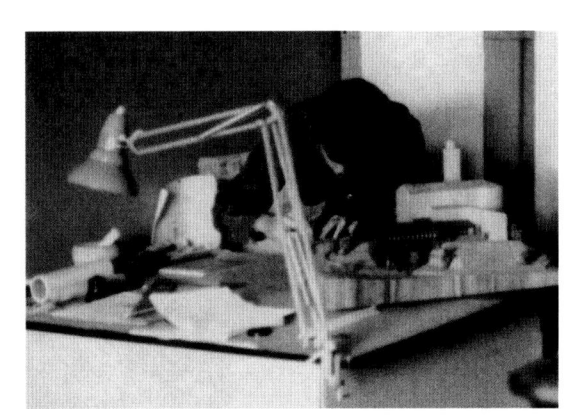

1. Young Mario Botta working on a model for the parish house project in Genestrerio, 1962
2. Studies at the Art college of Beato Angelico in Milan, 1963
3. Guido Gonzato, *Autoritratto* [Selfportrait], 1930, conté pencil drawing, private collection
4. Sketch of Dürrenmatt center in Neuchâtel, 2000

ing architect in his early adolescence by Tita Carloni, who had "taken him on to work as an apprentice in his studio". We will come back to this in a moment: but in the meantime it is worthwhile recalling that previously Botta had already often insisted on the singularity of that initial thrilling experience, to stress the value of a decisive and ineludible lesson.

"Not a single day would go by without me going to the construction site to check that work was in progress and being carried out the way I had planned it, and there discover building techniques and processes I had not known about up to then. And, furthermore, I could feel the pleasure and emotion in observing how a *place* was being transformed". Of course: "with all the linguistic doubts due to the *naivety* of the very first work, but nonetheless with the awareness of the role of the creativity present in a work of architecture". And, indeed, in his career, the so-called institutional studies, which will follow (2) and which we will speak about later, were anticipated by wide-ranging "building site experience". His journey appears to be "inverted" compared to the customary path, but it is at the same time reminiscent, if not of the circumstances of Palladio's training (which was, I would like to recall, *mutatis mutandis*, even too obvious), at least of the multiple and centuries-old history of the lapicides from his small homeland Ticino, who achieved supreme and glorious success in the major cultural centers in Italy and Europe after leaving the valleys and the lakes of their native land, their only baggage being the artisan expertise accumulated through the practice of the basic building techniques.

So much for that.

It would be superficial to underestimate the atmosphere that teenage Botta had to breathe in Carloni's studio, permeated – like other fervently active architecture studios in Ticino, the likes of Aurelio Galfetti (though with lecorbusierian inclinations); Livio Vacchini (with glances to Mies and Louis Kahn) – by neo-rationalist humors fuelled by Aldo Rossi's teachings, claiming the primacy of composition over function, the recovery of the typology issue, and paying attention to the relationship with the urban texture. Such a climate exhorted to a lack of scruples in the composition practice, but before that, to the consideration and admiration of the historic and natural heritage of the *place*: the rural houses as well as the dramatic spatiality of the small Romanesque churches; a "landscape", according to Dante Isella, with the "sparkling and nearly Manzonian air of the Pre-Alpine lakes and the sharp and at the same time friendly mountain cliff sides" – and with an attitude that Gianfranco Contini could see in another fellow countryman, the incredibly forgotten painter Guido Gonzato (3), for whom "not only was the syntactic inflection of the sentence important, the single word counted in its greatness and nobility", which will condition and regulate the geometrical variables. Consequently, Botta's initial "naivety" is only apparent and, vice versa, in substance, presumes what Sergio Bettini would have already, and maybe obscurely, defined "a fully-formed historical consciousness" according to which "the sense of reality, of nature" are concrete facts that meet in their plurality in a temporal succession of objects, forming the space and the time of experience"; they coincide "with the field of our *vivente experiri* (= *Erlebnis*)".

And this aspect deserves a note that recalls the peculiarity of Botta's training: the "inverse path", which he himself has never failed to point at with the appropriate emphasis – also in the 2009 interview, which we have taken the cue from – and the assiduous presence on the building site which developed with a "greediness for doing", bound to become a joyful daily habit, but that in the meantime represented a privileged occasion to accumulate a "wide-ranging experience" before starting his academic course of studies, and that would subsequently become an urge, an ineludible, binding need: the conquest, and practice of *timing*, i.e. the ability that distinguishes the artist, who therein, inasmuch "punctual emergency of time, unpredictable or at least indeterminable by the artist himself", "finds – we once again quote a memorable essay by Sergio Bettini, published just over half a century ago in 'La Biennale di Venezia' on the review *Arte e critica* – not only the freedom and the unconditional hazard of his creative 'discretion', but also the guarantee of success, the 'evidence' that what he does is a work of art".

"Hazard" and "guarantee". When Antonio Gnoli provokingly asked Botta to what extent chance had counted for him, in the interview we have taken the cue from, reminding Mario about the relationship he had with Friedrich Dürrenmatt, whose house in Neuchâtel he will later be called to intervene on, transforming it into a cultural center (4) (and this is one of his most inspired spatial gestures) and, considering that for the great writer it is above all chance that governs our lives, Mario gave an eloquent answer. "Chance always plays an important role. But every one of us has to be able to orient it. You cannot simply succumb to it. One day everything seems to be predictable, then you come across an image that you were not expecting; at that point you have to know if you want to use it, develop it or let it be": and it is necessarily the ability to master *timing*, the achievement of which requires a training and a trial and error period that "cannot take place in the academic-school system, but on the technical field, so to say of practice: just like a jump champion cannot learn from any lesson to find the right moment for the perfect takeoff; but he can be helped to reach it by training; becoming the master of his body and repeating the exercise incessantly; just like no teacher, as great as he may be, can really teach a violin virtuoso to keep the notes for the infinitesimal time more or less than the one schematically noted on the score; but only the full mastery of the in-

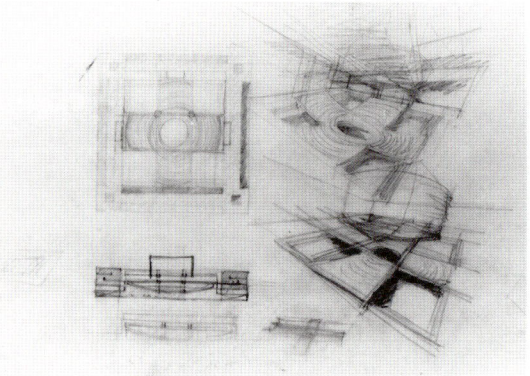

5. Dissertation at the IUAV – Architectural Institute of the University in Venice on July 31, 1969, from left: Mauro Lena, Giuseppe Samonà, Carlo Aymonino, Constantino Dardi, Carlo Scarpa, Valentino Pastor, Gian Ugo Polesello, Ignazio Gardella, Mario Botta
6. Sketch of the thesis project, 1969

strument and constant practice can lead him – if he manages – to get that *timing* right. *Timing* is eventually the secret of an expressive performance; the artist can only 'form' by learning the trade in the most technical sense of the term, until he reaches that technical automatism […] that grants him the *freedom* to repeat his colors incessantly, until 'something' warns him that he cannot change anything anymore: that he has seized the *timing,* precisely". Therefore, this is all there is to "the difference between the engineer and the architect (just like between the prose writer and the poet; the illustrator and the painter; et cetera), for example. The engineer measures and calculates within a 'given' time; whereas the architect applies the 'discretion' of his own *timing*": and therefore he does not verify, he creates "through that process which was already the rush of teenage Botta from the drawing table, where he felt at ease on his own, to the building site, "territory of constant learning" – as he himself defined it in a page of *Quasi un diario* (Firenze, Le Lettere 2003) -, "a difficult, rewarding but sometimes also unforgiving attempt" to *become* irreversible and indelible in architectural space: where, eventually, *timing* cannot do anything else but exclude any "wrong gesture" to materialize as a "right gesture".

When Mario, upon concluding the studies in Milan which gave him the necessary degree to enter university, has to choose the location for his university career in order to obtain the academic license and the legal authorization to practice his profession, he will not hesitate to recognize Venice as the place of his choice; and we could, non idly, question ourselves on the motivations for such a choice, which, in my opinion, transcends the awareness that the university in Venice was considered among the most dynamic and brilliant in Italy in the early 60's for the prestige of lecturers of the caliber of Giuseppe Samonà and Carlo Scarpa, without mentioning the others, whose teachings will in fact be decisive for the fortune of the young man from Ticino (5, 6). Something else, far more fascinating and binding, must have attracted and deeply captivated Botta: the city; as there he had the *chance* to meet and become friendly with a volcanic figure who taught art history, but also directed one of the city's cultural institutions, the Foundation Querini Stampalia: Giuseppe Mazzariol. He was the man who, in the light of the teachings of his own Master, i.e. that Sergio Bettini we mentioned above, could introduce Botta to the depths of Venice, explaining to him that if it is true that "all non-common cities are works of art […] and it cannot be said of them that they belong to the past since they live their own time in the present, i.e. they pass from shape to shape […] they live inasmuch there are living people who realize them in their time and therefore they are somebody's present experience […,]: no other city has such an openness, an inexhaustible interpretability like Venice". Thanks to the incomplete structure of its shape, it is not the object of mere and inert contemplation but

7. House in Stabio, 1967
8. Sketch of the Notre-Dame Cathedral in Paris, 1968

rather of immediate participation. As such, "it is possibly the most present city among all: because it has never been a 'classic' city – such as, for example Florence; it has always been and still is an open shape, versed in *time*, thus sorted out in color and rhythm", and "the city cannot be understood […] by means of classic contemplation, as a closed shape", it has to be "lived", since the secret of its *modernity* lies in its power of identification between our present time and its shape.

And as young Botta's familiarity with Venice gradually increased, he could not help perceiving an "expression of spatial *continuum* and therefore – unlike other cities founded in the Middle Ages or during the Renaissance, and maybe with the exception of Siena and Amsterdam – of a mainly urban value", and reach the irrevocable conviction that architecture "is not the tool to build in a place, but to build *that* place. It has to take into account its features, its identity, its being origin, in its own way", and this leads "to working on the territory of memory".

In another interview granted to Marco Bevilacqua for the daily *Il Mattino di Padova*, on the occasion of an exhibition of his work between 1993 and 2003 in the hall of the Palazzo della Ragione in Padua, Botta asserted that, today, "being modern […] means witnessing one's time" but as a "constant re-reading of the great past" and thus, "the territory the architect of the third millennium has to work on is the territory of memory". He must have had in mind the lesson which had a decisive impact, with Mazzariol and Venice in his youthful passion, when he asserted that "the model of the European city, which is the result of a millenary stratification, today more than ever offers the antibodies which can defeat the urban degenerations of the present time", fuelled by the "crisis of town planning, which is not able to respond in an adequate way to contemporary complexity" and even gives in to the wile of speculative building. Along these lines and from the very beginning, Botta exorcised the obscene seductions of the song of the mermaids of post-modernism in the omen of the vertigo of globalization. Of post-modernism he despised the confusion of styles with history, thus turning it into a caricature, and a need of memory limited to the remake of the tympanum and the column; of globalization he denounced the negation of the concept of place and the proclamation of the end of history. This is the moment he became aware of the need, in the spatial organization of human *Lebensraum*, of the indissolubility of the ethical and esthetic components; which entailed a lucid and ineludible consciousness of the architect's social responsibility, precisely verified by his awareness of being in the time of history.

In this respect, the meeting of the young talent from Ticino with Le Corbusier – brought about by the usual Mazzariol, who had vehemently wanted the "giant" in Venice to plan the new hospital *on the borders*

9. Sketch of the House in Riva San Vitale, 1970
10. Sketch for the house in Morbio Superiore, 1982

– must have been exciting, or even shocking, in what he could recognize in the old Master (Botta will later say, and has repeated even recently, "he was what Einstein was for physics. He brought the problems of the 20th century. He had an extraordinary faith in the possibility of redeeming society through space"); he accepted the challenge to tackle the open shape of the city, with the humility of questioning the programmatic and systematic *scientific methodology* of his *plan libre* in the presence of a historical value revealed in a space-time continuity, adapting the modulation of his architectural *machine*, and its functional distribution, to that of the spatial *continuum* of the urban site. Last but not least, the ripening of the "sense of reality and of nature" that had guided Mario upon his debut in architecture will find further solace and suggestions in Venice; once more through personal meetings.

With Louis Kahn, first *perceived* in the reproductions of his works in the pages of Vincent Scully's monograph at the time of his apprenticeship in Tita Carloni's studio in Lugano, later *rediscovered* and even helped in the work for the exhibition of his models, when the Estonian master arrived in Venice to plan the congress center, without success ("he asks me to measure the spaces; the diameters of the trees, the circumference of certain spaces, the height of others. I do so."). He stands at his side day and night, progressively discovering "his strength, intuition, intelligence", convincing himself that he "was a messianic figure of 20th-century architectural culture" who could have stemmed the post-modern culture which would flood America; he is enchanted by, and resolves to treasure, the radical but nonetheless constructive criticism towards the utopia and arrogance of the Modern Movement through the pursuit and definition of archetypal forms like *institutions*, the universality of whose social value is built on the sedimentation of memory of needs, above all functional to collective life as they materialize in an elementary geometric shape, which is capable of *placing itself in time* through the dynamic expressiveness of planimetric and volumetric aspects, supported by the choice of materials and regulated by light.

Then with Carlo Scarpa: he will take Mario to his graduation, fascinating him with his almost obsessive attention for detail, a combination of rigid artisan probity and aristocratic elegance; with his unspent and stubborn attention to the graphic testing of his *organic* spatial intuitions, as they claimed not to be staged in a dimension to be contemplated, but lived in.

If, on the one hand, Botta did not refrain from his independent design work during the period of the so-called academic training, which approached the end of the 60's, on the other hand, his work could not fail to be affected by the events the *student* was experiencing, almost enduring: and yet, a work like the residential house in Stabio (7), invented in 1965 and realized two years later, though being an evident "tribute

11. Frank Lloyd Wright, drawing for Masieri Memorial in Venice
Courtesy Frank Lloyd Wright Foundation, Scottsdale, AZ

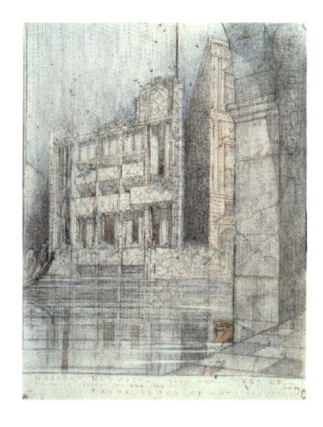

to Le Corbusier" (8), conceals the germs of future original developments (the multi-story structure of the interior; the in-between connections created by light effects rather than plastic elements; the use of un-polished reinforced concrete; the tension aimed at dynamizing the compositional geometry): seeds that would blossom between the mild, green, rolling hills and in the quiet diffused light of Ticino, during the 70's and in the following decade up to the 90's, in a sequence of true masterpieces, inaugurated by the family house in Cadenazzo, invented and realized between 1970 and 1971, which was embedded in an environmental context threatened by a wild urbanization of insignificant and mediocre one-family homes, like "a sort of mysterious pre-existence with the shape of restless stereometry, where openings are limited to large portholes placed at the extremes of the building" (E. Pizzi), and the sense of the *event* as a formal seal of a place reality will be revealed by the application on the farmhouse in Ligrignano, to recover and highlight the original profiles by inserting large cylindrical volumes in bricks bound by a regular weave of metallic profiles.

And, one after the other, the houses in Riva San Vitale (9), Ligornetto, Pregassona, Massagno, Viganello, Stabio, Morbio Superiore (10), Breganzona, Vacallo, Losone, Manno, Daro, Montagnola, Bernareggio, with an inexhaustible effusion of creative imagination but always in the relationship with the natural and historical landscape, which was never sidestepped, will materialize and lead to the creation of an extremely original language in the open form of an authentic, and new and innovative, architectural poetry, characterized by dialectics of geometry, color and light: the first far from rationalizing space in a mere timeless representation of an *idea*, the second articulating itself in delicate chromatic compositions, for effect of the latter – which is not abstract and fixed luminescence, to quote Bettini again, but "is identified in its changing direction and intensity according to the turning and changing of 'tempus'" – to assert itself in the modernity of spatial-temporal structure.

It is beyond doubt that in the meantime, the teachings of Le Corbusier, Kahn and Scarpa (with the crucial experience in Venice) are enriched by other impulses Botta is very aware of. In fact he has never failed to admit to them, and has even gone as far as listing them as *flashes* in the introductory section of this catalogue, indicating them as "emotions" of "elective affinities". Surprising are the references to Calder and Klee on the one hand, and Moore, Malevič and Mondrian, on the other; to Picasso and Wright, in the end. These artists – referring to the first five to start with – can be brought down to a form of *abstractism*, whose spatial-temporal dimension materializes in the acceptation of "empirical space in its existential reality" (quoting Bettini once again), entailing it, composing it, *building it* in time, i.e. by overcoming the du-

12. Sketch for the TCS Building in Hyderabad, 2003
13. Preliminary sketch for the church project in Mogno, 1986
14. Sketch of the Chapel on Monte Tamaro, 1990

alism of space-shape, "renouncing any dimensional precondition, contracting shape in unitary bulks, subtracted [...] to any corrosion, resolved in the ongoing search for their pure formal *quality*". On the other hand, Picasso, in the last season of his magnificent artistic adventure, enriched by the most astonishing experiences, but consistently oriented to the aim of entering, to quote Pierre Francastel, "dans l'espace qui, pour Dufy et Matisse, restait encore un object vu de dehors et décrit comme tel", proposes pictorial images, whose spatiality tends to coincide with the space the observer of the painting places himself in, involving the time of his existence, his *in der Welt sein*. With regards to Wright, Mario could not be uninformed about the vicissitudes of the Masieri Memorial (11) at the bend of Canal Grande towards the Basin of San Marco, and he may even have commented on the projects with Carlo Scarpa, perceiving the concern of the American master (which will later also become his own matter of concern) of generating "outdoor" spaces from the interior space, "where the subject establishes his existence", subordinating the compositional elements, starting from the walls, to the need of *informing* the continuity of his own space-time.

The same parsimony (not to say suspicion) that Botta uses the right angle with, appears to us as an explicit Wrightian legacy, and one can perceive, once more, an expedient which is consistent with his architectural thinking, hostile to the definition of closed, blocked objects – in one word: classic, which can be contemplated in their finiteness. Thus, in order to make up for, or to question, the marginality of the square or the rectangle, beside the circle, the ellipse, the curved lines, in Wrightian style, one can see his predilection emerge for the "incompleteness", the balance "instability" of the triangle, which is, as once again Sergio Bettini underlines, a figure "whose vertices protrude towards a space which is not included in the figure itself, which therefore expects to be completed, and appears as the symbol of a kinetic spatiality, projected in time". Thus, the buildings in Pregassona, Massagno, Viganello, Morbio, Vacallo, Daro, Bernareggio, have to be reviewed and compared to the apartment building in Novazzano, the Ransila building, the Banca del Gottardo and the Cinque Continenti Center in Lugano, the UBS headquarters in Basel, the library of the Capuchin Convent in Lugano, the audiovisual library in Villeurbanne, the Watari-um gallery in Tokyo, the theater and André Malraux Cultural Center in Chambéry, the churches San Giovanni Battista in Mogno, Beato Oderico in Pordenone, San Pietro Apostolo in Sartirana.

In fact, these works are the result of about two decades of architectural activity; during this, while having to tackle and realize the most manifold and elaborate typology issues, resulting in works of unmistakable originality and authentic architectural poetry, Botta gradually defines the basic structure of a geometrical language with variable shapes, which are never prospectively fixed in the purely contemplatable absolute of a closed plastic *individuum*, temporally tested in light and aroused by the *timing* hazard – and, therefore, dynamic, active, existential – which they establish with the natural and historical *site*. Thus a language, as we have already stated beforehand, that cannot be expressed by abstractions in the logic of being, fixing the certainty of an idea, but bound to justify itself first and foremost as being capable of materializing, with the will of *being* and through and at the head of an exhausting, graphic and building trial and error (documented by the architect's crowded notebooks: who will, not by chance, state that "beauty requires trial and error, you can only say that something is nice once you have tried it"), in the time of existence.

We are hence faced with a process that, in the moment it detracts the artistic quality of the result from the adjustment to an eternal and, so to say, neo-platonic canon, and connects it to the ethical need for the correct function ("a house – but it could also be a hotel, an office building, a bank – it is not only the square meters that constitute it", is what Botta will say in his interview with Gnoli; he cannot do anything else but retrace and realize it, in fact, in the *hic et nunc* of a *place*, since – and it is worthwhile reiterating a recurring expression used by Mario – doing architecture does not mean building *in a* place, but building *that* place, thus going down in the temporal flow of history.

Now, however, it is evident that such an attitude had a privileged opportunity of being applied in the first two decades of activity which, progressing from the universe of Ticino to the European scale, dealt and communicated with a territory rich in history and memory; "when you go to build in Siena, Venice, Amsterdam, you feel as if you were in paradise. These cities are the formal expression of history". But when the activity of the architect becomes *global*, and this is a condition that Mario will start facing, *more or less*, in the early nineties, the disorientation (no time, no place) could have been devastating; it could have caused the capitulation or the escape in the irresponsible expedients of post-modernism, even though acquired and practiced with irony. But this "is interesting only in literature. If done in stone and concrete it can turn into a serious problem" because "architecture is ineludible" and "cannot be switched off as if it were a program you don't like or put on the side like a disappointing book".

So what? how is it possible to accept the condition of global architect, willing to take on a supranational clientele, in a time when the subjection to a global point of view of architecture is challenged, in the consideration that – for example – "in Korea you can travel for hours and hours within a city where the oldest building is thirty years old", and in the disgust for the spaces of a contemporaneity, which *representing* the *non place*, according to Marc Augé denies time; and memory?

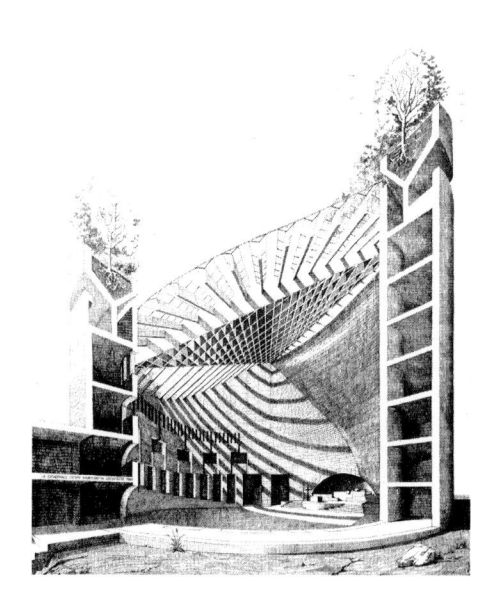

15. Perspective drawing of the Cathedral in Evry, 1988

Botta's answer sounds surprising and convincing, and its importance can be perceived by observing the elaboration of the *Museum* issue in Rovereto and in San Francisco (California).

Now, in the first case, the architect is concerned with entering the *time* of the city, by connecting and emphasizing the *continuum* of the streets – by making the street that separates the two *historical* buildings Alberti and del Grano, whose prospects look on the *historical* Corso Bettini, flow into a circular square, sealed by the bright discourse of the walls of the three stories, which enclose the spaces with explicit functions –, whereas in the second case, having to build within an inert built-up area, he avoids any confrontation with it, by choosing *old* materials, stones and bricks, that realize the assembly of the parallelepipeds constituting the building, by even denying the façade, replaced by the great *eye* that catches the dazzling *natural* outdoor light to channel it into the interior paths. Elsewhere, as in the case of the office building for Tata Consultancy Services in Hyderabad (12), India, it will be the immaculate plane of stones of the chosen site that will suggest the solution of a monolithic body emerging from that stony field, reinforced by the use of excavated materials, almost a primordial event, which nevertheless marks, in its evidence of being an artifact, the irruption of time and existence in the non time of eternity. In Botta, when he happens to be faced, as "global architect", with the deserts where he is called to by a furiously active clientele in every single corner of the globalized world, there is a sort of tension which animates him to play in a place where there is only a whirling silence of absence, the hazard of a possible present, capable of orienting a future (which is always a gamble) in the moment it develops into a past.

If this pertains to the overwhelming "need for expression", "stronger than any reason, than any risk" that distinguishes Mario (and that he himself recognizes), it is nevertheless unrelated, indeed contrary to any temptation of the colonizing arrogance that moves the conceited "star architect". It rather belongs to an ethical attitude that, in Botta's opinion (and we have already mentioned it), esthetic research cannot ignore: and that I would dare define Erasmian humanistic existentialism. Which, obviously – and eventually – includes the awareness of the sacred as a "cultural challenge"; a challenge that the architect has imposed upon himself by facing the explicit issues of the church and the synagogue. And so, if he has entrusted some of the most authentic expressions of religious space between the second and the third Millennium to us – from San Giovanni Battista in Mogno (13) to Santa Maria degli Angeli on Monte Tamaro (14); from Beato Odorico in Pordenone to the Cathedral of the Resurrection in Évry (15); from the Cymbalista Synagogue in Tel Aviv to the Church del Santo Volto in Turin – he is aware that the consciousness of the sacred must be present even when the architect faces *civil* issues, because existence, which materializes in memory and history, does not exclude the awareness of mystery: which is threshold and eternity.

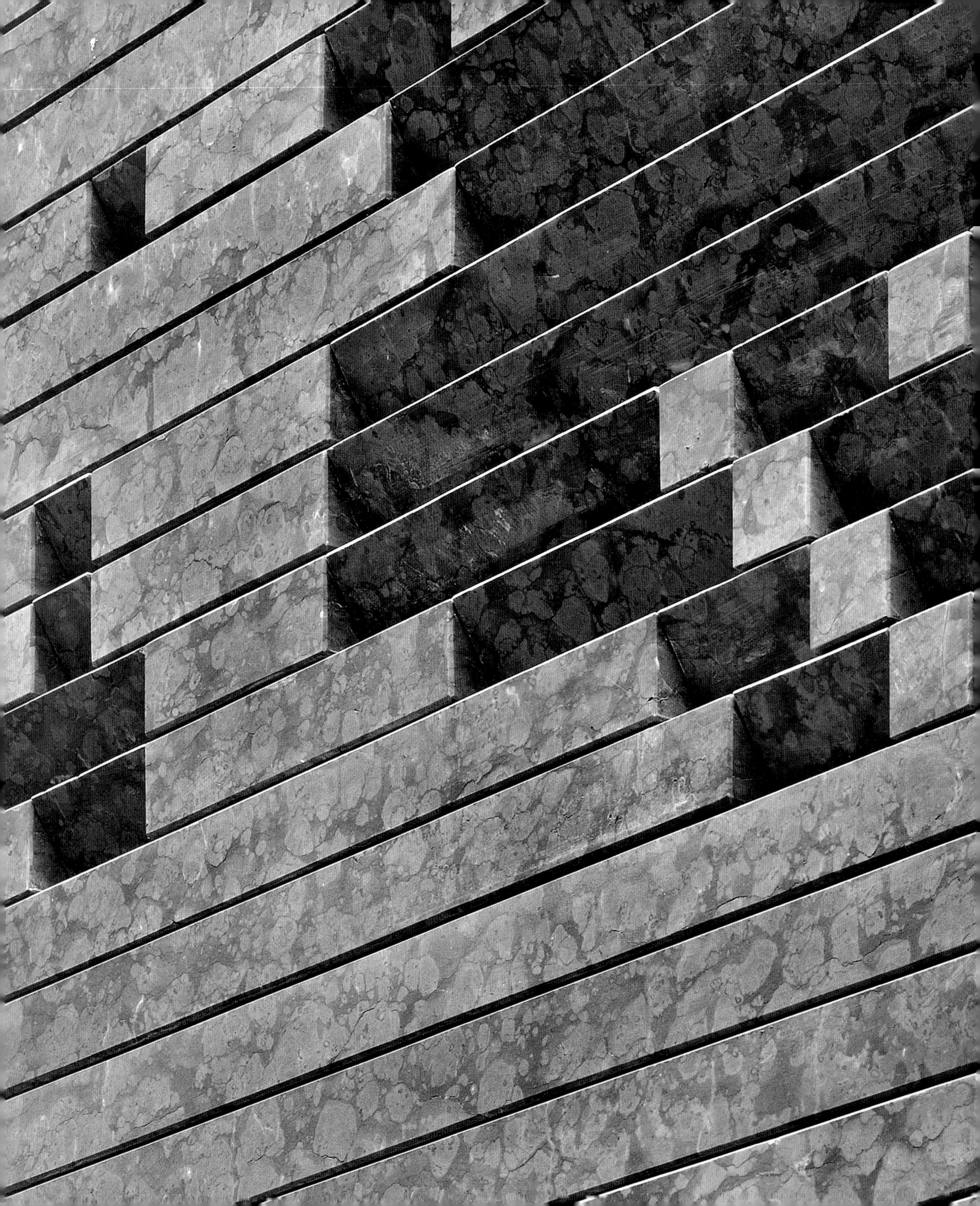

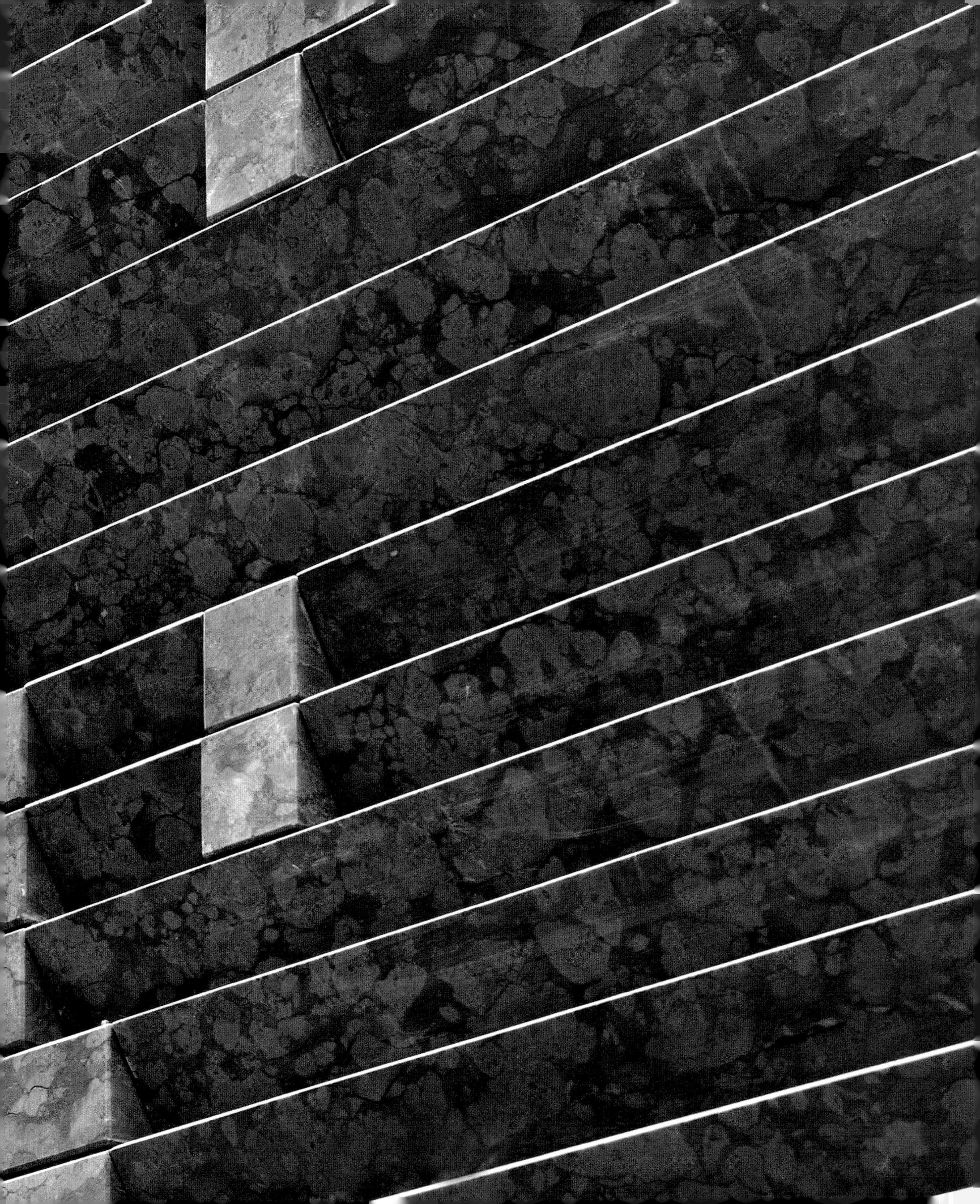

MARIO BOTTA AND SWITZERLAND
ROMAN HOLLENSTEIN

> "Per vivere una condizione universale credo sia necessario avere risorse profondamente locali."[1]
> M.B.

For a long time Swiss people mainly considered Ticino as a Mediterranean sanctuary, where they could enjoy life, drinking a glass of merlot wine under palm trees and cypresses. But in the 80's, suddenly, the media pictured a modern image of the southern Swiss canton. They reported of a new kind of architectural tourism and of people coming from all over the world, tramping through private yards, to photograph Mario Botta's villas. Also architects made pilgrimages to "southern Switzerland, listened to guided tours and debated in symposia"[2]. The Swiss enjoyed this new attention; for the first time after Le Corbusier's death, one of their architects had achieved worldwide consideration. Botta's expressive, Mediterranean architecture was replacing the Protestant, austere modern art, which in the 70's had sunk into functionalism, impeccable on the technical and material side, but lacking innovation and sometimes even a bit stupid on the formal and theoretical side[3].

EARLY SUCCESS

The successful trend started in late autumn 1975 with the exhibition *Tendenzen*[4] (1), organized by Martin Steinmann and Thomas Boga at the Federal Institute of Technology in Zurich (ETH). The show, dedicated to the new form of architecture in Ticino, came as a bombshell. Visitors were amazed above all by the primary geometrical forms, the axiality and the heavy materials used in Botta's one-family homes, which appeared to be monumental in spite of their small size. The news of the exhibition also echoed abroad. Last but not least also because of the caustic critique by Francesco dal Co, who dismissed Botta's unconventional family houses as "manieristic, typological and formal chimeras"[5] in the architecture magazine *Architecture d'aujourd'hui*.

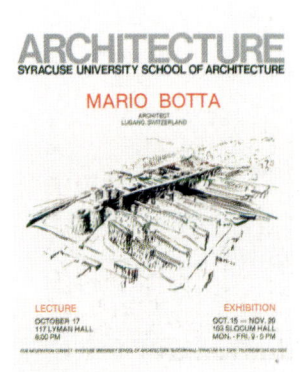

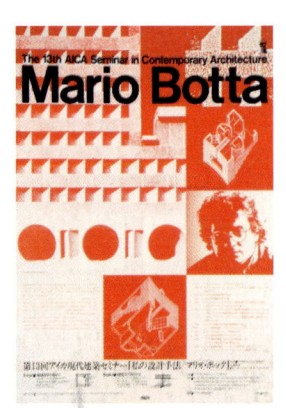

1. Poster of the exhibition *Tendenzen, Neuere Architektur im Tessin* [Tendences – New Architecture in Ticino], Zurich 1975
2. Poster of the exhibition and lecture at the Technical University of Vienna, 1977
3. Poster of the lecture and exhibition at the Syracuse University School of Architecture, New York, October 1989
4. Poster of the lecture held by Mario Botta in Tokyo and Osaka in 1986 at the international workshop AICA of contemporary architecture

Steinmann and Bruno Reichlin replied to the provocative attack by Dal Co on behalf of the Swiss architectural scene. They emphasized that the complexity of Botta's building displayed a "poetical intent" and defined Dal Co's argumentations as moralizing[6]. Only two years after this controversy, Botta's works were presented in a touring exhibition, which went from Vienna (2) to Geneva, via New York (3) and Rome. Also Kenneth Frampton concerned himself with Botta's architecture, stating that it was a classic example of "critical regionalism"[7]. This regionalism was a by-product of the Swiss federalist, multicultural climate, where Cantons act as small republics, fostering their linguistic, cultural and political distinctiveness. In this peculiar context, a handful of architects in Ticino, undisturbed by the national trends, managed to develop their own form of architecture, which, on the one hand, rejected the strident tones of post-modernism and, on the other hand, fought against the excesses of functionalism with neo-rationalist strategies. Soon also Dal Co stopped seeing "chimeras"; in 1985 he published the first wide-ranging monograph on Botta's work[8], which served as a backup publication for an exhibition in Venice. Thanks to his buildings and his lecturing activity, Botta soon became the most important Swiss cultural ambassador, traveling to countries such as Argentina, Japan (4), Canada or India. The most surprising fact was that the new star on the Swiss architectural scene had not studied at the ETH in Zurich. Nonetheless, he had come across the architectural wealth of ideas of the Swiss forge during his apprenticeship as an architectural draftsman in Tita Carloni's studio in Lugano. From Carloni, but also from the books of Zurich writer and architect Max Frisch, who he later referred to as "mon maître-à-penser" (my master of thinking) and "the clear-headed mind that controlled the follies of technological progress"[9] Botta learned to appreciate the ethical aspect of architecture, which upholds handicraft and aims at the perfection of details.

A SWISS ABROAD

With Carloni's and Frisch's teachings in mind, Botta completed his academic studies at the IUAV in Venice (5), where Carlo Scarpa and Giuseppe Mazzariol opened new architectural perspectives for the Swiss architect. Through his art history professor Mazzariol, who was attempting to promote contemporary architecture in Venice, Botta was introduced to Le Corbusier's office. While assisting his colleagues Julian de la Fuente and José Oubrerie, Botta had the chance to collaborate on the drafting of the hospital project in Venice, which unfortunately was never realized. Although he never met Le Corbusier himself, his work was influenced by the views

5. Model of the urban scale project in Bellinzona of Botta's final thesis at the University Institue of Architecture in Venice in 1969
6. Drawings by Mario made during his stay in Paris and after having met with Alberto Giacometti: "ripensando Giacometti" [rethinking Giacometti], 1968

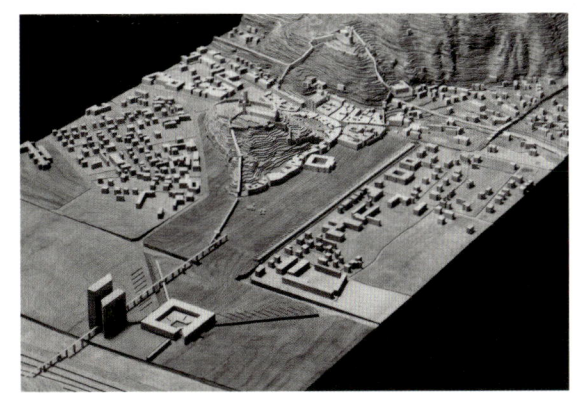

of his great fellow countryman. Botta also had a chance to feel his way of thinking in the legendary studio in Rue de Sèvres 35 in Paris, where he spent a couple of weeks working in August 1965, after Le Corbusier's sudden death.

Not only did Botta meet Lluís Sert and Oscar Niemeyer in Paris; he also visited Alberto Giacometti (6), who brought him down to earth by telling him that, being Swiss, he would get nothing for free: "Oh! Le pauvre, tu es suisse aussi. Tu devras faire tout tout seul!"[10] Botta was particularly struck by these words also because Giacometti too belonged to the Italian-speaking minority of Switzerland. Botta felt "as if the world that inspired him was also part of the world that safeguarded my roots"[11]. Henceforth it was clear to him that he would have had to fight like Giacometti if he wanted to be successful. He got a first chance to assert himself upon his return from Venice to Ticino, when he was asked to realize a one-family house in Stabio. Giuseppe Mazzariol later defined the resulting work "a flower for le Corbusier"[12]. In his dissertation, carried out under the supervision of Scarpa, he also dealt with his homeland, drafting a vision for Bellinzona, the capital of Ticino, which sowed the seeds for his later architectural and urban work. He dedicated himself to this urban project during the student unrest in 1968, with an "unbroken faith in architecture"[13], which was likely to have been fuelled by Giacometti's advice. Not even the risk of being "punched and despised by his fellow students"[14] managed to deter him from his work.

AMONG CULTURES

The need for urban development in Ticino and the pleasure he took in building were the main reasons that prompted Botta to return to Switzerland and "fight where one is born."[15] But he may also have been attracted to his homeland by that attachment to landscape, which is characteristic of the people in Ticino as it is to all Alpine people: "With regards to my work, it may well be that the peculiar landscape of the Mendrisiotto, with the mountains to the north and the open horizon to the south, is capable of conditioning my plastic sensitivity."[16] Not least therefore, he hoped that "my architecture is perceived to be rooted in and tied to the culture of my native land."[17]

In Lugano, far away from Venice's theory-burdened debates, Botta opened his own studio in 1970 – convinced that "if there is no building there is no architecture."[18] In Lugano he found a milieu where he could discuss and cooperate, but also measure himself with great architects like Luigi Snozzi, Livio Vacchini, Aurelio Galfetti and

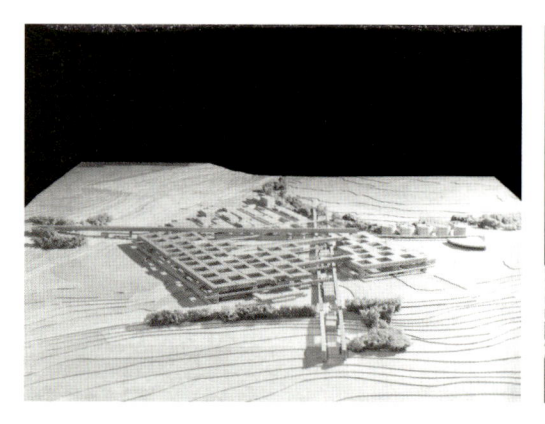

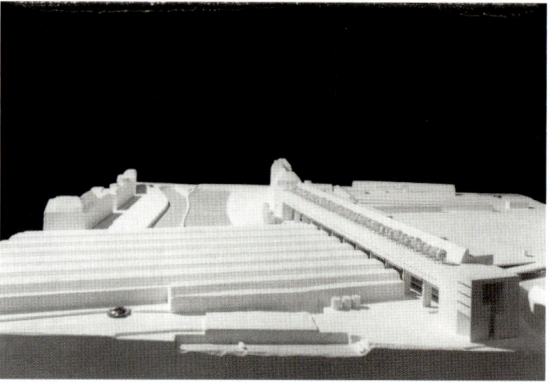

7. Model of the competition project for the new EPFL – Ecole Polytechnique Fédérale in Lausanne, 1970
8. Model of the competition project for the railway station-extension in Zurich, 1978
9. Poster of the Ticino Tourism agency
10. Reuse of a former farmhouse in Ligrignano, 1978
11. Church San Giovanni Battista in Mogno, 1996
12. Chapel Santa Maria degli Angeli, Monte Tamaro, 1996

Rino Tami. At that time, he would have not found such a stimulating environment in the near metropolis Milan, which he had felt very close to since high school. The most glorious piece of work of these early times in Ticino was the competition project for the new EPF campus in Lausanne (7), conceived by Botta in 1970 with Carloni, Galfetti, Snozzi and Flora Ruchat. This project, which unfortunately was not realized, was reminiscent of the cellular structuralism of Le Corbusier's project for the hospital in Venice.

Later on, he would once more team up with Snozzi for large-scale urban projects: in 1971 for the competition for a new administrative center in Perugia and in 1978 with the visionary project for the extension of the main station in Zurich (8), which Kenneth Frampton described as "one of the most brilliant demonstrations of neo-rationalism"[19]. But once again, a Swiss jury failed to recognize Botta's intuitiveness. In order to make up for the lack of large assignments in Ticino, besides participating to competitions, Botta concentrated on the realization of family homes. These works allowed him to polish his architectural language, similarly to the beginnings of young Le Corbusier. If, on the one hand, his villa Della Casa in Stabio (1967), conceived as a living machine, can be considered a tribute to Le Corbusier, on the other hand, the house Caccia in Cadenazzo (1971), characterized by the large oculi, can be seen as a homage to Louis Kahn, whom he worked for in Venice, once again through Mazzariol's mediation.

The tower house Bianchi in Riva San Vitale (1973) can be considered his first stylistically fully autonomous work. Like this small monument, also the minimalist, serial school complex in Morbio Inferiore privileges the elementary aspects and rejects any fleeting and purely functionalist nature of architecture. These and other works, like the underground library of the Capuchin convent in Lugano and the restructuring of an old farmhouse in Ligrignano (10), which formally appears to be inspired by Aldo Rossi's monument in Segrate (1965), turned Botta into the star of the international traveling exhibition *Architecture 70-80 in Switzerland*, which was inaugurated in the Kunsthalle Basel in 1981. Alongside Rossi, who taught at the ETH in Zurich in the 70's and who gave an important impetus to the development of a new Swiss German architecture, Botta had become an international representative of the neo-rationalist "tendenza". Last but not least, because, unlike his Italian colleagues, he could distinguish himself by brilliantly putting his theories into practice.

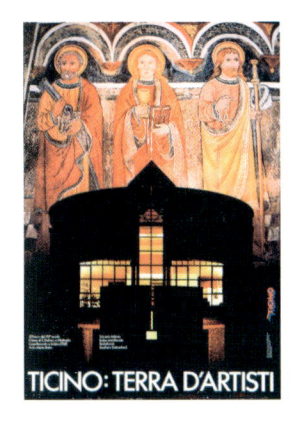

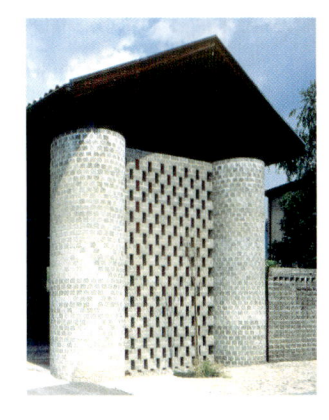

Botta's formal language reached full maturity in 1982 with the Romanesque-looking Casa Rotonda in Stabio, "which can be included in the demanding records of inventions and innovative ideas."[20] Here his architectural language, characterized by massive walls, deep clefts, recessed windows and skylights went beyond neo-rationalism. This work is a perfect example of how Botta manages to build a place, by emphasizing its urban morphology or rural topography in a critical, almost poetical way. The symbolic nature of this building, which would have later even influenced the realization of the cathedral in Evry, became the tourist landmark of Ticino as "terra d'artisti" in 1984 (9).

FROM LUGANO TO THE WORLD

However, Botta's hunger could not be satiated by miniature works, much as they may have been admired. Therefore, starting in 1980, he increasingly tried his luck by participating in international competitions: in Stuttgart and Berlin as well as in Guernica or Lyon. In 1982 he received his first large cultural and urban assignment in France with the project for the *André Malraux* theater in Chambéry (1982-87). In the same year his first Swiss building outside Ticino, the *Banque de l'Etat* in Fribourg, was inaugurated. In the meantime he was busy in the city of Lugano with two important projects: the *Ransila* business complex and the former *Banca del Gottardo* (today BSI), which is still considered one of the rare icons of bank architecture.

At the same time, the project for a building in the small mountain village of Mogno caused a stir in Ticino. Botta was asked to present a project for the reconstruction of a church which had been destroyed by an avalanche in April 1986. Enthusiastic about the idea of being able to render something to his homeland, whom he owed a lot to, starting from the landscape over to Romanesque architecture up to the stimulating architectural environment, he set to work, without asking for remuneration, and conceived a severe cylindrical building, which was intended to recall the "atavistic struggle between man and mountain."²¹

His project was widely criticized for being too radical for a small mountain village. Only after Botta himself intervened in the debate, did the grid-locked situation begin to loosen up. Nonetheless, the realization of his first religious building took so long that the churches in Pordenone and Sartirana in Italy and the Cathedral in Evry in Paris were completed before the church in Mogno was inaugurated in June 1996 (11). Only two and a half months later, the first mass was celebrated in the church on Monte Tamaro (12), a building which majestically inserts itself into the mountain setting of the upper Sottoceneri and which might almost be mentioned in the same breath as Le Corbusier's chapel in Ronchamp. From then on, Botta was reputed as the master of the

13. Tent for the 700 years anniversary of the Swiss Confederation set up in Bellinzona, 1996
14. Poster for promotion of the *Botta '91* chair designed for the 700-years celebration tent, 1991
15. Project for the extension of the Swiss Parliament building in Berne, 1991
16. House Caccia in Cadenazzo, 1971
17. Architects Herzog&de Meuron: The Blue House [Blaues Haus] in Oberwil, 1980

sacred, a title which brought in other important projects: from the Cymbalista Synagogue in Tel Aviv, realized for a Swiss patron, where the Romanesque, like in Mogno, had acted as a "sort of guide in the research"[23] to the majestic church Santo Volto in Turin.

THE ARCHITECT OF THE NATION

By the end of 1988, with the inauguration of the Banca del Gottardo in Lugano, it was not only the Swiss media who celebrated the 46-year-old architect as a hero. Subsequently, the number of prestigious assignments began to multiply and Botta was soon dealing with all kinds of buildings. One after the other, he conceived the Mart museum in Rovereto (1988-2002), the Museum of Modern Art in San Francisco, the city library in Dortmund and the monument *Cumbre de las Americas* dedicated to Santa Cruz de la Sierra in Bolivia, as well as a skyscraper in Seoul and an office building in New Delhi. Therefore, nobody was taken by surprise, when Marco Solari, in 1989, on behalf of the Federal Council, asked Botta, "the major media figure among our architects"[24], to design a temporary construction for the seven hundredth anniversary of the Swiss Confederation.

The celebrations were inaugurated in January 1991 under the mobile dome created by Botta, which had been set up on the castle rock in Bellinzona. "The miracle of Castel Grande"[25] (13, 14), as it was defined by exhibition expert Harald Szeemann from Berne, was later installed in other symbolic Swiss venues. Never before had an architect been able to mark some of the most beautiful locations in Switzerland with one of his works – albeit only temporarily. Botta, who in the meantime had been promoted to architect of the nation[26], was invited to take part in the competition for the extension of the Parliament Building in Berne (15). His project, which provided for a new, fan-shaped socle with administrative offices to be added to the main building situated above the river Aare, received the first prize. Unfortunately it was never realized because of high-pitched debates and the concerns about the cityscape, which had been declared Unesco world heritage.

In spite of this disappointment, Botta did not stop to pay attention to national issues. In 1992, on behalf of Roland Crottaz, the president of the Swiss University Conference, he realized a study on architectural training in Switzerland. This study triggered the creation of the Academy of Architecture in Mendrisio, which was inaugurated in 1996 and represents a humanistic alternative to the architecture departments of the Zurich and Lausanne-based Federal Institutes of Technology. Botta himself considers it a privileged, inspiring location for intellectual exchange. His commitment to the nation led the tireless architect so far that in 1993 he developed a model for the national exhibition *Expo 98* with Aurelio Galfetti, the historian Jean-François Bergier and other intellectuals. In the end, the exhibition only opened its doors in 2002, with a different concept. In November 1998, on the occasion of the 150-year-anniversary of the Federal Assembly, Botta was invited to the Parliament as representative of the Swiss cultural scene to hold a speech on "culture and politics" in Switzerland, whereupon he emphasized the "richness of diversity as a common heritage."[27] Botta, who considers himself Ticinese and Swiss, but also European and citizen of the world, had already emphasized five years earlier, in the Geneva daily *Le Nouveau Quotidien*, how important it is to "live Europe" in "a country that knows that it belongs to a history and a culture which go beyond its borders."[28]

CRITICAL VOICES

Botta's colleagues' envy grew parallel to his increasing triumph at the national level. They refused to accept that even Herzog & de Meuron were inspired by Botta's house Caccia in Cadenazzo (16) when they realized the "blue house" in Oberwil (17) in 1980, with its characteristic porthole windows, or that Botta had introduced the ornament developed starting from the material in Swiss architecture, and this long before Herzog & de Meuron had begun to celebrate the ornament with their signal tower in Basel, wrapped in copper strips. Previously, the two architects had concentrated on simple, nude cubes, like Roger Diener, Peter Märkli or Peter Zumthor, creating a minimalist but nevertheless evocative new Swiss simplicity, which owed a lot to Aldo Rossi's analog design strategy. These new developments started to marginalize Botta's Mediterranean architecture, which had dominated the Swiss architectural scene for several years. For Botta "didn't really fit into the new simplicity."[29] In fact, Botta has never really got over this paradigm shift: "I have the impression that Swiss-German culture has always looked on me with suspicion; my approach is too far from the aseptic language of the north."[30] Botta's Swiss German colleagues accused him of formalism and criticized him for repeating himself with his trademark-like buildings. But Botta saw his struggle for shape confirmed in Picasso's and Giocametti's[31] work. With regards to the school in Morbio Inferiore he had been criticized because his architectural principle, based on a "system of spatial formulas," failed to consider "the complexity of the creation of urban phenomena."[32] Therefore it was hardly surprising that Botta was not represented with one single building in the extensive ex-

18. Swiss stamps dedicated to two buildings: the house in Breganzona and the library in Villeurbanne, edition 1993
19. Sketch of the San Carlino, Lugano 1999
20. Theater alla Scala of Milan, 2004

hibition dedicated to recent Swiss architecture *Matière d'Art*, which took place in Paris in the summer of 2001. There were merely two brief mentions in the catalog.[33]

POPULAR ARCHITECTURE

But this debate only concerned the architectural scene. The public at large and the media have never stopped appreciating Botta for his modesty and affability. "The public perceives him as an advocate of the opening up of Switzerland. He has a clear opinion, which he does not hesitate to defend. You will hear him talk about refugee problems on the radio, he speaks about cultural policy on television, he is asked for his opinion on architecture in newspapers."[34] His open-mindedness made it easier for him to be in touch with artists and writers than with architects on the other side of the Alps. He became friendly with Max Frisch, who he had admired from early on, but also with Jean Tinguely and Max Bill.

Shortly after the death of writer and painter Friedrich Dürrenmatt, in 1992, his widow, Charlotte Kerr, asked Botta to draft a project for the Dürrenmatt museum in Neuchâtel, which was to be opened in 2000. While working on this project, he conceived the comprehensive Dürrenmatt exhibition, which was held in the Kunsthaus Zurich in 1994. "Planning for Dürrenmatt was also an adequate way to settle, at least in part, the debt of gratitude I felt towards that thorny fellow countryman, who in my eyes was so Swiss and at the same time so far from Switzerland."[35] In the same period, the pharmaceutical company Roche asked Botta to design a museum in Basel in honor of Jean Tinguely, who had died in 1991. The museum, the building of which was completed in 1996, has become a distinctive museological feature on the Rhine.

Further evidence of Botta's popularity in Switzerland after the late 80's is the fact that in 1992 and 1994 he was asked to design the stage settings for the ballet shows *Nutcracker* and *Medea* at the Opernhaus in Zurich and in 1995 for *Ippolito* at the Stadttheater in Basel. A commitment that he repeated in Zurich in 2009 for Rossini's *The Barber of Seville*. A further highlight in Botta's Swiss career, after the issue of two Botta post stamps (18) in 1993 to celebrate his 50th birthday, is represented by the Borromini celebrations in September 1999. With his model of the Roman church San Carlo alle Quattro Fontane (19), reproduced in its original dimension, and set afloat on lake Lugano near Villa Ciani, Botta managed to evoke a masterpiece in that very same landscape that "could have influenced Borromini's innate sculptural spirit since his childhood."[36]

21. Tschuggen Wellness center in Arosa 2006
22. Wellness center at Rigi Kaltbad, 2004, completed in 2012
23. Project for the new thermal baths in Baden, 2009

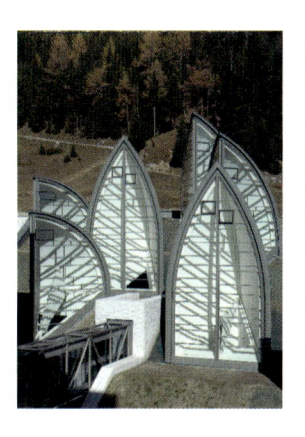

This project was particularly important for Botta, for he too connects the plasticity of his own architecture with the landscape and the light of Southern Ticino.

CULTURE AND LANDSCAPE

The wooden model, admired by hundreds of thousands of locals and tourists, was dismantled in 2003, in the same year in which Swiss television elected Botta to representative of Swiss culture. Was it a simple coincidence that at that time he was engaged in the realization of several cultural buildings all over the country? With the underground extension of the Bodmer Foundation in Cologny near Geneva, with the Werner Oechslin library in Einsiedeln as well as with the renovation of Museo Vincenzo Vela in Ligornetto and the medieval castle in Leuk, Wallis. In the same period he was also involved in planning the restoration and extension of the Scala in Milan (20), considered to be an intellectual stronghold for many from Ticino.

The Swiss national sports center on the Lago Maggiore and the spiral-shaped observation tower in the wooded hills of Jura, near Moron, prepared the ground for his tourism buildings. At first, the new wellness center of the hotel *Tschuggen* in Arosa (21), which was the expression of a new kind of poetics for Botta, caused bewilderment. If, on the one hand, its skylights light up like Christmas trees at night, on the other hand, the skylights of the wellness center on the Rigi resemble mysterious crystals. The new building on the Rigi (22) represents an added value for the world-famous panoramic mountain on Lake Lucerne. Furthermore, since Botta won the competition for the renewal of the thermal bath area in Baden (23), near Zurich, an urban quarter that dates back to the ancient Roman times, the master from Lugano has returned to the limelight in the German part of Switzerland.

Even though Botta sometimes describes Switzerland as "madre e matrigna"[37] (mother and stepmother) and believes that a prophet has no honor in his own country, up to today he has realized more significant buildings than any of his colleagues in every single part of Switzerland. Furthermore, several of his key works have been realized in Switzerland – from residential buildings, as well as schools, libraries, banks, museums and wellness centers, to churches and celebrative buildings. The only feature missing in this list is a skyscraper, after citizens in the village of Celerina, Engadine, voted against the realization of the fortress-like "Torre Botta" (24) in a referendum in March 2008. Nevertheless, Botta continues to promote Switzerland abroad. Recently, he man-

24. Preliminary project for a hotel tower and residences in Celerina, 2008

aged to point the way for a Swiss patron with the Bechtler Museum in Charlotte, North Carolina. In spite of his worldwide success Botta reiterates: "My affection for Switzerland does not prevent me from having a critical look."[38]

[1] "To live a universal condition I think it is necessary to have deeply local resources,"
Mario Botta in an interview with Roman Hollenstein, Lugano, January 26, 2010.
[2] Heinz Horat: "Häuser als Skulpturen in der Landschaft," in: *Neue Zürcher Zeitung*, 19.5.1984.
[3] Tita Carloni: "Alles andere als Pferde," in: *Tessiner Zeitung*, March 29, 1997, p. 9.
[4] The exhibition *Tendenzen*, organized by the ETH in Zurich, lasted from November 10 to December 12, 1975 and displayed 40 works by 20 architects as well as an architects collective.
[5] Francesco dal Co: "Critique d'une exposition," in: *Architecture d'aujourd'hui*, 1977, 190, p. 58–60.
[6] Martin Steinmann and Bruno Reichlin: "Critique d'une critique," in: *Architecture d'aujourd'hui*, 1977, 190, p. 58–60.
[7] Kenneth Frampton: "The Isms of Contemporary Architecture," in: *Architectural Design*, No. 52, 1982.
[8] Francesco Dal Co: *Mario Botta. Architectures. 1960–1985*, Milan 1985-New York 1986.
[9] Mario Botta: "Max Frisch," in: *Quasi un diario. Frammenti intorno all'architettura*. Firenze 2003, p. 215.
[10] "Oh! Poor you, you too are Swiss. You will have to do everything on your own!" Botta: "Atelier Giacometti (autunno 1965)," in: *Diario* (cf. note 9), p. 148.
[11] Cf. note 10.
[12] Giuseppe Mazzariol: "Un fiore per Le Corbusier," in: *Werk*, 1969, I, p. 227.
[13] Heinrich Klotz: *Moderne und postmoderne Architektur der Gegenwart*, Braunschweig 1984.
[14] Tita Carloni: "Tra conservazione e innovazione," in: *50 anni di architettura in Ticino 1930–1980*. A cura di Peter Disch. Bellinzona 1983, p. 10.
[15] Botta: *Diario* (cf. note 9), p. 40.
[16] Botta, cf. note 1.
[17] Livio Dimitriu: "Architecture and Morality. An Interview with Mario Botta," in: *Perspecta*, 1983, 20, p. 120–138.
[18] Botta: *Diario* (cf. note 9), p. 268.
[19] Kenneth Frampton: "Mario Botta and the School of the Ticino," in: *Oppositions 14*, New York 1979, p. 1-25.
[20] Alberto Sartoris in: *La casa rotonda*, Milano 1982, p. 84.
[21] Botta: "La chiesa di Mogno (aprile 1987)," in: *Diario* (cf. note 9), p. 62.
[23] Botta: *Diario* (cf. note 9), p. 42.
[24] Marco Solari in: *Mario Botta – la tenda, la tente, das Zelt*. Bellinzona 1991, p. 5.
[25] Harald Szeemann: "Das Wunder von Castel Grande," cf. note 24, p. 58 and p. 60.
[26] On September 7, 1991, the Zurich daily *Tages-Anzeiger* titled: "Mario Botta – unser Nationalarchitekt" and the architecture magazine *Hochparterre* celebrated the architect as "Botta national" (Nr. 11, 1991, p. 82-83).
[27] Botta: "Cultura e politica (ottobre 1998)," in: *Diario* (cf. note 9), pp. 183-184.
[28] Botta in: *Le Nouveau Quotidien*, Genève, September 27, 1993. quoting from: *Diario* (cf. note 9), p. 134.
[29] Benedikt Loderer: "Mit modernen Formen römisch," in: *Mario Botta. The complete works. Volume 3. 1990-1997*, Edited by Emilio Pizzi, Basel-Boston-Berlin 1998, p. 6.
[30] Botta, cf. note 1.
[31] Botta (cf. note 1) and Peter Disch: *Mario Botta. La ricerca negli anni ottanta*. Lugano 1990, p.7.
[32] Max Bosshard, Christoph Luchsinger, Annette Gigon, Mike Guyer: "Die Quadratur des Ortes," in: *Archithese* 3, 1984, p. 28-31.
[33] *Matière d'Art. Architecture contemporaine en Suisse*. Editor Centre culturel suisse à Paris. Basel 2001, p. 52-53 and 172-174.
[34] Benedikt Loderer, cf. note 29., p. 6.
[35] Botta: "Dürrenmatt a Neuchâtel," in: *Diario* (cf. note 9), p. 216.
[36] *Mario Botta. Architettura del Sacro – Prayers in stone*. Bologna 2005, p. 185.
[37] Botta, cf. note 1.
[38] Botta: *Diario* (cf. note 9), p. 266.

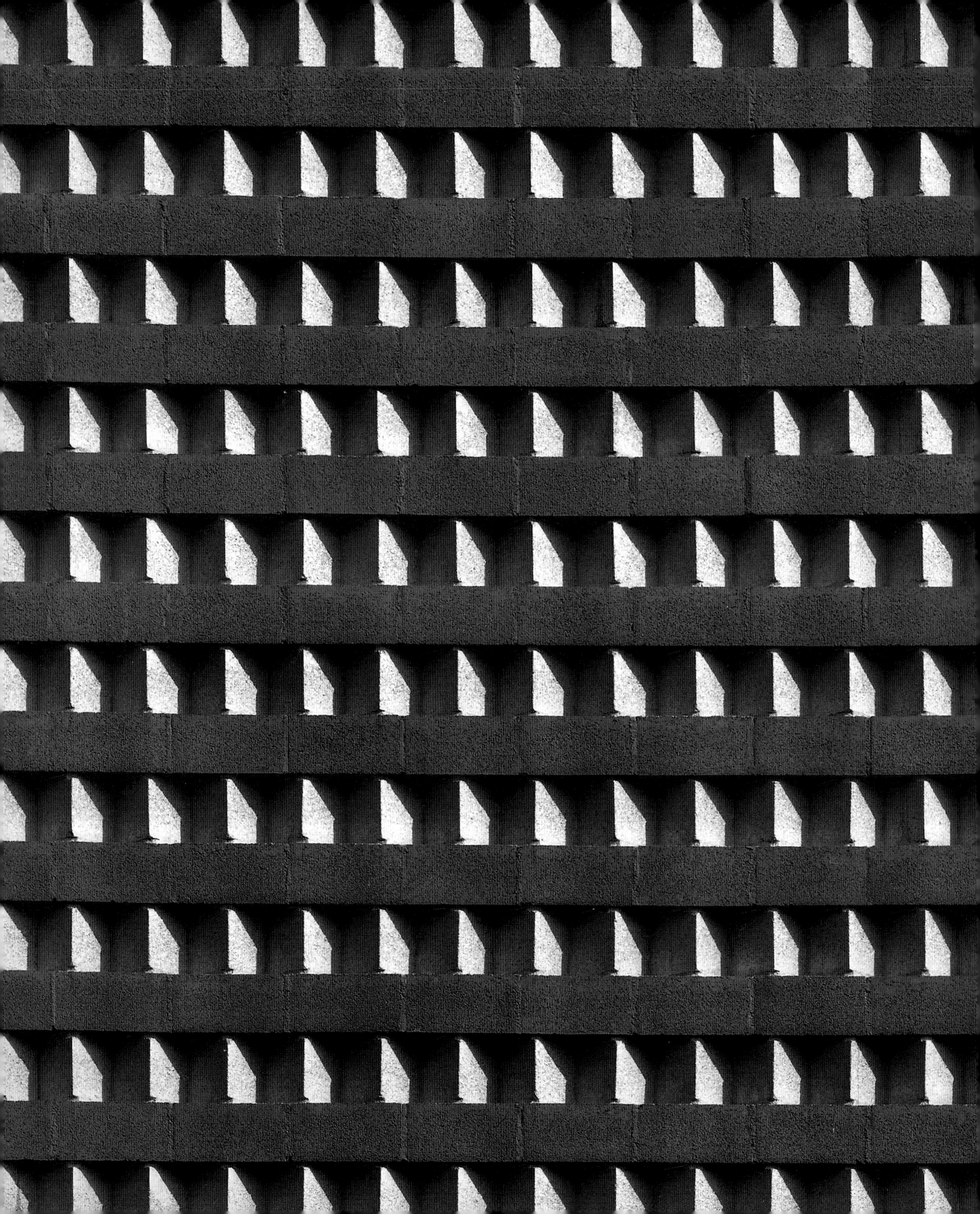

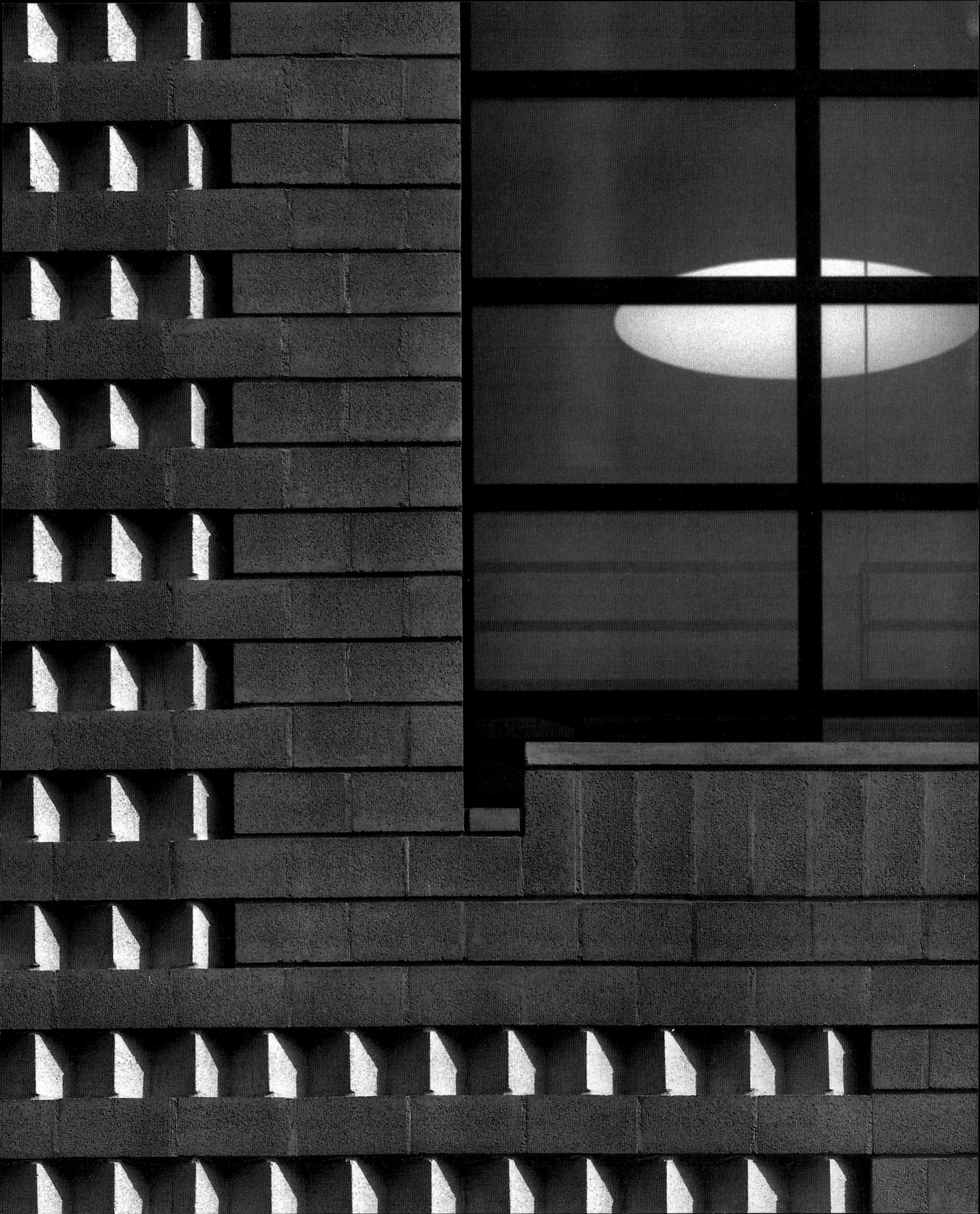

FROM THE VILLAGE TO THE CITY
JACQUES GUBLER

MB gives me *carte blanche* for an essay. Thank you Mario! Now, this white paper is waiting for typographical signs. I have read several kilograms of publications on and by MB: over 550 hectograms of books, magazines, catalogs, brochures, albums, newspaper cuttings, without considering the weight of CD ROMS. What else could be said? Twenty-five years ago[1], maybe even fifteen, it would still have been possible to present the "storia della quistione", to use Italo Svevo's exquisite wording. To draft a prudent path. To walk, without drowning, on the ink of printed paper, condensed in chronological order. From Martin Steinmann[2] (1975) to Kenneth Frampton[3] (1980, 1983), from Pierluigi Nicolin[4] (1982) to Virgilio Gilardoni[5] (1984), from Francesco Dal Co and Mirko Zardini[6] (1981, 1987) to Werner Oechslin[7] (1991), from Giovanni Pozzi[8] (1993) to Rudolf Arnheim[9] (1993), to reach the *Summa Felicitatis* published by Jean Petit[10] (1994).

In the 90's scholars still mentioned the "extraterrestrial" discovery of Botta's work (this is how the Parisian cartoonist Marc Reiser (24, 25), madly in love with the Casa rotonda in Stabio, called it and represented it): the polyphonic and controversial reception of strong, self-declared *primary* architecture. We had observed a debate arise in a Jurassic intellectual landscape, where the antithesis between *weak thought* and *negative*

1. Watari-Um art gallery, Tokyo, 1990
2. San Francisco Museum of Modern Art, 1995
3. Kyobo tower, Seoul, 2003

thought, *typological conformity* and *territorial changes*, idiomatic architectural *issues*[11] and/or *collective myths*, titillated the theoretical discussion from Venice to Turin, with a crucial stop in Milan, where books and magazines were published and then spread beyond the Alpine hills. Today, in three out of five continents, the presence of Mario Botta's "factories" (1-6) and portrait, the *thousand and more* achievements of the *Magister Mendrisiensis*, appear to shuffle the printed cards in a never-ending game of tarot or *monopoly*. This quantitative challenge entails risks for any form of narrative which wants to avoid *case study*: the study of a single project for a specific client in a single building site.

The difficulty paralyzing me lies in the lack of a history of "architecture as a mass medium" in the capitalist society of the past thirty years. Of course, the theoretical postulate of "architettura come mass medium" was launched in Italy with the publication, over forty years ago, of the book by Renato De Fusco of the same name[12]. Starting from the metaphor of architecture as an individual expressiveness and linguistic "message", the author describes a double crisis that involves the social meanings of art and language, aiming at a new critical, semiological interpretation. This program appears to exactly anticipate the practical work carried out empirically in Las Vegas by the trio Denise Scott Brown, Robert Venturi, Steven Izenour[13]. Till now, possibly due to my lack of canine sense of smell in the galaxy of contemporary artistic literature, I have failed to find a book which attempts to retrace the chronology, mechanisms and circuits in a comparison with such "architecture as a mass medium".

A book which should exist is still missing; something students in architecture schools well know when they look for THE book that could, in the time of one afternoon, turn out to be useful for their project for the next day. My answer to this shortage is: YOU have to write such a book. The book that I am missing would open with a first, elegant and contradictory chapter: the 1980 Venice Biennale. The book would have to make an attempt to understand the imbricated chronology of different occurrences: the importance of exhibitions in terms of iconographic source; the combined effect of exponential dragging between the application of computer science to the typographical composition and printing methods; the polemic attitude of magazines asserting exemplarity versus the magazines dedicated to the non-choice of random *remplissage*; the political aura of certain international competitions; the virtual representation of the envisaged project without incidents, negation of the long building times; the role of architecture as a strat-

4. Cymbalista Syngogue and Jewish Heritage center, Tel Aviv, 1998
5. Monument Cumbre de las Americas, Santa Cruz de la Sierra, 1996
6. Jean Tinguely Museum, Basel, 1996

egy used by multinationals to represent and reinforce *corporate identity*; the considerable increase, in large and small newspapers, of the pages dedicated to the picturesque images of houses and skyscrapers; the pop emergence of the movie image of architects; the inscription with full rights of architects in the *star system* hierarchy, possibly aimed at opening a welcome parenthesis in the wide-spread scenario of sportsmen meeting showgirls. I do not know this book, but it may exist.

In the meantime the condemnation of the *star system* has become the *fil rouge*, almost the a priori of any critique. Some authors side *against architecture*[14]. Using the same preamble, other authors try to re-establish the trade. In the mouths of architects, the worst offence is to throw the label of *star architect* in the face of the competing colleague. The caricature of "social Darwinism" prevails, in itself the caricature of the *Origin of Species* and the *Descent of Man*. I am not trying to defend the devastating system of global capitalism. I can see that in the past ten years the reformist idea of "cultural resistance", which arose from Germany's post-Hitler history and was introduced in architecture by Max Frisch and Luigi Snozzi, has been trivialized and is served *à toutes les sauces* in the most reactionary situations, from the protection of embryos to the protection of trees. Does inflation not appear also in the field of symbols and images, as Sigfried Giedion used to think?

WHEN THE ARCHITECT COLLECTS ELECTIVE AFFINITIES

I have had a social relationship with MB and his family for over thirty years. We have grown at a distance, without ever losing sight of each other. I harbor a bond of *respeto* for Mario, as they would say in Buenos-Aires. In this exhibition MB wants to reunite a constellation of people, dead and alive, under the illuminated sky of "elective affinities": he wants to gather friends, near and far, dead and alive, to illustrate *Encounters* in the cordiality of *Incontri*.

This brotherly invitation reminds me of the festive commemoration of Georges Baines's 80th birthday in 2006. The architect from Antwerp, who distinguished himself for the *poursuite* of modernity, took care of the set-up of his personal exhibition in Brussels himself. In the central room of the Ixelles museum he gave the *place d'honneur* to his deceased friends, whom he felt orphan of: first of all the couple Georges Vantongerlo - Max Bill. He depicted the electric meeting with the CoBrA group in the 50's (a dozen of key players from Copenhagen, Brussels, Amsterdam) and the amazing discovery of Japanese xylography, a con-

7. Mario Botta, 1959
8. Mario Botta, female nude, art college Milan, 1963
9. Mario Botta, female nude back, art college Milan, 1963

tinent he discovered through his friend Felix Tikotin, collector, architect and gallerist. To present himself to the public, Baines chose to display his collection of *coups de coeur*. His personal work was set in the background, with remote panels on the side galleries, which in turn looked down on the central area on the ground floor. A freshly published monograph gave information on his "complete works"[15]. I was very much impressed by this exhibition, where Baines seemed to say: "I am not alone, I have met friends who have helped me find my stubbornness". *Stubborn*, adjective: refusing to comply, agree, or give in; obstinate, according to the definition in the Collins Concise English Dictionary. In the course of modern history Baines's architecture exists as a collection of elective affinities.

While Narcissus drowns on the shore of the pond, pining for his own reflection, we know that our social existence depends on the existence of others. Roughly paraphrasing Simone de Beauvoir and Jean-Paul Sartre, we can repeat without excessive shame: "One is not born an architect, but becomes one". This is exactly what MB tells Jean Petit, as the latter tries to reconstruct the cultural *milieu* the architect comes from: "I was not born an architect, I have become an architect through the work of others that has nourished me."[16] Following this trail, Petit retraces the artist's personal path by means of Vasarian narration, from the cradle to the conquest of crucial cities.

ROLE TAKING: FROM ADOLESCENCE TO THE PROFESSION

The sociological concept of "role taking" comes from the field of psychology[17]. The ancestral theatricality of social life seems to be tied to the choice of an individual role and to the "organized reproduction of social interactions, thus to social integration. [...] In fact, roles *represent* institutions", writes Daniela Cherubini[18]. This theory implies an immediate consequence. The old positivist theory of the geographical and cultural *milieu* as the casting mold of existence is replaced by the chance of the individual to choose the orientation of his/her future. It is not only a matter of ascertaining that there is a centuries-old tradition of workers in the rural basin of the region Mendrisiotto and Ceresio, tied to the building of churches, villas, monuments, and that MB organically breathes the air of this region. It is just as important to answer the question: How come, in the cultural basin of the Mendrisiotto, where there is a great tradition of modern professional cycling (just as in the neighboring region Varesotto and in Flanders), MB is not the name of a

10. Mario Botta, nude back, Museum Vincenzo Vela, 1991
11. The Museum Vincenzo Vela, Ligornetto, before the restoration work
12. The Museum Vincenzo Vela in Ligornetto, 1883,
Wood engraving from a drawing of Bonamore, Official newsprint/journal of the Swiss national exhibition in Zurich,
Courtesy Museum Vincenzo Vela, Ligornetto
Federal Office of Culture, Switzerland

cyclist known for his feats as a *grimpeur* during the Giro d'Italia and the Milano-Sanremo? For a boy, role taking entails the choice of his profession. The same is true today for a girl. I remember the joke, read in Paris in 1959, when, after Sunday lunch, the young sister is asked: "Now tell me, what will you do when you grow up?" Answer: "I want to be a blind pianist." She had probably heard Art Tatum's music…

The "issue" of professional choice is related to the people a boy/girl manages to find, imitate and copy, during and after school. As Jean Petit has already shown, there is a relation between Botta's meeting with his first employer in Ticino, Tita Carloni, author of admirable tectonic configurations, and the discovery of his following teachers, tied to the city of Venice in the 60's: Carlo Scarpa, Le Corbusier, Louis Kahn. At first, the teenager MB follows an apprenticeship as an architectural draftsman. Later on, he will find the opportunity to study in a school of architecture. From Tita Carloni[19] we know that the 15-year-old boy was the first one to arrive at work in the morning and he would be the one who lit the coal stove. He would soon be able to draw complicated construction details, also in axonometry. Carloni recognizes his apprentice's *amour* for stonework. In the master's office the moral and cultural dimension of projects is their bread and butter. Soon MB starts practicing "Sunday architecture", which was common practice in Ticino in the 50's: small personal works for family and friends "to make up the poor wages."[20] During his apprenticeship he builds a small house looking south on a sloping plot of land near the lowland of Chiasso, which clearly referred to a model of his master Carloni. With the realization of this house, a decisive role taking emerges at the age of 16, when the boy sees his first project materialize in a building site. All his energy is funneled towards a result which is not easy, reminiscent of the often quoted exclamation: "I, too, am a painter". But what did Correggio want to say in front of Raphael? Maybe "I would also like this". We are not far from the childish dispute of the *jouet* and from the discovery of the world by playing with a handicraft.

VINCENZO VELA AND ALFONSO TURCONI

A chronological distance of four years separates the obtaining of his diploma as an architectural draftsman (1961) and his enrolment at the University of Venice IUAV (1964). What does the boy do between the ages of 18 and 21? He commutes between his mother's village, Genestrerio, where he builds the parish house, public confirmation and blessing of his role taking, and the attractive Liceo artistico Beato Angelico in

13-14. The Museum Vincenzo Vela, octagonal hall, 2001
15. Vincenzo Vela, statue of Alfonso Turconi set in the courtyard of Palazzo Turconi, todays Mendrisio Academy of Architecture
16. 100 Swiss Francs banknote showing Francesco Borromini's portrait and the drawing of the church Sant'Ivo alla Sapienza
17. The Swiss Federal Railways advertisement for the half-fare card using Francesco Borromini's portrait

Milan, where he obtains his artistic baccalaureate (8, 9). MB admits to Jean Petit that he studied at home in the mornings and then went to the Museo Vela in Ligornetto in the afternoons, three kilometers from the maternal cradle, to draw *sur la bosse* (10). I would like to depict the meeting of the young architect and the old sculptor Vincenzo Vela in a fairy-tale way. Vela does not offer Botta "elective affinities", which he can use without mediation in his training as an aspiring architect. He rather offers him an amusing break from the compulsory exercises he had to hand in at high school. So as not to waste time, he efficiently copies the pre-existing academic drawings directly, without going into the interpretation of plaster molds[21]. The primordial anti-academic ideology, breathed for the first time in Tita Carloni's studio and later confirmed in Venice, is likely to have been further reinforced in Ligornetto (11). However, I wonder if the assiduous visits to the nearby Vela house-atelier does not rather imply the discovery of an *artistic system*: a family sanctuary made up of father, brother and son, with sculptures and paintings, sketches and models, furniture and books, an art temple, almost swallowed up by *oubli*, an exciting mausoleum to be discovered and maybe even polished in a distant future (12). The renovation of the house and atelier will become a reality at the beginning of the following century; a real institutional resurrection, under the protective wing of the Swiss Confederation and thanks to the dynamism of the new director (13, 14).

In the Mendrisiotto of the 60's one could not forget the local saga of the Vela family, two brothers stonecutters and one son a painter. On the contrary, it was essential to remember them in the sense of Swiss patriotism. The work of sculptor Vincenzo Vela situates itself at the antipodes of two 19th century myths: the *self-made man*, the man who "starts from nothing" and becomes rich and famous, son of his own work, and the poor migrant, who makes a fortune in America to die better in his village, accompanied by the dignity of his capital. Vincenzo Vela progresses on the path of mechanical arts, which had become liberal arts. He escapes from the local, back-breaking stone quarries and achieves international fame in the Italian-French-Swiss triangle. It is not to the scope of this essay to present the adventure of his work. I would like to refer to the well-read publications by Gianna A. Mina Zeni, the museum director, which are published in the world wide web in an elegant website. Vela becomes popular for the commissions he receives in the cities of Milan, Lugano, Bergamo, Turin, where he illustrates Cavour's royal pantheon. He interprets the gestures of the great figures of 1848, like Daniele Manin, and of the subsequent Risorgimento. His Garibaldi dis-

18. Francesco Borromini, the cupola of Church San Carlino alle Quattro Fontane in Rome Courtesy Archivio dei Trinitari, San Carlo alle Quattro Fontane, Roma
19. Cross section of San Carlino in Lugano, 1999

plays a crushing energy. He represents history, from Spartacus to dying Napoleon, from the military alliance of Savoyard Italy with imperial France to declare war on Lombardy. He celebrates the Gotthard railway tunnel, which reinforces the geographical connection between Milan and Berlin.

Baudelaire used to say that sculpture of his time was a bore, *ennui*, and that photography "is not an art" but a mechanized production with no poetry. Vincenzo Vela proves the opposite, not only because he uses photography as a tool to verify shape, but because he succeeds in introducing dynamism in his sculptures. According to the criteria of art history, his work can be placed in the movement of social realism. However, this label does not consider his ability to translate the represented historical moment into a psychological moment: Spartacus's revolutionary uprising, Napoleon's daydreaming gaze while dying in exile. Let's take a close look at the monument dedicated to the memory of Count Alfonso Turconi, erected in the courtyard in front of the hospital in Mendrisio, the so-called Ospizio della Beata Vergine. Turconi, a landowner in the Mendrisiotto, is a figure of 18th century Enlightenment. Moved by physiocratic ideology, he developed agricultural experiences, whereas his interest for the French revolution pushed him to move his residence to Paris, where he died in 1805. In his will be bequeathed a capital donation for the construction of a hospital in Mendrisio, the building of which took place half a century later. The effigy of the donator, completed in 1868, takes possession of the central courtyard of the hospital. The base, made of Baveno pink granite, serves as a fountain. The figure itself is carved in Carrara marble. The sculptor's task is to depict an almost forgotten personality. Vela decides to portray Conte Turconi as a twin of Thomas Jefferson; tall, slender and elegant (15). However, the composition does not refer to the classical comparison. The body stands up from the chair, which is pushed back with the left hand. It is the moment of drafting the will. The momentum is the main subject. The left foot walks over the base the chair stands on in precarious balance. The result is a combination of a double psychological fact: the moment of decision-making and the offer of his last will.

In a second life, Alfonso Turconi will inhabit the courtyard of the Academy of Architecture of the Università della Svizzera italiana. The old hospital building is transformed into a school building, the result of an intelligent renovation carried out under Tita Carloni. The new school opened in 1996, following a teaching plan drafted by MB. I suggest considering the "Turconi", which is how students call the original building of the Accademia, the small pantheon in the Mendrisiotto: on the main staircase the busts of sculptor

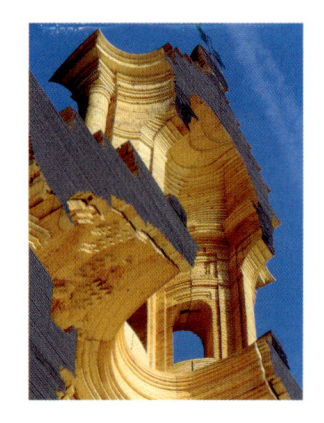

20. Detail of the small wooden cupola of San Carlino in Lugano, 1999
21. Three dimensional drawing of the small cupola of San Carlino, Lugano 1999
22-23. San Carlino, Lugano 1999

Vincenzo and his painter son Spartaco stand alongside a doctor and a politician. Furthermore, with the renovation of the Vela Museum in Ligornetto, carried out between 1997 and 2001, MB sets the stage for a reinterpretation of Vela's work. He turns the 19th century cavern into an energizing bath, illuminated by millions of bright particles. The architect follows the classic principle of shape breaking off from the base. He draws mobile steel bases, which the sculptures appear to levitate on. The white plastering of the room walls and of the central hall reflects the colors of the garden, a phenomenon which can be even better observed on rainy days. In a nutshell, the architect succeeds in actualizing observation and performs the transfiguration of the house/atelier into a place of education and discovery.

FRANCESCO BORROMINI: FROM BISSONE TO THE TIBER AND BACK TO THE SHORES OF LAKE LUGANO

Born in Bissone, a village on the shores of Lake Lugano, in 1559, Francesco Borromini was "resurrected" in Berne in 1976, when his portrait was printed on the 100 Franc note by the Swiss National Bank. His nervous face was depicted with fantastic engravings and combined with an architectural frame, a copy of Paolo Portoghesi's drawings for the church San Ivo alla Sapienza (16). The following decade, the Swiss Transportation Company used Borromini's anxious portrait on the flier promoting the sale of the yearly travelcard, valid on the Swiss railway network, at half price, exactly 100 Swiss francs (17). These details are clear evidence of the fact that Borromini had been "naturalized" in the last third of the 20th century and declared a Swiss citizen with full rights. The forth centenary of the artist's birth triggers a fundamental reexamination of his work. *Borromini e l'universo barocco* (18) is the title of an exhibition organized in Rome. On the same occasion, a symposium with the specialist *élite*[22] is held. Ticino was in the forefront in supporting this international effort, not only with a parallel exhibition, *Il Giovane Borromini*, set up in the Cantonal Art Museum in Lugano[23], but, most importantly, with a strong and amazing plastic event: the temporary staging of a cenotaph on the waters of Lake Lugano. I say cenotaph because it is the commemoration of a dead person in the absence of his physical remains, the result of an "un-catholic" suicide. The only remains are represented by the silhouette of the cross section of the church San Carlo alle Quattro Fontane (19). This *event* arises from MB's imagination; i.e. to take possession of the lakefront in Lugano to insert an unprecedented geometrical building. This is how the young *Accademia* in Mendrisio reveals its existence in the capital city[24]. MB succeeds in catching Borromini to create a *projet d'école*, as it is called at the Institute of Technology in Lausanne: a profiled research program which develops enthusiasm and emulation. But with an imperative deadline. Whereas in Lausanne a *projet d'école* financed by the National Fund for Scientific Research can protract for over a decade without any substantial practical result, the Ticino project had to materialize within a year. A Borromini Atelier is created. Students, assistants, teachers are invited to participate immediately. In the meantime, MB contacts Alessandro Sartor, professor for photogrammetric survey in the context of architecture at the Roman university Sapienza, who delivers the data of the San Carlo[25].

The reduced scale model, used for the exhibition, gives rise in MB's mind to the dream of a *blow up* in a 1:1 scale, a true urban *happening* (20). The aim becomes to install a provisional structure on the lakefront in the shape of a parallelepiped chest, where the cross section of the church is to be anchored. Two modern machines fuel the project: computerized axial tomography creates a stratigraphic vision of the body to be constructed, whereas a laser-operated "laminator", a system called LOM, leads to numerical modeling. This new experience is carried out in Lausanne in the group gravitating around architect Georges Abou Jaoudé, head of the *Laboratoire d'informatique et de visualisation* at the Lausanne-based Polytechnic[26]. Abou presents a model in a 1:33 scale, which is not only a solid object made of laser-cut paper, spreading a funny burnt smell, but a numerical model which, theoretically, can be applied to any scale of operation. De facto, these high tech machines manage to translate a project studied by the point of the *fixpencil* by the *architecte au fixpensil*. However, the final result is the opposite of *high tech* architecture: the assembly of ready-made panels, a clever, archaic and provoking DIY.

The first question refers to the location for the installation of the *folie* in the lake gulf by Lugano. The protected ducks and swans are not to be disturbed. Nevertheless, there is a central location, near a small square where sycamores frame the sculpture of Wilhelm Tell, a popular work by Vincenzo Vela, with the national hero waving the winning arrow in front of the "postmodern" and vulgar façade of the Casino. More importantly, the second question concerns the orientation of the structure. It is a matter of the physical perception of the happening. MB decides to make the most of the east-west axis, thus making the central facade of the concave cross section perceivable at a distance of 300-400 meters (21). In contrast, the short

24. Jean Marc Reiser at Mario Botta's exhibition opening at the French Institute of Architecture in Paris, 1983

walk on steel poles from the shore to the raft is a tribute to the north-south axis. From here there is a bizarre perspective from a picturesque point of view. The rising of the skylight cut in half appears like the reproduction of a curious fossil (22). To the one hundred or so articles which described the bewilderment provoked by the happening with a thousand and more clever references, I prefer Abou Jaoudé's metaphor, which talks of bones and skeletons. The squid bone looks like a profile without relation to the face. The vertical section, the autopsy of the San Carlino, is so strong that in the day-time it looks like a giraffe with its neck in the shape of a skylight. In the middle of the night it looks like an elephant: from west to east the distant night vision creates a plastic effect that could not be verified before the installation of the spotlights: the concave volume of the San Carlino projects itself like a convexity after sunset. This three-dimensional effect, observed by thousands of amazed tourists and citizens, could not be photographed. The night pictures only manage to illustrate the light surrounding the concave profile of the San Carlino. The spectacular effect of the yellow, honey-colored convexity disappears.

The other bizarre beauty of the San Carlino, *choc culturel*, focuses on the touch of magic that transforms Borromini's niceties into a "primary" or *brutalist* superimposition of fir wood panels. In 1999 newspapers and magazines describe either a dichotomy between past and present or a technological miracle worked in religious skepticism. Nobody notices that the San Carlino carcass needs an orthogonal netting of steel poles and braces to anchor its wooden structure. The building site IT program is not a secret, but nobody is interested in it. Now, in the aftermath of 11th September 2001, the prevailing feelings in 1999, Borromini's year, i.e. the expectation of the universal *bug*, are unremembered. The San Carlino could have become a sign of hope in the future. The San Carlino *folie*, at first rejected by the majority of the local population, now offers a new postcard of the city. Even the first opponents of the monument will attempt to defend its permanence. Is it possible that inflation, deflation, bubbles, takeovers concern not only banks, but also the trends and the symbols we live with?

I remember a fast ride on the highway between Mendrisio and Lugano in 2000. While Mario was driving, he carefully observed the geography of the lake to discover the geometrical traces that Francesco would have seized *in situ* and taken to Rome under his hat. This touching episode leads to the conclusion that MB communicated with Borromini as if he was a colleague still alive.

[1] In the first publication *Mario Botta. The complete works, Volume 1 1960-1985*, Birkhäuser Verlag, Basel-Boston-Berlin 1993, Botta's bibliography indeed already amounted to 600 publications twenty years ago. See pp. 247-254.
[2] Martin Steinmann, "Wirklichkeit als Geschichte, Stichworte zu einem Gespräch über Realismus in der Architektur", in Heinz Ronner et al., *Tendenzen, Neuere Architektur im Tessin*, Zürich, gta Verlag, 1975, p. 11. Steinmann develops the notion of *realism* as a rational answer, promoted by a group of young local architects, to the social needs of Ticino during and after the construction of the Gotthard highway.
[3] Kenneth Frampton, *Modern Architecture, a Critical History*, London, Thames & Hudson, 1980; 2nd increased edition, ibidem, 1985, pp. 313-14; and "Prospects for a Critical Regionalism", *Perspecta*, n. 20, 1983, pp. 147-172. *Critical regionalism* is referred to as the introduction of modernity in the local typology repertoire, interpreted in a poetic and tectonic way.
[4] Pierluigi Nicolin, "Note pour le second volume des oeuvres de Mario Botta", in Pierluigi Nicolin, François Chaslin, *Mario Botta, 1978-1982, Laboratoire d'architecture*, Milano/Paris, Electa/Le Moniteur, 1982 [*Mario Botta. Buildings and Projects 1961-1982*, Electa-Rizzoli, New York 1984] The architect from Ticino discovers Paris.
[5] Virgilio Gilardoni, "Gli spazi dell'uomo nell'architettura di Mario Botta. Note sulla biblioteca luganese dei Frati", Bellinzona, Archivio Storico Ticinese, vol. ann. 1984. On page 240 Gilardoni develops the metaphoric equation *workshop* equals *laboratory*.
[6] Francesco Dal Co, Mirko Zardini, *Mario Botta, Architecture 1960-1985*, Milano, Rizzoli, 1987; Francesco Dal Co, "Conversazione intorno all'architettura", in *Una casa*, Milano, Electa, 1989, pp. 81-87. Dal Co focuses on the metaphor of the *totem*. Zardini insists on the interpretation of myths.
[7] Werner Oechslin, "Introduction", in *Architectures 1980-1990, Entretien avec Pierluigi Nicolin*, Barcelona, Gustavo Gili, 1991, pp. 8-19. Summary of existing critique.
[8] Giovanni Pozzi, "Quattro istantanee per Botta", in *Sull'orlo del visibile parlare*, Milano, Adelphi, 1993, pp. 423-437. A subtle and heartfelt tribute, with an iconological note.
[9] Rudolf Arnheim, "Notes on Religious Architecture", *Languages of Design*, Vol.1, 3, August 1993, pp. 247-252. Commenting on the plan of the church in Mogno, Arnheim inserts the interaction of the circle and the ellipse in the *geometrical principles of the Age of Humanism* (p. 247). He observes that "the inherent religiosity of these shapes can inspire architects independently of their religious faith."
[10] Jean Petit, *Traces d'architecture: Botta*, Milano, Fidia Edizioni d'Arte, collana Panorama Forces Vives, 1994. MB opens the *album de famille* for the author and offers him a detailed biographical path, marked by deep friendship. Jean Petit's hidden autobiography projects into the shoes of the other.

25. Jean Marc Reiser, la maison ronde de Mario Botta - Mario Botta's round house

[11] See Oswald Mathias Ungers, *Architettura come tema, Architecture as Theme*, Milano, Electa, 1982.

[12] Renato De Fusco, *Architettura come mass medium, Note per una semiologia architettonica*, Bari, Dedalo libri, 1967.

[13] Robert Venturi, Denise Scott Brown, Steven Izenour, *Learning from Las Vegas*, Cambridge, MS, MIT Press, 1972.

[14] Franco La Cecla, *Contro l'architettura*, Turin, Bollati Boringhieri, 2008.

[15] Kenneth Frampton, Francis Strauven, Jacques Gubler, Luc Verpoest, *Georges Baines*, Gent, Ludion, 2006.

[16] Jean Petit, op cit, p. 303, "Je ne suis pas né architecte, je suis devenu architecte à travers le travail des autres qui m'a nourri […]."

[17] Excellent discussion in Daniela Cherubini, *Il concetto di ruolo nella teoria sociologica*, doctorate in applied sociology and methodology of social research, Milano, Bicocca, January 2007.

[18] Ibid., p. 7.

[19] Tita Carloni, "Les débuts de Mario Botta", in Jean Petit, op cit, pp. 325-326.

[20] Ibid., p. 325.

[21] Jean Petit, op cit, reproduces an example *à la sanguine*, p. 27.

[22] The wandering exhibition is inaugurated in the Palazzo delle Esposizioni in Rome, on December 16, 1999. The three-day symposium will follow in January 2000. The research results are published in *Borromini e l'universo barocco*, by Richard Bösel and Christoph L. Frommel, Milan, Electa, 2000. Vol. 1, texts by Joseph Connors, Robert Stalla, Richard Bosel, Christoph L. Frommel, Heinrich Thelen, Paolo Portoghesi, Martin Raspe, Marcello Fagiolo, Werner Oechslin, Elisabeth Kieven. Vol. 2, catalog of works.

[23] Catalog *Il giovane Borromini, dagli esordi a San Carlo alle Quattro Fontane*, by Manuela Kahn Rossi and Marco Franciolli, Milano, Skira, 1999.

[24] Of the three departments opened in 1996, two (the school of economics and the school of communications) are located in Lugano, whereas the school of architecture, the *Accademia*, is located in Mendrisio. The Università della Svizzera Italiana will decide to adopt the English name "University of Lugano."

[25] Rolando Bellini, Fabio Minazzi, *Mario Botta per Borromini: il San Carlo sul lago di Lugano*, Varese, Edizioni Agorà, 2000, p. 17.

[26] Georges Abou Jaoudé, "Cattedrale di carta", in *Mario Botta, Borromini sul Lago*, by Gabriele Cappellato, Milano, Skira, 1999.

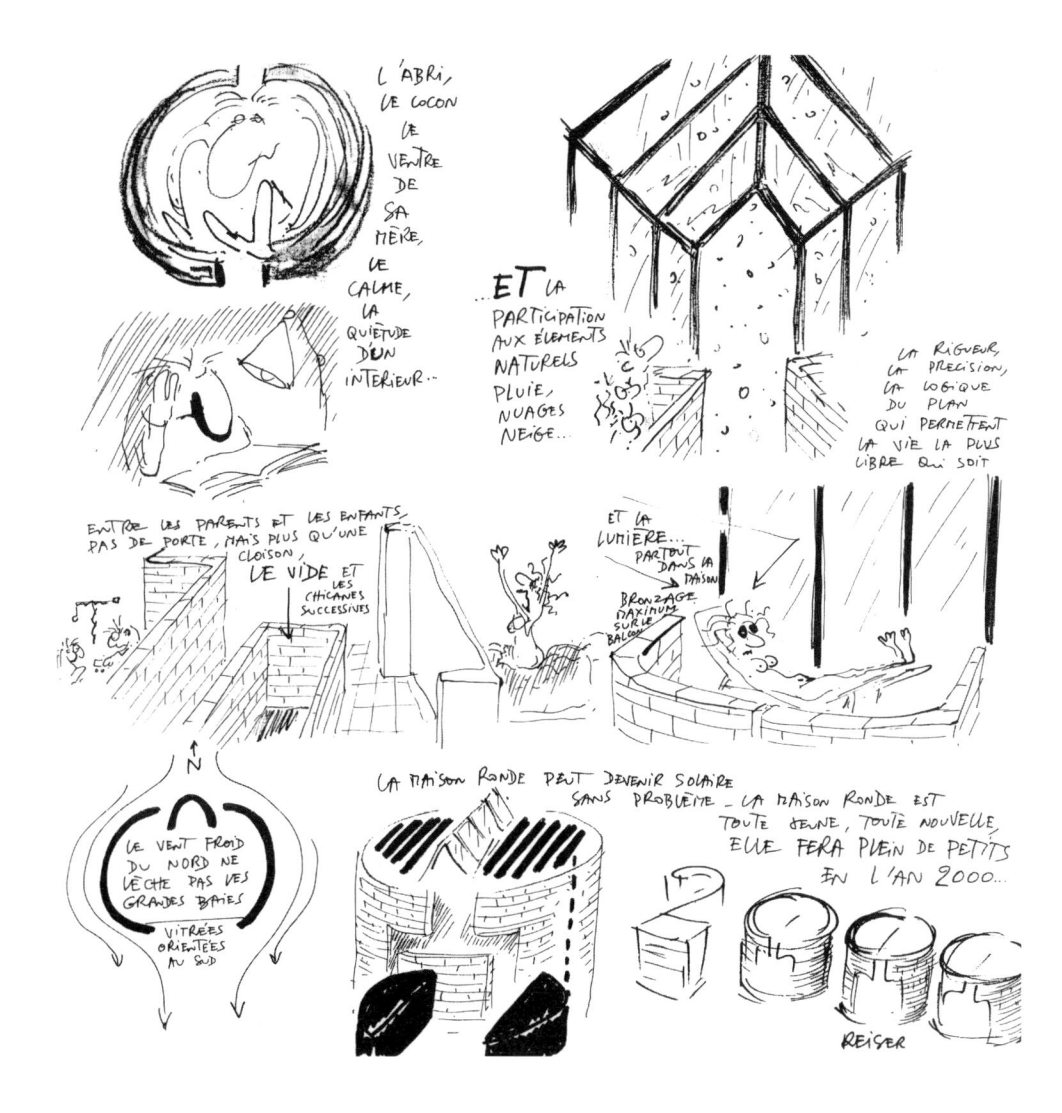

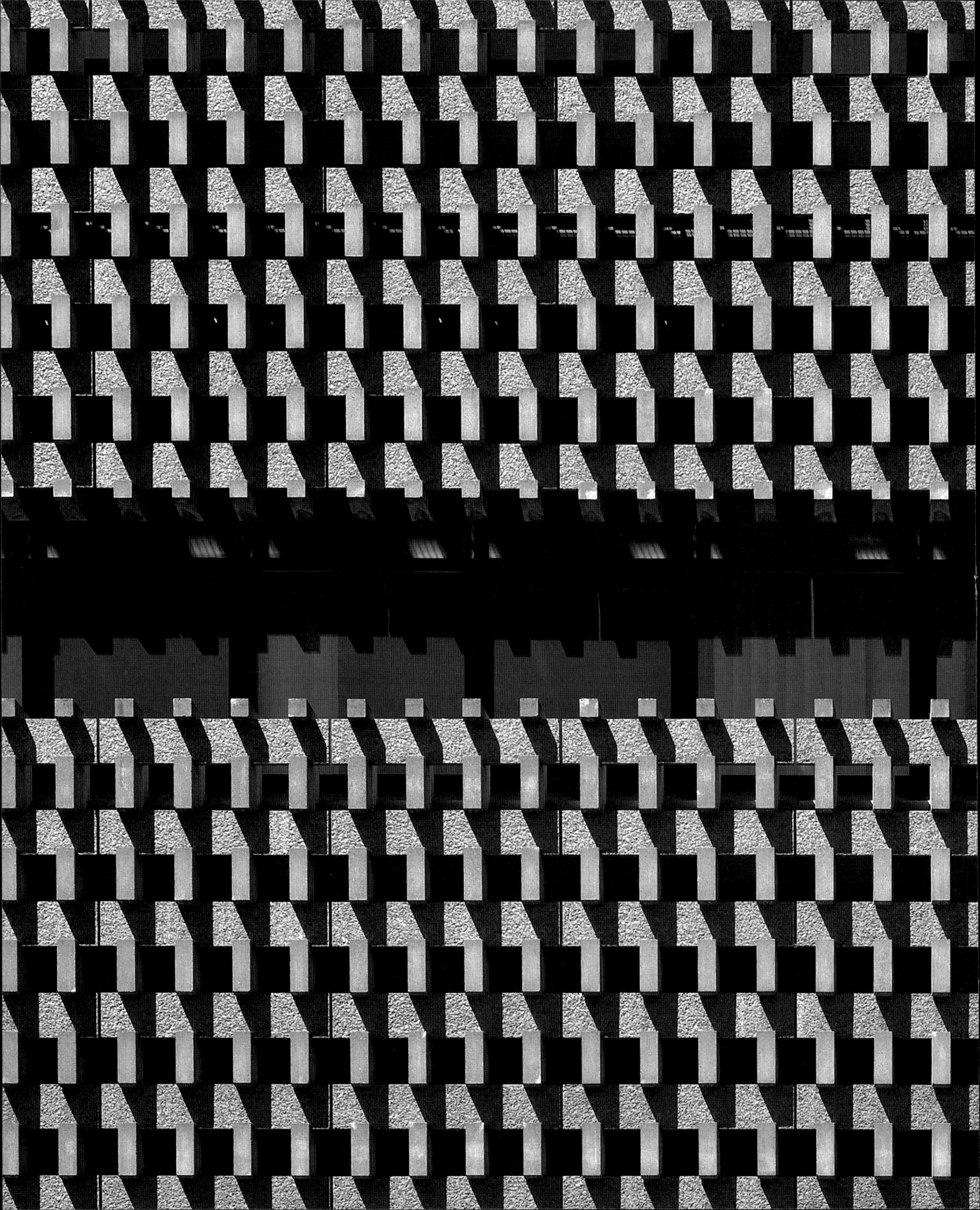

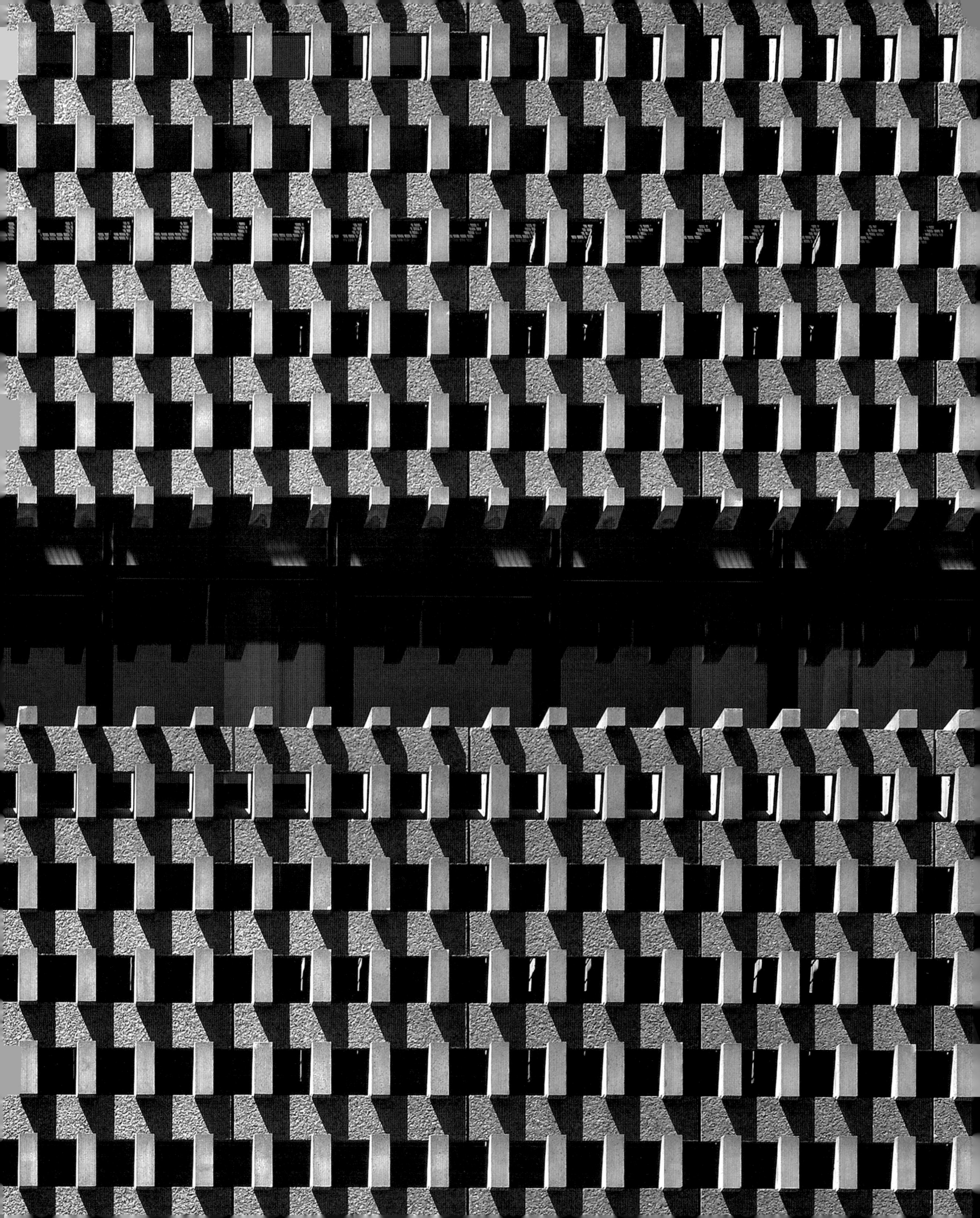

LIBRARIES

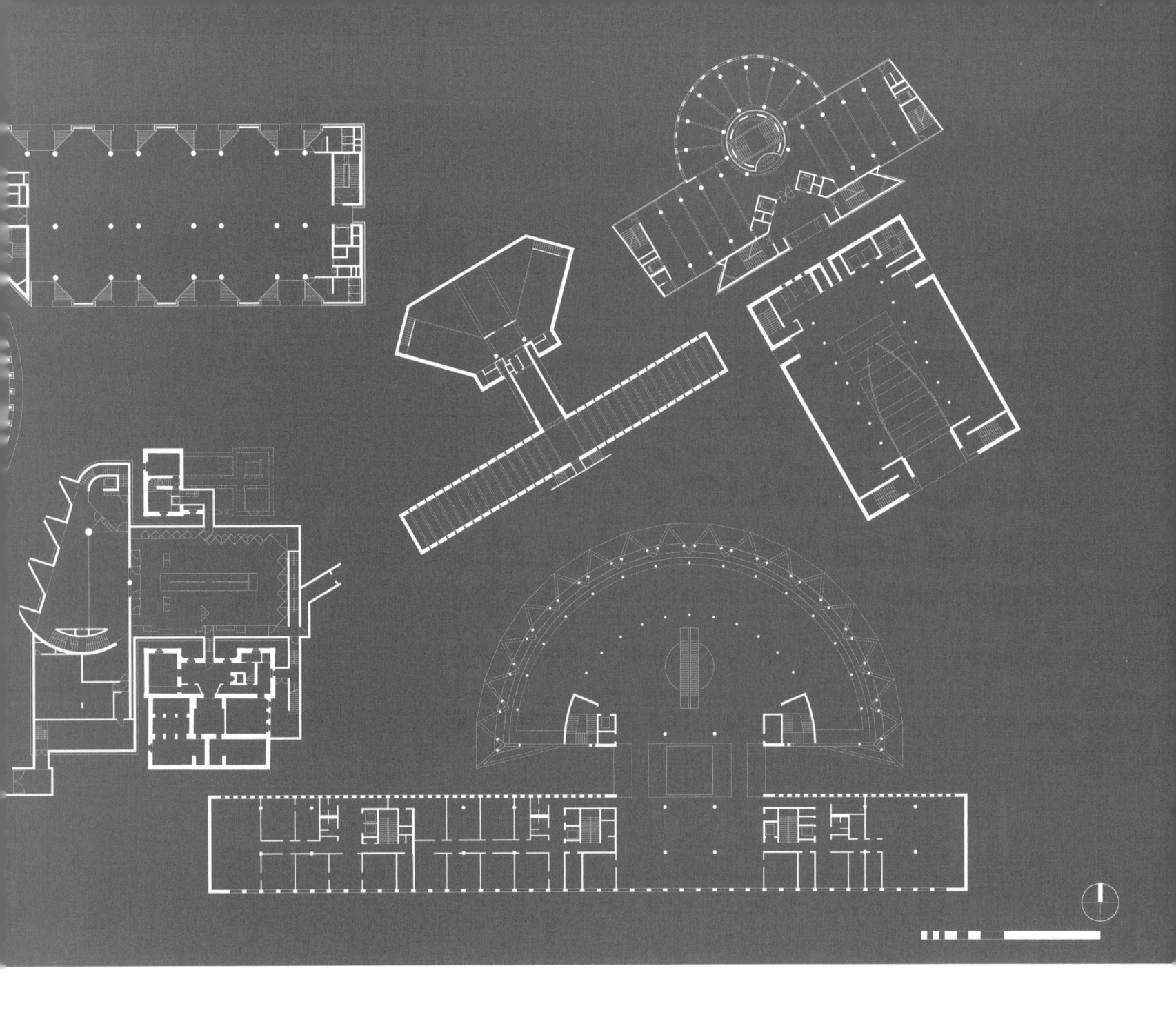

Libraries are the spaces in which our knowledge and memory are kept alive and safeguarded. They are the cases containing the thinking and the hopes of the past generations. Thus the spaces for the reading and the preservation fill up with presences and sacred messages we recognize as an heritage of mankind. Libraries permit us to voice a larger history that goes beyond our human time limits. For this reason they take on symbolic aspects. They become emerging or monumental presences reaffirming their exceptional nature and their collective meanings over the surrounding domestic background.

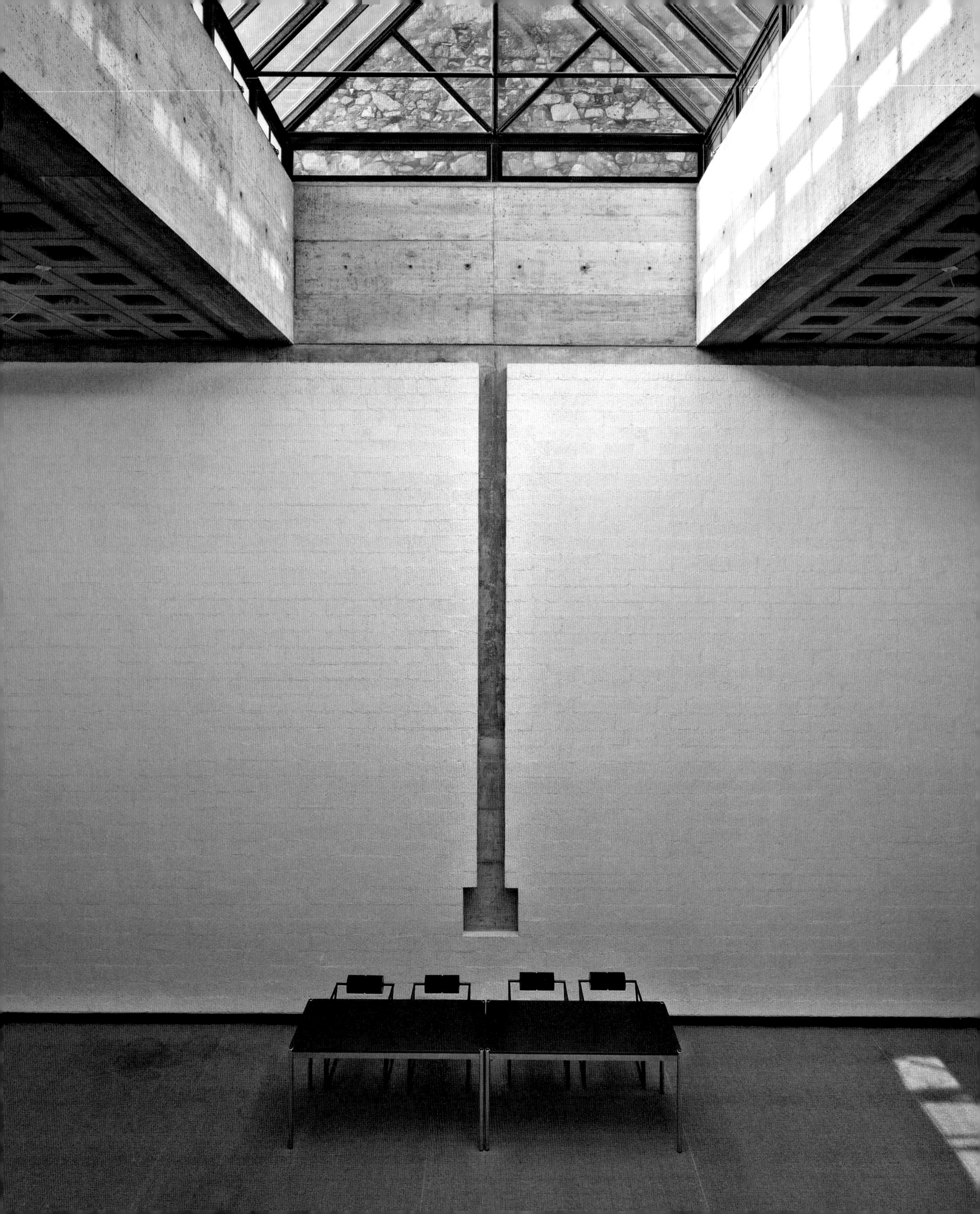

LIBRARY AT THE CAPUCHINS CONVENT
LUGANO – SWITZERLAND

1976-1979

Archive: n° 023
Project: 1976
Construction: 1976-79
Client: Monastery of the Capuchin Friars, Lugano
Site area: 7'200 m² / 77'500 s ft
Floor area: 900 m² / 9'688 s ft
Volume: 3'800 m³ / 134'196 c ft

The 17th-century monastery lies on the hillside between the historic centre of the city and the built-up area around the station. The aim of the project was to revive the collective character of the entire structure, realizing a public library, and later the restoration of the convent. The building is set underground and leaves unchanged the plan of the old convent. The interior offers a reading and reference room on two floors that opens around a central space. A skylight that emerges from the garden and establishes an immediate visual relationship with the church above illuminates the core and highlights the axis of the library marked by a deep vertical cut in the wall.
The long book storeroom delimits the underground structure towards the city. A vertical element with the elevator links the library to the offices located in the above convent.

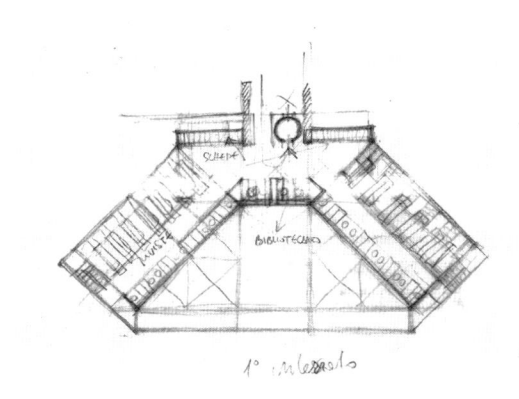

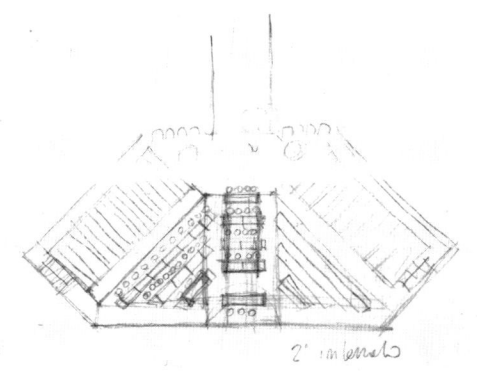

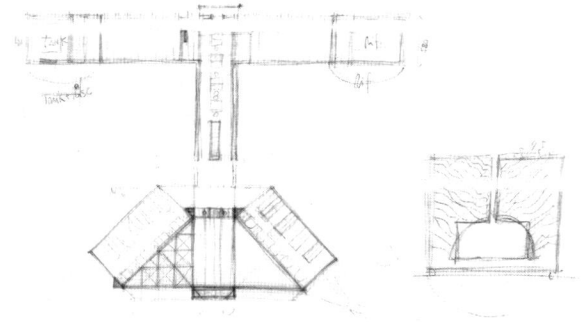

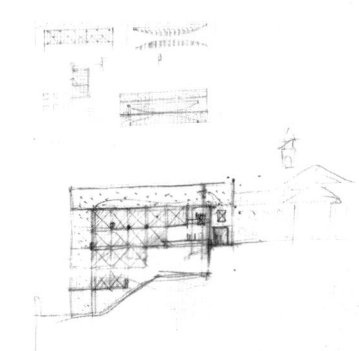

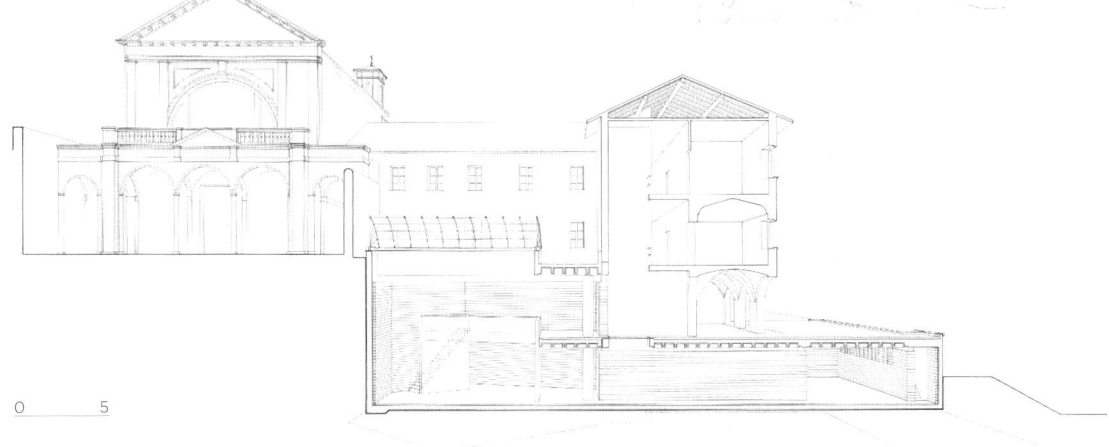

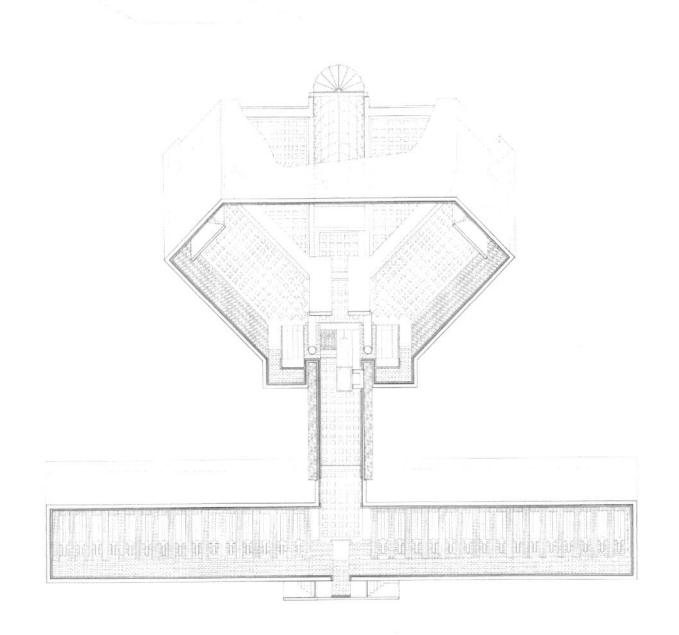

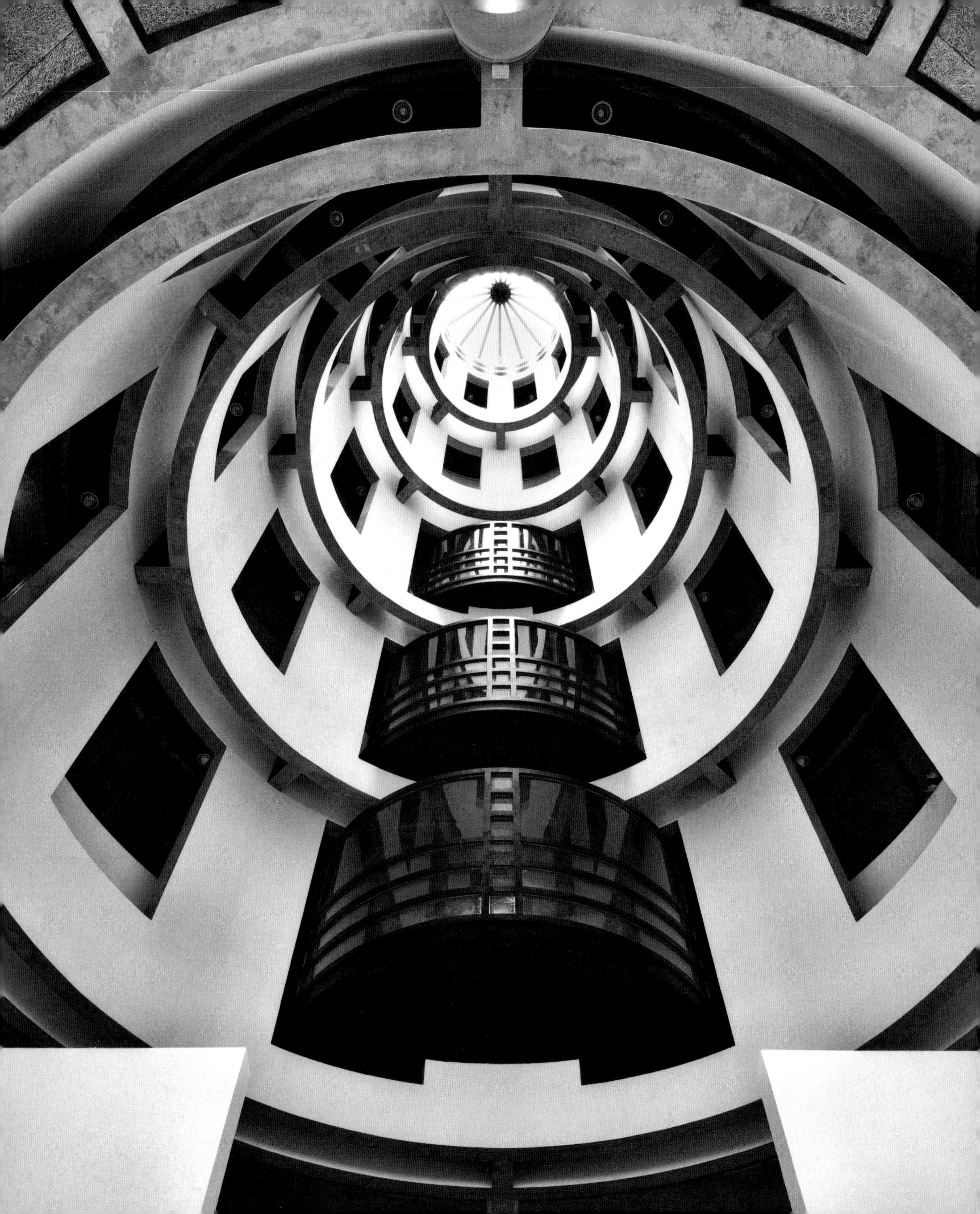

MAISON DU LIVRE, DE L'IMAGE ET DU SON
VILLEURBANNE – FRANCE

1984-1988

Archive: n° 084
Competition project: 1984
Construction: 1985-88
Client: City of Villeurbanne
Site area: 5'400 m² / 58'125 s ft
Floor area: 5'580 m² / 60'063 s ft
Volume: 18'000 m³ / 635'664 c ft

The building is set within the continuous urban front along avenue Emile Zola. The entrance façade projects itself forward with respect to the glass brick walls connecting with the neighboring buildings. A deep vertical cut forms two symmetrical walls, in whose corners the stairwells are set. The pattern of the street façade, clad in alternated colored bands of stone, also characterizes the cylindrical volume on the rear courtyard. Same as the main front, the cylindrical volume is detached from the surrounding buildings by means of connecting parts faced with glass bricks. The interior space presents a central cavity, rising up from the ground floor to the roof. It shapes a light well made of concentric rings, around which the reference rooms are located and from which the glassed-in volumes containing the librarians' desks emerge.

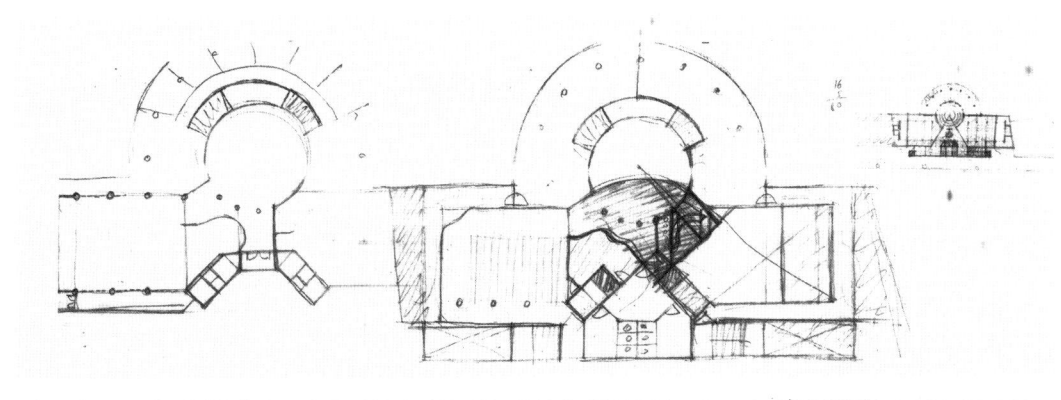

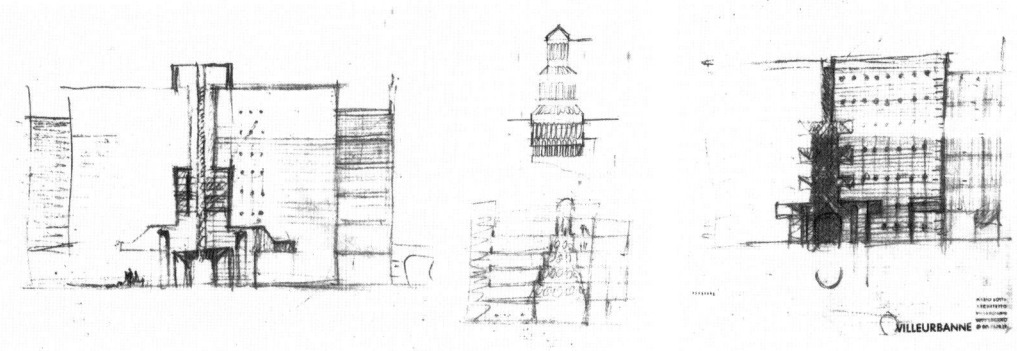

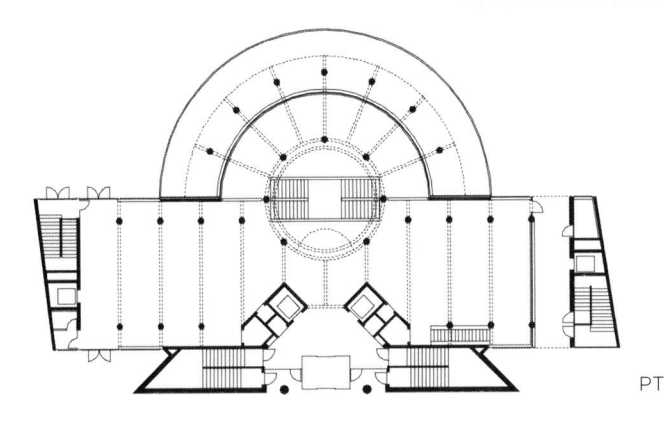

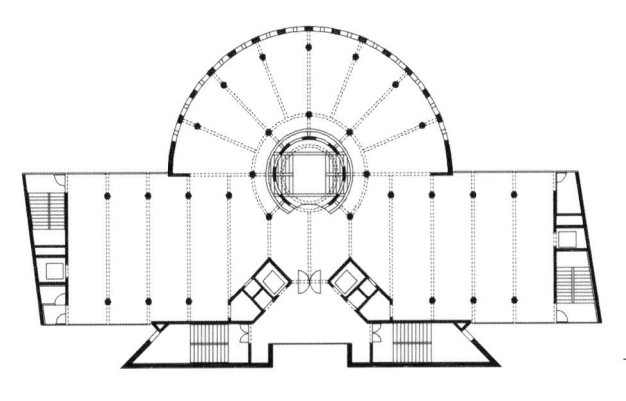

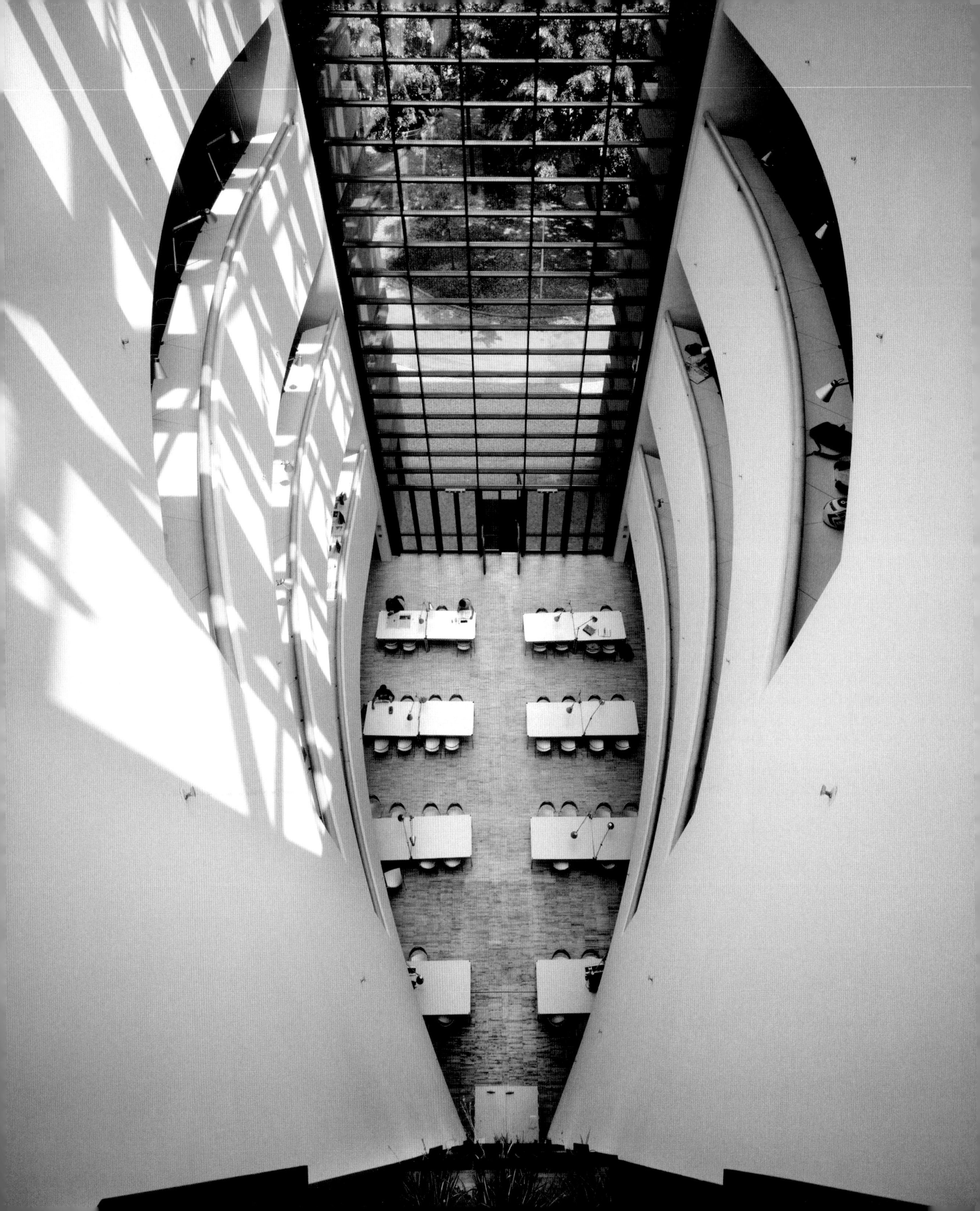

LIBRARY TIRABOSCHI
BERGAMO - ITALY

1995-2004

Archive: n° 278
Project: 1995
Construction: 2002-2004
Client: City of Bergamo
Partner: arch. Giorgio Orsini
Site area: 9'360 m² / 100'750 s ft
Floor area: 3'130 m² / 33'691 s ft
Volume: 17'500 m³ / 618'006 c ft

The Tiraboschi library is the core of the inter-librarian system including all the Bergamo-based libraries. The building is strategically located near the university, between a major city street and a green area. Towards the main road, the solidity of the massive brick wall is only interrupted by a thin cut that widens near the entrance. Inside, the building develops on five level all facing the central void illuminated by roof lights. Opposite the entrance, a wide window front along the whole height of the building opens the reading galleries towards the backyard planted with trees.

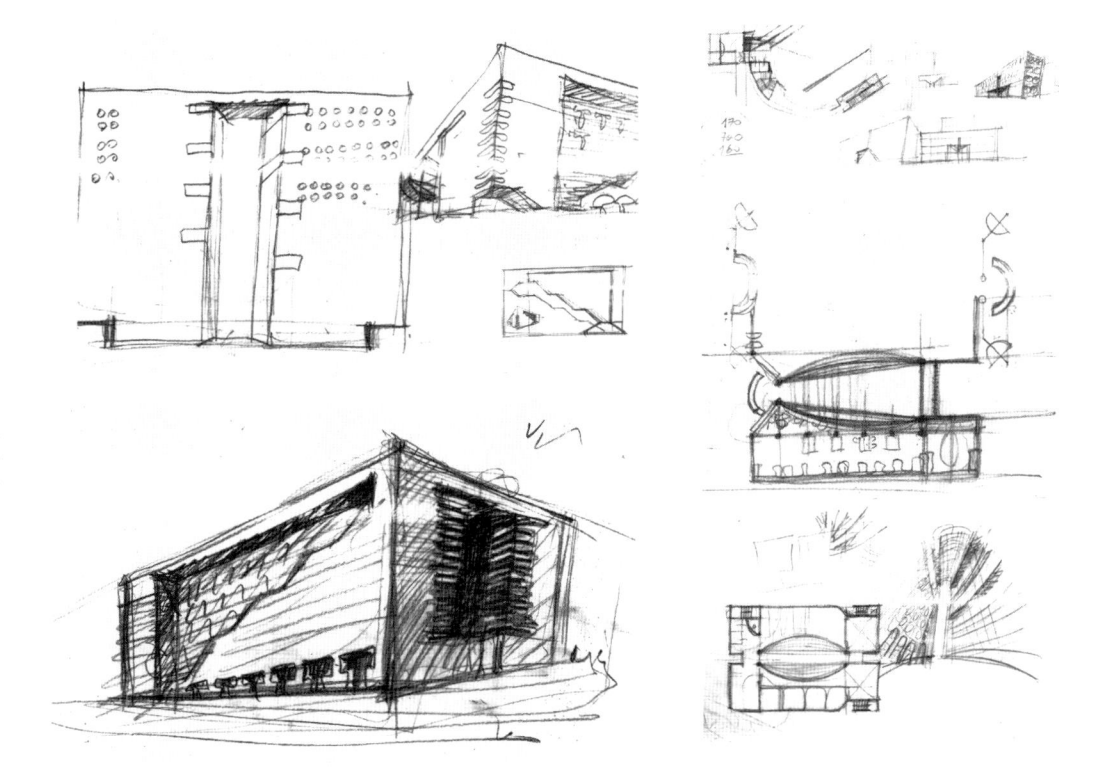

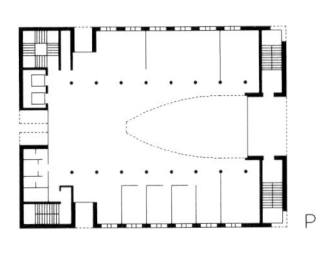

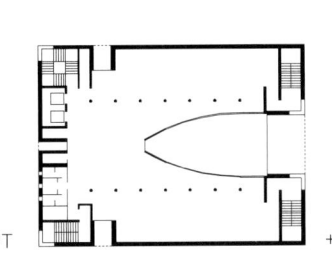

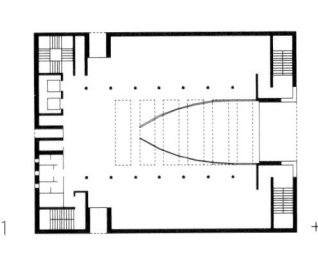

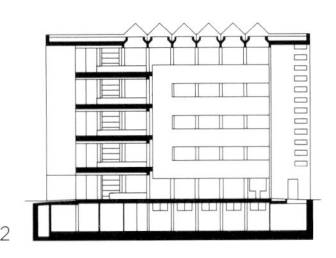

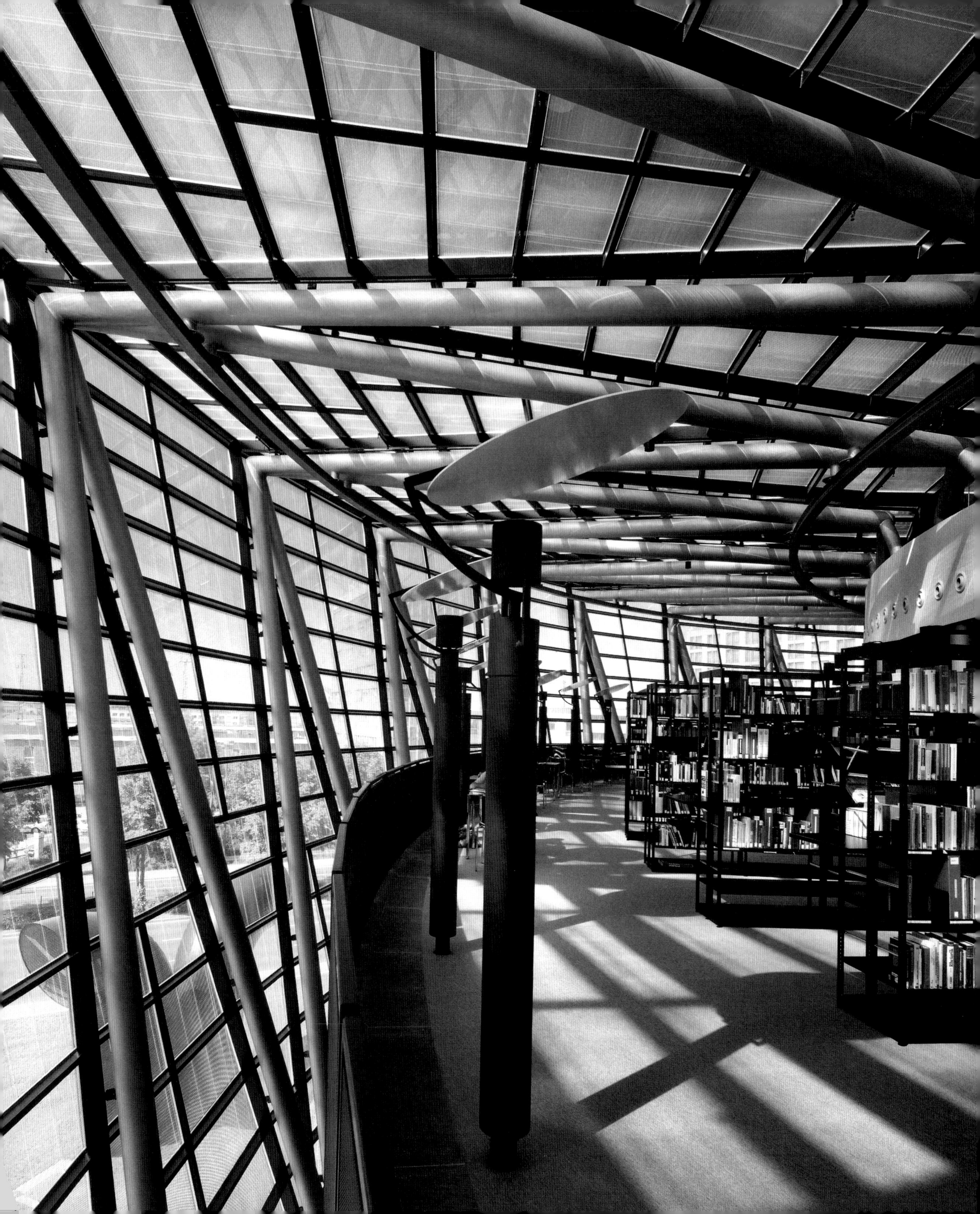

MUNICIPAL LIBRARY DORTMUND – GERMANY

1995-1999

Archive: n° 297
Competition project: 1995
Construction: 1997-1999
Client: City of Dortmund
Partner: arch. Gerd Vette, eng. Klemens Pelle
Site area: 7'000 m² / 75'347 s ft
Floor area: 14'130 m² / 152'094 s ft
Volume : 53'735 m³ / 1'900'000 c ft

The library is located between the historic town and the empty urban space in front of it with the 19th-century railway station. It consists of two distinct buildings, in shape and volume, in material as well as in use. One, an upside down truncated half-cone houses in a one and open space different floors with the reception area, the library catalogues and the reading rooms. The other, a long orthogonal building for offices and storages, is characterized by a progressive tapering on the different floors. The entrance to the library is set at ground floor in the junction of the two different volumes. The interior allows at a glimpse the distribution of paths on the two floors of the library and the connection to the facilities located in the body next to it. The cone presents itself as a high-tech building, with a steel and glass structure becoming the characteristic for the building. Inside, the round joists of the two floors withdraw from the structures of the piers of this wrapping, standing free in all of their height. The Dortmund library shows a complex of building which breaks with the traditional unitary typology proper to libraries, in order to respond through its layout to the historic morphology of the city.

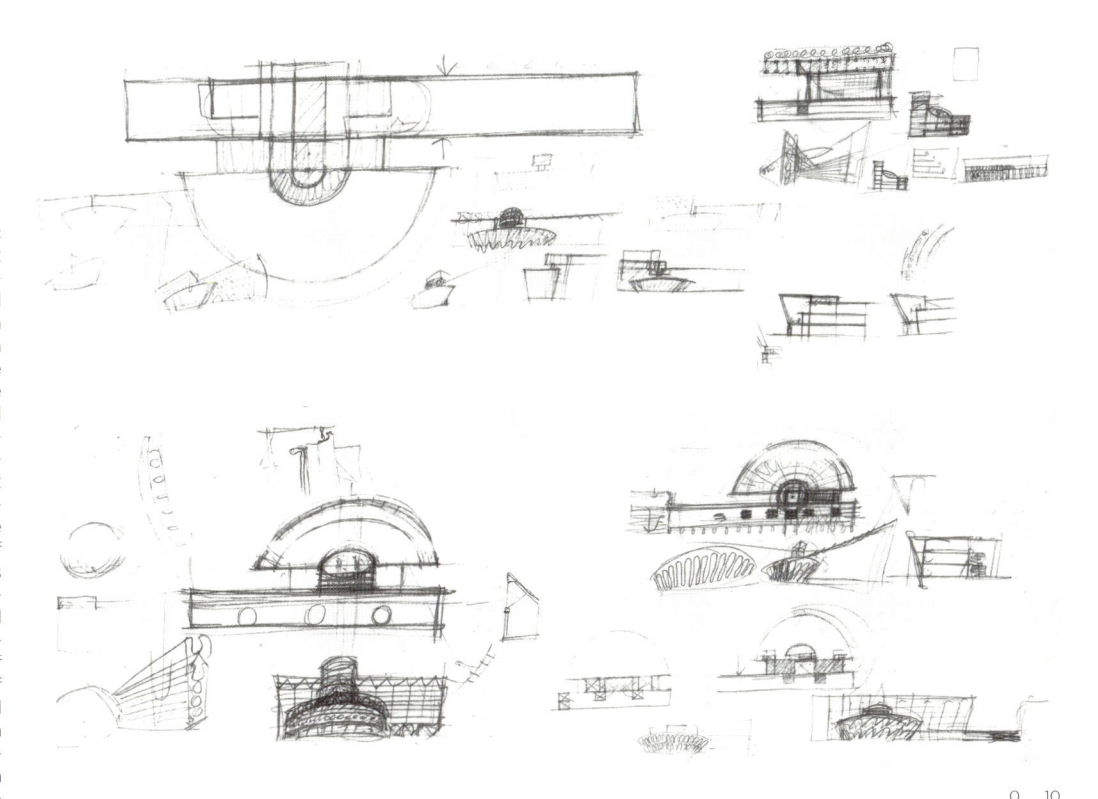

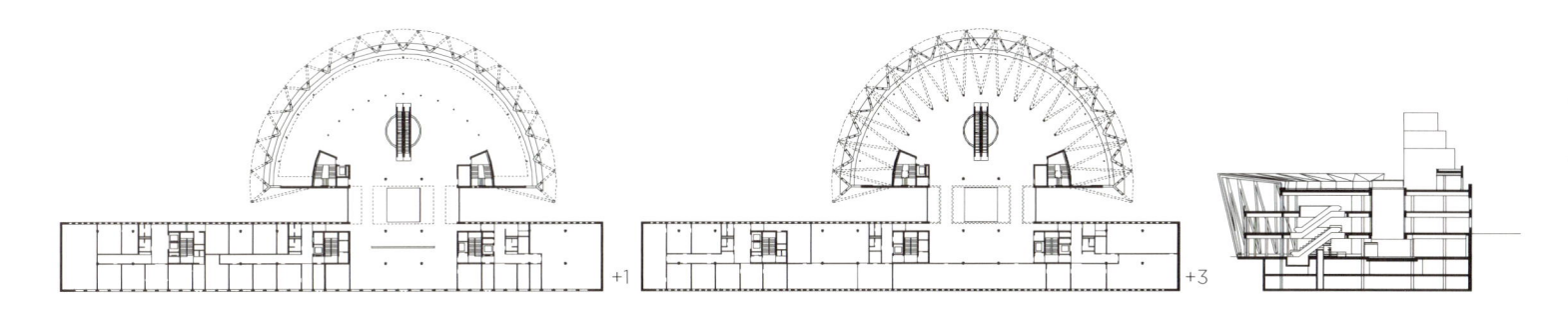

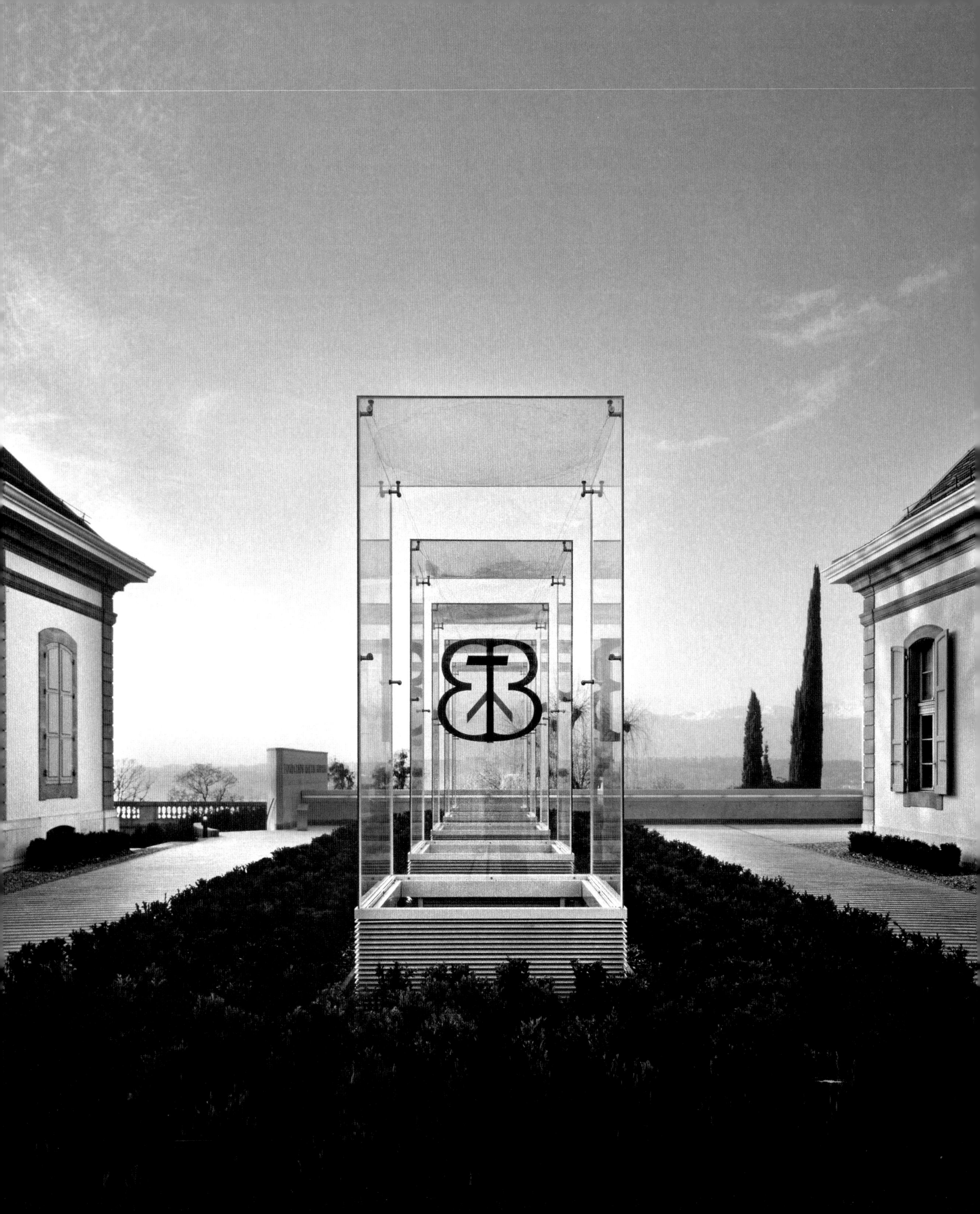

MARTIN BODMER FOUNDATION
COLOGNY – SWITZERLAND

1998-2003

Archive: n° 353
Project: 1998
Construction: 2000-2003
Client: Martin Bodmer Foundation
Site supervision: Studio Archilab, Pully
Site area: 5'500 m² / 59'201 s ft
Floor area: 1'280 m² / 13'777 s ft
Volume : 9'000 m² / 317'832 c ft

The Library located in Cologny, near Geneva, host the collection of manuscripts and documents that constitutes a cultural heritage remarkable for its quality and rarity. Bodmer considered his collection not only as a library, but also as a 'museum of documents that trace the history of the human mind'. The extension of the foundation is set between two early 20th-century villas in a large estate and consists of a two-storey hypogeal construction linked to both of the villas. The exceptional nature of the preserved documents suggested the idea of considering the building as a "concealed jewel case" with nothing emerging from the ground except five glass elements. Skylights, that enable natural light flow into the underground exhibition area. Their geometrical shapes slightly interfere in the perception of the surrounding landscape and delicately reveal the underground presence. The access to the new museum's extension happens from the garden, crossing a sunken courtyard on the lakeside of the property. Inside, the exhibition spaces are distinguished by the contrast of the daylight tangling the suspended artworks that are placed in the center of the new building, and the soft punctual light on the rare books behind the showcases along the walls. The space appears almost boundless and mutable, only delimited by the arrangements of the books, each of them held by a specific designed iron support.

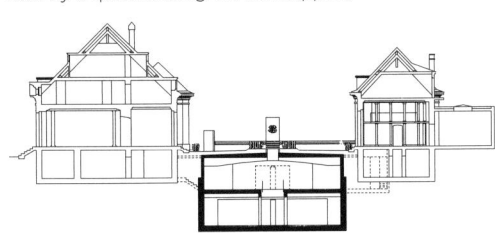

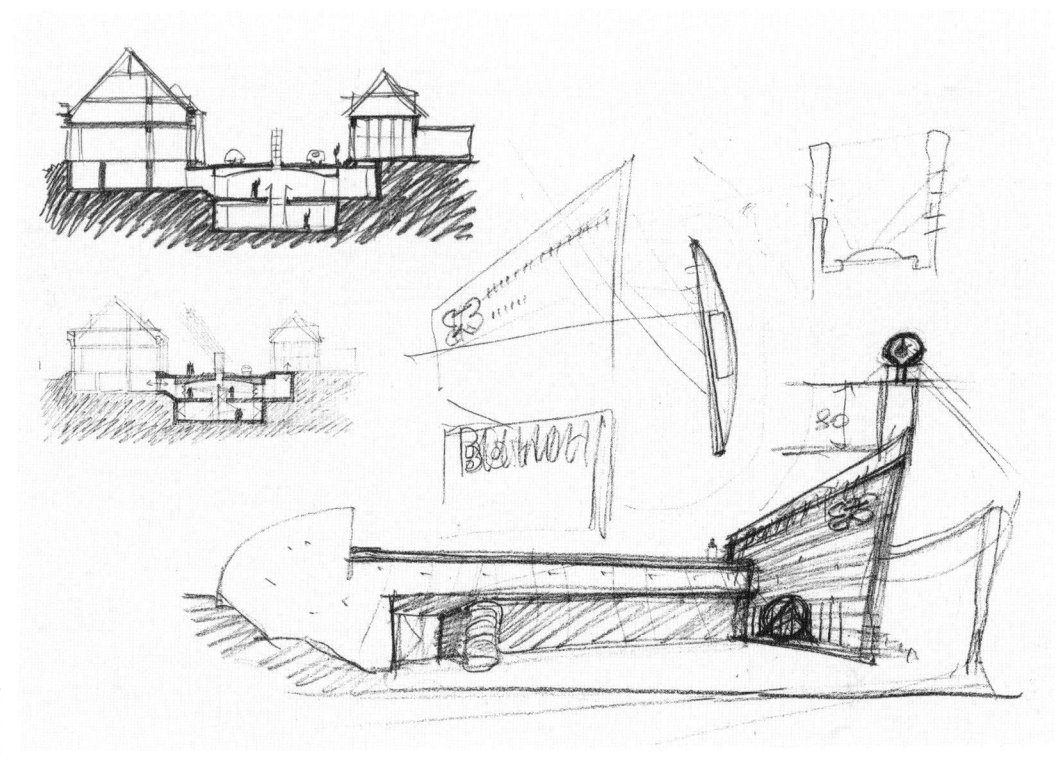

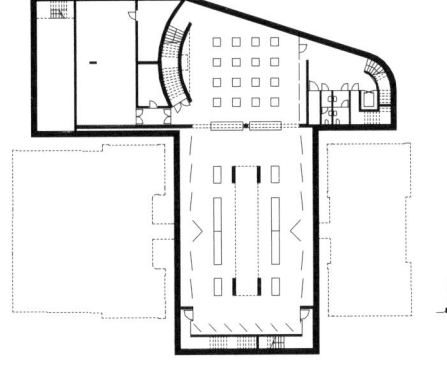

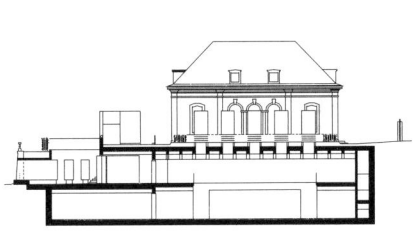

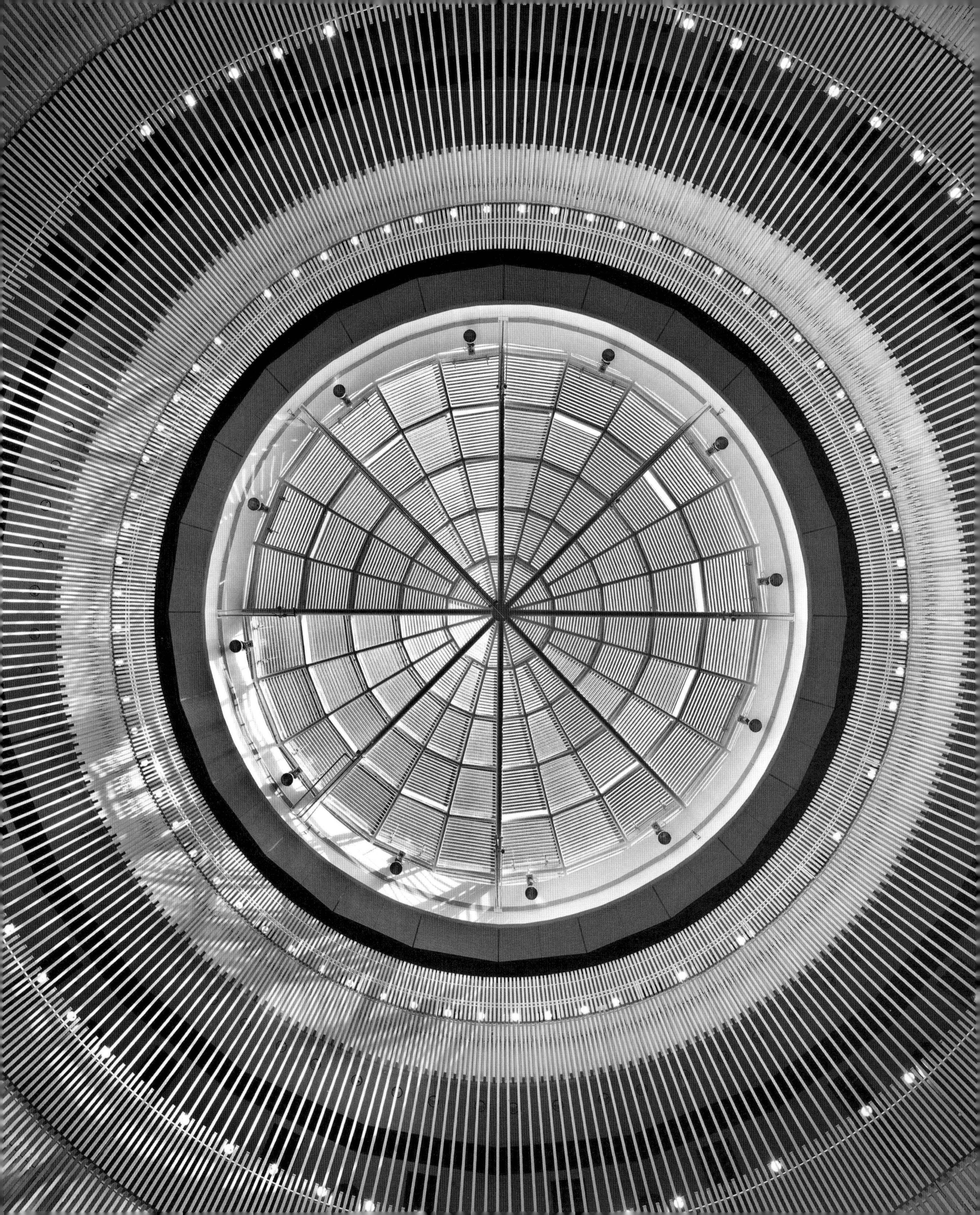

TSINGHUA UNIVERSITY LIBRARY
BEIJING – CHINA

2008-2011

Archive: n° 637
Project: 2008
Construction: 2009-2011
Client: Shanghai Real Estate (Group) Co. Ltd.
Shanghai Shentong Underground Railway Assets Managements CO. Ltd
Partner architect: ECADI - East China Architectural
Design & Research Institute Co., Ltd Shanghai
Area: 20'000 m² / 215'278 s ft
Floor area: 16'000 m² / 172'222 s ft above ground
Volume: 70'000 m³ / 2'470'000 above ground

The library is composed of a rectilinear volume marked by a balanced sequence of large windows used to form the rhythmical composition of the façade. It is treated as a single, full-height body in which to insert the large circle of an overturned conical volume with recessed openings. Open in different directions toward the greenery to activate a free flow of students and visitors, the library features an inner central space, the library's core, covered by a large skylight, forming a perspective toward the sky and a full-height courtyard faced by the three levels of the reading rooms, that are sheltered by a screen composed of wooden slats. The insulated masonry and the stone cover guarantee a good energy performance throughout the year, adapting to the hot summers and the cold winters of Beijing, while all interior spaces feature linear and tempered materials to enhance a warm and essential atmosphere of a place devoted to knowledge and memory.

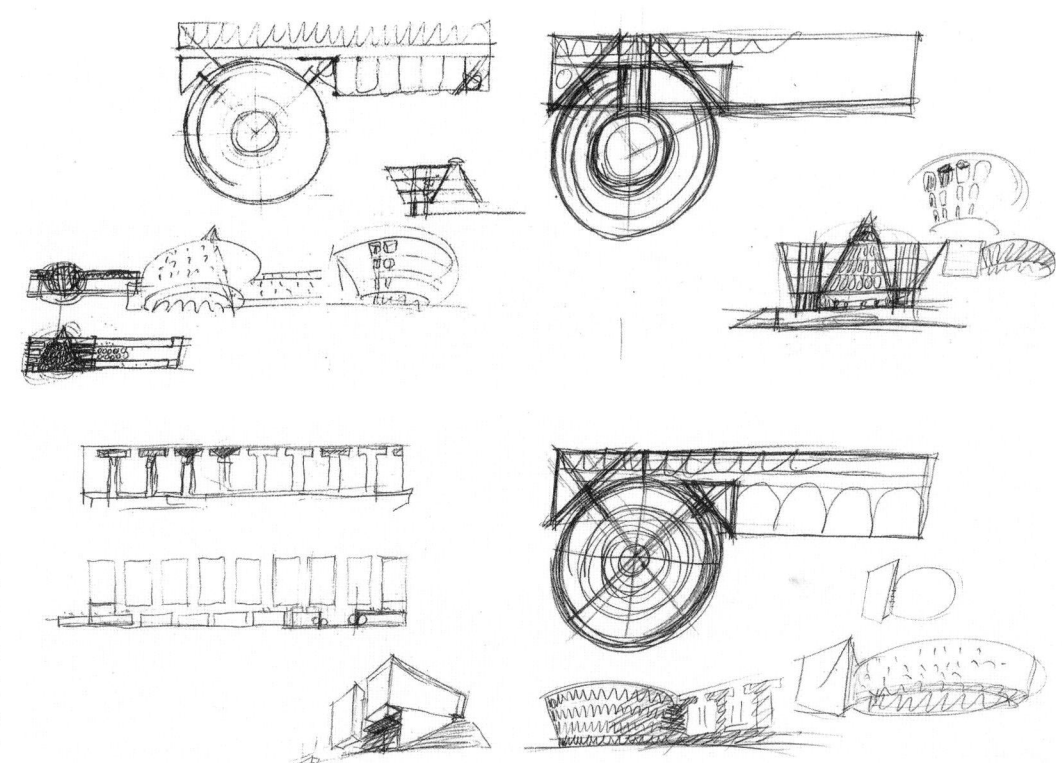

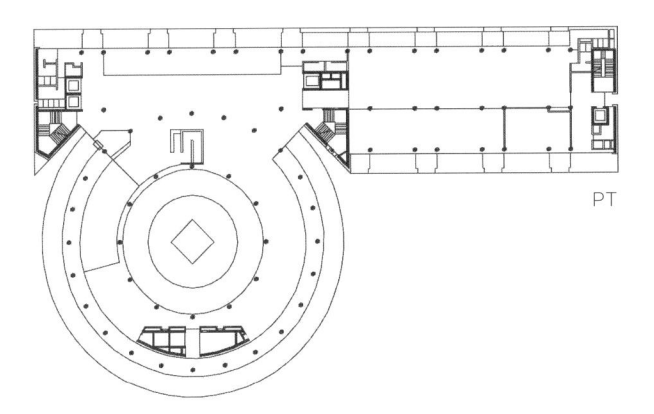

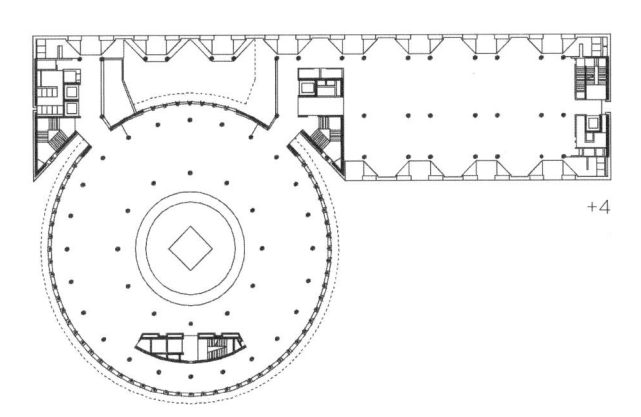

MUSEUMS

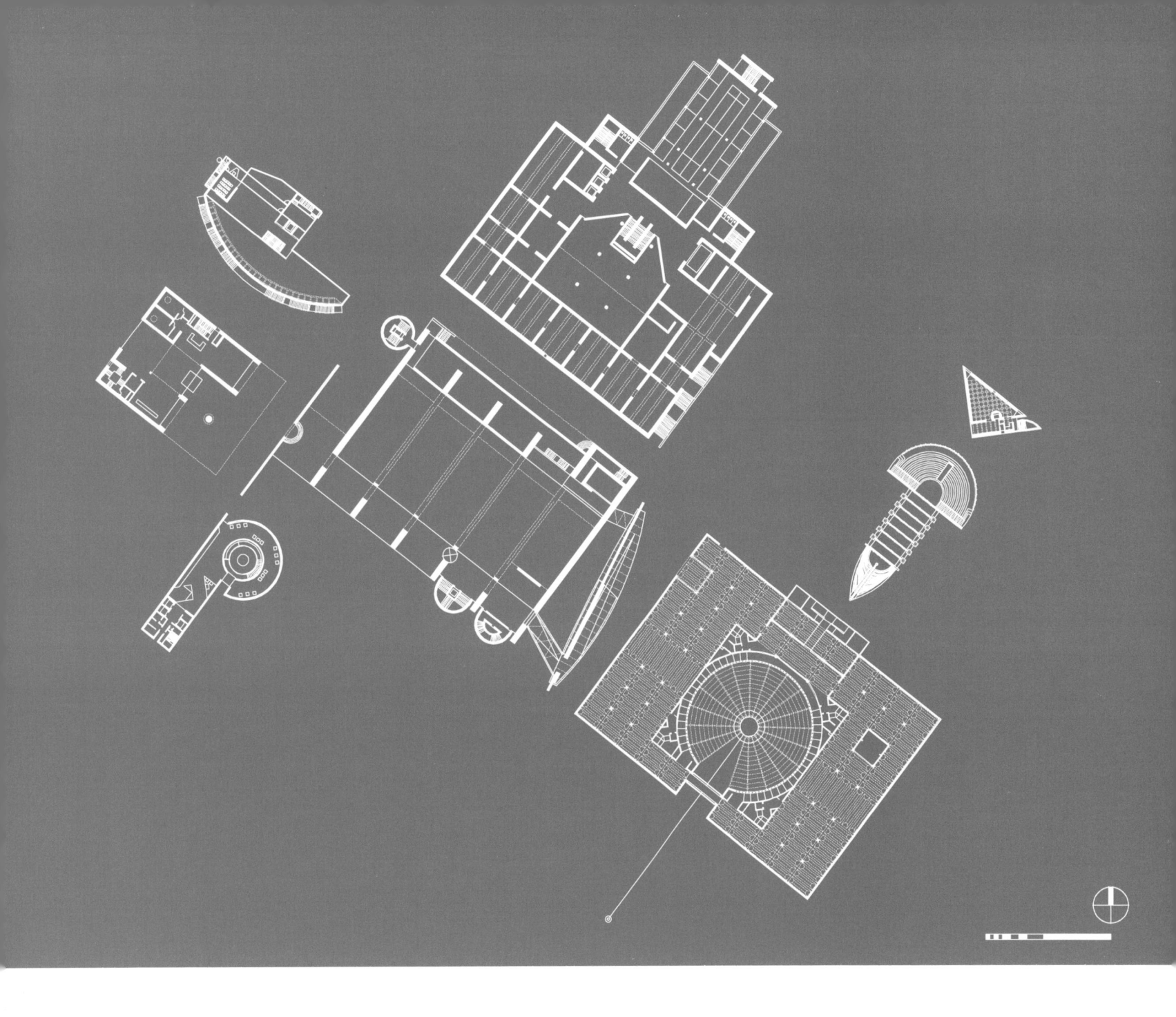

The critical fortune that led to the construction of many museums in the second half of the 20th century, is perhaps proportional to the loss of values of the communities that promoted them. A strong society does not need special "containers" for marks or lost values and it should not bestow on them an attention detached from everyday life engagements. Museums all over the world have changed. They have become new meeting places, sometimes for entertainment, that satisfy a more widespread free time. The architect has to interpret these new hybrid institutions considering these contradictions.

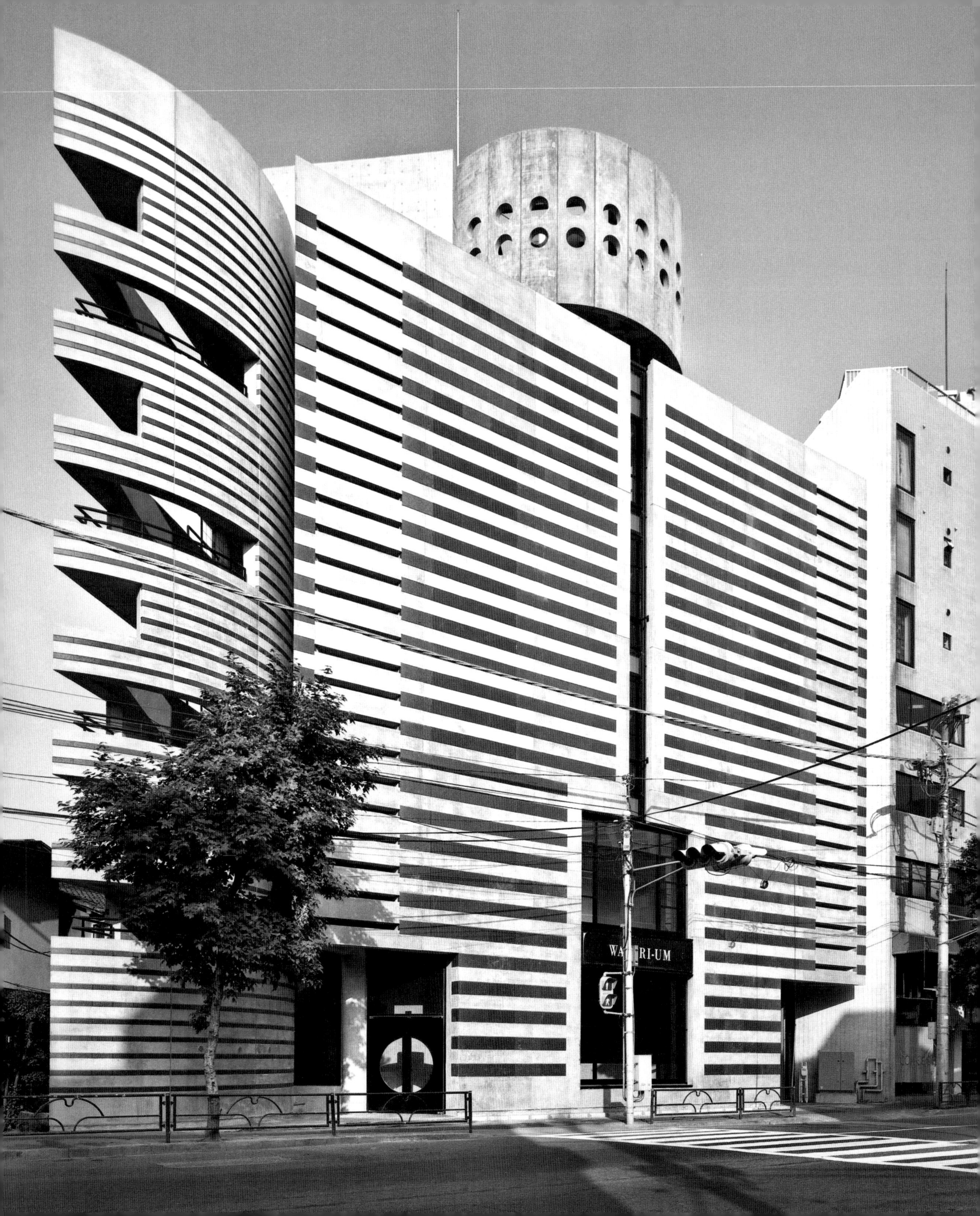

WATARI-UM ART GALLERY
TOKYO – JAPAN

1985-1990

Archive: n° 099
Project: 1985-88
Construction: 1988-90
Client: Hiroshi Watari
Partner: Takenaka Corporation
Site area: 157 m² / 1'690 s ft
Floor area: 627 m² / 6'749 s ft
Volume: 3'650 m³ / 128'898 c ft

The art gallery stands in a densely populated urban area, in the Shibuya-ku district. It occupies a triangular plot and is confronted with three different situations: a major thoroughfare, a side street and a smaller construction to the rear. The main façade is characterized by the alternation of black stone slabs with unfinished, precast concrete elements and by a long vertical cut ending at the base in a rectangular opening. The entry is on the corner where the front meets the cut-out silhouette of the emergency stairway. This latter is pushed outward, beyond the building's size, so to gain exhibition surface along the side walls. The top of the building is crowned by cylinder with round wholes that incorporates technical facilities. The building is articulated over five levels above ground and a basement, linked by a single vertical connection. The exhibition spaces are on the first three levels and, in spite of their limited dimensions, they appear larger thanks to the simple layout.

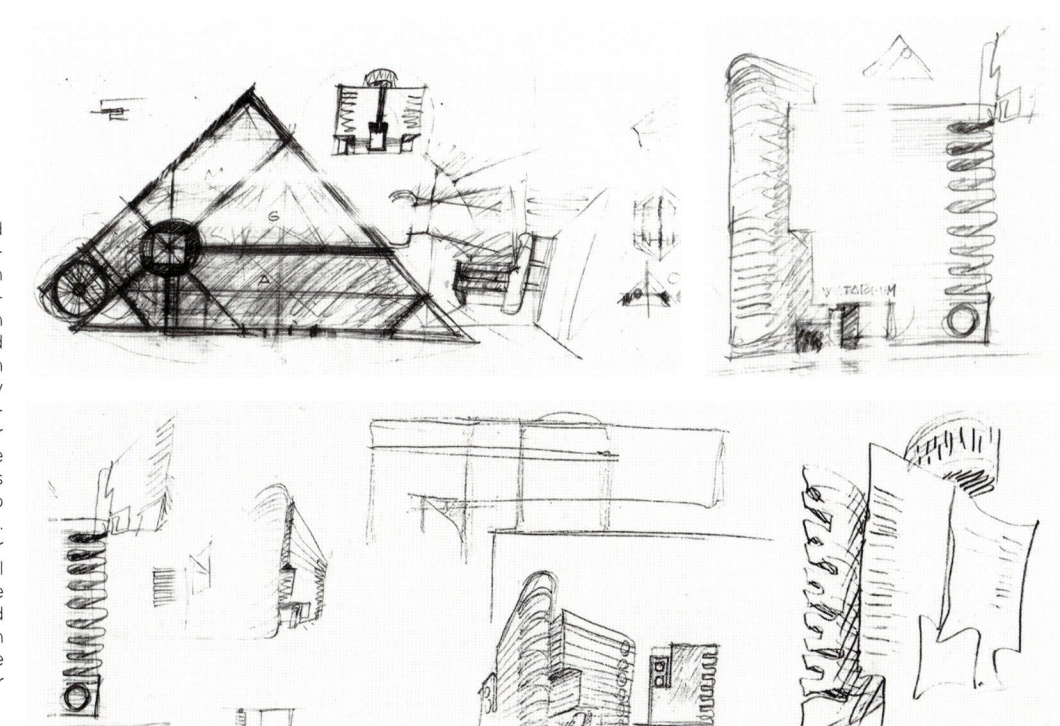

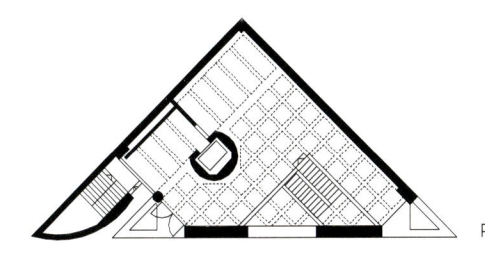

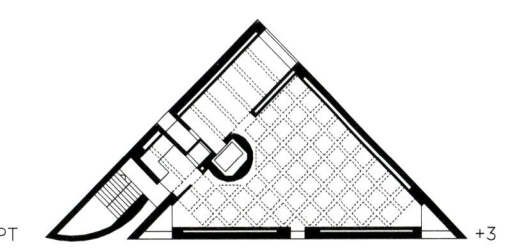

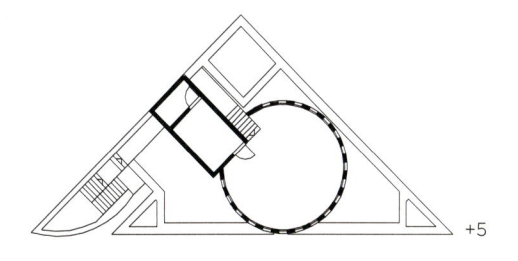

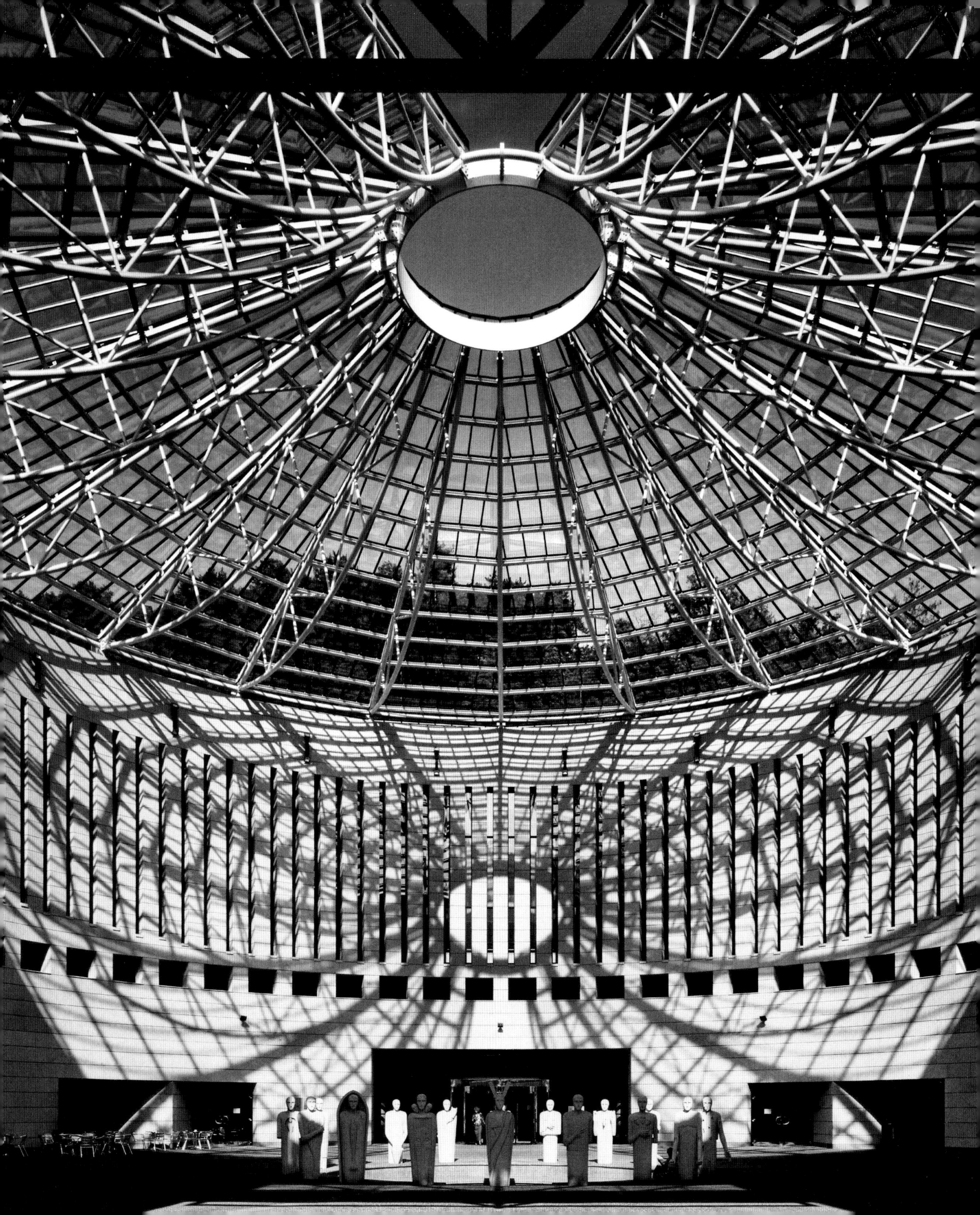

MART MUSEUM OF MODERN AND CONTEMPORARY ART OF TRENTO AND ROVERETO - ITALY

1988-2002

Archive: n° 156
Project: 1988-92
Construction: 1996-2002
With: Engineer Giulio Andreolli
Client: City of Rovereto, Autonomous province of Trento
Site area: 29'000 m² / 312'153 s ft
Floor area: 20'800 m² / 223'889 s ft
Volume: 140'000 m³ / 4'944'000 c ft

The museum is located along corso Bettini, in proximity or rather in the back of the two main buildings Palazzo Alberti and Palazzo del Grano. The project follows an axial composition and is organized along the lane between the wings of the two historical buildings, that introduce to the central plaza covered by an impressive glass dome. The public plaza as the core of the new culture center gives access not only to the museum, but also to all related services as the library, lecture hall and restaurant, distributed all around. The museum's facilities cover three floors above and one underground with exhibition rooms of different sizes and different light sources. Circulation to and through the galleries guides around the inner courtyard with a staircase system set on the back. Light comes in from above through a regular grid of skylights. The way the building relates to the city, the transition from the outdoor public space to the interior and the ability to understand the spatial structure are essential elements in the design of this museum. The building offers a sensitive interpretation of the existing urban texture and a strong spatial relation with its surrounding, and immediately consolidates itself as a main part of the town.

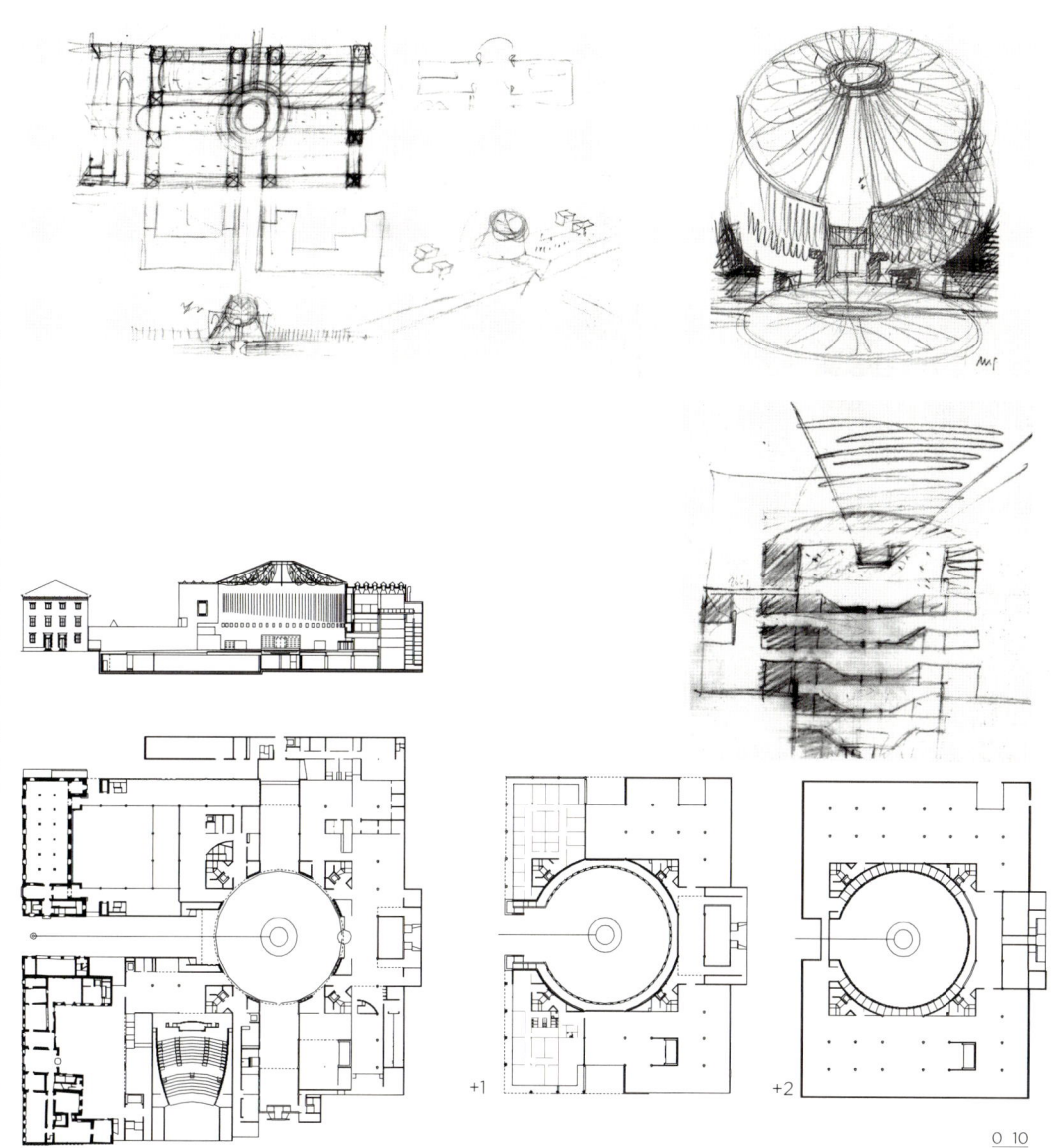

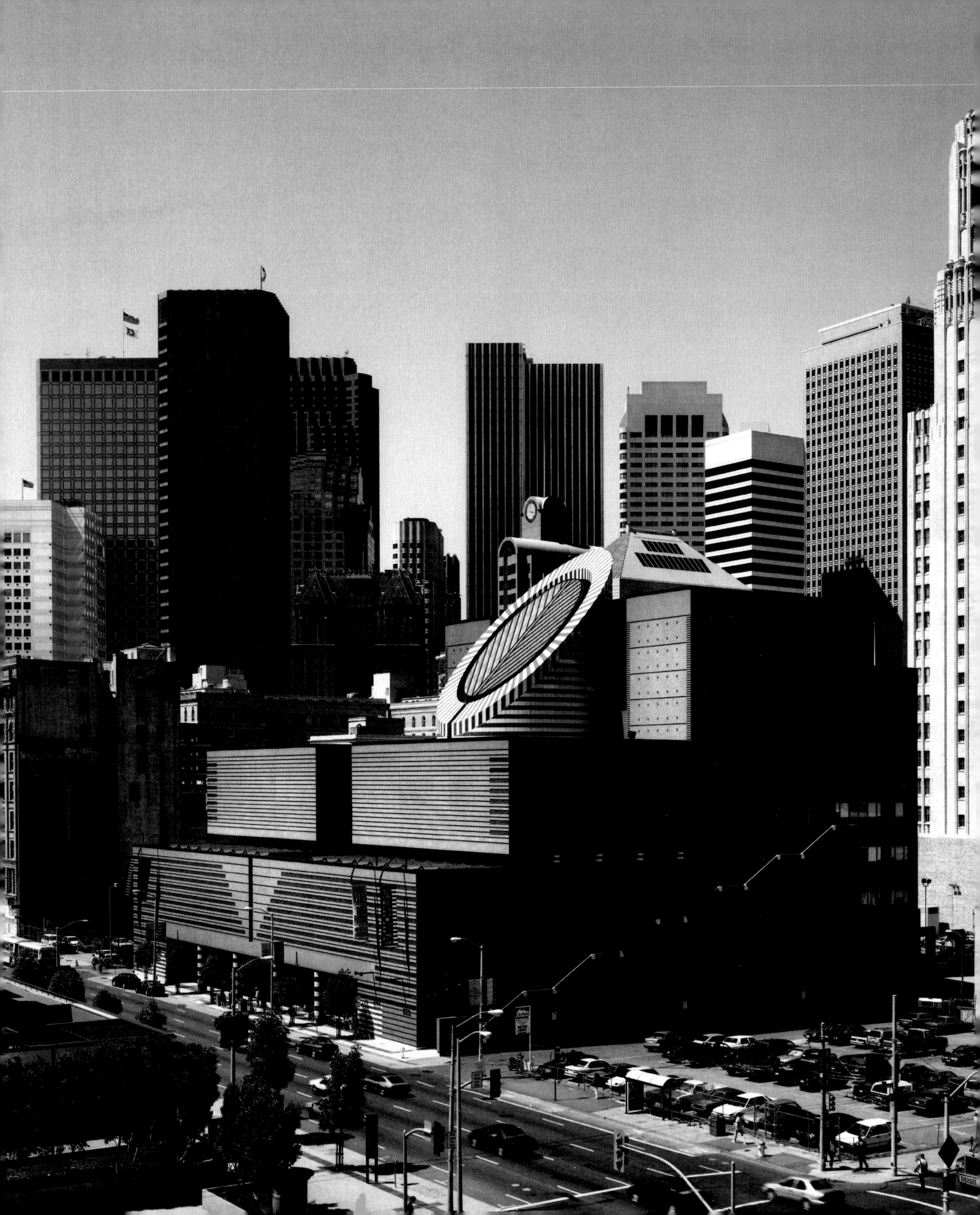

MOMA MUSEUM OF MODERN ART
SAN FRANCISCO – USA

1989-1995

Archive: n° 162
Project: 1989/1990-1992
Construction: 1992-1995
With: Hellmuth, Obata & Kassabaum Inc., San Francisco
Client: San Francisco Museum of Modern Art
Site area: 5'575 m² / 60'000 s ft
Floor area: 18'500 m² / 199'132 s ft
Volume: 100'000 m³ / 3'531'400 c ft

The museum is located in the Yerba Buena district, in an area surrounded by skyscrapers. In contrast with the vertical tension of this latter, the MoMA seems anchored to the ground. Its orthogonal and terraced volume, composed by a steel structure covered with brick clad precast panels, expands horizontally. The central skylight, impressive for its size and with the shape of a truncated cylinder becomes an "eye" towards the city and illuminates the lobby beneath. The ground floor dominated by the sculptural presence of the staircase offers a wide hall with the reception and information desk, library, cafeteria, event space and educational facilities. The central void rises through all levels and is to be considered the gravity center of the museum. All galleries reveal a subdued and calm architecture devoted to the work of art. Compared to the "abstract" image of the downtown at the back, the building shows itself with a strong "figurative" appearance.

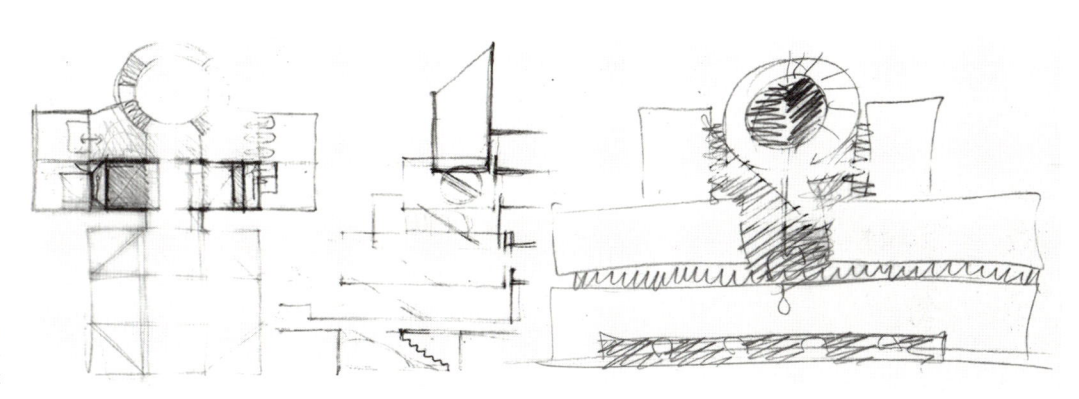

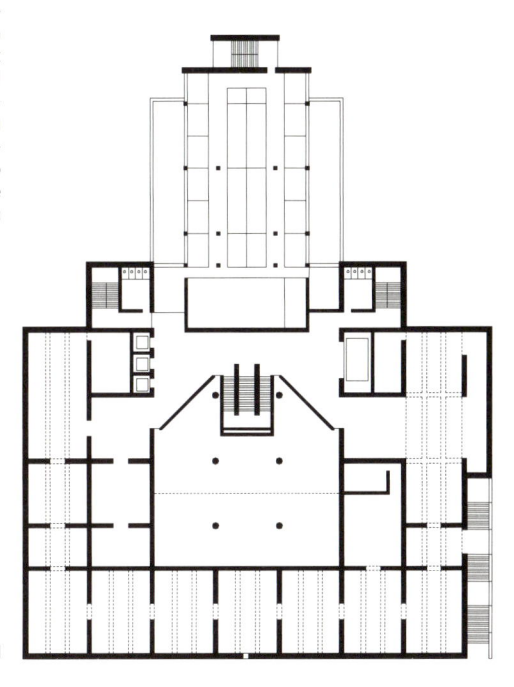

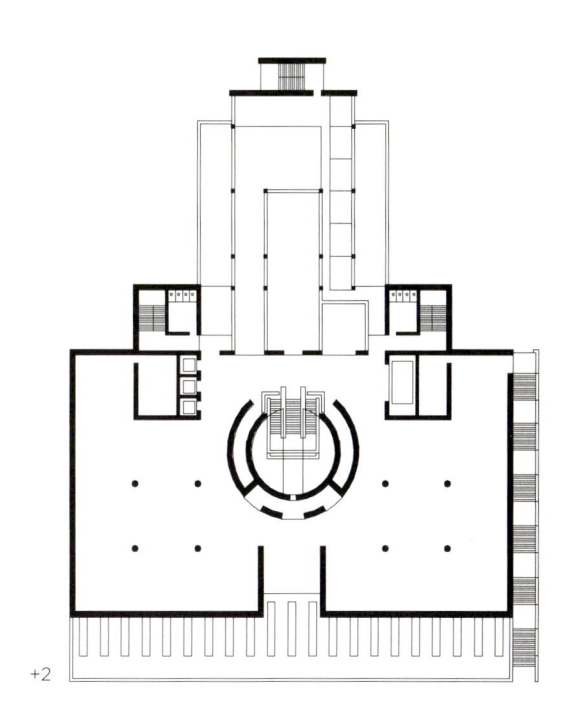

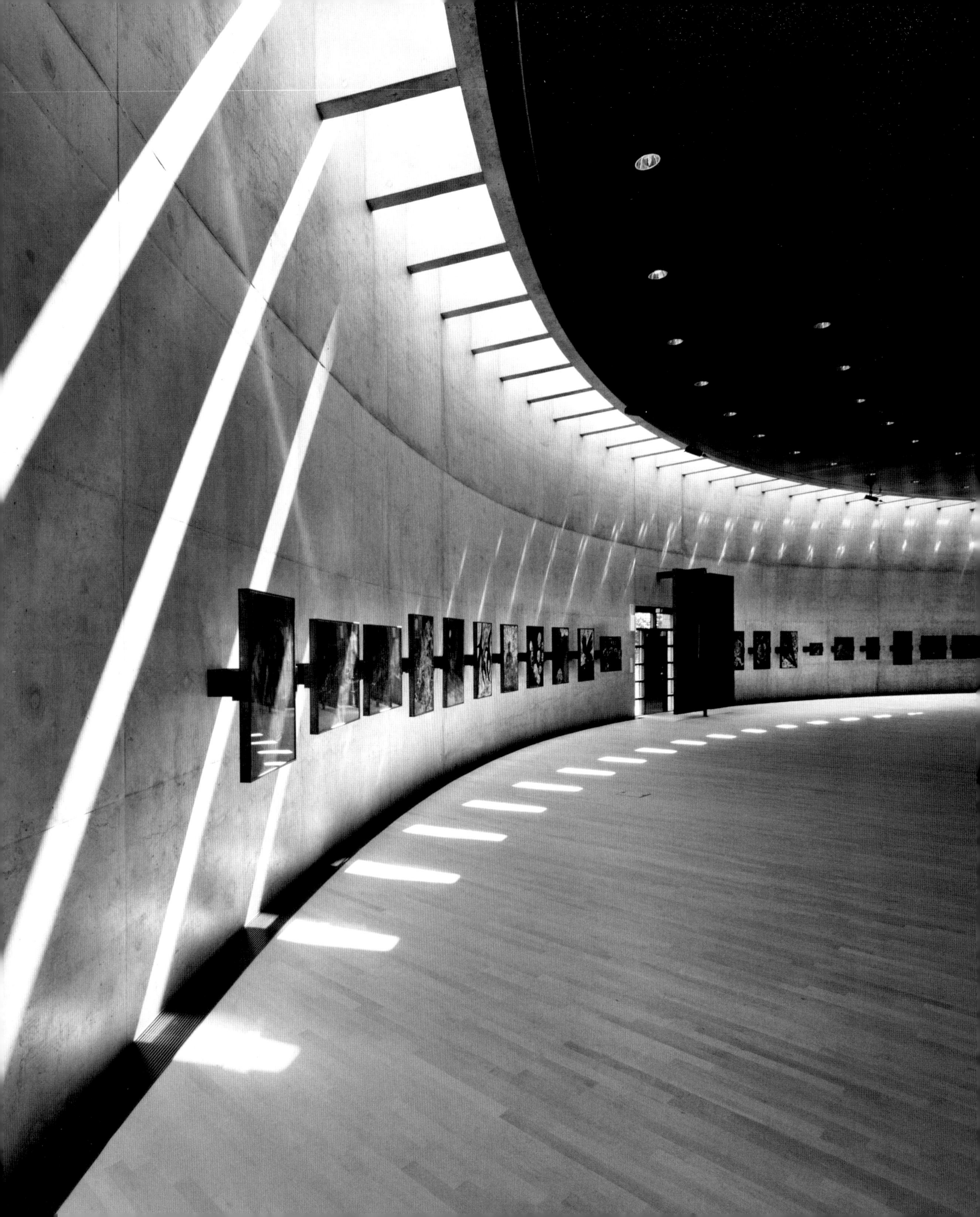

DÜRRENMATT CENTER
NEUCHÂTEL - SWITZERLAND

1992-2000

Archive: n° 228
Project: 1992/95-97
Construction: 1997-2000
Client: Swiss Confederation,
Federal Department of Finance
Partner: arch. Urscheler & Arrigo SA
Site area: 4'200 m² / 42'208 s ft
Floor area: 820 m² / 8'826 s ft
Volume: 4'700 m³ / 165'980 c ft

The small museum conserves the graphic work and paintings by the Swiss author Friedrich Dürrenmatt. Set on a hilly site, the museum is built underground, next to Dürrenmatt's former private house that beside the author's original library now hosts several public services, the offices and the coffee shop, to allow the new spaces to be totally used for exhibition purposes. The construction penetrates the body of the mountain through three levels and expands downward in an arc towards the valley as "bowels" whose convex form resurfaces from the steeply sloped terrain. On the outside just the curved stone wall and the tower reveal the presence of the museum spaces beneath, while the large terrace invites to enjoy the great panoramic view towards the lake. The use of grey slate blocks as exterior cladding enhances the massiveness and texture of the walls. Visitors approach from the street in the back, enter the museum through a small lobby between the house and the tower and move downstairs to the main exhibition floor. Roof lights along the edge of the building illuminate the underground exhibition spaces.

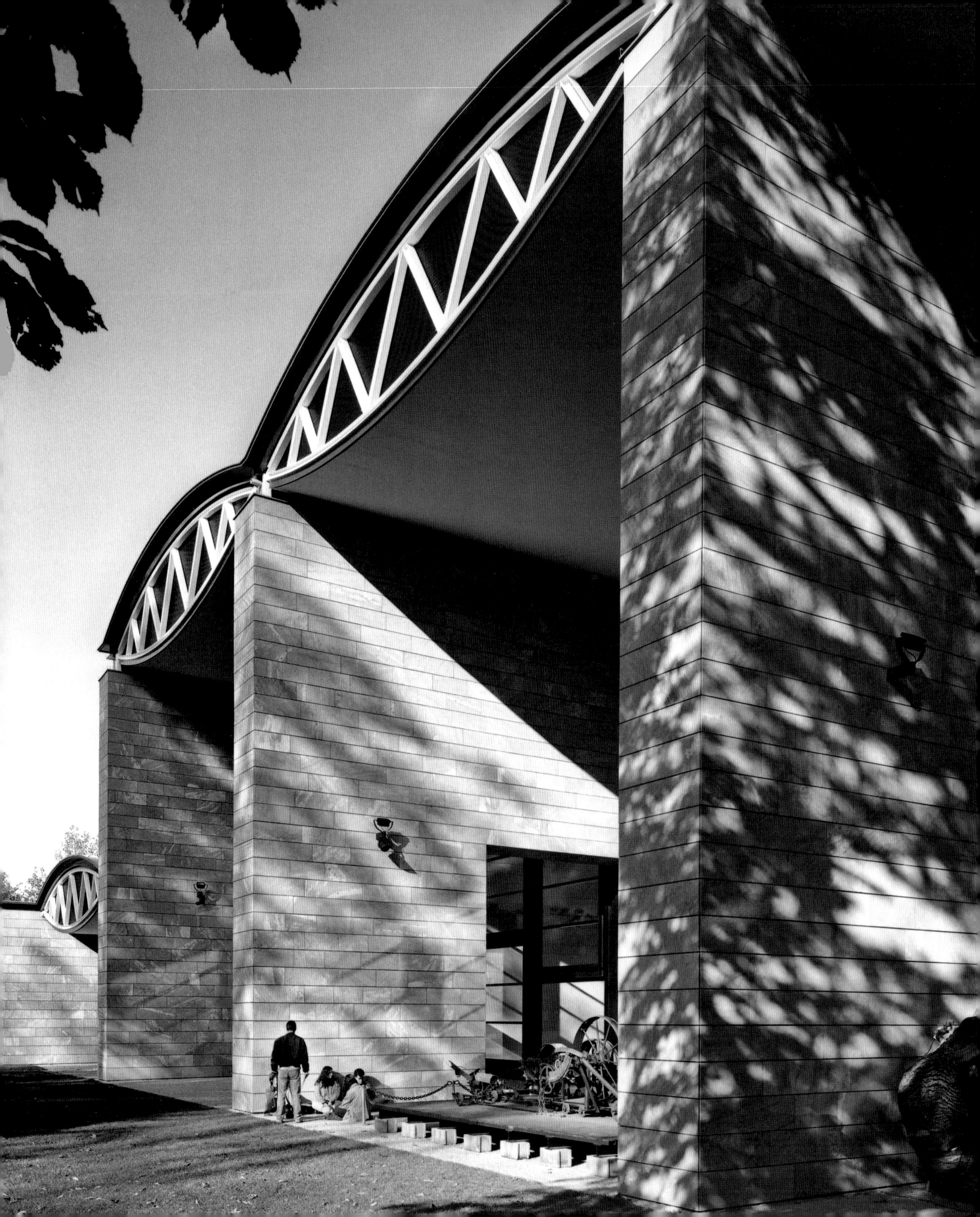

MUSEUM JEAN TINGUELY
BASEL – SWITZERLAND

1993-1996

Archive : n° 229
Project: 1993
Construction: 1994-1996
Client: Hoffmann-La Roche AG, Basel
Partner: GSG Baucontrol, Basel
Site area: Park 28'450 m² / 306'233 s ft
Floor area: 6'057 m² / 65'197 s ft, where of 2'866 m² / 30'849 s ft for exhibition purposes
Volume: 54'150 m³ / 1'912'290 c ft

The museum is set along the eastern side of the 19th-century Solitude Park, facing the Rhine River and at the end of a motorway bridge. Thus, the building is an attempt to re-design the urban void between the 20th-century fabric of the city and the edge of the motorway. Each building front responds in a different way to the prevailing urban conditions. On the east, next to the traffic lane, the building's massive wall and elevated volume are shaped to create a barrier protecting the museum's area. On the west side, facing the park, the volume opens towards the garden with a wide portico, characterized by a series of arches. The north side provides a covered entrance to the park and the museum. The south front faces the river with a strong formal element: a slightly curved glass walkway takes the visitor along the magnificent river view before entering the galleries. The itinerary through the exhibition spaces on four different levels ends in the large open space on the ground floor. Complying with the spirit of Tinguely's kinetic art, movement becomes primary in this museum, it becomes part of the museum experience.

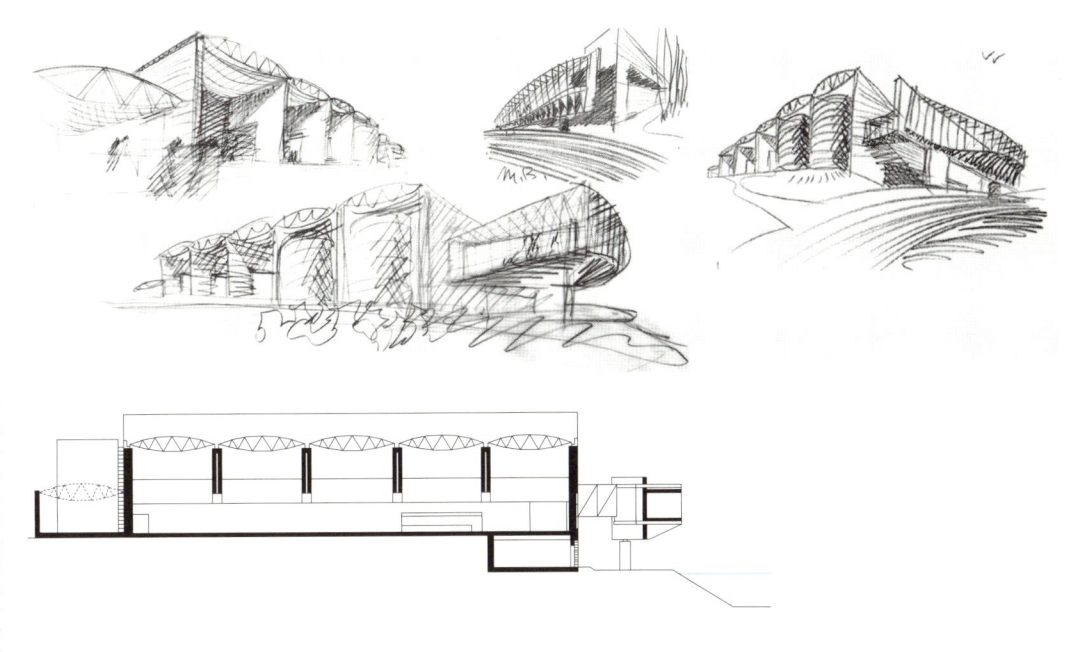

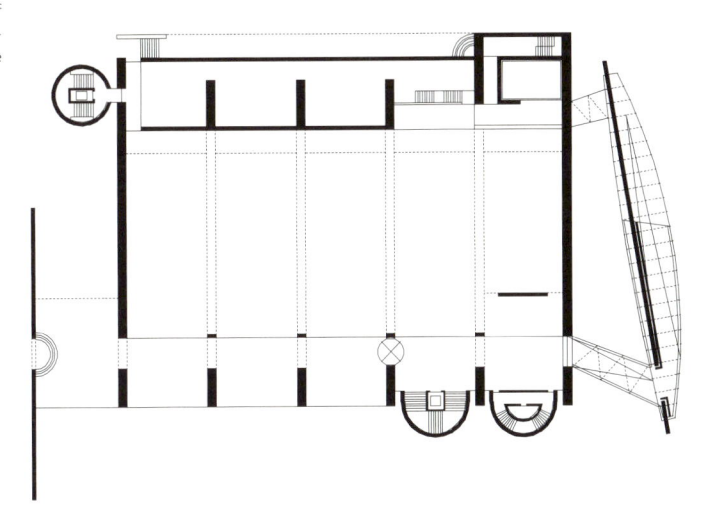

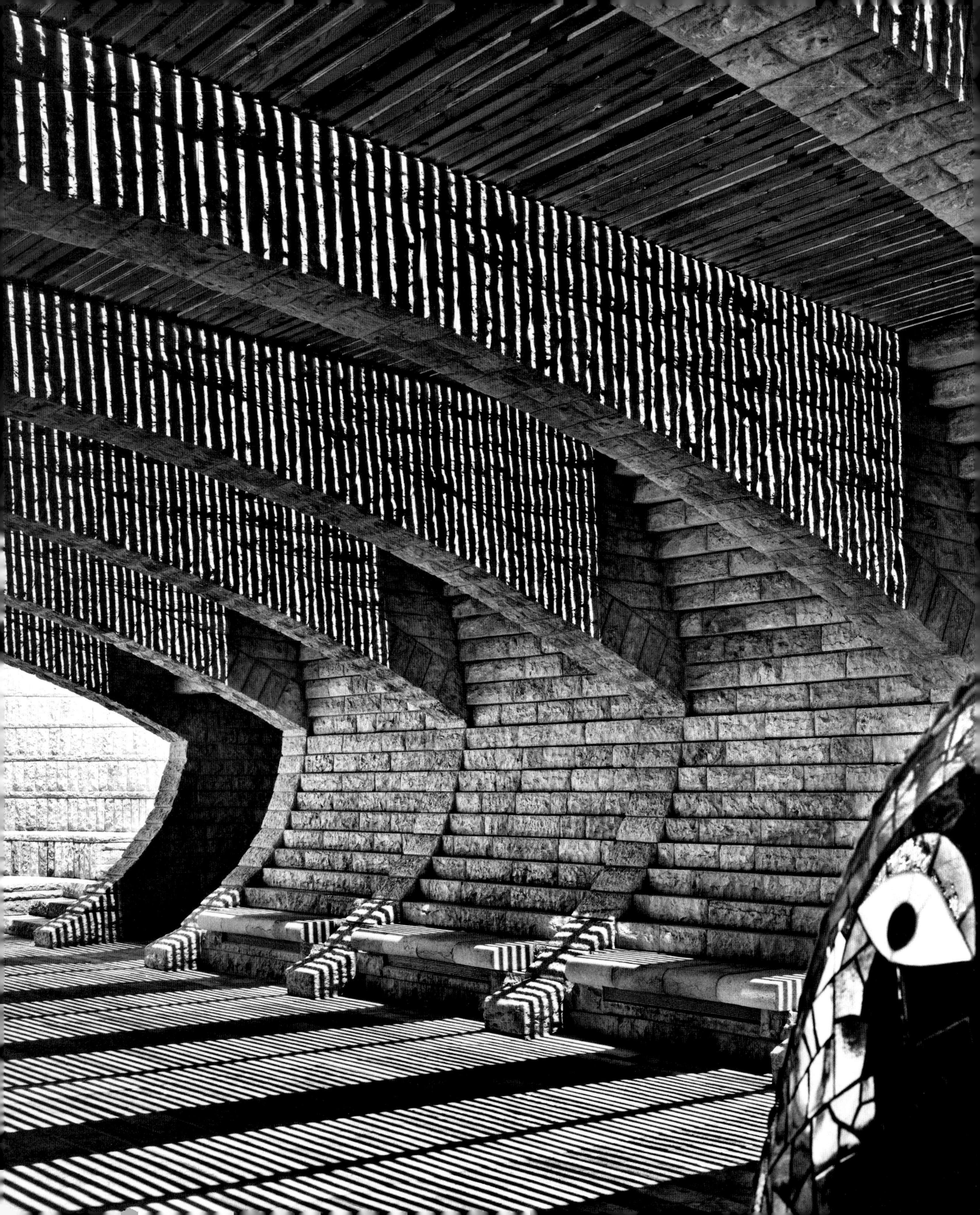

NOAH'S ARK
JERUSALEM – ISRAEL

1995-2001

Archive: n° 283
Project: 1995-98
Construction: 1999-2001
With: Niki de Saint Phalle
Client: The Jerusalem Foundation -
City of Jerusalem,
director of the zoological gardens,
Shai Doron
floor area: 670 m² / 7'212 s ft
Volume: 2'700 m³ / 95'349 c ft underground

The project for Noah's Ark was sparked by the profound friendship with Niki de Saint Phalle. The idea was taken as an opportunity to exploit the complementary talents and the feeling of expression with a sense of complicity, going beyond the ideological and cultural disquisitions that characterise different worlds. The ark located in the zoological gardens of Jerusalem has been thought in low-relief, as an imprint in the ground and fossilised in the yellow local stone. The ensuing space is presented to visitors as a path marked by a tempo of dream-like moments, with a descent into the main underground volume that resembles a shady stone "belly" crossed by a rivulet and marked by the regular succession of arches. Big colored animals fill the patch of grass around the structure. The man-sized underground spaces of the ark and the hollows in the sculptures promote the play for which the project was conceived.

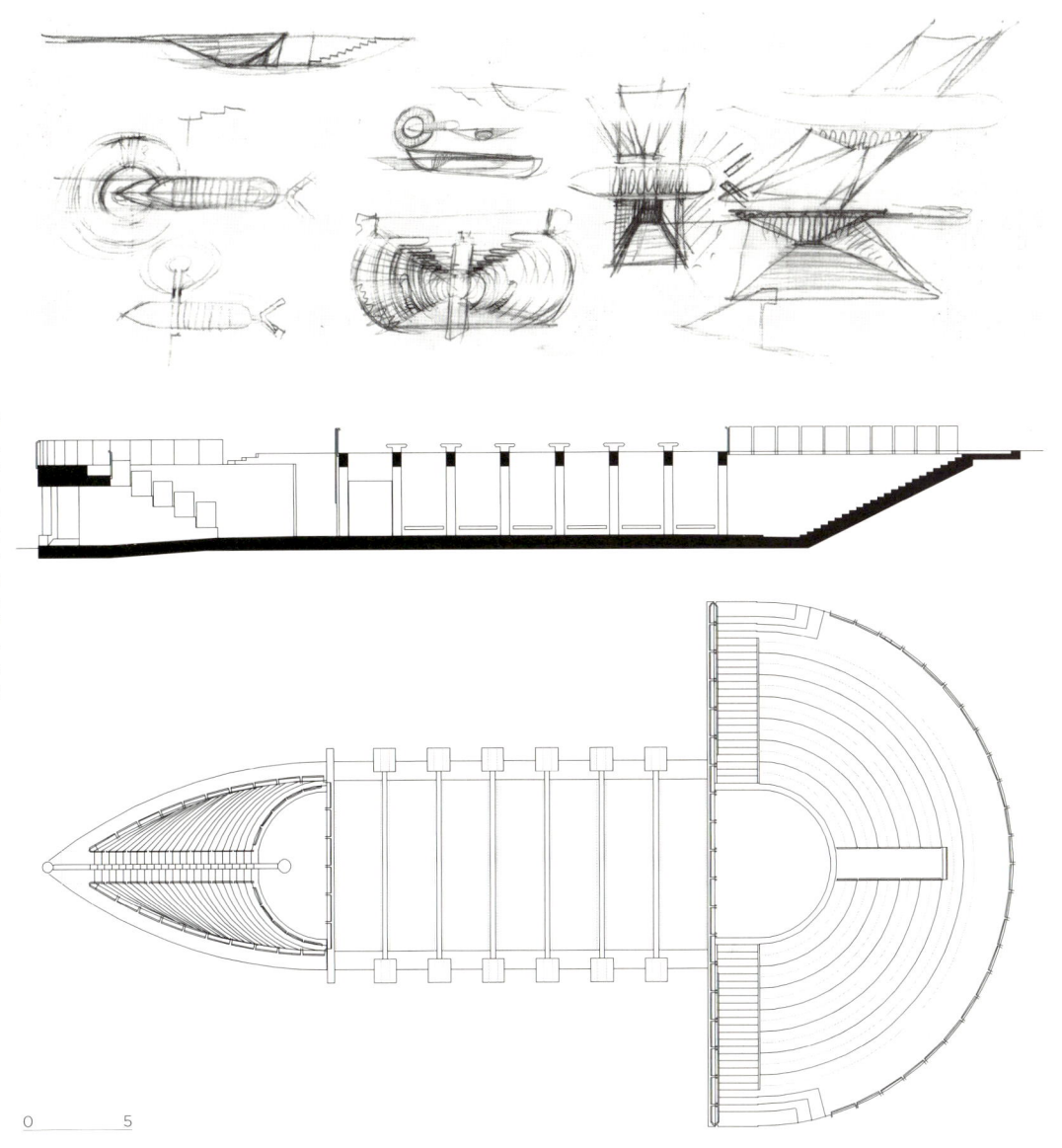

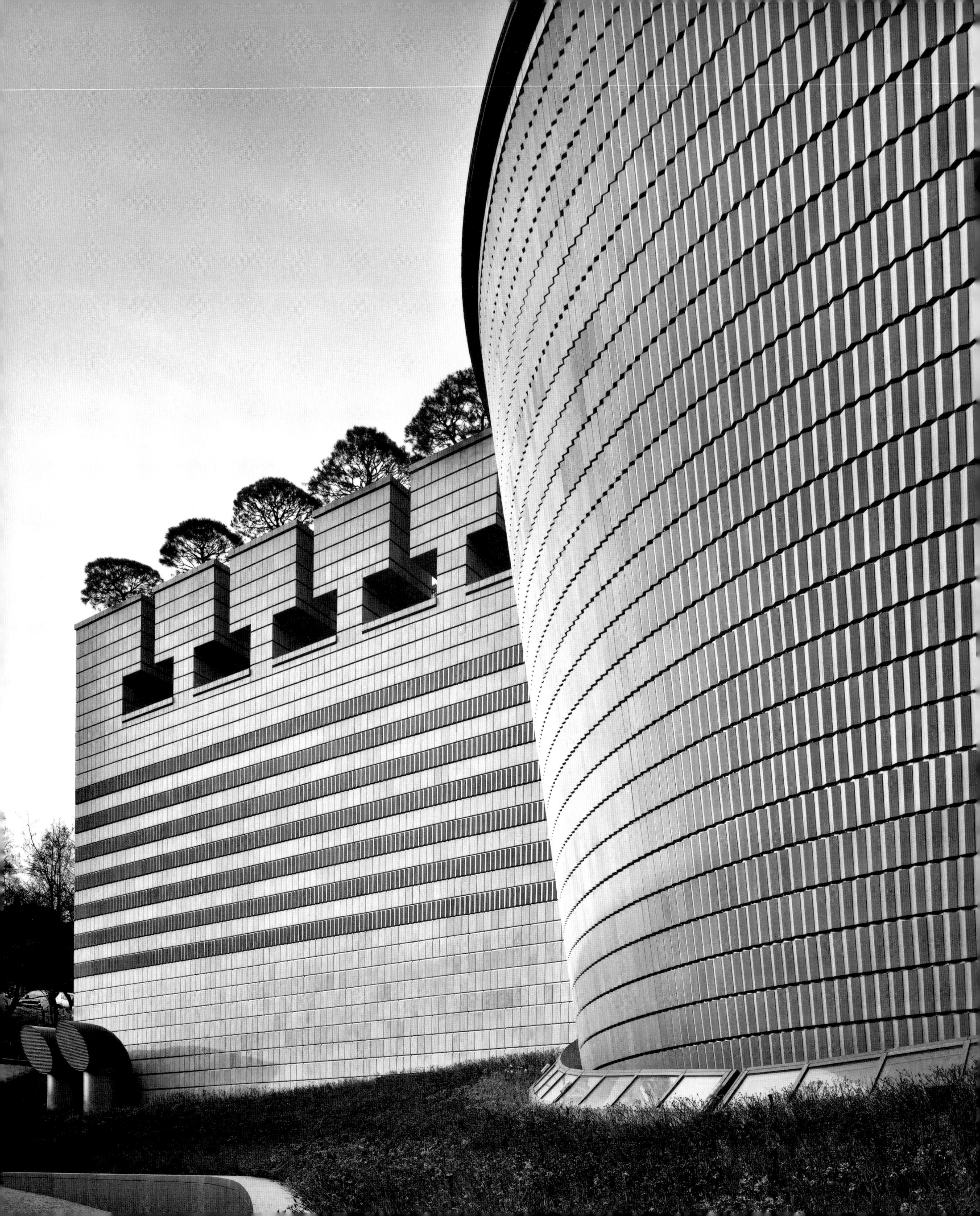

LEEUM SAMSUNG MUSEUM OF ART
SEOUL - SOUTH KOREA

1995-2004

Archive: n° 299
Project: 1995-97/2002
Construction: 2002-04
Client: Samsung Foundation for Culture
Partner: Samoo Architects & Engineers, Seoul
Site area: 2'333 m² / 25'112 s ft
Floor area: 10'000 m² / 107'639 s ft
Volume: 42'000 m³ / 1'483'216 c ft

Half way up a hill in Hannam-dong, three different buildings, two museums and one educational center for children create the new cultural center of Samsung foundation. The Leeum museum for ancient art is set back and on higher ground compared to the other buildings and therefore becomes the landmark of the new urbanization plan proposed by the Foundation. The museum, with an important part underground where the three cultural entities meet, is an isolated object rising from a green slope that connects the roads above and below. The building consists of two primary shapes: a parallelepiped coupled with an inverted cone. The exterior is further enhanced by the expressive language of the façade texture: smooth, flat terracotta tiles combined with special V-sectioned elements create a natural effect of subtle shades under the natural light. The visit starts on the top floor and steps down the bright central stairs that unwinds along the curved walls of the cone. In contrast to the dim light of the exhibit spaces, the large glass roof enlightens the central core down to the main lobby.

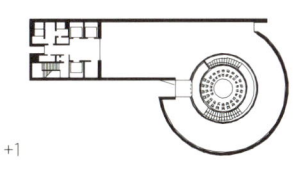

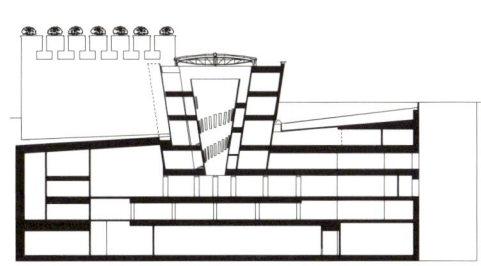

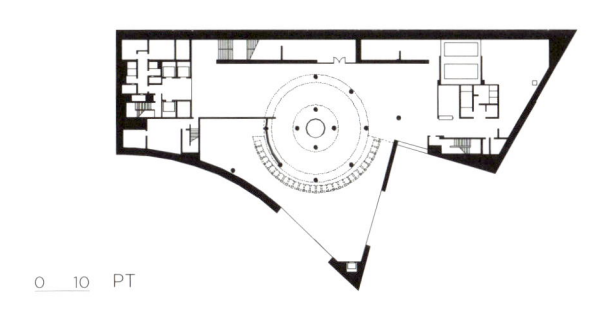

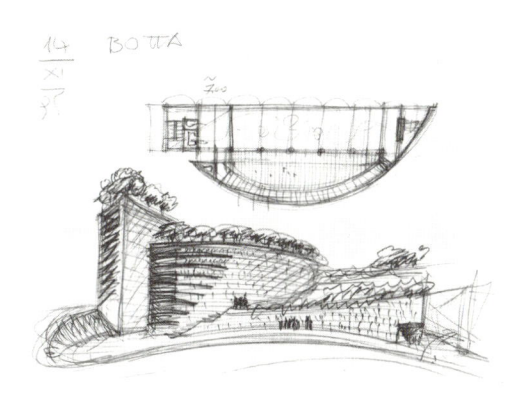

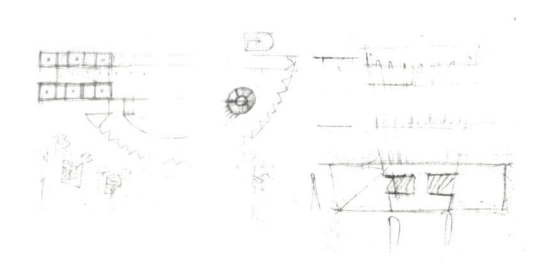

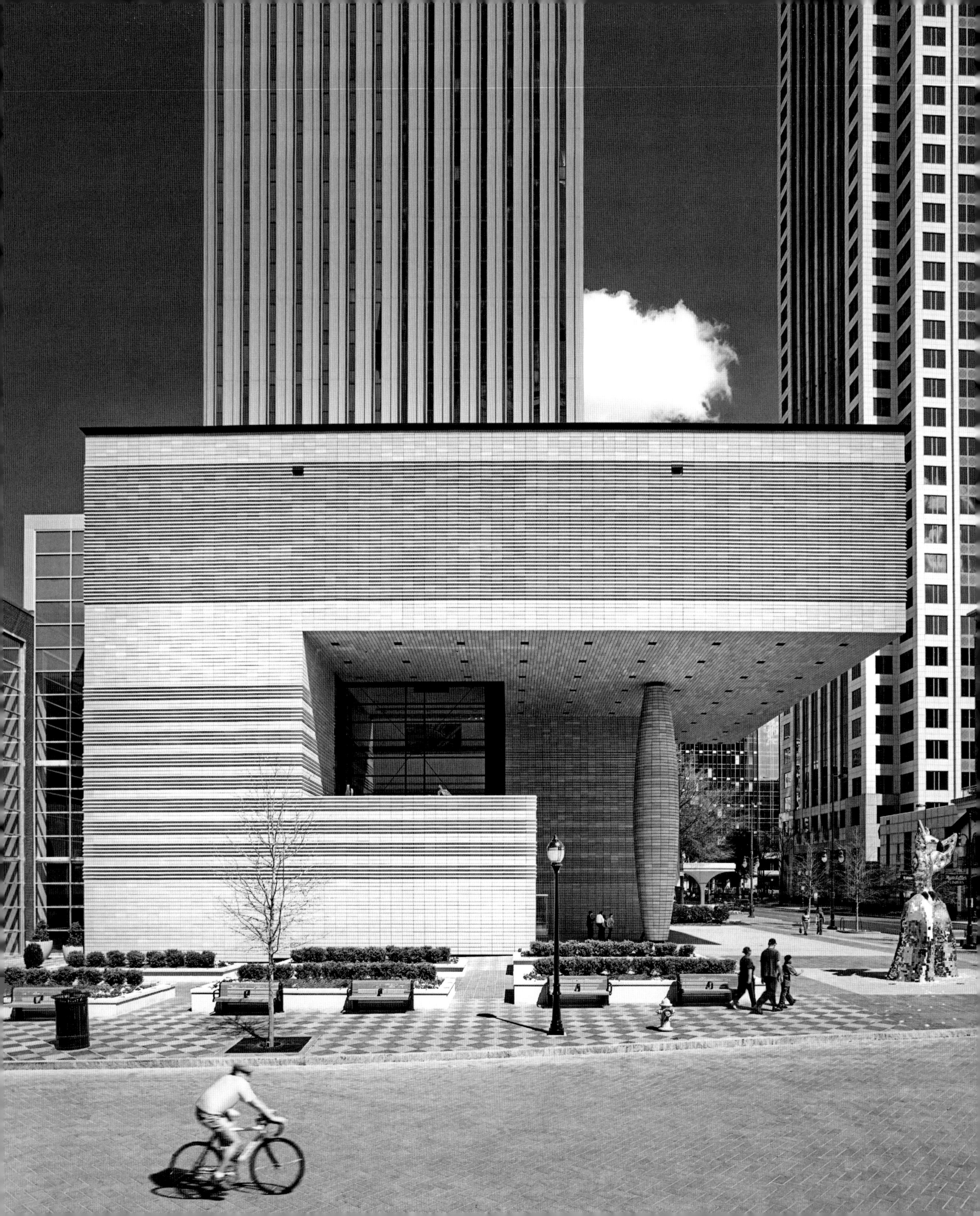

BECHTLER MUSEUM OF MODERN ART
CHARLOTTE – USA

2000-2009

Archive: n° 424
Project: 2000-2005
Construction: 2007-2009
Client: Andreas Bechtler
Partner: Wagner Murray Architects PA, Charlotte
Site area: 1'912 m² / 20'580 s ft
Floor area: 2'490 m² / 26'802 s ft
Volume: 16'992 m³ / 600'067 c ft

The museum is located in downtown Charlotte, a city that has undergone a rapid urban development in recent years. It houses the works of art of the Andreas Bechtlers' collection with important artists such as Tinguely, Niki de Saint Phalle, Picasso, Giacometti, Matisse, Mirò, Degas, Warhol, Le Corbusier, Léger. The cube-shaped building is hollow inside to offer an outdoor public courtyard that is outlined by the plastic volumes at the back. The four-storey structure is characterized by the soaring glass atrium that extends through the core of the museum and diffuses natural light throughout the building thanks to a system of vaulted skylights. Despite its modest dimensions, a great plastic force is created by the play of solids and voids. It can be thus defined as an architecture-sculpture where the voids mark a new urban space sheltered by the fourth floor gallery jutting out from the core of the building and supported by a huge single column rising from the plaza below. The choice of the materials for the interior spaces and the terra cotta exterior cladding provide the museum with a rigorous, though elegant simplicity.

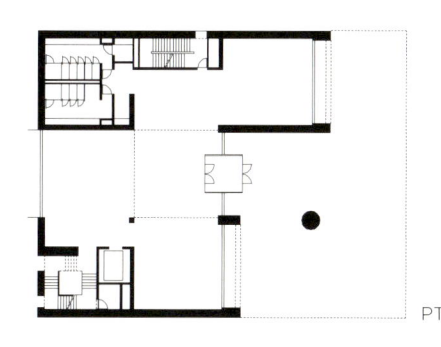

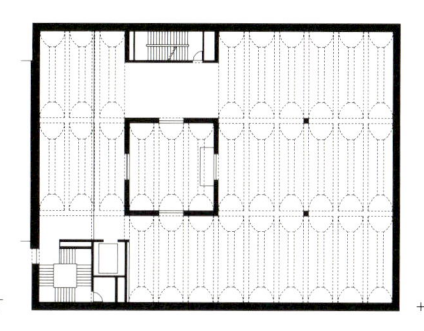

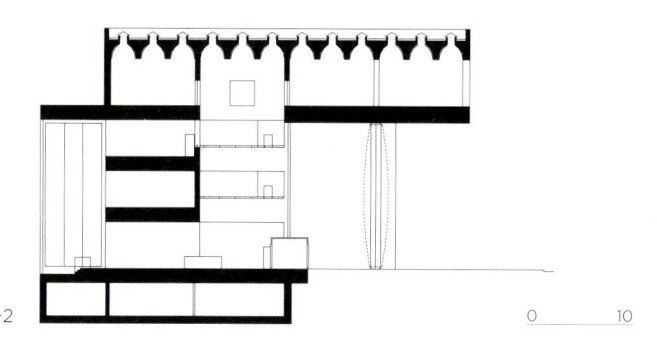

THEATERS

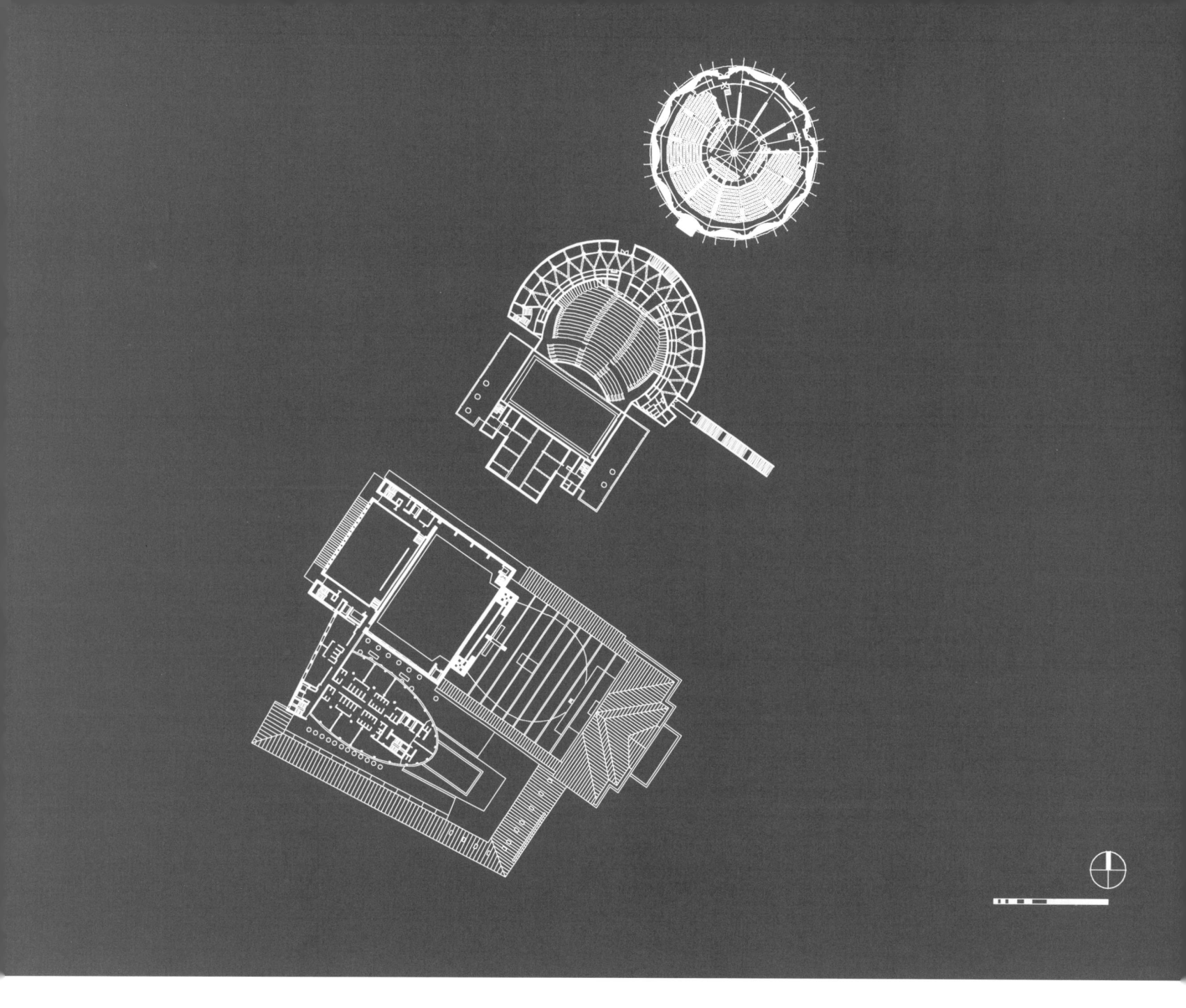

Theatres are buildings in which people live emotions evoked by the collective imagination: spaces, facilities and stage machines to present events that allow man to go beyond everyday life. The need to dream distant realities we can identify with and share with other men, is an elementary one. In the history of the European city, theatres have always had privileged positions and particular meanings. For this reason, they often represent a urban structure able to ordinate, sometimes to subordinate, the conjunctive fabric of the surrounding territory.

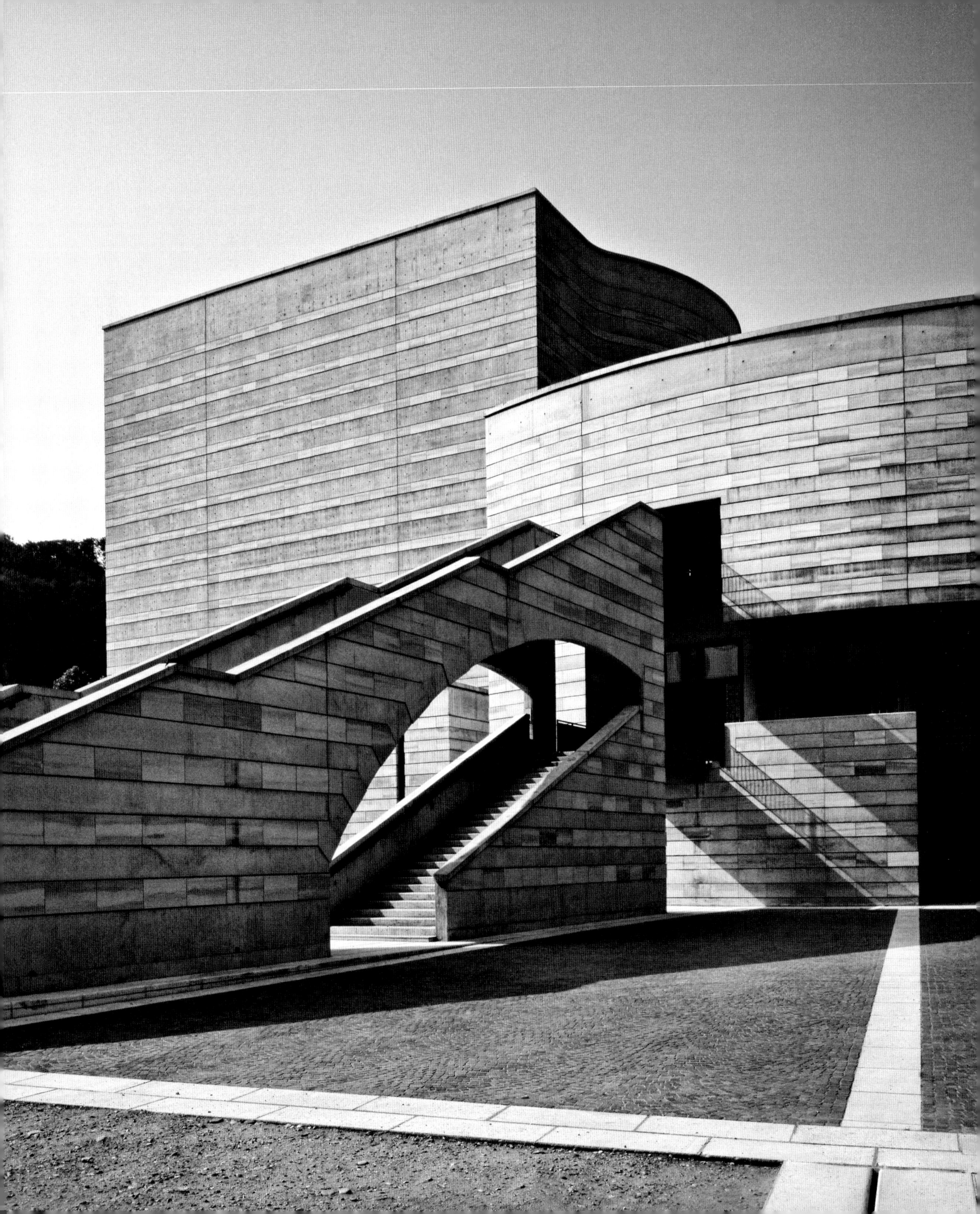

THEATER AND CULTURAL CENTER ANDRÉ MALRAUX
CHAMBÉRY - FRANCE

1982-1987

Archive : n°068
Competition project 1982
Construction: 1983-87
Client: Municipality of Chambéry
Site area: 7'600 m² / 81'805 s ft
Floor area: 9'800 m² / 105'486 s ft
Volume: 82'000 m³ / 2'895'00 c ft

The project arises from an architecture competition calling for the restoration of a 19th-century Napoleonic military barracks and for the construction of a multi-use complex. The new building is set outside the existing quadrilateral, interpreted as an external foyer. It only just touches the historical building to accentuate the perception of tension created by the two volumes. The different functions of the complex are organized within three volumes: the parallelepiped that houses the technical facilities, the stage tower and artist's room, the circular volume of the theater itself that represents the key point in the layout and as a third element, the emergency stairs, linked to the two levels of the theater hall and delimiting as an autonomous construction an new urban square. Whereas the administrative services are located within the east wing of the Napoleonic quadrilateral, the public entrance follows a path through the historical courtyard.

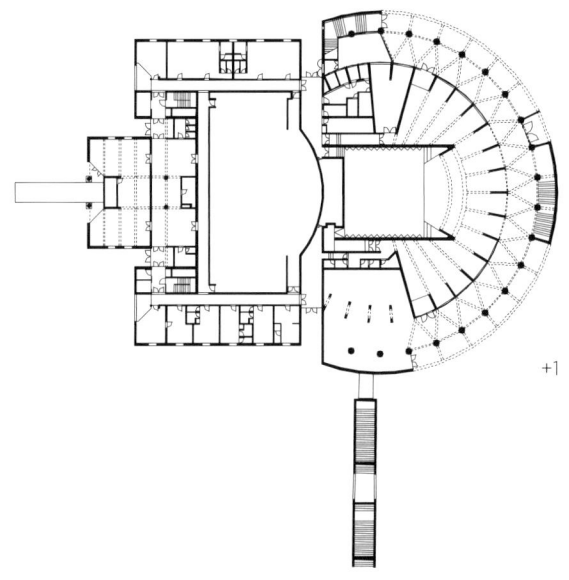

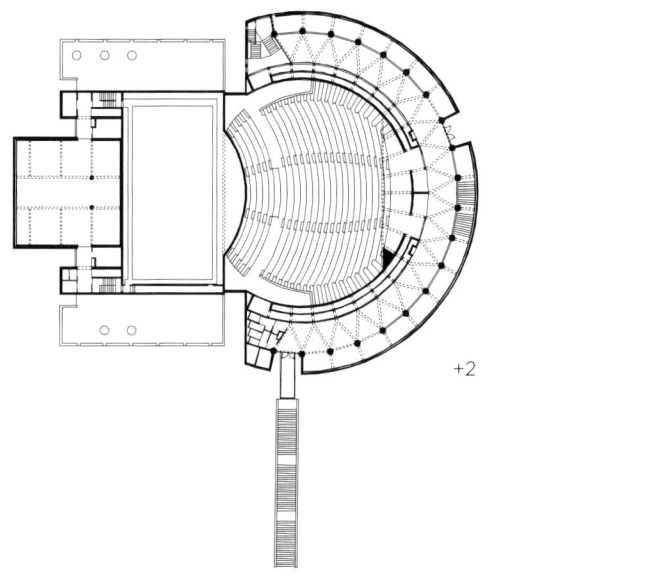

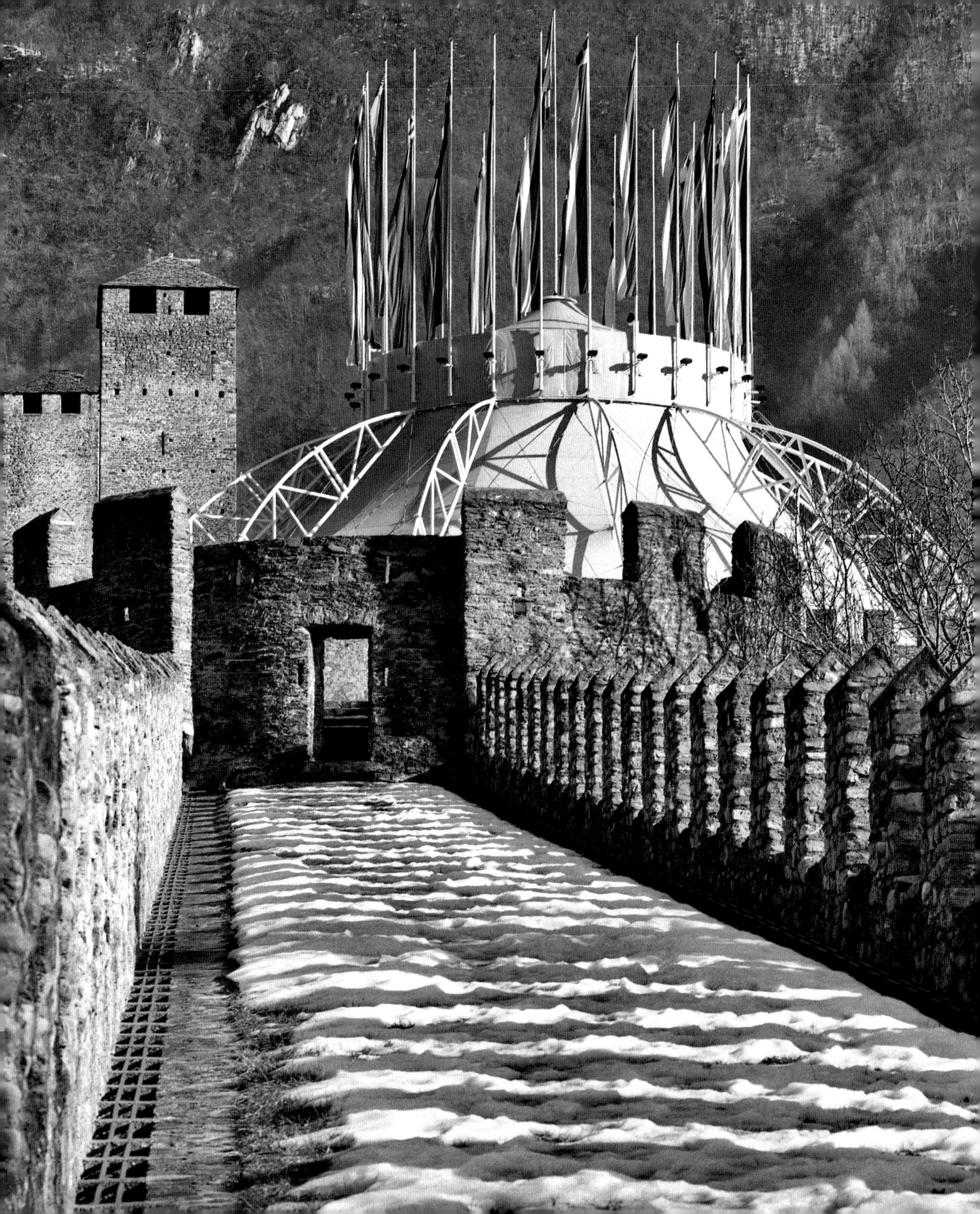

THE 700TH ANNIVERSARY CELEBRATION TENT
BELLINZONA - SWITZERLAND

1989-1991

Archive: n° 169
Project: 1989
Construction: 1990-91
Client: Swiss Confederation
Floor area: 1 540 m² / 16'576 s ft
Volume: 13'000 m³ / 459'000 c ft

"I imagined a structure able to shape a primary image in the landscape – a dome – something simple and precise, contemporary and archaic at the same time, thus capable to resist the confused jargon of the fragile "modern" culture and to become a point of reference and of dialogue in the different contexts". The large tent was designed on the occasion of the celebrations for the 700th anniversary of the Swiss Confederation in 1991, with a diameter of more than 40 meters, a height of 33 meters, it offered approximately 1900 seats. The reticular frame of thirteen metal ribs and stabilized with guy-wires, consisted of white tubular steel elements that held the suspended bright tent. On top the structure converged into a crown surmounted by the colored flags of the Swiss Cantons. Within the space of a year, the tent was set up in several Swiss and European cities.

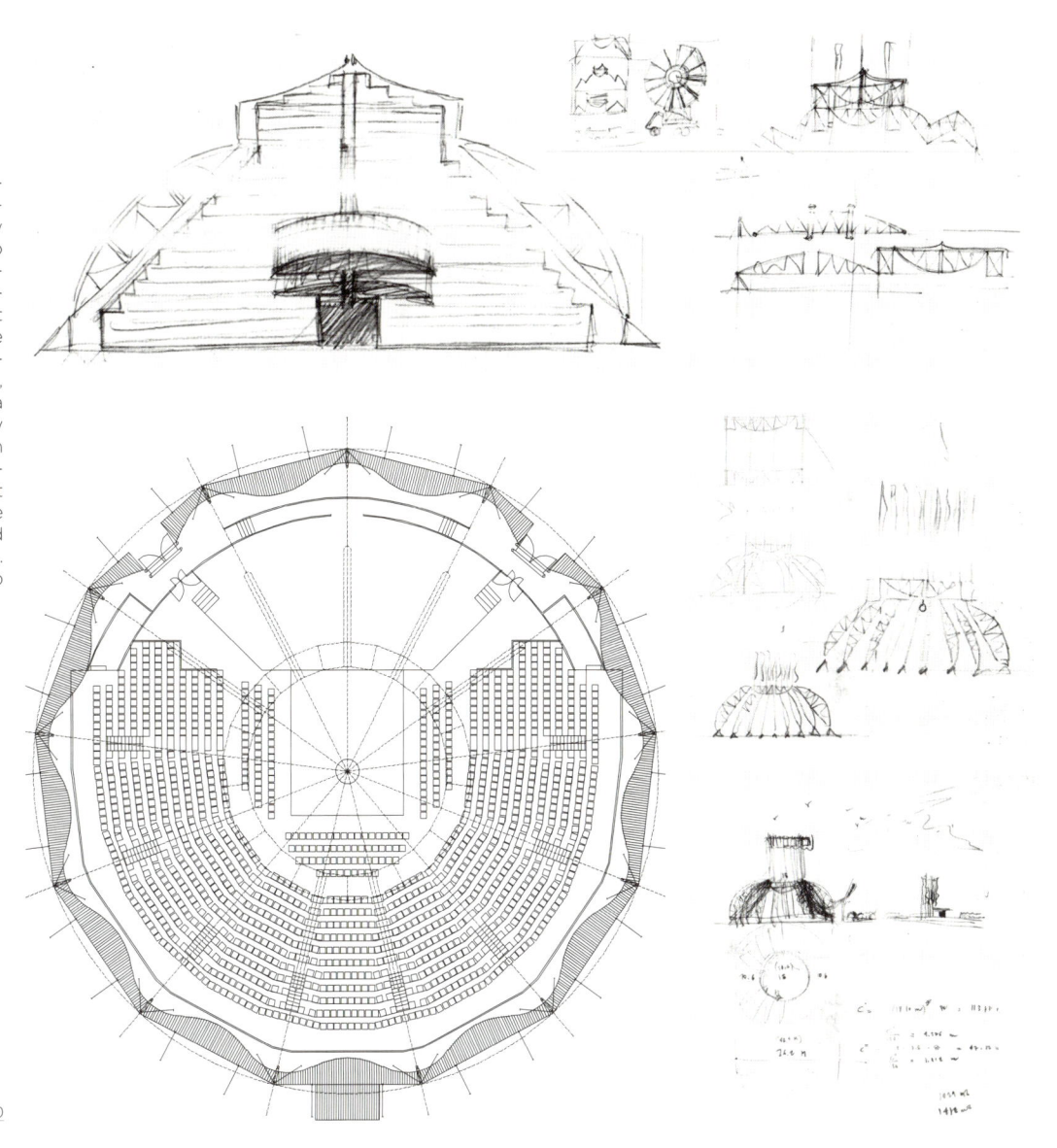

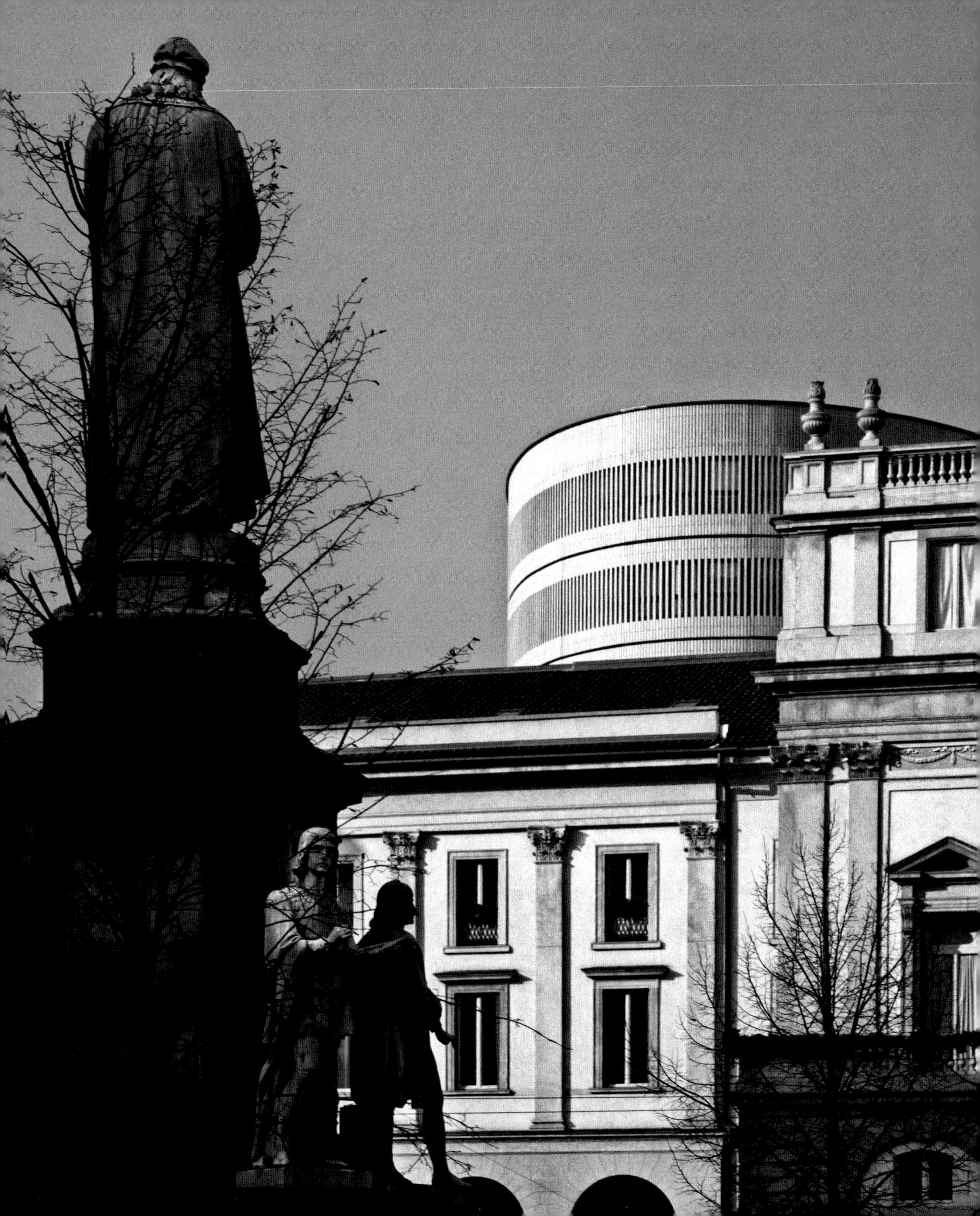

RESTORATION OF THE THEATER ALLA SCALA
MILAN - ITALY

2001-2004

Archive: n° 448
Project: 2001
Construction: 2002-2004
Client: Municipality of Milan
Volume of the new extension only:
130'000 m³ / 4'590'906 c ft
(above ground: 95'000 m³ / 3'355'000 c ft
underground: 35'000 m³ / 1'236'000 c ft

The restoration and extension of the Theater alla Scala affected a wide triangle of the city. From the square in front of the historic building the lot extends along Via Filodrammatici on one hand, and along Via Verdi until the former San Paolo bank on the other. The architectural project regarding the extension developed two new volumes surmounting the eaves of the existent neoclassical building: the raising of the stage tower in the shape of a parallelepiped, – with all technical requirements and rehearsal rooms to fit –, set in the main axis to reinforce the layout of the Piermarini theater, and next to it, an elliptic volume housing the artists' dressing room that hovers above the historical buildings. A conservative restoration was provided for the monumental parts of the theater and its original structure as the Piermarini hall and the 19th-century annex buildings, whereas the new parts, that are set back from the street front, want to express a contemporary and "abstract" architectural language to contrast with the "figurative" one of the historical urban landmark.

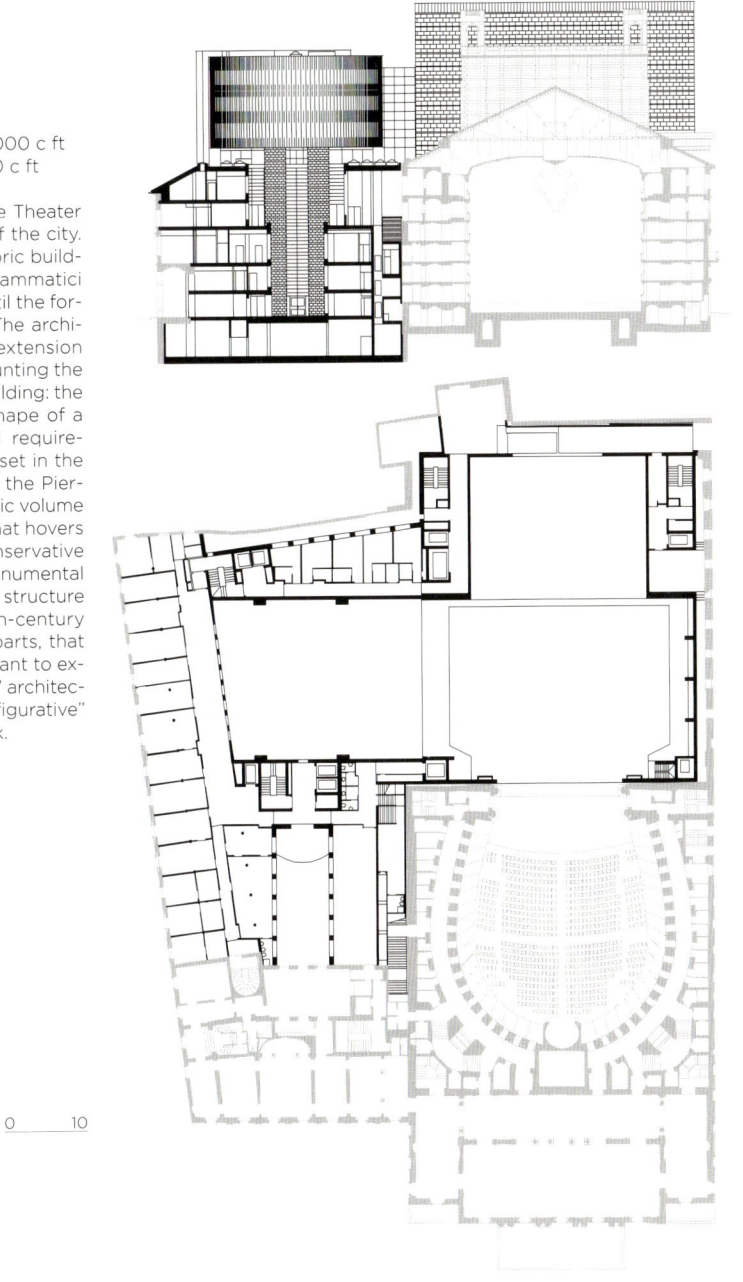

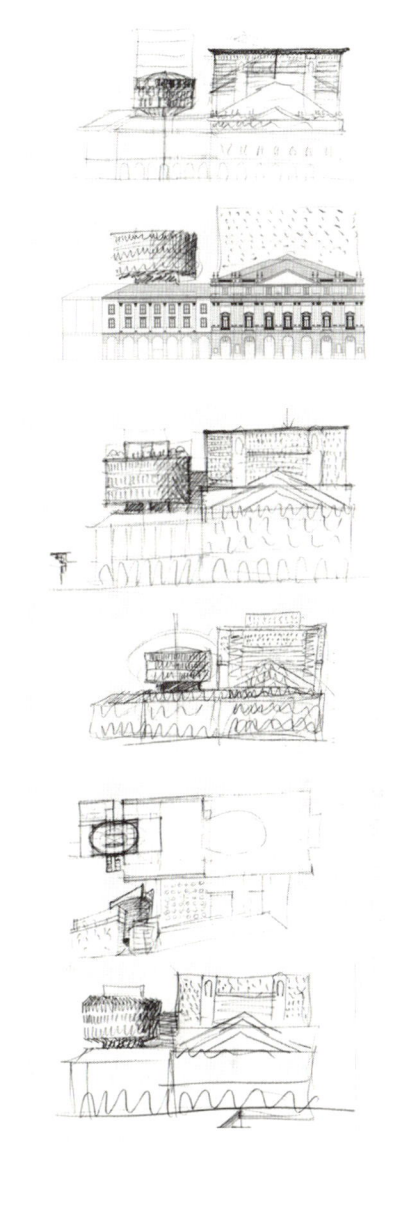

SACRED SPACES

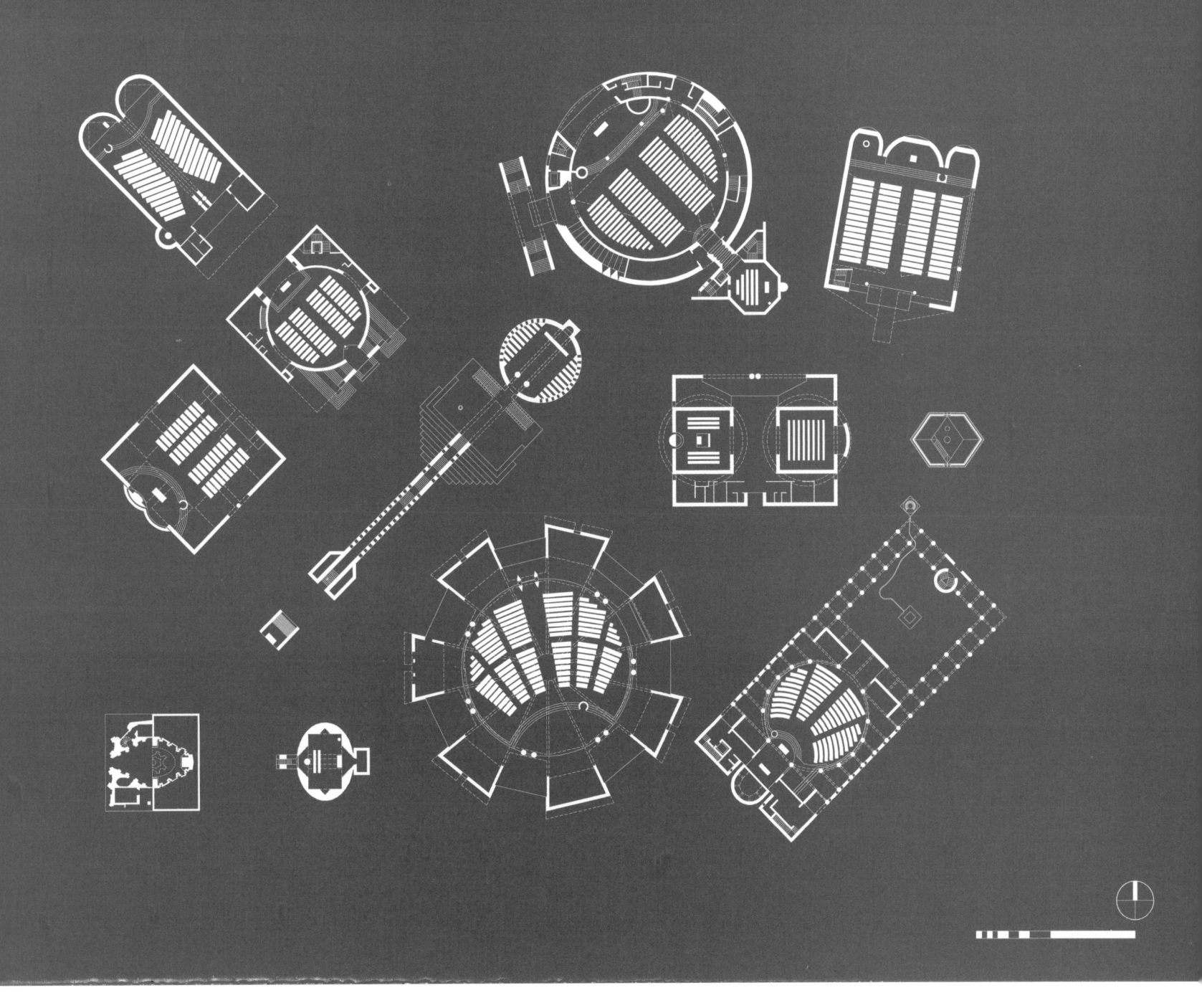

Architecture hides the idea of the sacred. It requires the transformation of a condition of nature into one of culture and this happens through the work and the spirit of man. To build a church nowadays entails a comparison with the break and the ethical-aesthetical twisting brought about by the 20th-century Avant-gardes towards every form of expression. The organization of the sacred space, aiming for contemplation, silence and prayer, does not elude this historical-artistic condition. Architects must work within this new reality, orphans as they are of models that meet the hopes and the contradictions of the believers.

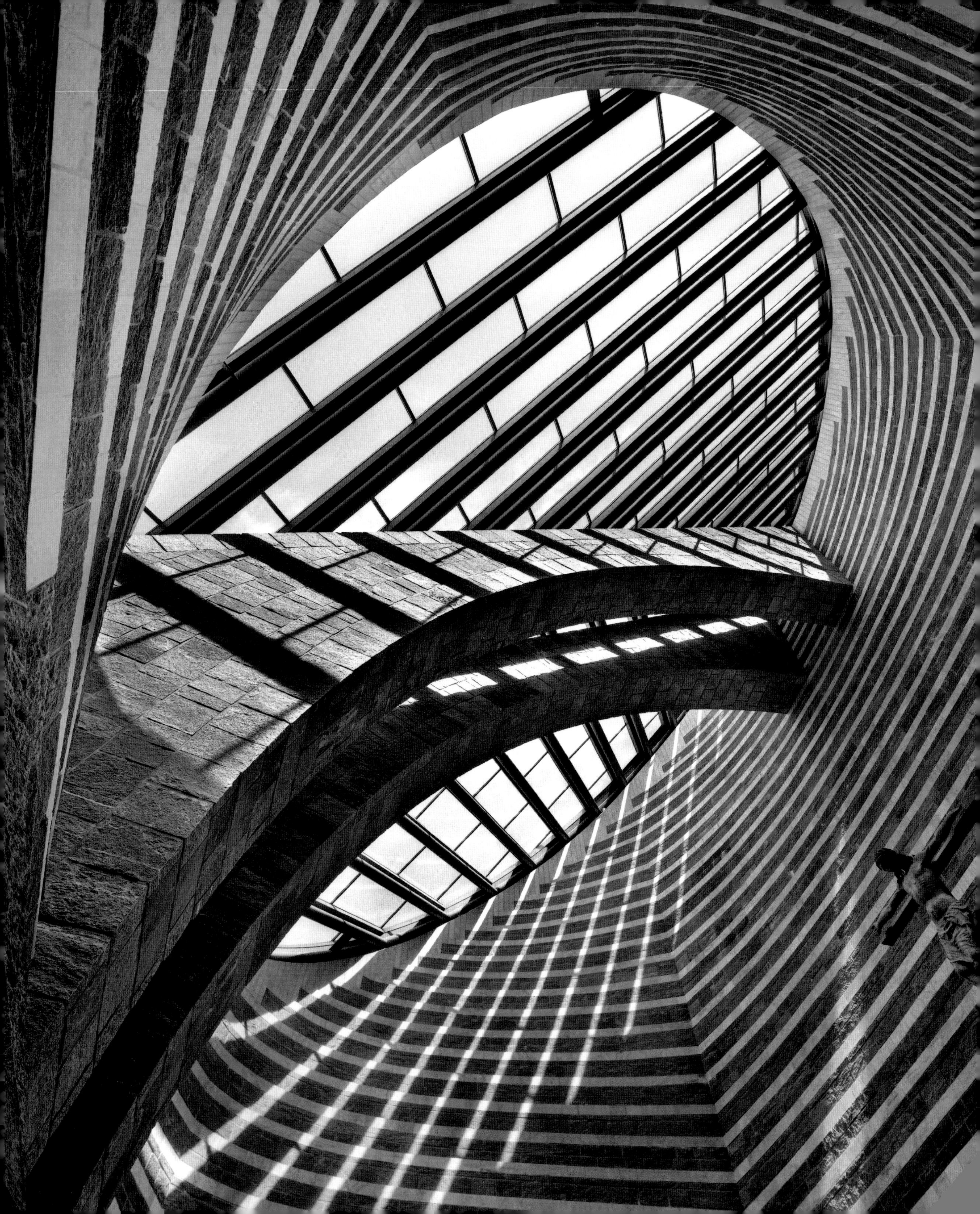

CHURCH SAN GIOVANNI BATTISTA
MOGNO – SWITZERLAND

1986-1996

Archive: n° 113
Project: 1986-1992
Construction: 1990-98
Client: Mogno Church Reconstruction Association
Partner: arch. Gianluigi Dazio
Site area: 178 m² / 1'916 s ft
Floor area: 123 m² / 1'324 s ft
Volume: 1590 m³ / 56'150 c ft

In 1986 an avalanche overwhelmed the village of Mogno in the Maggia Valley and carried the small 17th-century chapel away. The new church rises up on the same site of the former chapel and, though it preserves the relatively modest dimensions of the hall, it introduces a new image and architectural language. A language and expression that conveys a contemporary dimension, yet mediated by an archaic meaning thanks to the interplay of essential shapes: a rectangle inscribed within an external ellipse that widens into a circle at roof level. By means of its cylindrical volume and the massive stone walls, the building aims to resist any future natural disaster.

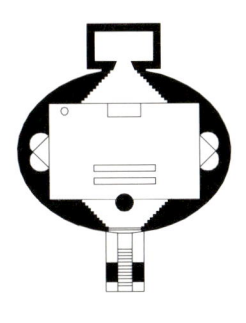

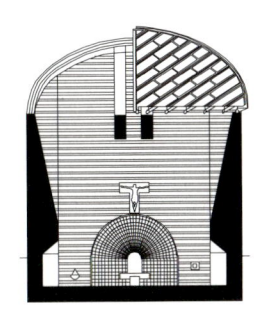

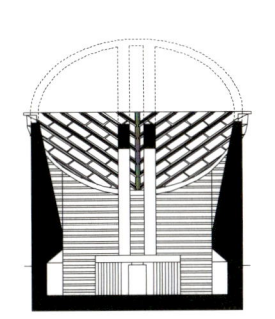

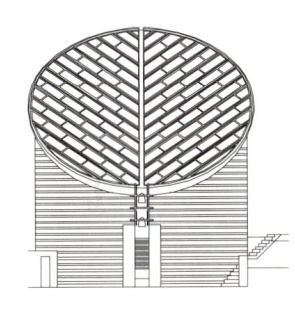

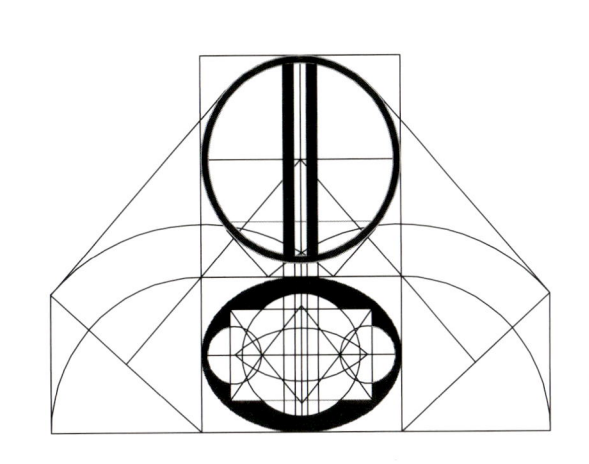

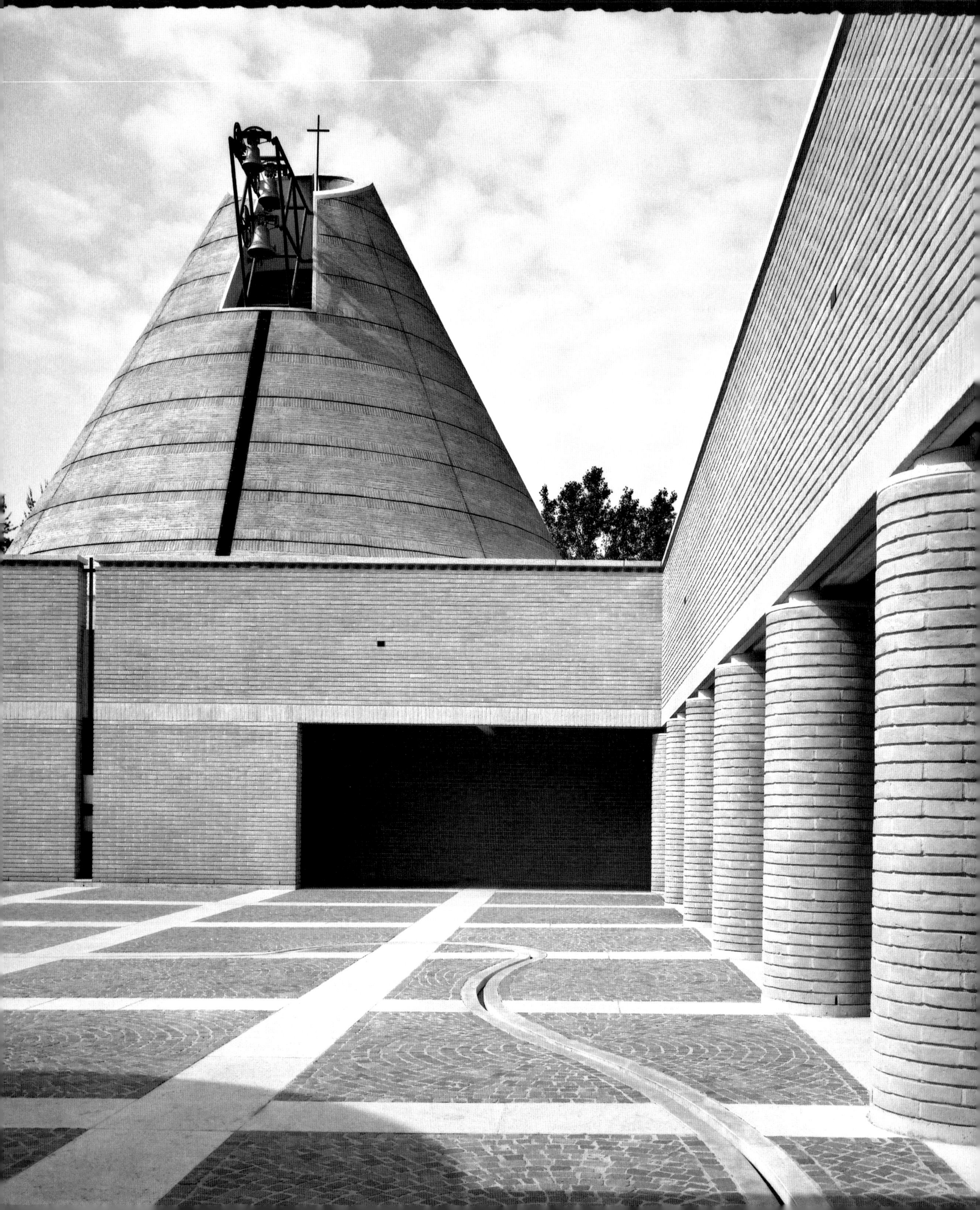

CHURCH BEATO ODORICO
PORDENONE – ITALY

1987-1992

Archive: n° 124
Project: 1987
Construction: 1988-1992
Client: Parish of Beato Odorico di Pordenone
Partner: Eng. Piero Beltrame, Giorgio Raffin
Site area: 3800 m² / 40'902 s ft
Floor area: 1020 m² / 10'979 s ft
Volume: 8800 m³ / 310'770 c ft

The church is characterized by a simple and unified structure, a kind of urban block enclosing the courtyard, the ambulatory, the ancillary services and the high part of the church in the shape of a truncated cone. The theme of the centrality, achieved by inscribing a circle on a square base, is linked to a clear direction. The colonnade borders of the cloister-shaped parvis create a secluded space as filter towards the urban surroundings. Within the four-sided portico a vertical slit on the main axis interrupts the continuous wall. The exterior image highlights the homogeneous character of the building with respect to the fragmentariness of the urban context. Inside, the space acts between the central conical volume and the lower side areas that merge outside into the rectangular boundary delimiting the building.

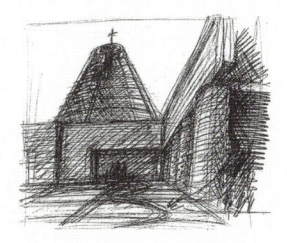

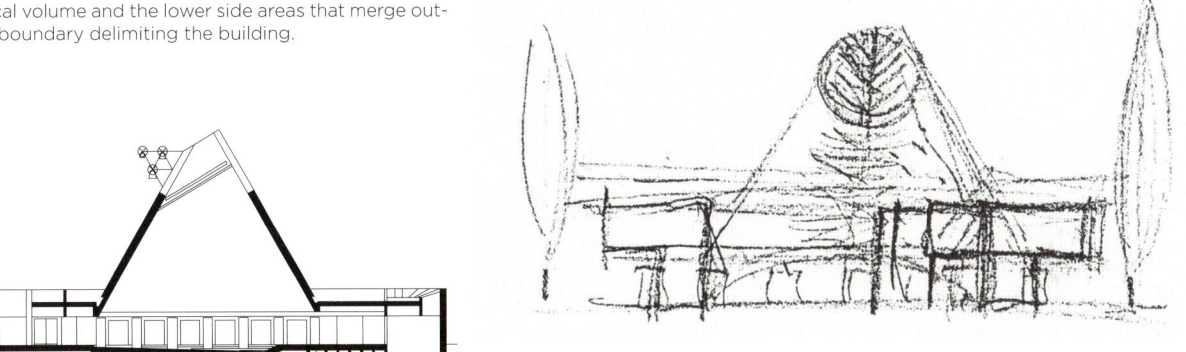

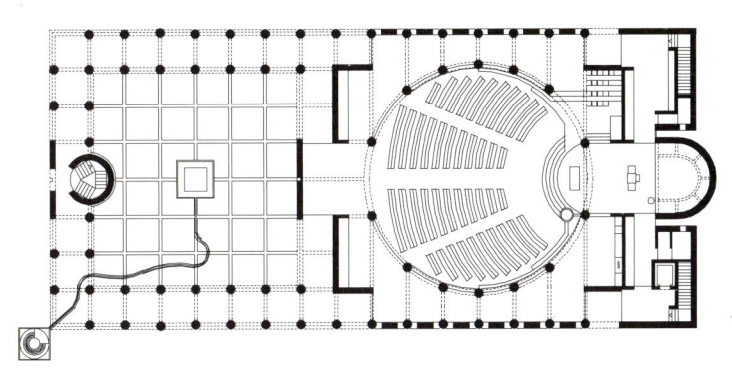

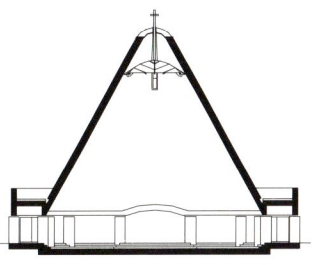

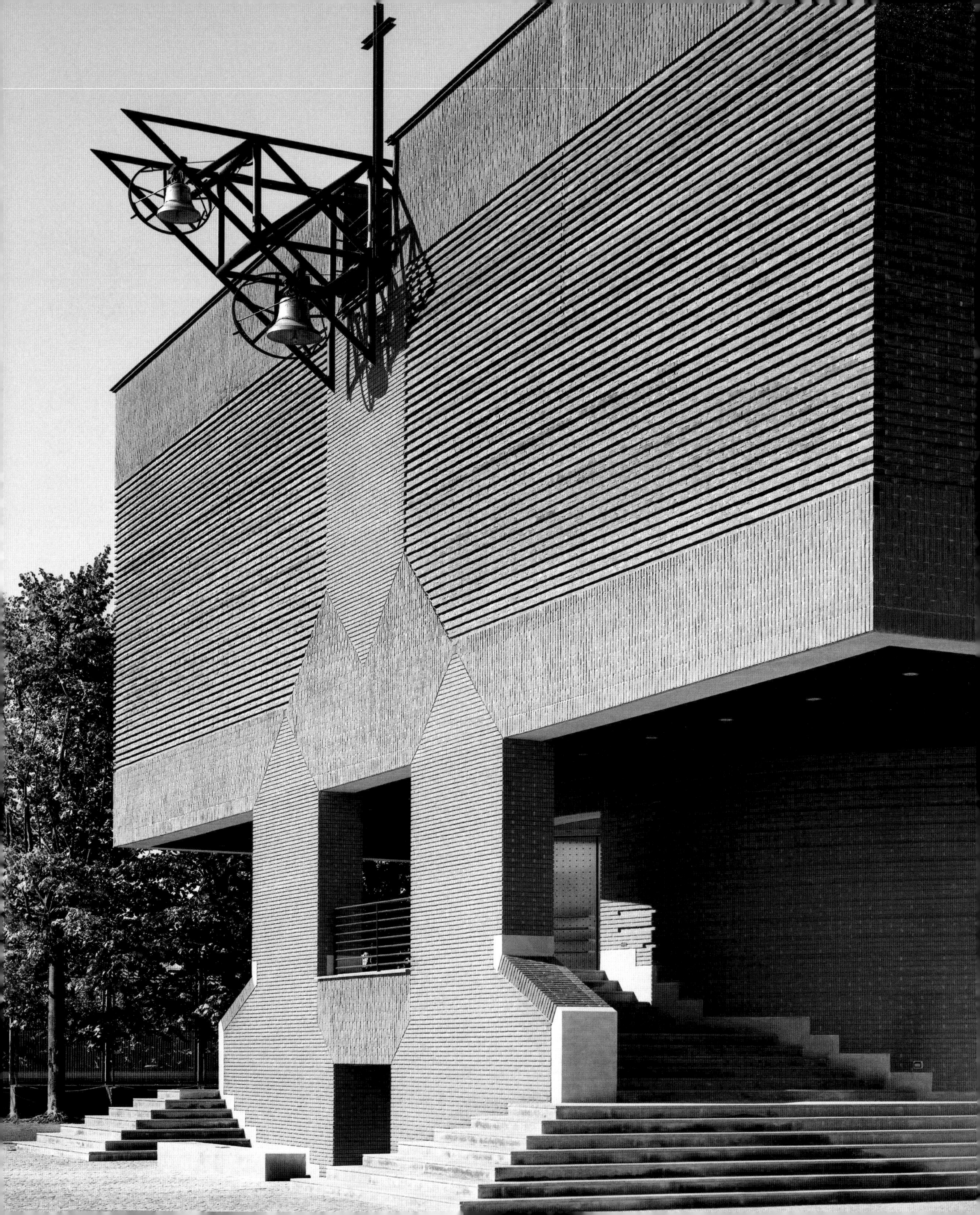

CHURCH SAN PIETRO APOSTOLO
SARTIRANA – ITALY

1987-1995

Archive: n° 132
Project: 1987-1992
Construction: 1992-95
Client: Parish San Pietro Apostolo, Sartirana
Partner: arch. Fabiano Redaelli, Anna Bruna Vertemati
Site area: 1'600 m² / 17'222 s ft
Floor area: 620 m² / 6'674 s ft
Volume : 9'800 m³ / 346'084 c ft

The architectural idea for the Church San Pietro Apostolo is based on a geometrical construction generated by the interpenetration of a cube and a cylinder. The prism forms the outer envelope while the cylinder defines the space designed for the faithful. A large portal, cut into the primary form of the mass, marks the entrance that is accessible from two side staircases. The main front tidiness is only interrupted by the cut with the belfry. The mass of the cylindrical ring within the cube rises from the floor, transforming itself into a two-floor women's gallery. The roof, detached from the external shell, is characterized by a series of coffers that recreates the base cube. Direct light comes in through the onyx filter of the wide arch-shaped opening behind the altar, and indirect light through the skylights set above the galleries.

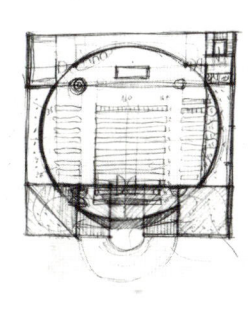

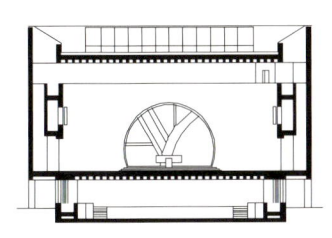

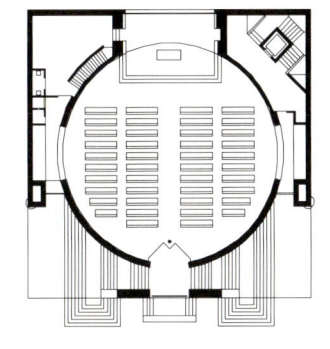

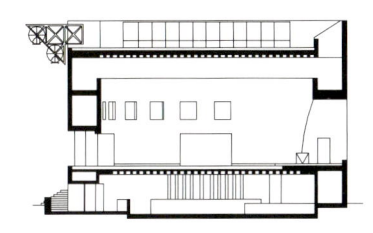

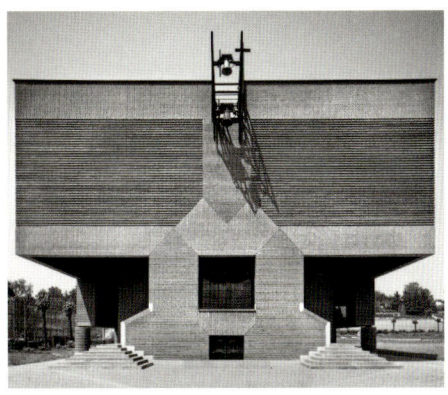

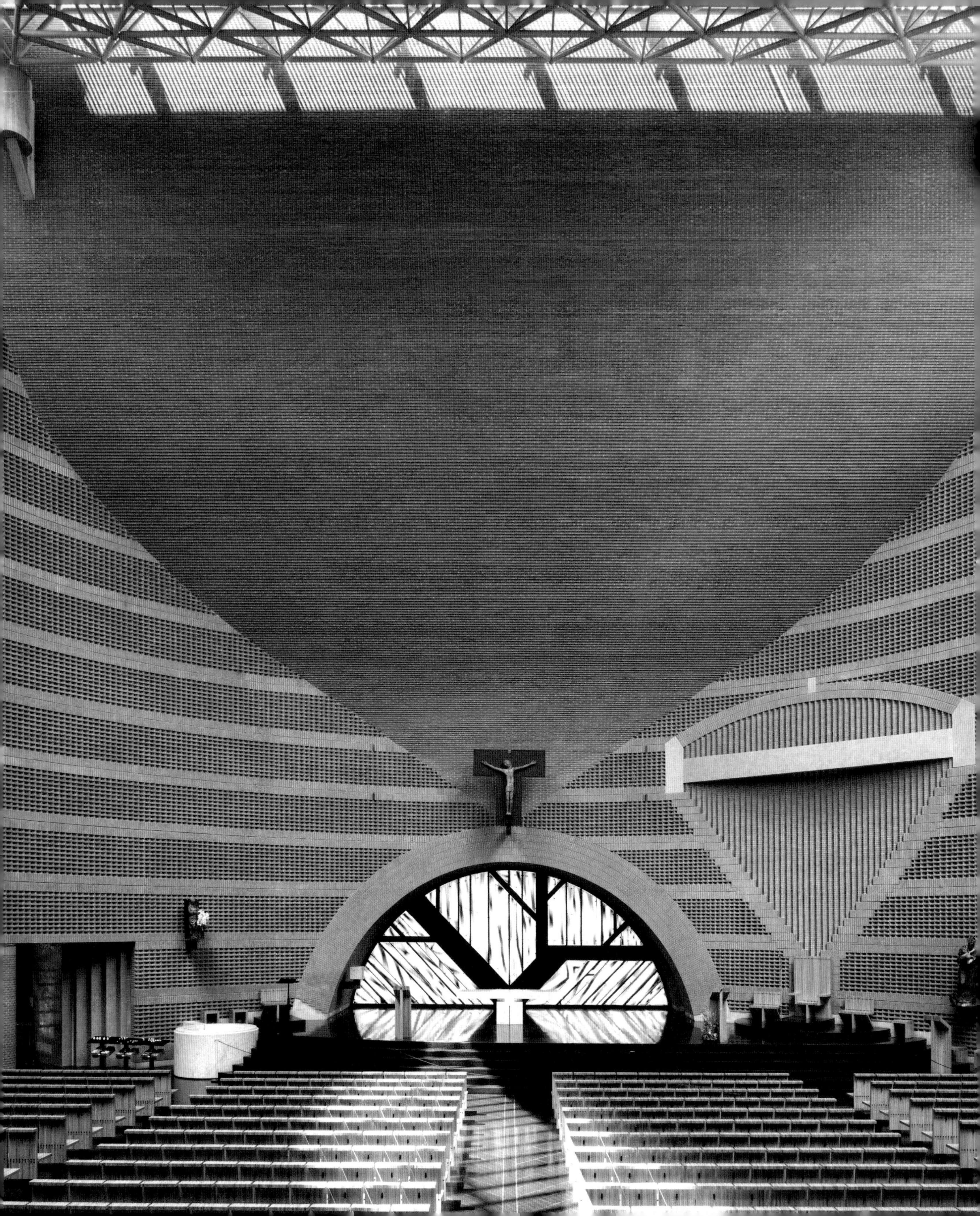

CATHEDRAL OF THE RESURRECTION
ÉVRY - FRANCE

1988-1995

Archive: n° 143
Project: 1988-1992
Construction: 1992-95
Client: Diocese of Évry Corbeil Essonnes
Project management: Philippe Talbot&Associés
Site area: 1'600 m² / 17'222 s ft
Floor area: 4'800 m² / 51'667 s ft
Volume: 45'000 m³ / 1'589'160 c ft

"I thought of the design for the House of God in the hope of making a house for man." It is a simple and homogeneous structure, formed by a cylinder cut diagonally. The uppermost part of the building overlooks the square while the lowest part borders with a residential complex. The cathedral opens towards the sky by means of the glass connection between the circle of the base and the triangle of the roof. The choice of placing a series of trees at the top of the building evokes a green halo suspended above the city. The cylindrical volume negates the very idea of a façade: it is the inclined surface of the triangle inscribed within the circle that indicates the church orientation. Inside, there is a given hierarchy between the central space designed for the faithful and the border areas for services on the different levels. The intersection of the cylinder with the linear connection of one side of the roof provide the apse with a particular shape, all enhanced by the texture of the bricks.

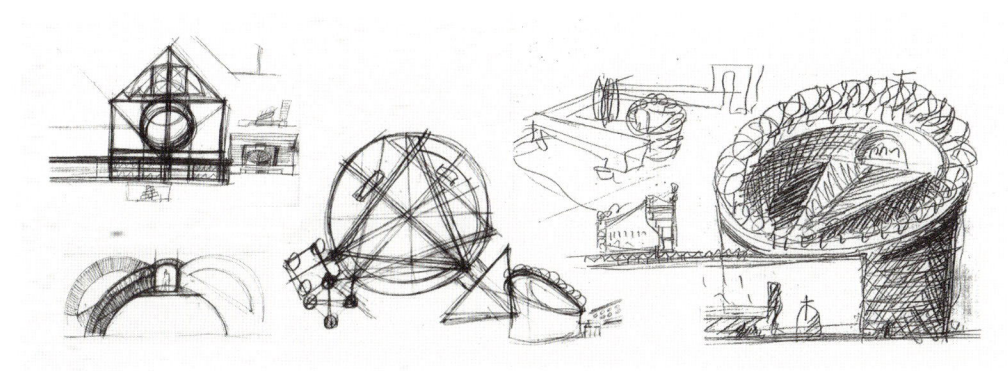

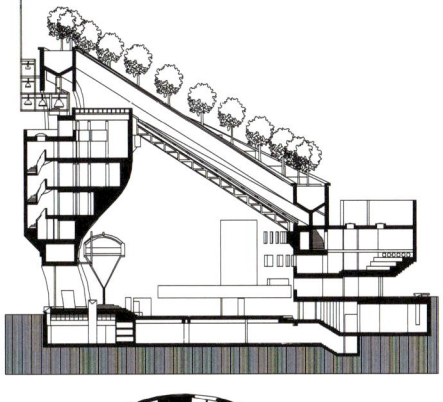

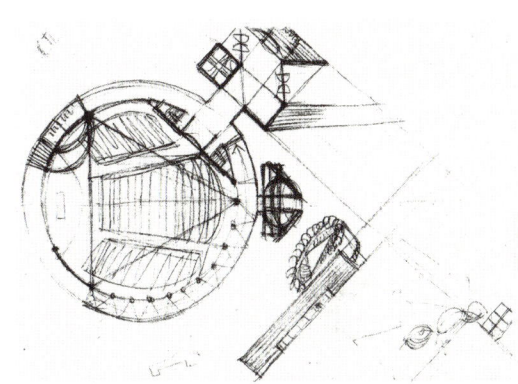

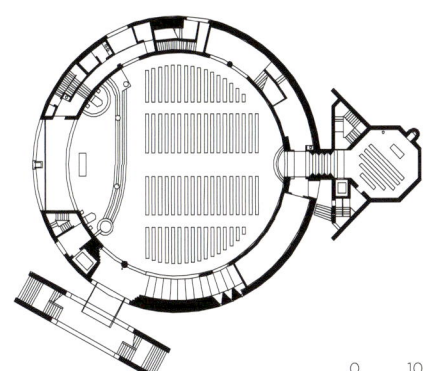

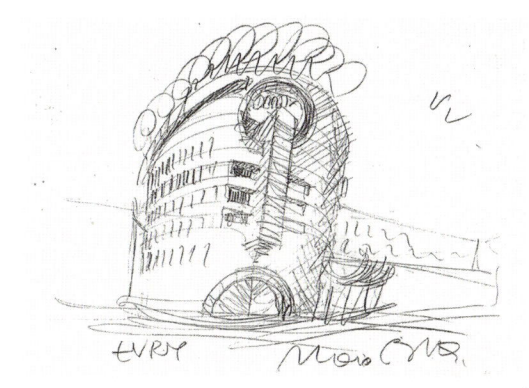

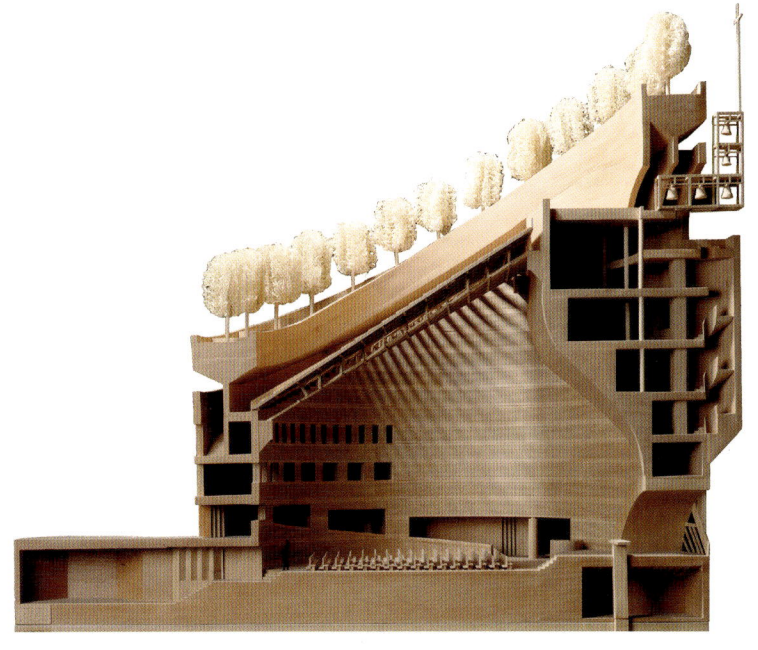

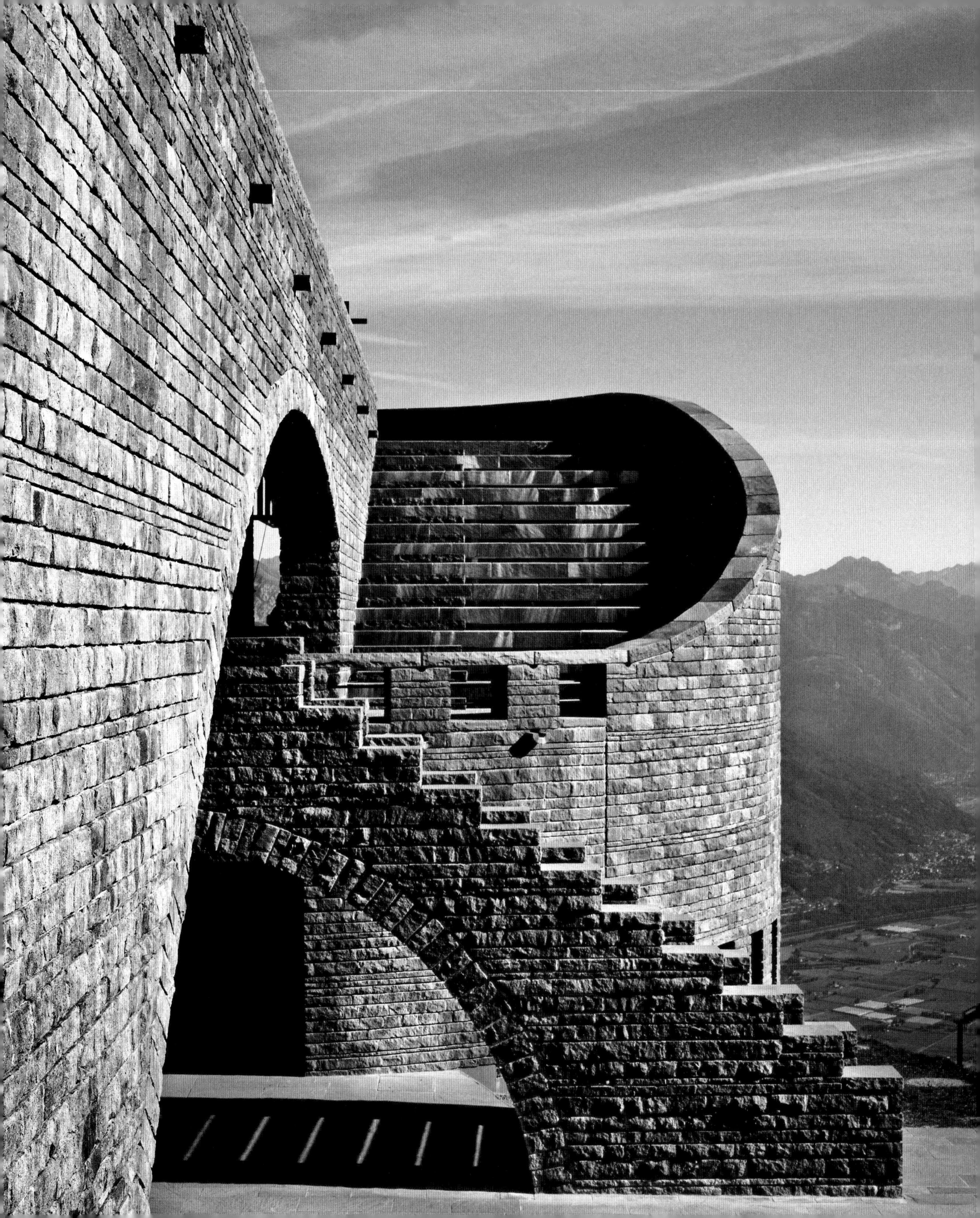

CHAPEL SANTA MARIA DEGLI ANGELI
MOUNT TAMARO - SWITZERLAND

1990-1996

Archive: n° 188
Project: 1990-92
Construction: 1992-96
Client: Egidio Cattaneo
Artist: Enzo Cucchi
Floor area chapel: 184 m² / 1'980 s ft
Floor area outer walkway: 150 m² / 1'614 s ft
Volume: 2'820 m² / 99'587 c ft

From a natural slope of the mountain the building extends into space to reach solidity in a cylindrical volume. Visitors can walk two paths: either along the walkway leading to a lookout across the valley or, following a path in between the walls downstairs towards the church entrance. The internal space is divided into three naves and characterized by the contrast between the circular walls, covered with blackened lime mortar, and the linear white outlines of the ceiling. Two heavy columns are set at the entrance of the lower central nave, which ends in the small apse that protrudes from the main volume. In this small space, the intense zenithal light draws attention to the sign of prayer displayed by two hands depicted on the wall by Enzo Cucchi, the Italian artist who also realized the engravings applied in the embrasures of the twenty-two small openings along the curved walls. The chapel by means of its articulated building work and the simple forms set within a natural morphology, defines a new and unexpected perception of the surrounding landscape.

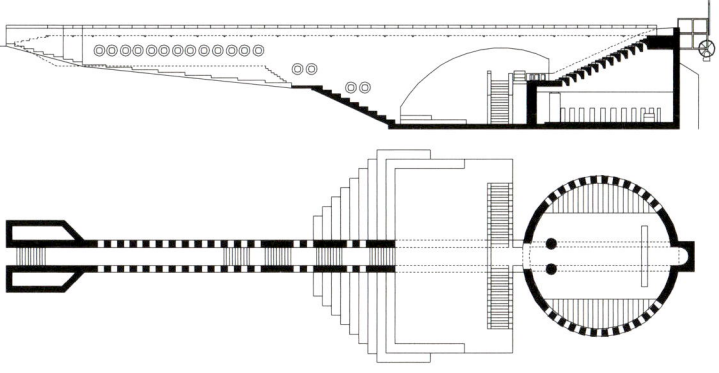

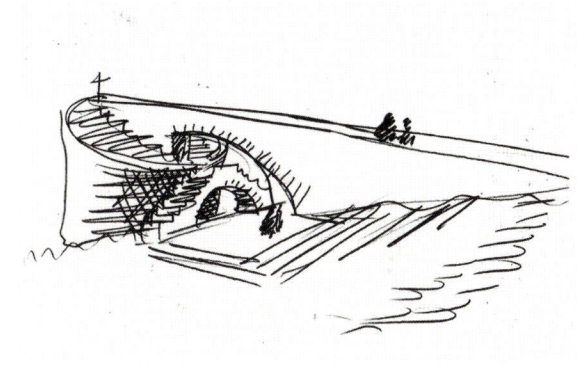

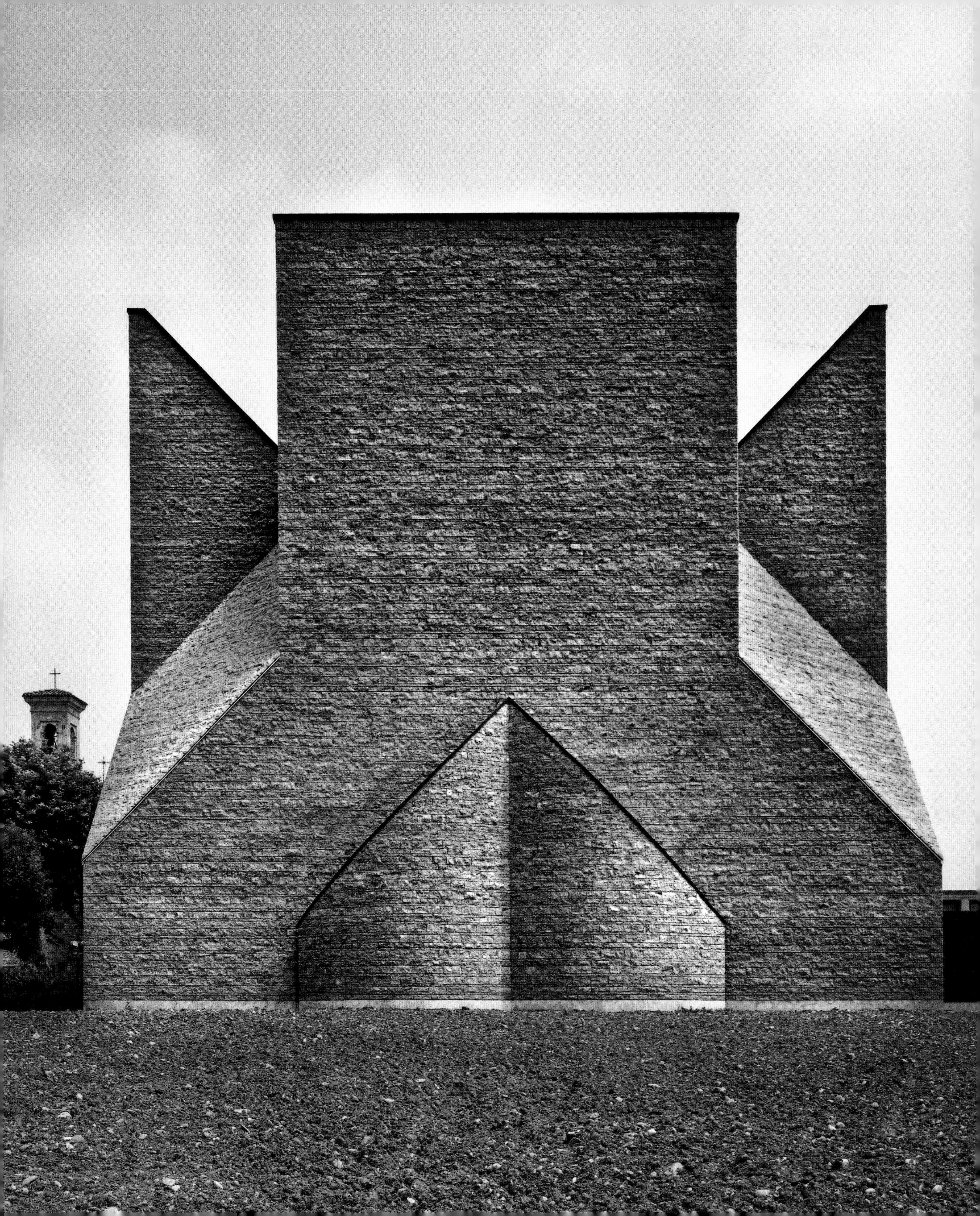

CHURCH PAPA GIOVANNI XXIII
SERIATE – ITALY

1994-2004

Archive: n° 265
Project: 1994-2000
Construction: 2001-2004
Client: Parish S.S. Redentore, Seriate
Partner: arch. Guglielmo Clivati
Sculptor : Giuliano Vangi
Site area: 26'300 m² / 283'091 s ft
Floor area: 2'137 m² / 23'002 s ft
Volume: 16'500 m³ / 582'692 c ft

The site of the new church dedicated to Holy Pope Giovanni XXIII is located close to the 17th-century church of San Alessandro Martyr in Paderno-Seriate, south of the city of Bergamo. The complex is composed of a square volume of the church, set in the center of the assigned area, and a long linear body surrounded on two sides by a colonnade that houses the services and the parish works. To enhance the unity of the complex, all volumes are clad with a split Verona stone. The interior of the church space offers itself as a one and only volume marked off by the perimeter walls and filled with daylight generated by the four roof lights. Polished Verona stone is also part of the interior finishing, not only for the floors but also as a high plinth running along the walls and the liturgical furnishings (altar, pulpit and chair) and supporting the wall panels made of gold-plated wooden lath, that evoke an ancient technique and tradition. A stone clad twin apse completes the presbytery and reveals a bas-relief by the Italian artist Giuliano Vangi.

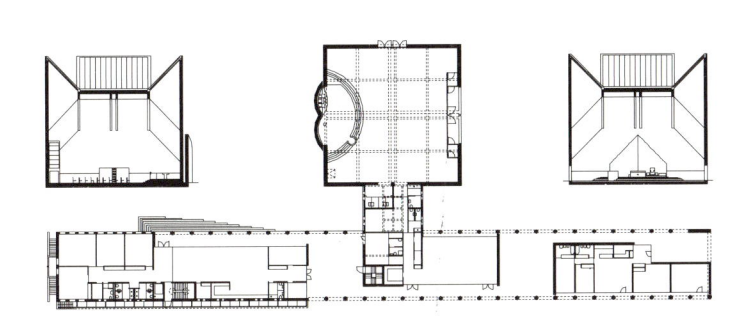

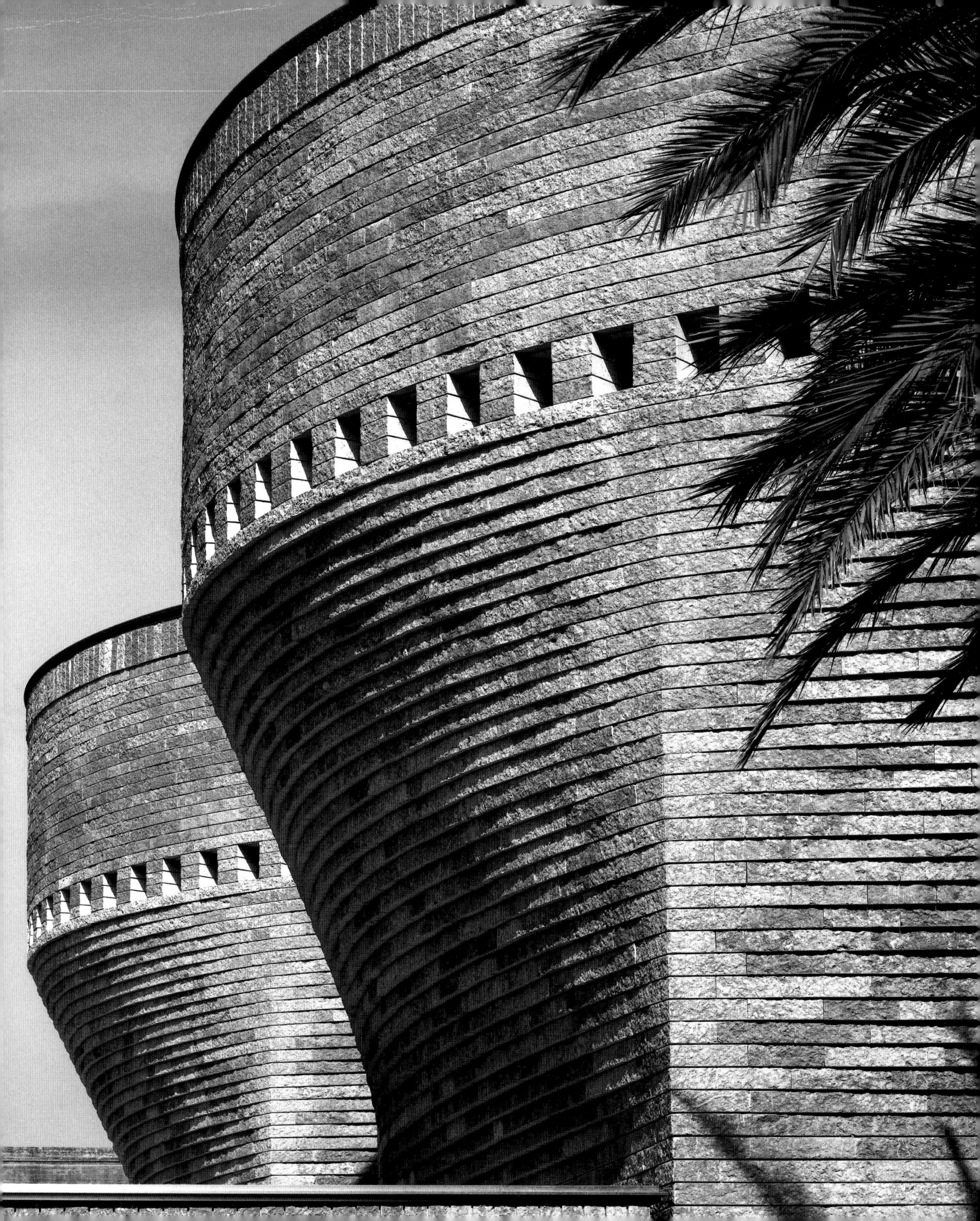

THE CYMBALISTA SYNAGOGUE AND JEWISH HERITAGE CENTER
TEL AVIV – ISRAEL

1996-98

Archive: n° 314
Project: 1996
Construction: 1997-98
Client: Paulette and Norbert Cymbalista
Partner: Arthur Zylberzac
Civil engineering: Shmaya Ben-Abraham
Floor area: 800 m² / 8'611 s ft
Volume: 7'325 m³ / 258'680 c ft

A place for prayer and a place for discussion, a synagogue and a conference hall, a crossroads for the religious and the secular. The concept for the project – to be built within the campus of Tel Aviv University – was helped by the clients' clear ideas about what they wanted: two spaces that were separate in functions but united as a symbol expressing the common quest for spirituality. From a unique rectangular base two identical square volume arise, both turning and open up into a circular shape. On top of each body the inscribed square roof creates four arch segments to let daylight in and flood down the interior gold sandstone walls, that characterizes the interior spaces. All exterior façade are clad in split red Verona stone. The base gathers the shared services and activities, well distributed around the two main spaces. Only the interior fittings reveal the different functions of the two halls.

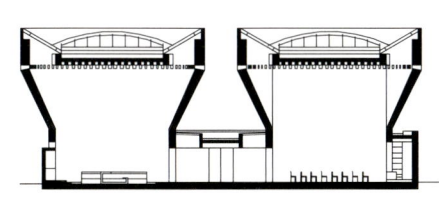

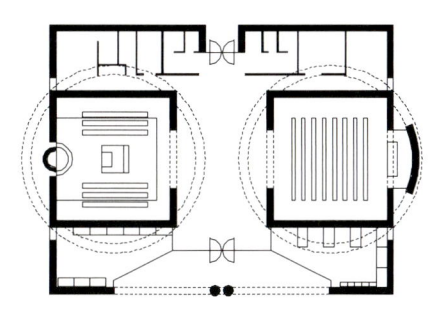

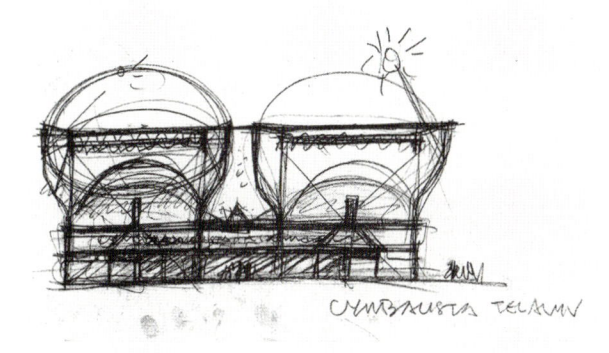

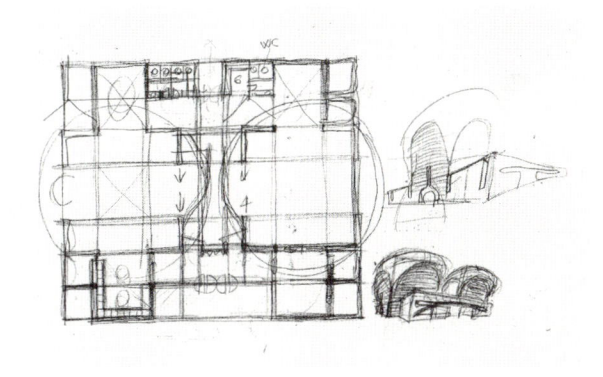

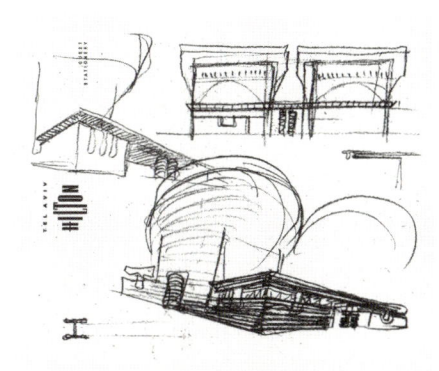

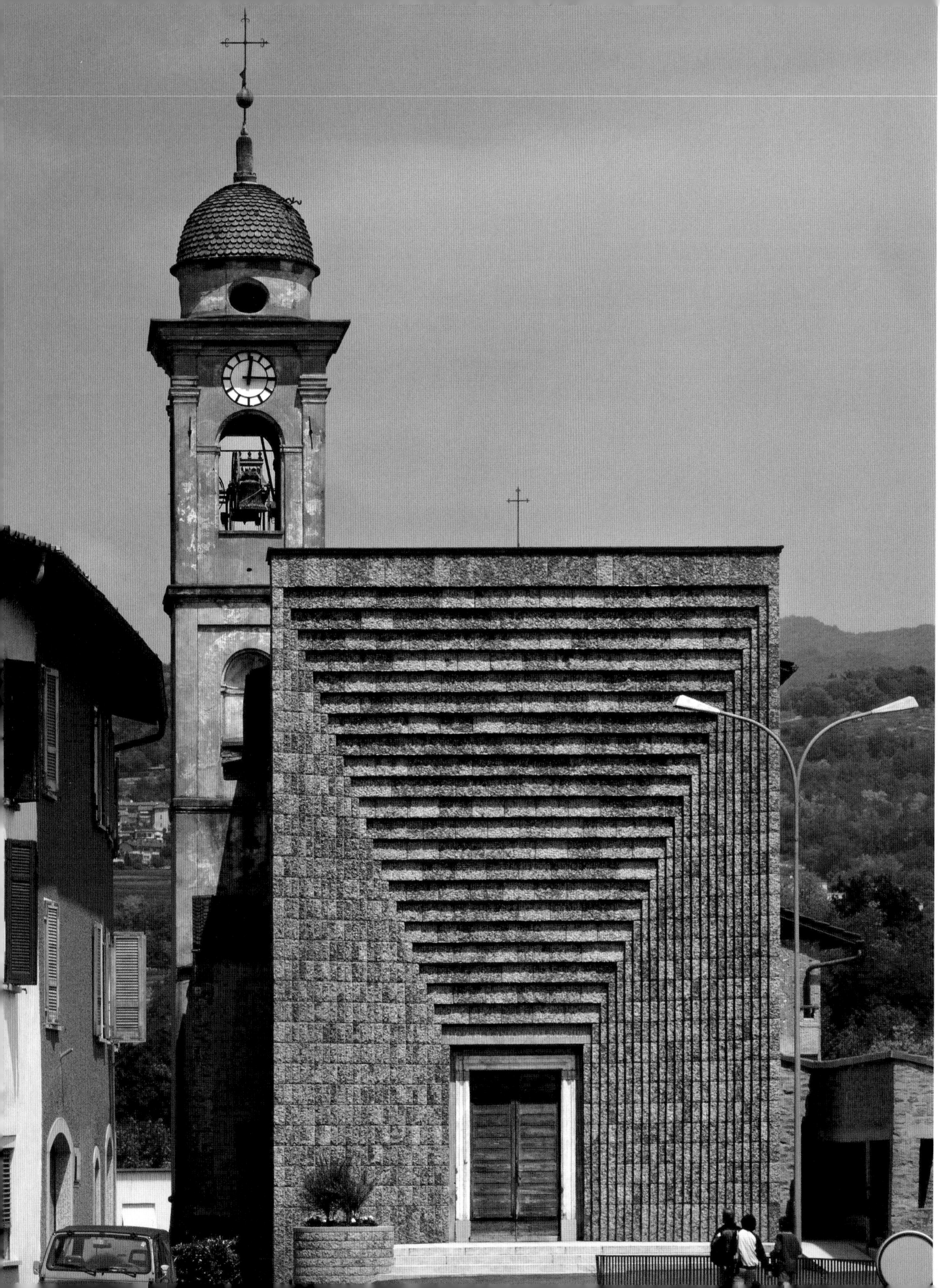

FAÇADE OF THE CHURCH SANT'ANTONIO ABATE
GENESTRERIO – SWITZERLAND

1999-2003

Archive: n° 371
Project: 1999
Construction: 2002-2003
Client: Parish of Genestrerio

The intention was to realize a new stone façade, worked in split Verona stone, to create a contemporary artefact in contrast to the 17th-century church building at the back. The new entrance gate is detached from the existent church front by a clear cut and widens on all side like a bellow up to a depth of three meters. This project was paralleled by the renovation of the parvis to create the levels required to link the new entrance with the existing square and the parish house, Botta's first architectural work. In 2009, the local artist Selim Abdullah created a bronze door to replace the former wooden one.

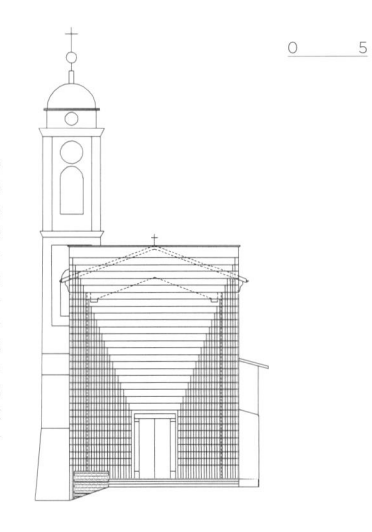

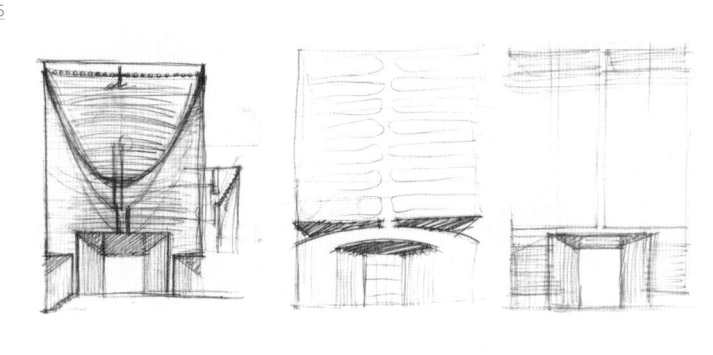

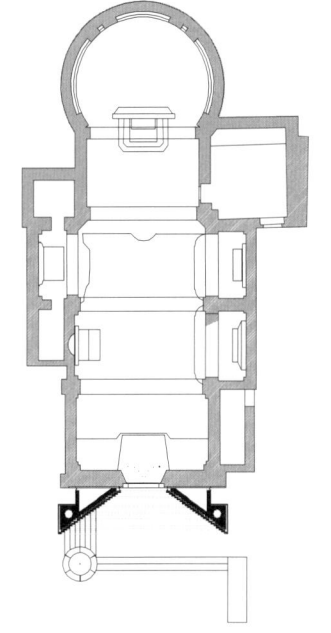

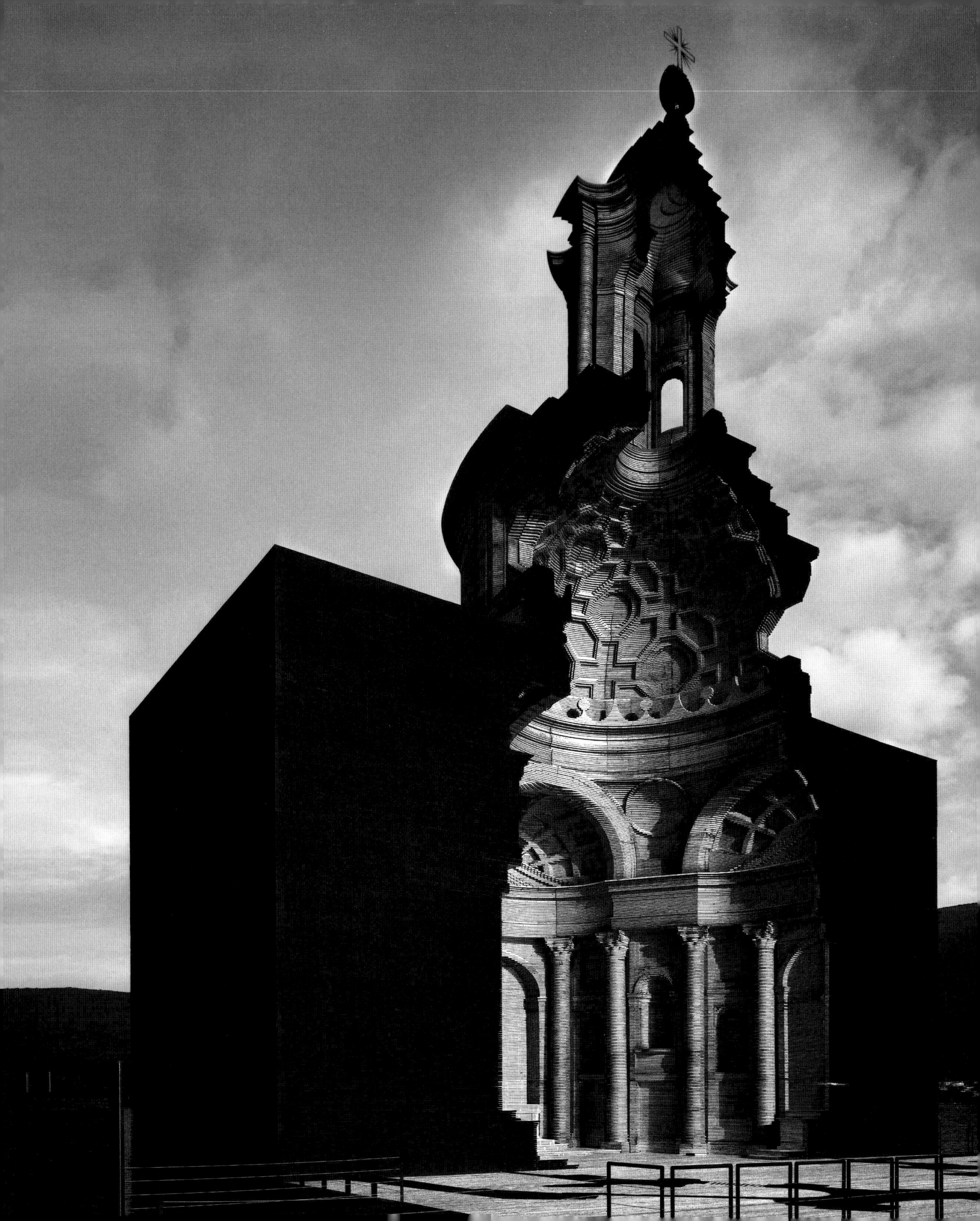

SAN CARLINO
LUGANO – SWITZERLAND

1999-2003

Archive: n°376
Project: 1999
Construction: 1999
Dismantling: 2003
Promoters: University of Lugano;
Academy of architecture Mendrisio

The life-size wooden model represented the cross section of the San Carlo alle Quattro Fontane Church in Rome. It was built in 1999 to commemorate the 400th anniversary of the birth of Francesco Borromini and to celebrate the exhibition at the Museo Cantonale d'Arte in Lugano. The contribution of an employment programme, supported by the University of Lugano and the Academy of architecture of Mendrisio made it possible to achieve an extraordinary undertaking in very little time thanks to the involvement of dozens of unemployed workers, as well as architects, draftsmen, carpenters and craftsmen. The wooden model was placed on a square platform anchored a few meters from the shore, on the lakefront of Lugano. The wooden structure, nearly 33 m high, was composed of 35'000 planks with thickness of 4.5 cm, modularly mounted with a hollow joint of 1 cm and held together with steel cables fixed to an important steel frame. San Carlino graced Lugano lakeside until October 2003.

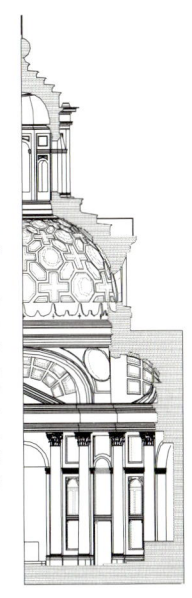

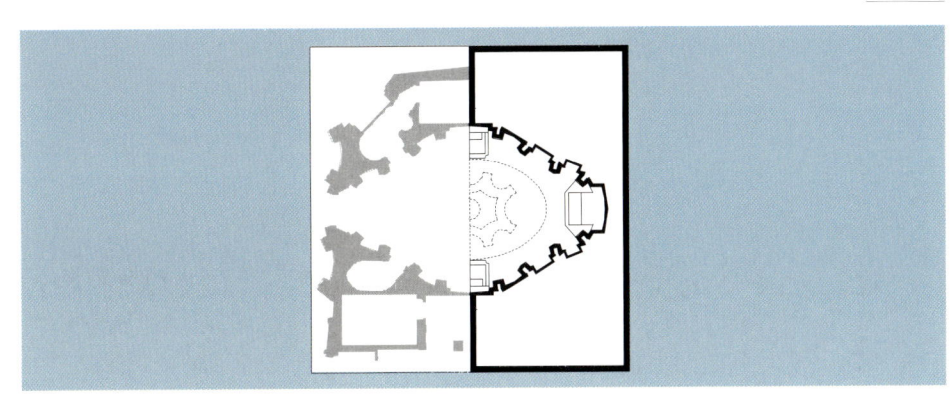

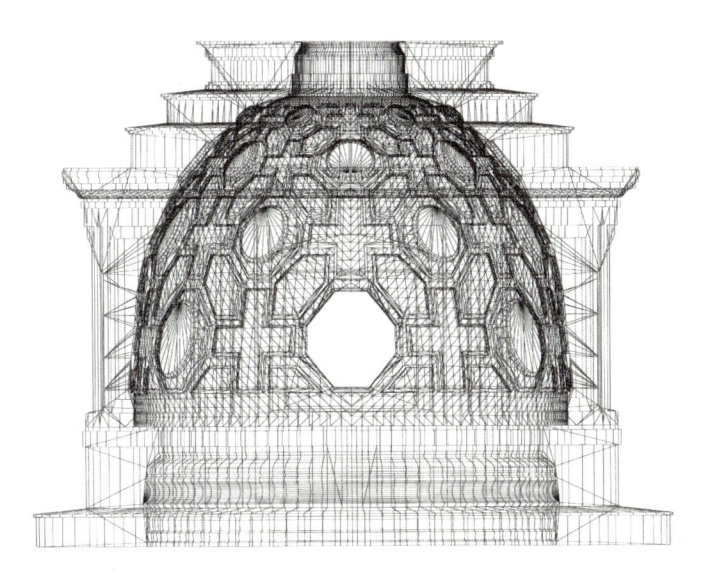

0   5

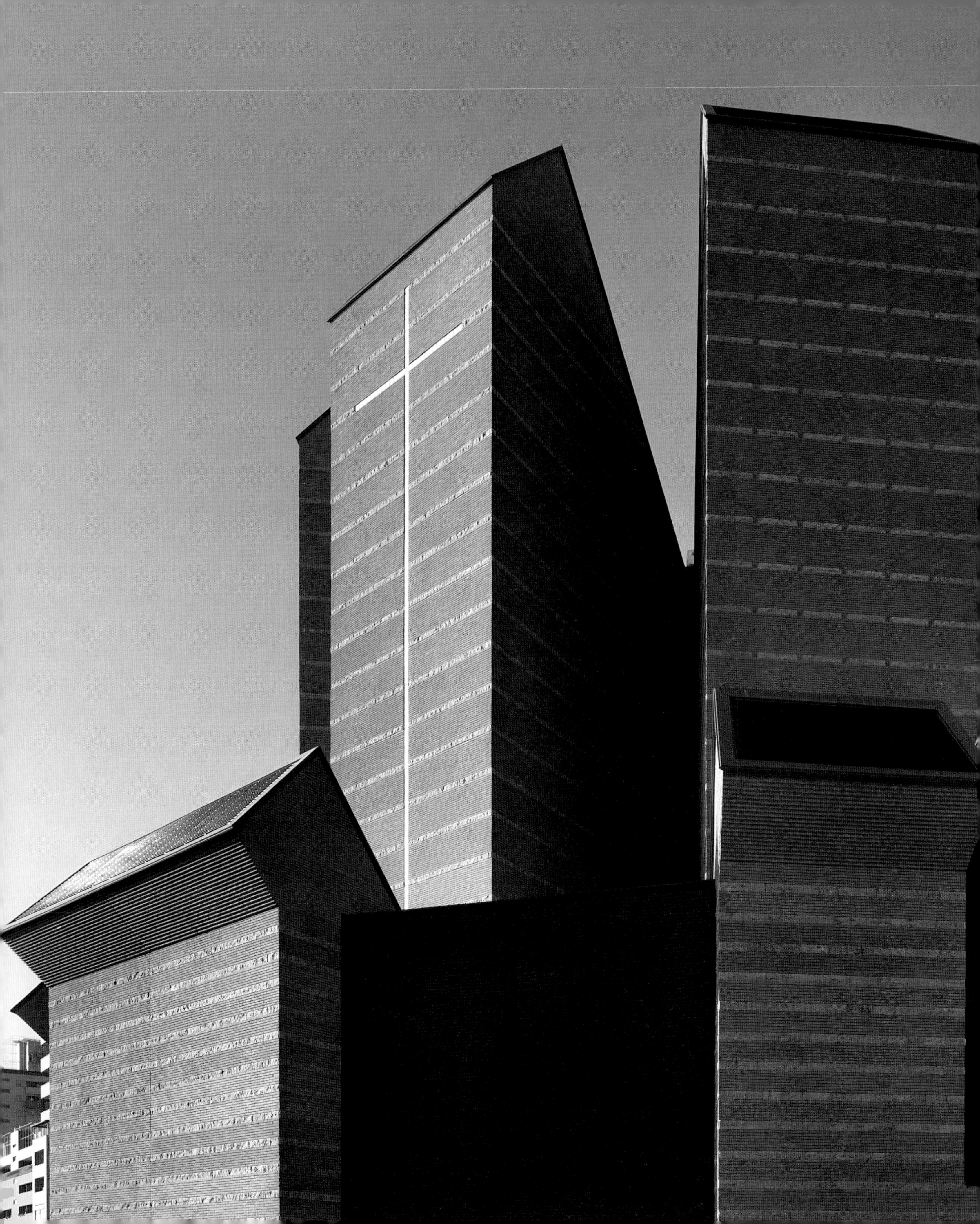

CHURCH SANTO VOLTO
TURIN – ITALY

2001-2006

Archive: n° 429
Project: 2001
Construction: 2004-2006
Partner: Studio O. Siniscalco, Turin
Client: Archdiocese of Turin, Cardinal Severino Poletto
Site area: 10'000 m² / 107'639 s ft
Floor area: 26'300 m² / 283'091 s ft
Volume: 125'000 m³ / 4'414'333 c ft

The central plan of the church is surrounded by seven towers added with lower bodies of the chapels that, through their truncated top, also act as skylights. Inside, the pyramidal roof shape embraces the wide hall and through the alternation of solids and voids generates a suggestive play of light and shadow in the central space. Following the clients' requests, the face of Jesus impressed on the "holy shroud" has been reproduced through a skilful interweaving of stone worked as a texture, enhanced by the daylight. As a reminder of the workers' culture on this area, the smokestack from the former steelworks has been conserved and added with a lightening steel spiral. The church connects to the urban surrounding by the lower building running along two sides with offices of the metropolitan curia, apartments, a weekday chapel, a presbytery and various structures for education and recreation as well as an underground conference hall.

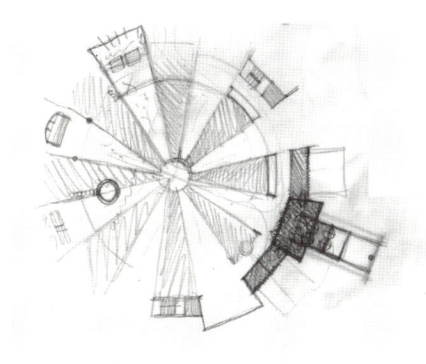

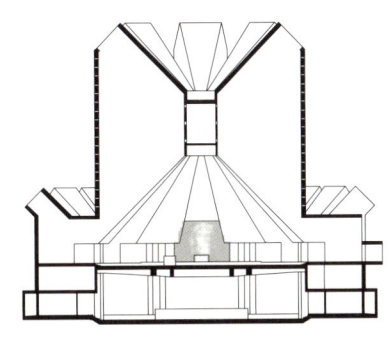

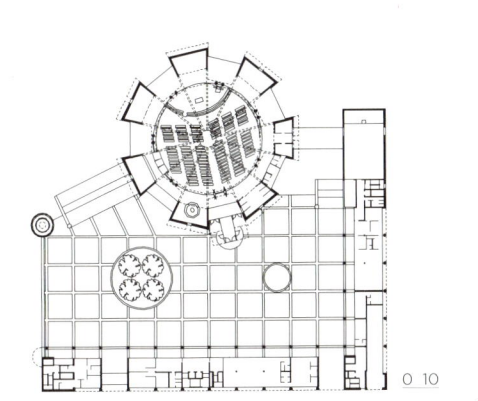

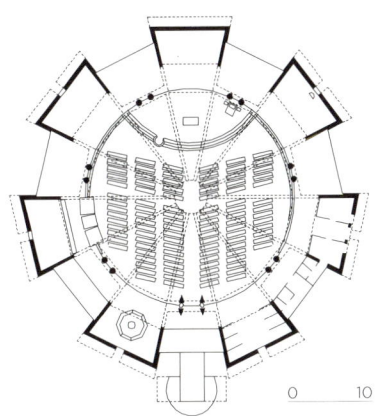

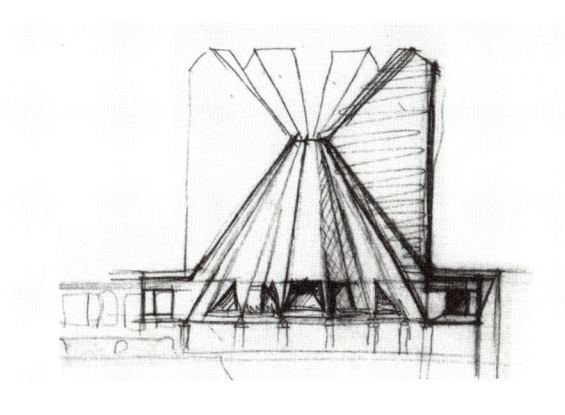

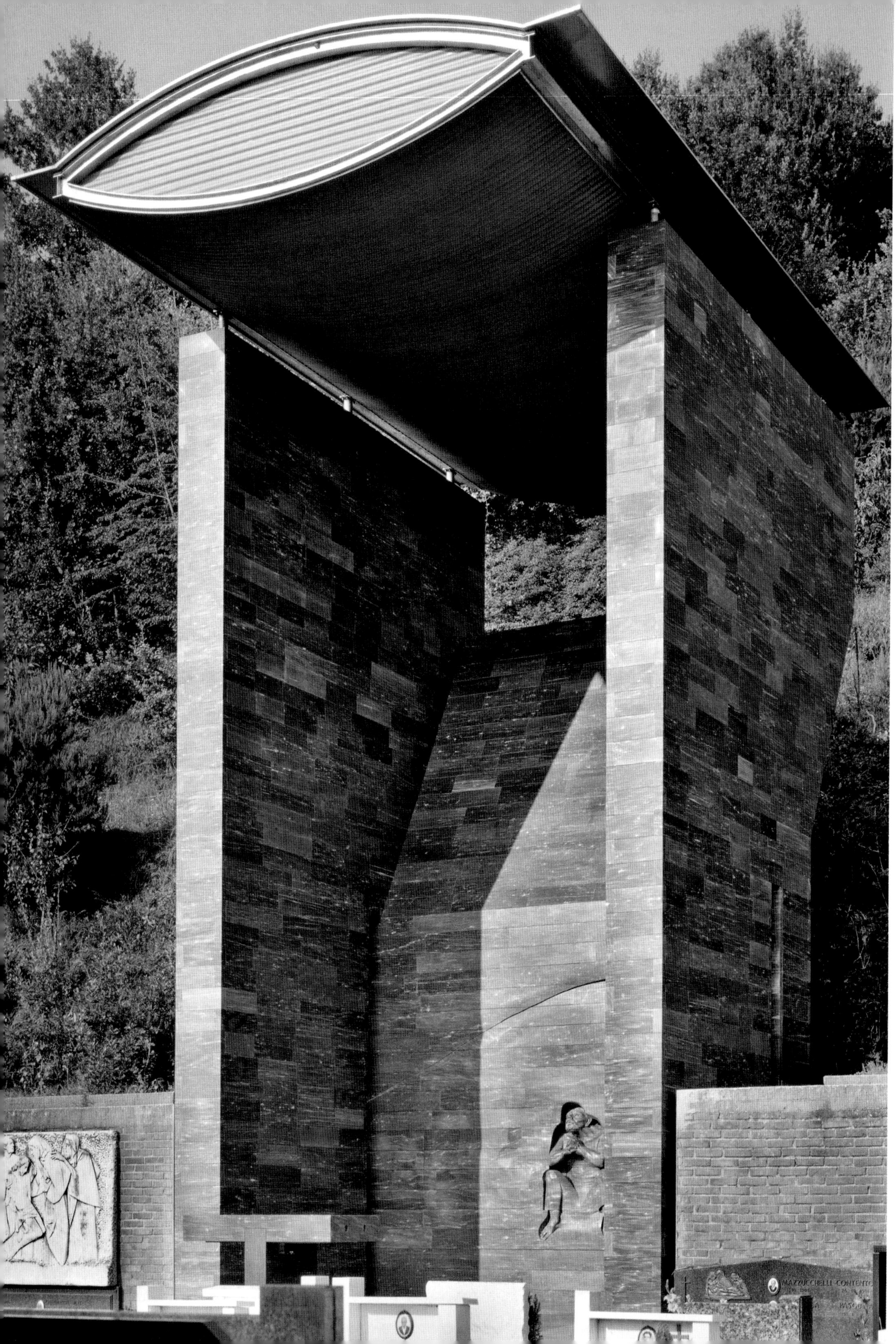
MAZZUCCHELLI CONTENTO

FUNERARY CHAPEL
AZZANO DI SERAVEZZA - ITALY

1999-2001

Archive: n° 439
Project: 1999
Construction: 2000-01
Client: Fondazione Mite Gianetti D'Angiolo o.n.l.u.s.
Sculptor: Giuliano Vangi
Partner: Engineers Marco and Ugo Davini
Volume: approximately 170 m³ / 6'000 c ft

Extremely austere in form, the chapel is set on a base from which the altar juts out along the front. On three sides, it is defined by walls that rise impressively from the ground to tilt towards the mountain, as if following its slope. The roofing is a lightweight lens-shaped metal structure that extends towards the valley to cover the altar, and it is slightly detached from the bearing walls to offer visitors a glimpse of the sky as they approach. The bearing structure is made of reinforced concrete clad with polished local Bardiglio Cappella marble that is velvety grey in colour, also used for the altar. The Italian Sculptor Giuliano Vangi used the marble of the back wall as a bas-relief portraying Job in the desert.

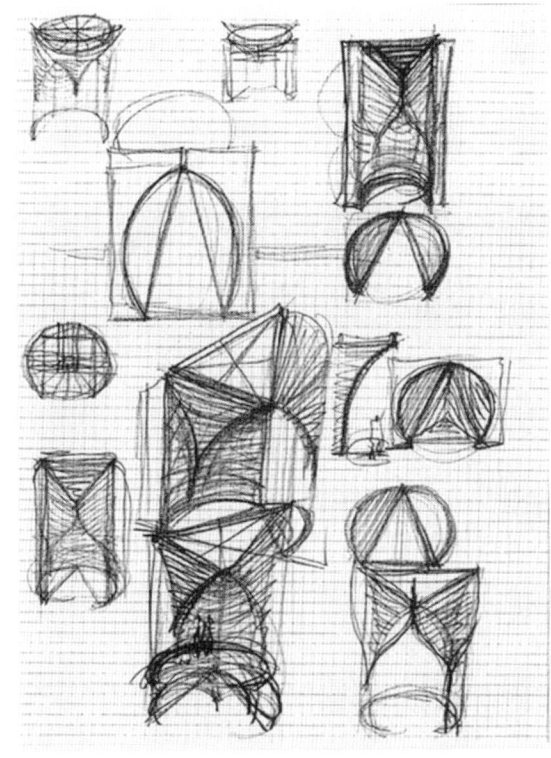

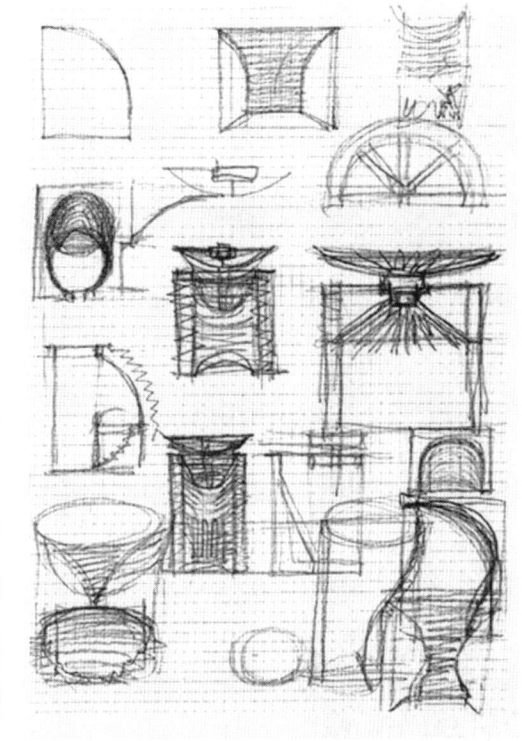

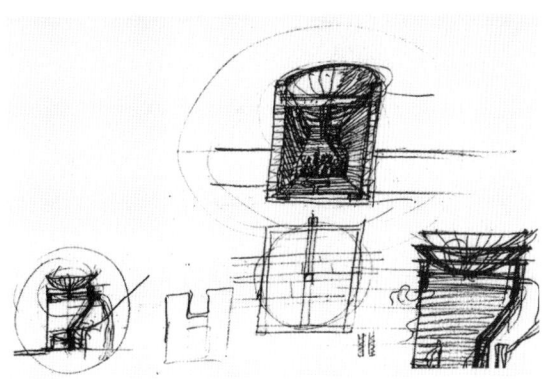

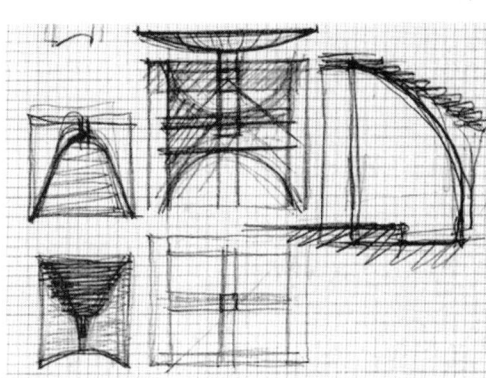

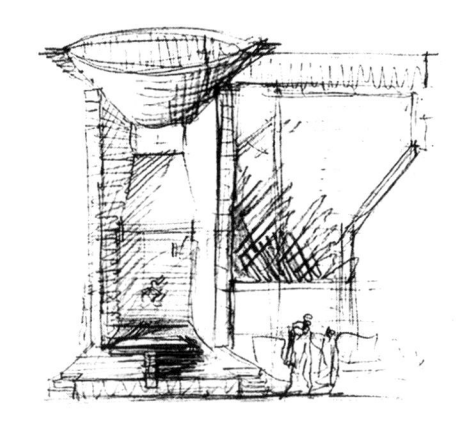

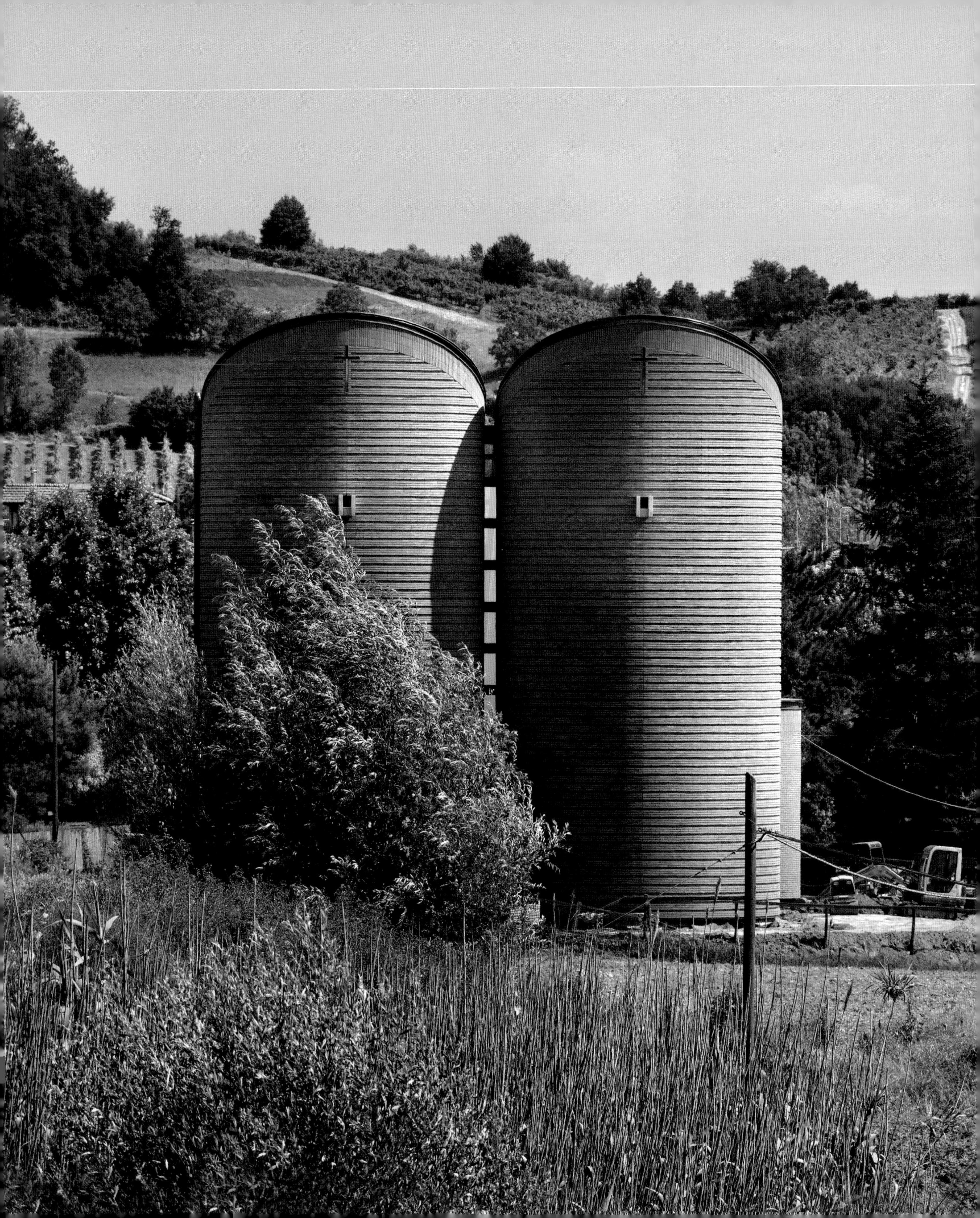

CHURCH SANTA MARIA NUOVA TERRANUOVA BRACCIOLINI - ITALY

2005-2010

Archive: n° 461
Project: 2005-2007
Construction: 2007-2010
Partner: arch. Mario Maschi
Client: Parish archbishopric of Santa Maria Bambina
Artist: Sandro Chia
Site area: 2'459 m² / 26'469 s ft
Floor area: 595 m² / 6'405 s ft
Volume : 4'700 m³ / 165'980 c ft

One can make out the new construction from the central square of the city, just beyond the historic center. The simple north-facing bi-apsidal structure defines a single internal space that is divided into two naves by a longitudinal skylight. The project aims to highlight the presence of the apsidal bodies and, meanwhile, to make the naves disappear. The exterior cladding is in terracotta bricks while the interior is in white stucco. Along the longitudinal skylight, a series of glass engravings by the Italian artist Sandro Chia virtually outlines a third nave.

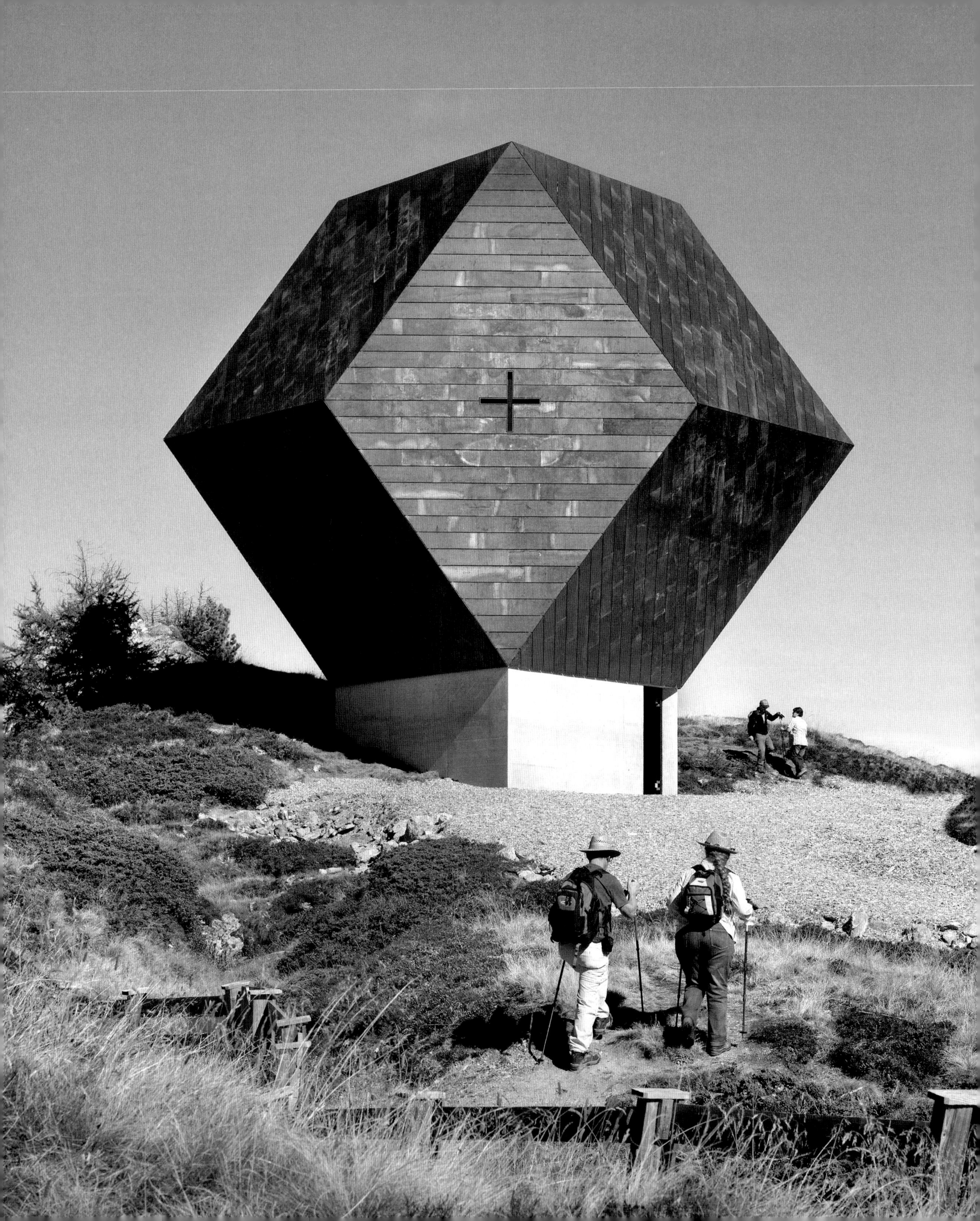

GARNET CHAPEL
PENKENJOCH ZILLERTAL - AUSTRIA

2011-2013

Archive: n° 708
Project: 2011-2012
Construction: 2013
Client: Josef Brindlinger, Christa und Georg Kroell-Brindlinger
Partner: Architect Bernhard Stoehr, Besto
Engineers: Konrad Merz, Merz Kley partner
Site area: delimited area 600 m² / 6'458 s ft
Floor area: 40 m² / 430 s ft
Volume: 750 m³ / 26'486 c ft
Artist: Markus Thurner for the wooden icon of Blessed Engelbert Kolland

The chapel gets its name from the particular mineral (garnet) that, in nature reminds a rhombic dodecahedron. The construction is set on top of a mountain at 2087m masl, next to a pond and overlooking to the north the lower Zillertal. The new building comes in the shape of a rhombic dodecahedron, set on a concrete base, with a wooden structure and covered in sheets of corten steel. From the base at ground level a staircase leads to the interior space where the visitor perceives at a single glance the evenness of the geometrical space. One single opening on the top offers a light source that brings to life the even surfaces of the walls, clad in larch wood lath. The magic of this space is the uninterrupted thanks to the light that comes streaming on the walls whose identical regular shapes produce different effects depending on the hours of the day.

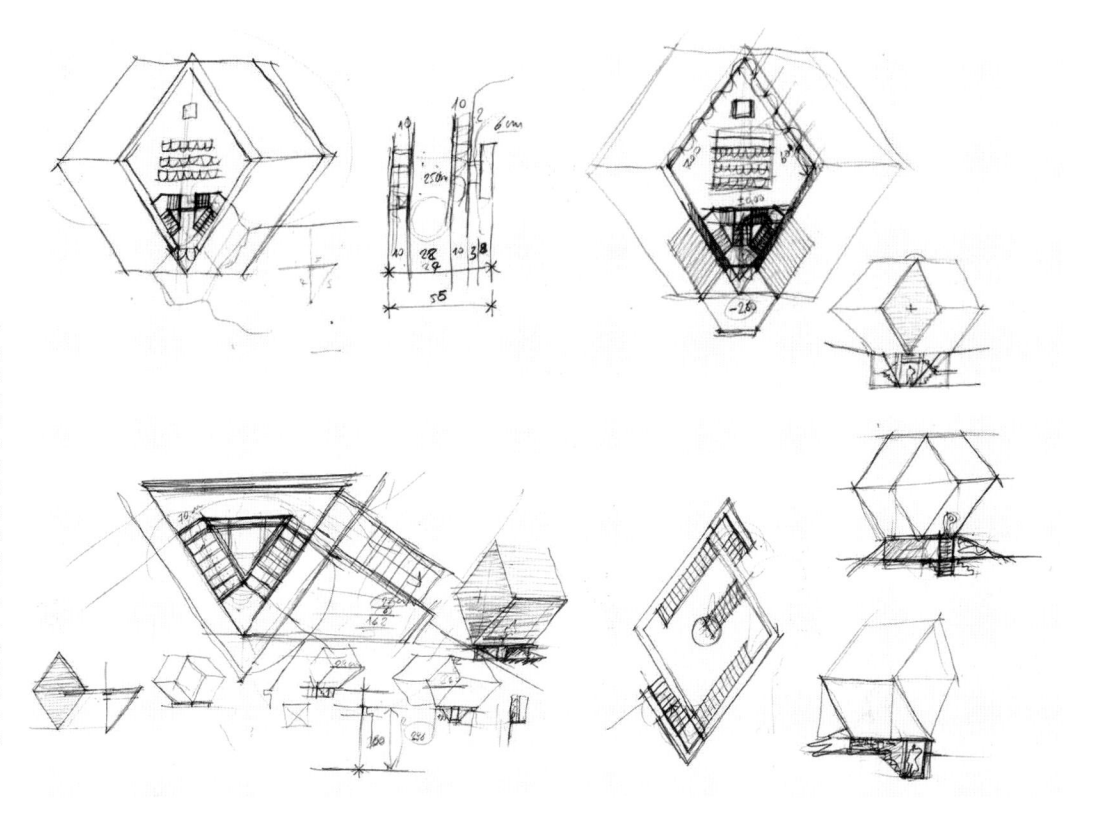

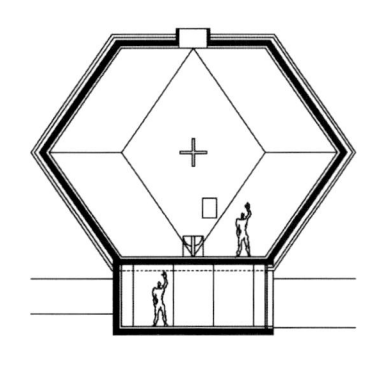

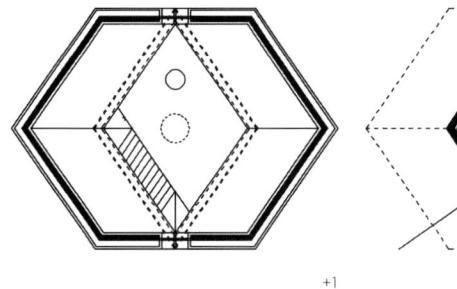

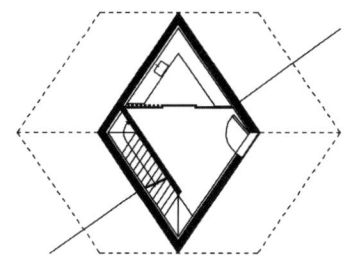

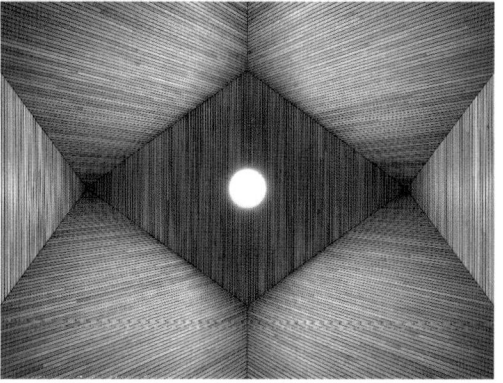

Fernando Garzoni, *Le mani di Enzo Cucchi e di Mario Botta*
Ricordo di una gita magica con Robert e June [Leaf]
Per Mario, maggio 1995, Fernando
(The hands of Enzo Cucchi and Mario Botta
I remember a magical trip with Robert and June [Leaf]
For Mario, May 1995, Fernando),
polaroid prints on cardboard with gouache,
9.84 in. x 11.81 in.
Private Collection

di Mario Botta Ricordo di una pipa magica
per Mario maggio 1995 fernando

AFTERWORD
MARIO BOTTA

> "The past as a friend"
> Louis I. Kahn

Fifty years have passed since I planned and built my first work of architecture as a young and eager "draftsman" apprentice.

At that time I was animated solely by an uncontrollable passion, which over the course of time I understood to be the underlying reason for this profession of mine: to build, stone on stone, to create and mold living space. A profession that aims at achieving that condensation of usefulness and beauty we call architecture.

Now, half a century later, I still feel disarmed vis-à-vis the mystery of the creative process; I have more experience but no certainty with regards to the responsibility of participating in the historical evolution (with the creation of living space), which inevitably, sometimes mercilessly, reflects the expression of the moral, civil, esthetic history of our time. Works of architecture become part of the real world within this context of continuous change; created as single actions they become collective works, signs of life and hope; and architects only discover at a later time that they were simply interpreters of these changes.

For this exhibition I have decided to present some works that, in my opinion, highlight my work career and, at the same time, raise some topical issues surrounding the cultural debate. They do not claim to be exemplary and I am aware of the limits and contradictions of a partial and anecdotic work in a historical time characterized by sweeping changes, be they induced by electronic revolution or globalization.

Nevertheless, in spite of the ongoing changes, the requirements concerning the shapes of space for living, working, cultural and spiritual activities are still a constant for architects, just like, and even more importantly, the landmarks concerning the city and its historical stratification; the city intended as the most advanced model of aggregation known by mankind, where the work of architecture finds its deepest reason for being.

The relationship that the new creation manages to establish with the surrounding context remains the primary issue for any form of architecture, in the search for a new quality of environmental balances.

THE TERRITORY OF MEMORY

It may sound anachronistic and out-of-place to emphasize the decisive role that the territory of memory plays in today's architectural planning process, given the specific historical context we live in and the fact that its models are inevitably influenced by the constant rushing and by the speed of changes, which swallow events day after day. This attitude may appear to be far from the prevailing concerns, especially for an architect who is constantly called upon to give shape to new life conditions.

And yet in our time, the territory of memory is a privileged space of interpretation and research, which is still able to nurture thoughts and hopes in the world of architecture: in all my life I have never met "creative talents" without a cultural obligation towards the past.

In more general terms, it is possible to observe that resorting to memory gives the measure of time to the modernity of the invention and enables a relation to be established between the new reality and a history that belongs to us, as it is the history of humanity at large. "The past as a friend", to use Louis I. Kahn's words, is not simply a poetical metaphor, but a real and true working condition in the culture of time, where it is possible to meet precious affinities and teachings, which are full of wisdom and prove to be useful when facing the complexity of the contradictions of our time.

The texture of memory is a living reality which interests us like philosophy or art history; it is a condition that follows us day after day through the achievements mankind has realized in the attempt to understand the human condition.

Looking at the past without prejudices is a way to actualize experiences which have already been consumed, rich in presences which have shaped our own identity in the course of time.

"J'existe car je me souviens" is an ineluctable condition of life that the architect, possibly more than others, has to be fully aware of as he is called upon to deal with the challenges of the creative act, which entails a transition from the well-known condition of the past to a new, unknown condition, which will forge the future.

Of course, all of this has nothing to do with the nostalgic attitude which takes obsolete life forms from models of the past and seeks to propose them again in the present.

The past, or rather the memory of the past, belongs to us only in so far as it succeeds in realizing itself in new life forms which meet the expectations of the present; it is our interpretations that legitimate the use of historical achievements and values.

In the creative process there is a condition of reciprocity between the present and the past; if on the one hand it is possible to recognize an "authentic modernity" (as it meets the needs of our time) in a historical legacy, on the other hand, it is just as evident that there is an "antiquity of the new" when the invention is able to communicate or evoke memories of times gone by or of other cultures. The works of great artists such as Picasso, Moore, Klee, Giacometti are an example; by means of an unmistakable sign of our times they have managed to convey an intense relationship with the memory of the great past.

The hidden shapes of our own origins reemerge unexpectedly in the features of the novelty, they turn up like "friendly" figures, which recall remote conditions and allow us to rediscover traces of our history. Their presence becomes the crucial condition around which the reasons of our ethical and social commitment develop. They become antibodies that help us face the traps and the precariousness of our being.

The past brings experiences which have already been consumed and which can be re-interpreted from a distance, far from the contingent reasons, from the urgencies and the pressures beleaguering the new needs.

The current architectural planning process grants less and less time for critical reflection, which is yet necessary to understand the reasons for "doing", to rediscover the intrinsic meaning of transformations.

Consequently, the memory of the past plays an even more fundamental role in preventing the new creations from turning into fragile and isolated tiles in the continuous process of work and history.

Nowadays, we are aware that the speed of transformation is directly proportional to oblivion: the faster the process of transformation becomes, the faster we are induced to forget.

The fragility of the culture of our time (ideas, life style, increase in consumption) leaves us bereft of examples and achievements that we could continue to draw on. We are asked to intervene in environmental contexts which inevitably alter the existing balances (spatial, social, economic and esthetic).

In comparison with the recent past, when environmental transformations were the result of slower processes, which lasted over a longer period of time and were almost imperceptible, generation after generation, nowadays we are confronted with fast and sweeping changes that create unease and uncertainty. Our need to belong to a territory, where we can find ourselves, is endangered: the "global" world inevitably weakens "local" certainties.

In this situation it may well be that the architect has stronger tools than other professionals, since he intervenes in a physical context where the laws of nature, from the alternation of seasons to the flowing of the solar cycle, maintain their ineluctability as conditions that can influence the ongoing transformations.

Works of architecture are usually built to last in time, beyond the life of the architects themselves, and consequently they will inevitably convey their messages to the future generations and start bearing a memory of their own.

The inertia needed for the action of "doing" becomes an antidote to the schizophrenia of transformations.

For an architect it is pleasant to imagine that his/her work will become, at least partially, history for future generations. However, for strong and shared values to emerge, the architect must work with rectitude and humility.

Making it possible for architecture to reflect the hopes of one's time has been the underlying commitment of the whole culture of the Modern Movement during the 20th century; a legitimate, ambitious goal that we know is still present in the spirit of every architecture.

THE "SACRED" SPACE

The work of architecture bears in itself the idea of the sacred.

The first act characterizing the architectural fact is the gesture of laying a stone on the ground, thus transforming a condition of *nature* into a condition of *culture*.

The work of building gives a physical shape to the space molded by the spirit of man.

By means of a "finished" configuration, the architect inevitably searches for a condition which evokes the infinite. Erecting a wall is a way to define a space, but at the same time it also creates a reference that makes it possible to interpret the surrounding context.

It is architecture itself that calls for the search of limits, between outside and inside, between light and shadow, between full and empty, between microclimate and the immensity of the universe in the accomplishment of a new immaterial reality. Beyond the threshold, the space of the "sacred" is modeled according to the different cultures and their forms of expression.

Indeed, in architecture the space of the "sacred" requires the presence of a threshold, a condition which separates inside and outside. This peculiarity is typical of architectural practice, which erects walls to create spaces.

The idea of threshold implies the condition of passage, of transition from a known situation to an unknown reality; the threshold intended as a limit expresses an expectation and a hope towards a "different" condition.

Beyond the "finished" product of architecture begins the immensity of the universe. But it is possible to speak of the need of "infinite" only through the "finite", within the completeness of the built work.

Space speaks to the spirit of man beyond its physical configuration, as Le Corbusier observed with regards to "ineffable space": "It is time to let an intuition rise, rich in experiences gained, assimilated, maybe forgotten and unconsciously reemerged. Space is within us, a work of architecture can evoke it and it can reveal itself to those who deserve it, to those who connect with the world created by this work, another world. Then the doors to a deep immensity open, erasing walls, chasing contingent presences and working the miracle of ineffable space."

The immensity prompted by the spaces created by the architect is a condition of the spirit, which, as le Corbusier mentioned, lies first of all within the soul of every single individual.

It is with this awareness that the architect creates and gives shape to spaces, with the aim of offering a better life condition in history and within the contradictions of his time. Besides the technical and functional aspects the architect pursues signs and spaces that can speak to the spirit and to the sensitivity of man, so that the ideal of beauty he aspires to can find its completion in the built shape.

Beauty is a form of possible truth in space-building, a state of mind which radiates joy in the experience of living. The beauty of architecture, intended as a form of intelligence, of culture, of knowledge, is a token of the ethical and social commitment that sometimes happily meets the expectations of mankind.

Architecture has this potential of renewing feelings which make it possible for man to be reconciled with the culture of his time, with the expectations of his soul.

To draw a space that makes it possible for people to cross the limits of the known reality is a legitimate aspiration, which has accompanied the history of mankind. This condition is evident in the historical stratification of cities, which are rich in symbolic values that go beyond everyday life.

The temple as a landmark building is a permanent feature in the organization of the "polis". Spiritual activities have always required special, dedicated spaces, albeit in different shapes; festivities, rituals, moments of prayer and silence, moments of reflection are events that recur in the course of life. In our modern, secularized society, apparently distant from the call of the spirit, it may sound out of place to speak of this kind of need. On the other hand, it is true that the various forms of religion have always accompanied mankind like a primordial and mysterious need.

The need for sacredness is present in every culture, also in those that appear to be far from it; the search for the infinite flows into the need for a new beauty that requires us to share our feelings with those of other people.

A city without places for the spirit is not a city.

It is surprising to ascertain that the places of the "sacred" have kept the simple condition of a space stretching between earth and sky; a condition of welcome, silence, meditation, rich in ancestral memories.

Compared to the living, working, leisure and institutional activities that man has built in time, the architecture of the "sacred" distinguishes itself from the "monumental" presences of collectivity by means of signs that enunciate symbolic values and contribute to enrich the stratification of the "polis".

The space of the "sacred" appears "different" compared to the other models of civil life; it is a space generated by the relationship with the context, by light, materials, geometries, where feelings rise from the tensions existing within the very same work of architecture. Of course, also from an architectural point of view, the space of the "sacred" requires to be charged with a spirituality that is able to reconcile us with the challenges of the past and the precariousness of the present. By taking risks on certain intuitions, the architect is granted, every now and again, the privilege to develop creative solutions.

There is no preset architectural standard, but a constant starting all over again, an uncertain groping which is questioned, from time to time, by the nature of the context, by history, by the prevailing sensitivity, in the search for architectural solutions that can lead to a condensation and a measure, where man can feel he is the key player in the silence of his own solitude and at the same time, if he wants to, part of a collective ritual.

Mario Botta during the rehearsals for the mise-en-scene of the *Barbiere di Siviglia* at the Opera in Zurich, December 2009

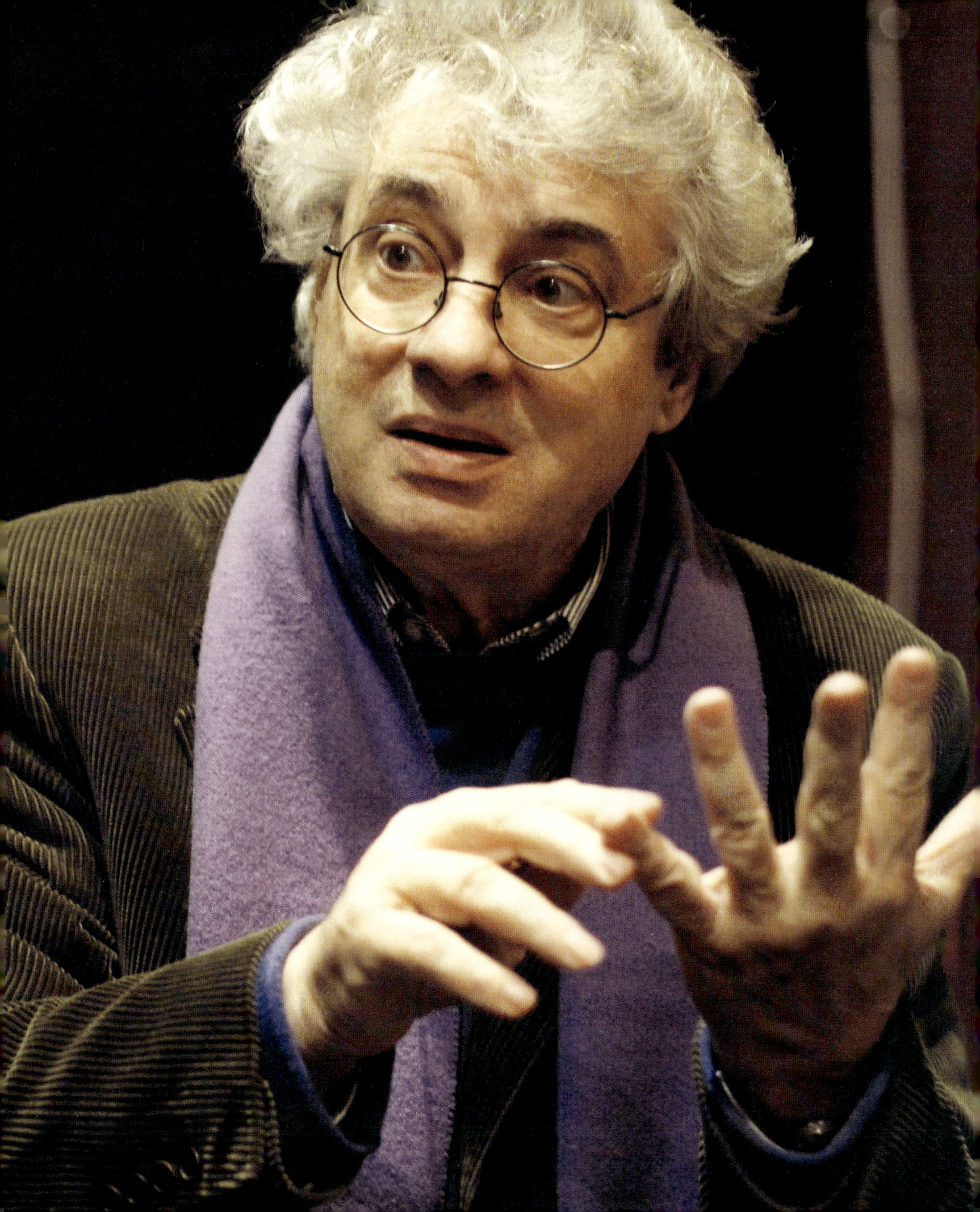

APPENDIX

BIOGRAPHY

Born in Mendrisio, Ticino, on April 1, 1943. After an apprenticeship in Lugano, he first attended the Art College in Milan and then studied at the University Institute of Architecture in Venice. Directed by Carlo Scarpa and Giuseppe Mazzariol he received his professional degree in 1969. While studying in Venice, he had the opportunity to meet and work for Le Corbusier and Louis I. Kahn.

Botta's professional career began in 1970 in Lugano. Known for his single-family houses in Ticino, his work encompasses many other building types including schools, banks, administration buildings, libraries, museums and sacred buildings. Along his work he teaches extensively in giving lectures, seminars and courses in architectural schools in Europe, Asia, North- and South America.

He served as visiting professor at the Ecole Polytechnique Fédérale in Lausanne in 1976, and at the Yale School of Architecture, New Haven, USA in 1987 and since 1983 he is entitled professor of the Swiss Polytechnic Schools. From 1982 to 1987 he was a member of the Swiss federal commission of fine arts.

Botta has always been an excellent instructor and is committed to helping others learn his trade, which led him, in 1996, to become one of the founders of the Accademia di architettura in Mendrisio (Switzerland). Today he continues to teach there as a Professor and he held the directorship in 2002-2003 and 2011-2013. By teaching at the Academy of Architecture, and as the chairman of the award jury of the BSI Architectural Foundation, Botta is able to impart his knowledge of a profession that is, first and foremost, his passion.

Since the beginning of his career, Botta's work has been recognized internationally and honored with prestigious awards such as:

1986   Chicago Architecture Award, USA
1995   European Culture Award, Karlsruhe, Germany
1996   Merit Award for Excellence in Design-AIA, California, USA
1999   Chevalier dans l'Ordre national de la Légion d'Honneur, Paris
2003   Swiss Award for Culture, Zurich
2005   Grande Ufficiale al Merito della Repubblica Italiana, Rome
2006   European Union Prize for Cultural Heritage Europa Nostra, The Hague (Netherlands)
2007   International Architecture Award, The Chicago Athenaeum Museum of Architecture and Design
2010   The Golden Award for Global Contribution in Architecture, Architecture + Design
        & Spectrum Foundation, Kuala Lumpur

A honorary member of numerous cultural institutions he has been conferred the title of *honoris causa* in different universities in Argentina, Greece, Romania, Brasil and Switzerland. Mario Botta lives and works in Mendrisio, Switzerland.

1. Mario's wife Maria Botta in the former office in Lugano
2. Mario Botta, Tobia Botta, Niki de Saint Phalle, Giuditta Botta in la Jolla, San Diego in 1996
3. Maria Botta with Tadao Ando and Tommaso Botta
4. Tullio Pericoli, Portrait of Mario Botta, 2009
Oil and pencil on canvas, 35 ⅜ in. x 35 ⅜ in.

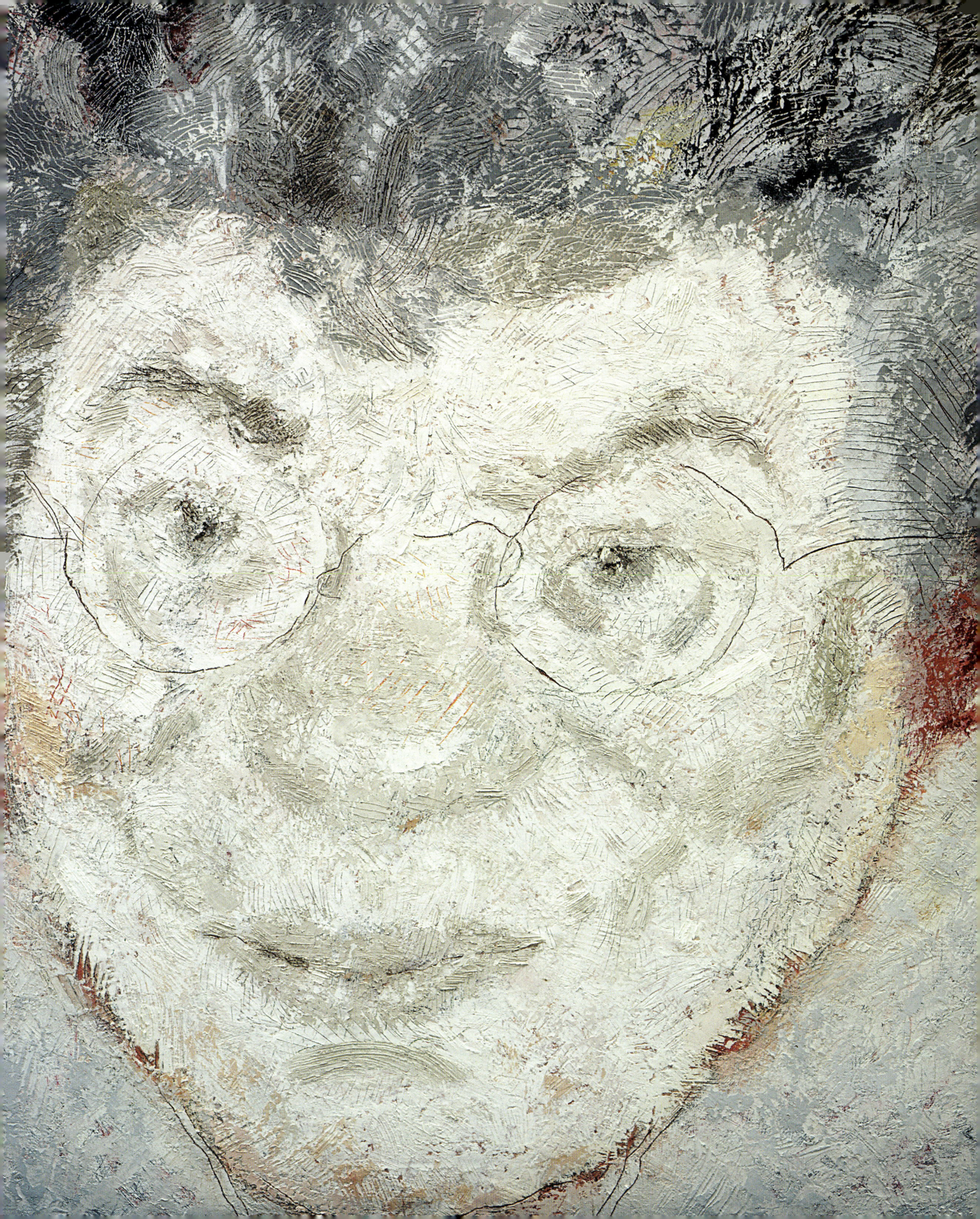

LIST OF WORKS
1959-2013

S = first draft, preliminary study
P = Project
C = Construction
CP = Competition project

1959-1969

001 Chapel San Fermo
Genestrerio, CH
S 1959

002 Family house
Morbio Superiore, CH
P 1959, C 1959

003 Parish house
Genestrerio, CH
Consultant architect Tita Carloni
P 1961, C 1962-1963

004 Family house, Stabio, CH
P 1965, C 1966-1967

004a Chapel of the Bigorio Monastery,
Sala Capriasca, CH
with architect Tita Carloni
P 1966, C 1966

005 Unified middle school
(project at IUAV- University Institute of
Architecture Venice)
S 1966

006 Family house,
Genestrerio, CH
P 1966, C 1967

007 Graduation thesis at IUAV,
Venice, I -
Mentors: Giuseppe Mazzariol, Carlo Scarpa
1969

008 Masterplan for the EPFL
Lausanne, CH
With architects Tita Carloni, Aurelio
Galfetti, Flora Ruchat, Luigi Snozzi
CP 1969

1970

009 Urban redevelopment EPUL,
Lugano, CH
P 1970

010 Elementary School,
Locarno, CH
CP 1970

010a Family house,
Ligornetto, CH
P 1970

011 Family house,
Cadenazzo, CH
P 1970, C 1970-1971

012 Extension of the railway station,
Zurich, CH
Group of architects and engineers: Giovanni
Buzzi, Aurelio Galfetti, Christina Göckel, Marco
Krähenbühl, Flora Ruchat, Luigi Snozzi, Ivo
Trümpy, Renzo Lucchini, Pietro Martinelli
CP 1970

1971

013 Public swimming-pool,
Bissone, CH
CP 1971

014 Business headquarters,
Perugia, I

with architect Luigi Snozzi
CP 1971

015 Two family house,
Vacallo, CH
P 1971

016 Family house
Riva San Vitale, CH
P 1971, C 1972-1973

1972

017 Office building,
Chiasso, CH
CP 1972

018 Kindergarden,
Stabio, CH
CP 1972

019 Altar of San Lorenzo Cathedral,
Lugano, CH
P 1972

020 Middle school,
Morbio Inferiore, CH
P 1972, C 1972-1977

1973

021 Family house,
Caslano, CH
P 1973

022 Meeting room at Bigorio Monastery,
Sala Capriasca, CH
P 1972, C 1972

023 Library of the Capuchin Monastery,
Lugano, CH
P 1973-1976, C 1976-1979

1974

024 House renovation,
Morbio Superiore, CH
P 1974, C 1974

1. 004
2. 016
3. 020
4. 045
5. 049
6. 067
7. 076

The initial number refers to the
chronological numeration of
Mario Botta's archive.
The red stands for the works
presented in this catalog.

025 Primary school,
Coldrerio, CH
CP 1974

026 Residences,
Rancate, CH with architect Luigi Snozzi
CP 1974

027 Convention center,
Samedan, CH
CP 1974

1975

028 House restoration,
Coldrerio, CH
P 1975, C 1975

028a Family house,
Villa Luganese, CH
P 1975

029 Family house,
Manno, CH
P 1975

029a House restoration,
Manno, CH
S 1975

030 Family house,
Ligornetto, CH
P 1975, C 1975-1976

1976

031 Family house,
Maggia, CH
P 1975, C 1976-1977

031a House renovation,
Cureglia, CH
S 1976

032 House renovation,
Ruvigliana, CH
P 1976, C 1976-1977

1977

033 Public gymnasium,
Balerna, CH
P 1976, C 1977-1978

034 Heat station building,
Ticino Neuropsychological hospital,
Mendrisio, CH
S 1977

035 Restoration and conversion
of the Ligrignano farmhouse,
Morbio Inferiore, CH
P 1977, C 1977-1978

036 House restoration,
Riva San Vitale, CH
P 1977, C 1977-1978

037 Craft Center I,
Balerna, CH
P 1977, C 1978-1979

038 House restoration,
Coldrerio, CH
P 1977, C 1978-1979

1978

039 State Bank,
Fribourg, CH
CP 1977, C 1978-1982

039a House restoration,
Dalpe, CH
S 1978

040 Extension of the railway station,
Zurich, CH
With architect Luigi Snozzi
CP 1978

1979

041 Family house,
Caviano, CH
P 1979

042 Family house,
Pregassona, CH
P 1979, C 1980

043 Urban redevelopment
of the *Rosshofareal*,
Basel, CH
CP 1979

044 Craft Center II,
Balerna, CH
P 1979

045 Family house,
Massagno, CH
P 1979, C 1980-1981

046 Row houses,
Riva San Vitale, CH
P 1979

1980

047 Office building,
Brühl, D
CP 1980

048 Family house,
Viganello, CH
P 1980, C 1980-1981

049 Family house,
Stabio, CH
P 1980, C 1981-1982

050 Private hospital and nursing home,
Agra, CH
CP 1980

051 House restoration,
Castel San Pietro, CH
P 1980

052 City center redevelopment,
Stuttgart, D
CP 1980

053 Science center,
Berlin, D
CP 1980

054 Renovation of the public lido,
Lugano, CH
CP 1980

055 House renovation,
Breganzona, CH
S 1980

056 House restoration,
Toscolano sul Garda, I
P 1980, C 1981

057 Multipurpose hall,
Estavayer-le-Lac, CH
CP 1980

1981

058 Family house,
Comano, CH
P 1981

059 Building restoration for hotel facilities,
Chiasso, CH
S 1981

060 *Quartier Mandinet* – urban planning,
Marne-la-Vallée, F
CP 1981

061 Residences IBA
Internationale Bauausstellung, Berlin, D
P 1981

062 Family house,
Lugano, CH
S 1981

063 Picasso Museum,
Guernica, E
CP 1981

064 Family house,
Mendrisio, CH
P 1981

065 Family house,
Origlio, CH
P 1981, C 1981

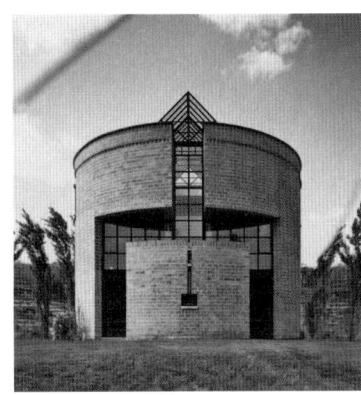

066 Restoration of the Capuchin Monastery and refurbishment of the church,
Lugano, CH
P 1981, C 1981-1982

067 Ransila 1 office building,
Lugano, CH
P 1981, C 1982-1985

1982

067a Hotel,
Melide, CH
S 1982

068 Espace culturel André Malraux,
Chambéry, F
CP 1982, C 1984-1987

069 Design: chairs *Prima* and *Seconda* for Alias 1982

070 House restoration and conversion,
Morcote, CH
P 1982, C 1982

071 Office building, *Place de la gare TGV*,
Lyon, F
CP 1982

072 Car showroom,
Agno, CH
P 1982

073 Family house,
Ronco, CH
S 1982

074 Family house,
Morbio Superiore, CH
P 1982, C 1982-1983

075 Urban redevelopment,
Klösterliareal, Berne, CH
CP 1982

076 BSI Bank (ex-Gottardo),
Lugano, CH
CP 1982/83, C 1984-1988

1983

077 Design: table *Terzo* for Alias 1983

078 Guardian's house, Villa "La Brise",
Beaulieu-sur-Mer, F
S 1983

079 Family house,
Aldesago, CH
P 1983

080 Townhall,
Rancate, CH
CP 1983

081 Reorganisation of Piazza Cavour, Ancona, I
CP 1983

082 Professional training school,
Cantù, I
P 1983

083 Siemens headquarters,
Munich, D
CP 1983

1984

084 Maison du livre, de l'image et du son,
Villeurbanne, F
CP 1984, C 1985-1988

085 Family house,
Bellinzona-Daro, CH
P 1984

086 Family house,
Breganzona, CH
P 1984, C 1986-1988

087 Exhibition design *Carlo Scarpa 1906-1978*,
Galleria dell'Accademia, Venice, I
With architect Boris Podrecca
1984

088 Design: chair *Quarta* for Alias 1984

089A Design Guscio for the exhibition *Le affinità elettive*,
Triennale di Milano, I
1984

089 House renovation,
Venice, I
S 1984

1985

090 Design: chair *Quinta* for Alias 1985

091 Design: armchair *Il Prinicipe*, *Re e Regina*, *Orientale-Occidentale* for Alias 1985

092 Design: lamp *Shogun* for Artemide 1985

093 a/b Design: Silver Jugs with Cleto Munari 1985/1989

094 Ransila 2 office building,
Lugano, CH
P 1985, C 1988-1991

095 Renovation and new urban settlement, Campo di Marte alla Giudecca,
Venice, I
CP 1985

096 Showroom ICF,
Design Center New York, USA
P 1985, C 1985

097 Offices and laboratories,
Geneva, CH
CP 1985

098 Family house,
Bosco Luganese, CH
P 1985

099 Watari-um art gallery,
Tokyo, J
with Takenaka Corporation
P 1985-1988, C 1988-1990

100 Urban residence quarters,
Turin, I
with Pierpaolo Maggiora,
Filippo Barbano, Mario Deaglio
P 1985

100a Offices and residences IBA Internationale Bauausstellung, Berlin, D
Partner: architects Bendoraitis, Gurt und Meissner
P 1985/1988, C 1989-1991

101 Provincial Parliament,
Pordenone, I
P 1985

102 Row houses,
Pregassona, CH
P 1985

103 Renovation of former Casa d'Italia,
Bellinzona, CH
P 1985, C 1985

104 Residential and office building,
Lugano, CH
P 1985, C 1987-1990

105 Urban redevelopment of Molino Nuovo area,
Lugano, CH
P 1985

106 Exhibition design *Mario Botta Architetture 1960-1985*,
Venice, I
with Achille Castiglioni
1985

1986

107 Renovation of State Bank
Bellinzona, CH
P 1986

108 Family house,
Morbio Inferiore, CH
S 1986

8. 086
9. 104
10. 116
11. 121
12. 123
13. 139

109 Family house,
Bottmingen, BL
S 1986

110 Urban development of Bicocca area,
Milan, I
CP 1986

110a Design: wand lamp *Fidia*
for Artemide 1986

111a Design: door handles FSB,
Brakl, D 1986

111b Design: table *Tesi*
for Alias 1986

112 Two family house,
Daro-Bellinzona, CH
P 1986, C 1990-1991

113 Church San Giovanni Battista,
Mogno, Valle Maggia, CH
Partner: architect Gian Luigi Dazio
P 1986/1992, C 1992-1996

114 Shopping center and hotel
Manzana Diagonal,
Barcelona, E
CP 1986

115 Bank building,
Basel, CH
Partner: Burkhardt & Partner, Basel
CP 1986/1988-1990, C 1990-1995

116 *Centro cinque continenti*
offices and residences,
Lugano-Paradiso, CH
with architect Gianfranco Agazzi,
P 1986, C 1990-1992

117 Family house,
Cavigliano, CH
P 1986, C 1988-1989

118 *Caimato* building,
Lugano-Cassarate, CH
P 1986, C 1989-1993

119 Apartment building,
Lugano, CH
CP 1986

120 Art gallery Thyssen-Bornemisza,
Castagnola-Lugano, CH
CP 1986

121 Urban redesign of Piazzale della Pace,
Parma, I
with architect Giorgio Orsini,
P 1986/92, C 1998-2002

122 Office building,
Lugano, CH
S 1986

123 Family house,
Vacallo, CH
P 1986, C 1988-1989

1987

124 Church Beato Odorico,
Pordenone, I
Partner: Piero Beltrame, Giorgio Raffin
P 1987, C 1989-1992

125 Interior of the UBS headquarter,
New York, USA
CP 1987

126 Family house,
Manno, CH
P 1987, C 1989-1990

127 Urban redevelopment,
Naples, I
P 1987

128 Exhibition design
Une architecture-trois habitats
École des Arts Décoratifs,
Geneva, CH
1987

129 Archeological Museum,
Neuchâtel, CH
CP 1987

129a Family house,
Savosa, CH
S 1987

130 Private dock,
Vésenaz, CH
S 1987

130a Design: chair *Latonda*
for Alias
1987-1988

131 Family house,
Losone, CH
Partner: architect Ennio Maggetti
P 1987, C 1988-1989

132 Church San Pietro Apostolo,
Sartirana di Merate, I
With arch. Fabiano Redaelli
and Anna Bruna Vertemati
P 1987, C 1992-1995

133 Commercial and residential building,
Chiasso, CH
P 1987

133a Bank Bruxelles Lambert,
Geneva, CH
With architect Urs Tschumi
CP 1987/1988-1990, C 1992-1996

134 Family tomb Ruppen,
Lugano cemetery, CH
P 1987, C 1992

134a Family house,
Gloucester, Mass., USA
P 1987

135 Refurbishment of a professional studio,
Geneva, CH
P 1987

136 Pavilion, Cureglia, CH
S 1987

136a Artist's workshop,
Novazzano, CH
S 1987

136b Design: armchair Obliqua
for Alias 1987-1988

136c Design: lamp Melanos
for Artemide 1987-1988

1988

137 Urban development Porte d'Aix area,
Marseille, F
With architect Aurelio Galfetti
CP 1988

138 Residence settlement,
Castelfranco Veneto, I,
With architects Luciano and Mario Gemin
P 1988, C 1994-1997

139 Residences,
Novazzano, CH
With architect Ferruccio Robbiani
P 1988, C 1990-1992

140 Renovation of the State Bank,
Bellinzona, CH
P 1988-1990, C 1990-1992

141 Via Nizzola residential and office building,
Bellinzona, CH
P 1988, C 1990-1991

142 Studies for an outdoor lamp
1988

143 Cathedral of the Resurrection,
Evry, Corbeil-Essonnes, F
Project management: Philippe Talbot &
Associées
P 1988-1992, C 1992-1995

144 New facade for the National work bank
Buenos Aires, RA
With architect Haig Uluhogian
P 1988, C 1988

145 Dimitri Theater,
Ascona, CH
S 1988

146 Administration building,
Offenburg, D
S 1988

147 Private residence,
Montreux, CH
S 1988

148 Renovation of Rothschild Bank,
Lugano, CH
P 1988

149 Multipurpose and cultural center,
Palermo, I
P 1988

150 Shopping center
Le Torri Cintoia, Florence, I
With architect Alberto Ortona,
CP 1988, C 1989-1992

151 Swisscom building,
Bellinzona, CH
P 1988-1992, C 1992-1998

152 Residential building,
Melide, CH
S 1988

153 International workshop
Napoli Sotterranea,
Naples, I
P 1988

154 Row houses,
Vacallo, CH
P 1988

155 Redesign of Piazza Cortevecchia,
Ferrara, I
P 1988

156 Mart – Museum of modern and
contemporary art of Trento and Rovereto,
Rovereto, I
With engineer Giulio Andreolli
P 1988-1992, C 1999-2002

157 Urban redevelopment of Vallée du Flon,
Lausanne, CH
With architect Vincent Mangeat
CP 1988

158 Urban developement,
Montpellier, F,
With architect Aurelio Galfetti
CP 1988

158b Theater,
Lugano, CH
S 1988

158c Design: lamp *Zefiro*
for Artemide 1988

1989

159 Family house,
Daro-Bellinzona, CH
Partner Ennio Maggetti
P 1989, C 1990-1992

160 Gas station building,
for Agip
P 1989

161 Family house,
Maienfeld, CH
P 1989

162 MoMA - Museum of Modern Art,
San Francisco, Ca, USA
With Hellmuth, Obata & Kassabaum Inc. SF
P 1989-1992, C 1992-1995

163 Office building,
Lugano, CH
P 1989

164 Family house,
Cologny, CH
Partner: architect Roger Chartiel
P 1989, C 1991-1993

165 Family house,
Aeugst am Albis, CH
P 1989

166 House extension and barn
Manno, CH
P 1989, C 1990-1991

167 National library of France,
Paris, F
CP 1989

168 Residential building,
Padova, I
With architect Nico Schiesari
P 1989

169 Tent for the 700° anniversary
of the Swiss Confederation, Bellinzona
(Sils-Maria, Brunnen, Basel, Berne, Lausanne
Geneva, Bruxelles),
With engineers Passera&Pedretti
P 1989, C 1990-1991

169b Design: chair *Botta '91*
for Alias 1991

170 Theater and redesign of the lakefront,
Lugano, CH
S 1989

171 Residence and showroom,
Zofingen, CH
Partner: architect Werner Schmutz
P 1989, C 1991-1993

172 Design: writing desk *Robot*
for Alias 1989

173 Cable car station,
Nara, CH
S 1989

174 Winery,
Napa Valley, Ca, USA
S 1989

175 Administration buildings,
Lugano, CH
S 1989

176 Administration building,
Bellinzona , CH
S 1989

177 Family house,
Montagnola, CH
P 1989, C 1991-1994

178 Office building,
Pusan, ROK
With Samoo architects, Seoul
P 1989, C 1993-1997

179 Kyobo building,
Seoul-Secho, ROK
P 1989-1995

180 HYPO-Bank,
Regensburg, D
CP 1989

181 Headquarters,
Bettlach, CH
S 1989

182 Residential building,
Carouge, CH
S 1989

183 Shopping center,
offices and theater, Varese, I
With architect Aurelio Galfetti,
CP 1989

183a Design: arm watch *Eye*
for Alessi
1989

1990

183b Design: rugs *La cattedrale*, *Marenza*,
483 nero e *483 verde rame*
for Lantal Textiles
P 1990, C 1991

184 Stand Sbarro '90, International motor
show, Geneva, CH
1990

185 CST – Swiss national youth sport center,
Tenero, CH
CP 1989/1996-98, C 1998-2001

186 Cultural Center,
San Sebastian, E
CP 1990

187 Residences and offices,
Steinfelsareal, Zurich, CH
P 1990

188 Chapel Santa Maria degli Angeli,
Monte Tamaro, CH
P 1990-92, C 1992-96

188a Exhibition design
*Mario Botta, Enzo Cucchi,
La cappella del Monte Tamaro*,
Museo d'arte cantonale, Lugano
P 1993, C 1994

189 *Palazzo del cinema*,
Venice, I
CP 1990

190 Design: studies for an ashtray
1990

191 Piazza Marconi center,
Vimercate, I
With architect Fabiano Redaelli,
PC 1990, C 1999-2001

192 Headquarters of the editorial
La Provincia, Como, I
with architect Giorgio Orsini
P 1990, C 1992-97

193 Casinò, Campione d'Italia, I
With architect Giorgio Orsini
P 1990/1998-00, C 2000-06

194 Roof for the rail net hub,
Chiasso, CH
S 1990

195 Family tomb Hernaus,
Lugano Cemetery, CH
P 1990, C 1991

196 Commercial and office center,
Mogliano Veneto, I

With architects Luciano Gemin, Giovanni Trevisan
S 1990

197 Administration building,
Lugano, CH
S 1990

198 Residences,
Carouge, CH
S 1990

199 New townhouse,
Cologny, CH
S 1990

200 Offices,
Rümlang-Zurich, CH
P 1990

201 *La Fortezza* offices and residences,
Maastricht, NL
Partner: Hoen Architecten bna
P 1990-1997, C 1997-2000

1991

202 Office headquarters
Merate, I,
With architect Fabiano Redaelli
P 1991, C 1995-1997

203 Thermoselect building structure,
Fondotoce-Verbania, I
With engineers Passera&Perdetti
P 1991, C 1991

204 Stand Sbarro '91, International motor show,
Geneva, CH
P, C 1991

205 Gas station,
Mendrisio, CH
S 1991

206 Family house for the children's village,
Rajsko-Oswiecim, PL
P 1991

207 Family residences,
Gorle, I
P 1991

208 Headquarters of the Swiss cancer league,
Berne, CH
Feasibility study 1991

209 Extension of the Swiss Parliament building
Berne, CH
Feasibility study 1991

210 Exhibition design
Mario Botta architectures 1980-1990,
Swiss cultural center, Paris-Musée Rath, Geneva
1990/1991

211 Research center and laboratories *Mapei*,
Robbiano-Mediglia, Milan, I
P 1991

212 Piazzale alla Valle quarter,
Mendrisio, CH
Partner: architect Silvano Sangiorgio
P 1991/95, C 1996-98

213 Gap Inc. Headquarters,
San Francisco, Ca, USA
S 1991

214 Ten row houses and villa,
Bernareggio, I
With arch. Anna Bruna Vertemati
and Fabiano Redaelli
P 1991, C 1995-1997

215 Renovation and extension
for a new convention center
Forum Engelberg, CH
S 1991

1992

216 State Museum,
Munich, D
CP 1992

217 Design: Screen *Nilla Rosa*
per Alias 1992

218 Cultural center,
Nara, J
CP 1992

219 Three family houses,
Montagnola, CH
P 1992

220 Office headquarters,
Geneva, CH
P 1992

221 Library Werner Oechslin,
Einsiedeln, CH,
Partner: arch. Hanspeter Kälin & Partner
P 1992/96, C 1998/2001-2004

222 Design: flower vase
for Munari
1992

223 Court roof for Sopracenerina
building,
Locarno, CH
P 1992, C 1993

224 Residences,
Monte Carasso, CH
P 1992, C 1994-1996

225 Stage design *Der Nussknacker*,
Opera, Zurich, CH
P 1992, C 1992-1993

226 Renovation of a stone barn,
Cadro, CH
S 1992

227 Home for elderly,
Novazzano, CH
P 1992, C 1995-1997

228 Friedrich Dürrenmatt center,
Neuchâtel, CH
Partner: architects Urscheler&Arrigo SA,
P 1992/95, C 1997-2000

229 Jean Tinguely Museum,
Basel, CH
Partner: Georg Steiner GSG Baucontrol,

14. 151
15. 159
16. 185
17. 221
18. 224
19. 227

P 1993, C 1994-1996
(first project Frenkendorf 1993)

230 OTAF Laboratories,
Sorengo, CH
P 1992/98 – ongoing

231 Offices, Milan, I
S 1992

232 Extension of a medical center,
Castagnola, CH
P 1992, C 1992

233 Row houses,
Merate, I
S 1992

234 Commercial and residential building,
Merate, I
With arch. Fabiano Redaelli e
Anna Bruna Vertemati
P 1992, C 1995-1997

235 Offices Dong Sung Roo,
Taegu - Seoul, ROK,
With Dow Group Architects
P 1992, C 1995-1998

236 Family house,
Mendrisio, CH
S 1992

237 Private residence,
Seoul, ROK
S 1992

238 Redesign of the townhouse square,
Morbio Superiore, CH
S 1992

239 Sporting hall,
Rivera, CH
S 1992

240 Urban development schemes for former Grand Hotel Palace area, Lugano, CH
S 1992

241 Family house,
Mendrisio, CH
S 1992

242 Extension of the *La Fonte* Foundation,
Viganello, CH
P 1992

1993

243 Family house,
Barbengo, CH
S 1993

244 Family house,
Dardagny, CH
P 1993

245 Office and commercial building
Alexanderplatz,
Berlin, D
CP 1993

246 Office building,
Mendrisio, CH
S 1993

247 Agip gas station,
Lyon, F,

With architect Marc Givry
CP 1993

248 Swiss Business Center,
Moscow, RUS
P 1993

249 Design: studies for a cloth stand
1993

250 Noise barrier on Viale Galli
and highway A2 South, Chiasso, CH
With engineers Grignoli, Martinola, Muttoni
P 1993, C 2002-2004

251 Event stage, Cornaredo stadium,
Lugano, CH
S 1993

252 Kyobo Offices,
Sangue-Seoul, ROK
P 1993, C 1994-1995

253 Residences,
Rovio, CH
P 1993

254 Building renovation,
Mendrisio, CH
P 1993-97, C 1998-2001

255 Two family house,
Ligornetto, CH
P 1993

256 Stage design *Medea-Fragment*,
Opernhaus, Zurich, CH
P 1993, C 1994

257 Design: Pins for the Swiss Cancer League
1993

258 *La Rinascente* shopping mall,
Milan-Lambrate, I
S 1993

259 Scientific high school,
Città della Pieve, I
With architect Giorgio Orsini
P 1993, C 1999-01

260 Row houses,
Vedü Alto-Merate, I,
With architect Fabiano e Ivo Redaelli
P 1993/2007, C 2008-2010

261 Thermoselect building structure,
Riazzino, CH
S 1993

262 Contempary Art Museum,
Zaragoza, E
CP 1993

263 Service area, highway A2 south
Quinto, CH
CP 1993/96, C 1997-1998

264 Municipal house and bank,
Cevio, CH
S 1993

265 Pope John XXIII Church and Pastoral center, Seriate, Bergamo, I,
Partner: architect Guglielmo Clivati
P 1993-94/2000, C 2001-2004

266 Restoration and reuse of a farm,
Rancate, CH
S 1993

267 Exhibition design *Friedrich Dürrenmatt*,
Kunsthaus Zurich, CH
P 1993, C 1994

1994

267a Expo '98
Proposal for the Swiss national exhibition,
with arch. Aurelio Galfetti, Prof. Remigio Ratti,
Jacques Pilet, Prof Jean Bergier
P 1994

268 Design: *Charlotte* chair
1994

269 Redesign of a square,
Camorino, CH
S 1994

270 Opera House,
Cardiff Bay, GB
CP 1994

271 New Parliament,
Namur, B
With architect Jean Pierre Wargnies
CP 1994

272 Urban redesign,
Legnano, I
With architect Riccardo Blumer
S 1994

273 New urban quarters former Appiani area,
Treviso, I
Partner: engineer Piero Semenzato
P 1994-2002, C 2004-2011

274 Redesign of Place de Paris,
Bruxelles, B
With architects Ph.D. Bloos and J.-P. Hoa
P 1994

275 Urban development OLVA,
Alessandria, I
S 1994

275a Renovation of the
Querini Stampalia Foundation, Venice, I
With architects Luciano and Mario Gemin
P 1993-1995, C 1996-2012

1995

276 Home for elderly and disabled,
Città di Trevi, I,
With architect Giorgio Orsini
P 1995

277 Shopping Mall,
Florence, I
S 1995

278 *Tiraboschi* Library,
Bergamo, I
With architect Giorgio Orsini
P 1995, C 2002-2004

279 Family house,
Muzzano, CH
P 1995, C 1997

280 Stage design *Ippolito*,
Theater Basel, CH
P 1995, C 1995

281 Design: studies for a table
1995

282 Villa at Monte Verità,
Ascona, CH
S 1995

283 *Noah's Ark* – Sculpture park
Jerusalem, IL,
With Niki de Saint Phalle,
Partner: architect Henry Raviv, Miller&Blum
P 1995, C 1999-2001

284 Design: watches *Blumenzeit* and *Disco*
for Mondaine
1995-96

285 Office building Werde-Areal,
Zurich, CH
S 1995

286 New Lobby Kyobo Building,
Seoul, ROK
P 1995, C 1995

287 Residences,
Bergamo, I
S 1995

288 Swatchmobil Smart Showroom
CP 1995

289 Residences, museum and library,
Carouge, CH
S 1995

290 Civic center,
Gorduno, CH
S 1995

291 Remodelling of the shop Wohnbedarf,
Zurich, CH
S 1995

292 National Basket center,
Fribourg, CH
P 1995

293 Residences,
Merate, I
S 1995

294 Restoration and renovation of
the Vincenzo Vela Museum
Ligornetto, CH
P 1995, C 1999-2001

295 Sintetica SA factory,
Mendrisio, CH
P 1995

296 Office and apartment building,
Pariserplatz, Berlin, D
CP 1995

297 Municipal Library,
Dortmund, D
Partner: arch. Gerd Vette,
eng. Klemens Pelle
CP 1995, C 1997-1999

298 Entrance gate Tarot Garden
by Niki de Saint Phalle,
Garavicchio, I
Partner: architect Roberto Aureli
P 1995-1997, C 2001

299 Leeum – Samsung Museum of Art,
Seoul, ROK
With Samoo Architects&Engineers,
P 1995-1997/2002, C 2002-2004

300 Private residence,
Seoul, ROK
S 1995

301 Pier at Faliro,
Thessaloniki, GR
With architects Morfo Papanikolaou,
Irene Sakellaridou, Maria Pollani
P 1995

302 Urban development,
Gordola, CH
Feasibility study 1995

303 Redevelopment of the former
agriculture union area,
Pordenone, I
S 1995

304 Installation for the exhibition
Design and Identity. Aspects of European Design,
Louisiana Museum,
Humlebaek, DK
P 1995, C 1996

305 Refurbishment of a private House,
Gandria, CH
S 1995

1996

306 Extension of Cassa di Risparmio,
Perugia, I
With arch. Giorgio Orsini
S 1996

307 Redesign of Lützowplatz,
Berlin, D
With Niki de Saint Phalle
S 1996

308 Nord Landesbank Headquarters,
Hannover, D
CP 1996

309 Renovation of Fondazione Rinaldi offices,
Morbio Superiore, CH
P 1996, C 1996

310 Renovation of RNB bank,
Lugano, CH
P 1996, C 1996-1998

311 Theater,
Pescara, I,
With architect Giorgio Orsini
S 1996

312 Benkert factory,
Altershausen, D,
Partner: Domo GmBH, Planungsgruppe
P 1996, C 1997-1999

313 National Galleries of Scotland,
Glasgow, GB
CP 1996

314 The *Cymbalista* Synagogue
and Jewish Heritage Center,
Tel Aviv, IL
Partner: Arthur Zylberzac
P 1996, C 1996-1998

315 Shopping malls,
Milan and Florence, I
With architect Riccardo Blumer
S 1996

20. 225
21. 273
22. 275a
23. 256
24. 294
25. 316

316 *Cumbre de las Americas* Monument,
Santa Cruz de la Sierra, BOL
With Luis Fernandez de Cordova & Roda srl
P 1996, C 1996

317 Kolonihaven Pavilion,
Copenhagen, DK
P 1996, C 1996

318 Chinese art museum,
Parma, I
S 1996

319 Design: hanging lamp *Mendrisio*
with Dante Solcà
for Artemide 1996/1998

320 Family tomb,
Stabio, CH
P 1996, C 1997

321 Residences and Municipal hall,
Viareggio, I
P 1996

322 Danish National and State Archives,
Copenhagen, DK
CP 1996

323 Avalanche shelters,
Nara, CH
S 1996

324 Extension of Epper Museum,
Ascona, CH
S 1996

325 Building renovation,
Mendrisio, CH
P 1996

326 TCS - Tata Consultancy Services Offices,
Noida-New Delhi, IND
Partners: architect Snehal Shah,
engineers Arvind G. Kelkar
P 1996-1997, C 1999-2002

327 Business center,
Saint Petersburg, RUS
P 1996

327a Tomb of Jean Marc Reiser,
Montparnasse cemetery, Paris, F
P 1996, C 1997

1997

328 Parking area, Lugano, CH
S 1997

328a Façade renovation of BSI Bank,
Mendrisio, CH
S 1997

329 Philharmonic hall,
Luxembourg, L
CP 1997

330 Kyobo Tower,
Seoul Seocho, ROK
With Chang-Jo Architects, Inc.
P 1989-1997, C 1999-2003

331 Design: studies for a door handle 1997

331a/b Design: watches MB
for Pierre Junod 1997/1998/2000

332 Orselina-Cardada funicular
station and cableway,
Locarno, CH,
With architect Paolo Pedrazzini
P 1997, C 1998-2000

333 Cultural and regional center,
Ascona, CH
S 1997

334 Presbytery for the cathedral
Santa Maria del Fiore, Florence, I
CP 1997

335 Tapestry for the Abbey
of Moutier d'Ahun, F
P 1997, C 1997

336 Cycling stadium,
Lausanne, CH
CP 1997

337 Auditorium and church,
Treviso, I
P 1997

338 Interchange hub of the
Swiss post public transport,
Bellinzona, CH
S 1997

339 Recovery of the former funicular station
of Campione-Sighignola, Campione d'Italia
Feasibility study 1997

340 Casino,
Saxon, CH
S 1997

341 New bridge,
Regensburg, D
With engineers Passera & Pedretti
CP 1997

342 *Würth* Museum,
Schwäbisch Hall, D
CP 1997

343 Hotel complex,
Saint Petersburg, RUS
S 1997

344 Spa, medical center and tourist resort,
Acquarossa, CH
S 1997

345 Lake and mountainside parking areas,
Morcote, CH
P 1997

346 Renovation of Cantonal Art Museum,
Lugano, CH
S 1997

347 Church and ecumenical center,
Malpensa airport, Milan I
P 1997

348 Family tomb, S. Lucia del Piave,
Treviso, I
P 1997, C 1998

349 Cathedral, Fàtima, P
CP 1997

350 National Bank of Athens, GR
With Morfo Papanikolaou,
Irena Sakellaridou, Maria Pollani
CP 1997/1998, C 1999-2001

351 Hotel complex,
Rochers-de Naye, CH
S 1998

352 State bank auditorium,
Fribourg, CH
P 1998

353
Fondation Martin Bodmer, Cologny, CH
Partner: studio Archilab
P 1998, C 2000-2003

353b Exhibition design
Mario Botta. Emozioni di pietra,
Palazzo Reale, Naples, I 1998

1998

354 *Campo Marzio* area development,
Lugano, CH
S 1998

355 Bank building,
Luxembourg-Kirchberg, L
S 1998

356 *Glacier 3000*-funicular station and tourist facilities,
Les Diablerets, CH
Partner: arch. Jean Nicollier & Robert Pilloud
P 1998, C 1999-2001

357 Multipurpose hall,
Montauban, F
CP 1998

358 Family house,
Königsberg, D,
Partner: Domo GmbH Planungsgruppe
P 1998, C 1998-1999

359 Exhibition design *Nag Arnoldi*,
BSI Bank (ex Gottardo),
Lugano, CH
P/C 1998

360 Design: 13 ceramic vases,
Atelier Rossicone, Milan 1998

361 University center at Milan Polytechnic
Institute, Bovisa-Gasomteri, Milan, I
CP 1998

362 Sanctuary of Notre Dame de Montara,
Maghdouche, RL
P 1998

363 Rock art museum,
Val Camonica, I
S 1998

364 Moron tower, Malleray, CH
With eng. Stampbach, Angelo Mongillo
P 1998, C 2000-2004

365 *La mattonata*
reconstruction and new walkways,
Assisi, I
P 1998

366 Crossair Lounge, Euroairport,
Basel-Mulhouse, F
S 1998

367 Design: SFMoMA watch,
Mondaine 1998

368 Interiors of Swisscom headquarters,
Milan, I
P 1998 , C 1998

369 Redesign of the exit area of the
Uffizi Gallery, Florence, I
CP 1999

370 Office building,
Chicago, USA
S 1999

371 Church façade Sant'Antonio Abate,
Genestrerio, CH,
Partner: arch. Flavio Pozzi
P 1999, C 2002-2003

372 Office and apartment complex,
Deventer, NL
Partner: Studio I'M architecten
P 1998-1999, C 2007-2009

373 Nordrhein-Westfalen
representation quarters,
Berlin, D
CP 1998

374 Residential building,
Carouge, CH
S 1998

375 Church Santa Maria Nuova,
Terranuova-Bracciolini, I
S 1998

376 San Carlino, wooden model,
Lugano lakefront, CH
With engineer Aurelio Muttoni,
Elio Ostinelli
P 1999, C 1999 (dismantled 2003)

377 Design: Jugs *Mia* and *Tua*
For Alessi 1998

377b Exhibition design
Mario Botta. Licht und Materie,
Deutsches Architektur Zentrum Berlin, D
P 1998, C 1999

1999

378 Hotel and apartments,
Schio, I
P 1999

379 Thermoselect building structure,
Giubiasco, CH
P 1999

380 Petra Winery,
Suvereto, I
P 1999-2000, C 2001-2003

381 Harting Headquarters,
Minden, D,
Partner: Planungsgruppe Minden:
Ing. Klemens Pelle, Petersen Ingenieure
PM Waltke und Halstenberg
P 1999, C 2000-2001

382 Cultural center and art gallery,
Münster, D
PS 1999

383 TCS Tata Consultancy Services offices,
Hyderabad, IND
partners: arch. Shashi Dhume, Pune Kartik Punjabi,
Shoba Bhopatkar , ing. Pangasa Semac
P 1999, C 2001-2003

384 Synagoge, Mainz, D
CP 1999

385 *Denver Millenium Marker*,
Denver, Colorado, USA
CP 1999

386 Auditorium,
Buenos Aires, RA
S 1999

387 Design: urban furniture *Pausa*
for Benkert, Königsberg, D
1999-2000

388 *King Fahd* National Library,
Riyadh, KSA
CP 1999

389 Administration buildings,
Bellinzona, CH
S 1999

390 Multipurpose and cultural center,
Varese, I
P 1999

391 Pediatric clinic, Padua, I
With arch. Gabriele Cappellato
P 1999

392 Design: studies for an outdoor lamp
1999

393 Residence buildings,
Fehlmann-Areal, Winterthur, CH
CP 1999

394 Renovation of the Leuk castle,
Leuk, CH
Partner: Studio Archpark AG
P 1999-2003, C 2003-2011

395 Church,
Reinach, CH
P 1999

396 Civic center and offices,
Denver, Colorado, USA
CP 1999

397 Museum and arts & crafts school,
Savièse, CH
S 1999

398 Urban redevelopment of the
SNCF railways properties,
Principality of Monaco
P 1999

399 University of Trento, I
With arch. Emilio Pizzi
P 1999, C 2004-2006

399a University library,
Trento, I,
With arch. Emilio Pizzi
P 1999/2005

400 Golf Club House,
Maastricht, NL
P 1999

401 Design: PET and glass bottle for *Valser*
water
P 1999, since 2001

402 Redesign of Piazza della Libertà,
Travagliato, I
P 1999

26. 326
27. 350
28. 364
29. 380
30. 381

403 New Opera House,
Oslo, NOR
CP 1999

404 Former Grand Hotel Palace area,
Lugano, CH
Feasibility study and competition program
1999

2000

405 Design: Glassware
for Cleto Munari 2000

406 Convention center, Engelberg, CH
S 2000

407 Renovation of an old manor farm,
Morbio Inferiore, CH
P 2000, C 2002-2004

408 Artwork arrangement
Cappella Sacromonte,
Varese, I
P 2000

409 Weekend houses,
Cardada, CH
Partner: arch. Ennio Maggetti
P 2000, C 2001-2002

410 University library
Rostock, D
CP 2000

410a Exhibition design
Mario Botta. Modelli di Architettura,
Centro OIKOS Bologna, I
P/C 2000

411 Shopping mall,
Mannheim, D
P 2000

412 Residences and Hotel
Jerusalem, IL
P 2000

413 Museum Udo und Annette Brandhorst
Stiftung,
Munich, D
CP 2000

414 Extension of the Swiss National Museum,
Zurich, CH
CP 2000

415 Residences,
Ascona, CH
P 2000

416 Green cross headquarters,
Mendrisio, CH
S 2000

417 Offices,
Lugano, CH
S 2000

418 Design: graphic design
for Kambly biscuit box
2000

419 Masterplan, Borgo Verde,
Vimodrone, Milan, I
S 2000

420 Mosque,
Strasbourg, F
CP 2000

421 Hotel complex, Lazise,
Lago di Garda, I
P 2000

422 Roof for central bus terminal,
Lugano, CH
With engineers Passera&Pedretti
P 2000, C 2001-2002

423 Headquarters of the
National Insurance Company,
Athens, GR
With architects Morfo Papanikolau, Irena Sakellaridou
CP 2000/2004, C 2004-2006

424 Bechtler Museum of Modern Art,
Charlotte, North Carolina, USA
Partner: Wagner Murray Architects
P 2000/2005, C 2007-2009

425 Contractor's association offices and
school SSIC, Gordola, CH
P 2000

426 Design: coffee cup
for Harting 2000

427 Residential complex,
Zermatt, CH
P 2000

427a Auditorium San Teonisto,
Treviso, I
S 2000

2001

428 Residences La vista,
Haarlemmermeer, NL
Partner: I'M architecten
P 2001, C 2008

429 Church Santo Volto,
Turin, I
Partner: eng. S. Dalmasso, Studio O. Siniscalco,
P 2001, C 2004-2006

430 Building renovation,
Vimercate, I
With architect Ivo Redaelli
P 2001

431 Hotel Grand Resort Lagonisi,
Lagonisi Island, GR
S 2001

432 Exhibition design of *Bortoluzzi*,
Art museum Mendrisio, CH
2001

433 Two family house,
Oberägeri-Zug, CH
S 2001

434 Urban development with residences
and offices,
Arcore, I
S 2001

435 Vimodrone – office towers
Borgonovo-Milan, I
P 2001, C 2007-2008

436 Tomb Giuseppe Buffi,
Bellinzona, CH
P/C 2001

437 Blessed Adolph Kolping Parish church
and centre,
Attendorn, D
P 2001, C 2006 (Parish center only)

438 Kindergarden,
Rosà, I,
With architect Giorgio Orsini
P 2001, C 2003-2004

439 Funerary chapel,
Cemetery of Azzano di Seravezza, I
With eng. Marco and Ugo Davini
P 1999-2000, C 2000-2001

440 Golf Club Hotel,
Colla Val d'Elsa, I
P 2001

441 BEIC European Library,
Milan, I
CP 2001

443 Offices De Monarch,
Den Hague, NL
P 2001

444 Office and residential building,
Leipziger Platz, Berlin, D
CP 2001

445 Fountain, Parco San Grato,
Carona, CH
P 2001

446 Hotel and residences,
Miami, Florida, USA
S 2001

447 New urban square,
Guastalla, I
P 2001

448 Restoration and renovation of the Theater alla Scala in Milan, I
Restoration work and assistance: architect Elisabetta Fabbri,
Structural engineers: BMS, Milano,
Projectmanagement: Ing. Antonio Acerbo
P 2001, C 2002-2004

449 Multipurpose hall,
Val Camonica, I
P 2001

450 Renovation and extension
of a private residence, Paris, F
PS 2001

450a Design: Vase *Tronco*
for Alessi 2001

2002

451 Requalification
and revitalisation of the old port,
Trieste, I
P 2002

452 Masterplan and re-urbanisation schemes
Falck areas, Sesto S. Giovanni, I
Feasibility study 2002

453 Complex of shops, offices and residences
Prague, CZ
CP 2002

454 Reception facilities for the faithful devoted to Padre Pio, Pietrelcina, I
P 2002

455 Design: Glass bottle
2002

456 Masterplan,
Val d'Arno, I
P 2002

457 Redesign of the main square,
Genestrerio, CH
P 2002

458 Racetrack facilities,
Monza, I
S 2002

459 Thalassotherapy center,
Spotorno, I
With arch. Fabiano Redaelli
S 2002

460 Art Center Tsinghua University,
Beijing, CN
CP 2002/2004

461 Church Santa Maria Nuova
Terranuova Bracciolini, Arezzo, I
Partner. architect Mario Maschi
P 2002/2004-2007, C 2007-2010

462 *Memorial 9/11*, Pentagon,
Washington, USA
CP 2002

463 Family houses,
Kilchberg, Zurich, CH
P 2002

464 Design: Book binding for
La Biblioteca Wittockiana 2002

465 Auditorium and multipurpose hall,
Bürgenstock, Stans CH
S 2002

466 Office and residential towers,
Pescara, I
Partner: Ing. Gianni Raducci, Caldora SpA
P 2002 C ongoing

2003

467 Administration, residential and hotel complex,
Segrate, I
P 2003

468 Public parking area
Piazza Marconi and new pier,
Stresa, I
S 2003

469 Masterplan,
Montecchio, I
P 2003

470 Mariinsky Theater,
Saint Petersburg, RUS
CP 2003

471 Headquarters for National builders' association, Lecco, I,
Project management: engineer Esilio Riva, ANCE
P 2003, C 2006-2008

472 Library, lodgings and students residence,
Cesano-Maderno, I
S 2003

473 Klinikum Minden, D,
With Planungsgruppe Minden,
CP 2003

474 Office and residential building
Unter den Linden, Berlin, D
CP 2003

475 Redesign of the church pavis,
Monselice, I
P 2003, C 2007-2009

476 Tschuggen
Bergoase– Spa and wellness center,
Arosa, CH
With arch. Gian Fanzun AG
CP 2003, C 2004-2006

477 Fountain,
Trento, I
S 2003

478 Urban redevelopment
of the former ABB areas,
Lodi, I
P 2003

479 Renovation of Dürrenmatt Kerr house,
Neuchâtel, CH
S 2003

480 School building,
Camposampiero, I
P 2003

481 Museum center,
Carrara, I
P 2003

482 Multipurpose hall,
Giussano, I
P 2003

483 Residences Parco Talenti,
Roma, I
P 2003

484 Urban requalification,
Busto Arsizio, I
S 2003

485 Family house,
Corteglia, CH
P 2003, C 2005-2007

486 Urban redevelopment with residence towers,
Genova, I
P 2003

486a New Parliament, Sofia, BG
With engineer Giulio Andreolli
CP 2003

486b Exhibition design
Mario Botta. Luce e Gravità [*Light and Gravity*]
Palazzo della Ragione a Padova, I 2003

486c Niguarda Hospital, Cà Granda,
Milan, I
S 2003

2004

487 Interiors for RSI television studio,
Comano, CH
2004

31. 383
32. 435
33. 476
34. 509

488 Spa and wellness center Eden Roc,
Ascona, CH
P 2004

488a Convention center Eden Roc,
Ascona, CH
P 2004

489 Samsung Offices, Seoul, ROK
With Samoo Architects & Engineers
P 2004, C 2005-2009

490 Re-design of Piazza Porta Mulina,
Mantova, I
P 2004

491 Art gallery Post,
La Fortezza building,
Maastricht, NL
P/C 2004

492 Tourist port facilities,
Cefalù, Sicily
P 2004

493 Office building,
Gallarate, I
Partrner: architect Luca De Risi
P 2004, C 2012

494 Urban development of Cornaredo area,
Lugano, CH,
With Daniela Baroni,
arch. Paolo Bürgi, Ing. Giovanni Pedrozzi,
Ing. Martino Singenberger-Emch+Berger AG
CP 2004

495 Piazza Castello urban requalification,
Lugano, CH
With arch. Giuditta Botta, Tobia Botta,
Tommaso Botta
CP 2004

496 Convention center Campo Marzio,
Lugano, CH
With arch. Giuditta Botta, Tobia Botta,
Tommaso Botta
CP 2004

497 Tourist facilities Bellavista,
Monte Generoso, CH
S 2004

498 Residential building and mall,
Silea, I
P 2004

499 Art and architecture museum,
Mendrisio, CH
Feasibility study 2004

500 Mineral bath and spa,
Rigi Kaltbad, CH
Partner: MLG Generalunternehmung
P 2004, C 2010-2012

501 Renovation of Istituto Don Bosco,
Maroggia, CH
S 2004

502 Cable car Tschuggen,
Arosa, CH
With arch. Gian Fanzun AG
P 2004, C 2005-2006

503 Movable puppet theater
Teatro dei sensibili of Guido Ceronetti
P 2004, C 2007

504 Design: Fountain pen
for Caran d'Ache 2004

504a Design: Table *Bello!*
for Horm srl 2004

505 Terrace roof, restaurant BSI building,
Lugano, CH
P 2004

506 Hospital,
Vimercate, I
With arch. Ivo Redaelli
P 2004

507 School campus,
Locride, I
CP 2004

508 Auditorium,
Rimini, I
P 2004

509 Office and residential building on
former Campari area,
Sesto S. Giovanni, Milan, I,
With architect Giancarlo Marzorati
P 2004, C 2007-2009

510 Renovation of a family house,
Genestrerio, CH,
With architect Giuditta Botta
P 2004, C 2006-2007

2005

511 Cultural center and museum,
Ascona, CH
CP 2005

512 Chianti cultural center,
Radda del Chianti, I
P 2005

513 Exhibition design
Mario Botta. Architettura del Sacro,
Plaster casts gallery, Art Institute, Florence, I
2005

514 Exhibition design
Mario Botta, Teatro alla Scala,
Milan, I
2005

515 Re-qualification of
former railways north properties, Saronno, I
S 2005

516 Building renovation,
Massagno, CH
P 2005

517 Winery Moncucchetto
and renovation of the farmstead,
Sorengo-Lugano, CH
P 2005, C 2007-2010

518 Chapel devoted to Mother Teresa,
Mosalp, Toerbel, CH
P 2005

519 Redesign of a piazza,
Perugia, I
P 2005

520 Reconditioning of the middle school
Morbio Inferiore, CH
P 2005, C 2011

521 Bipielle Professional training campus
Pieve Fissiraga, Lodi, I
S 2005

522 Synagogue Hall of Fame,
Berlin, D
CP 2005

523 New Opera,
Lausanne, CH
CP 2005

524 Subway hub station, Naples, I
P 2005, C ongoing

525 Power house,
Ferrero Piemonte, I
S 2005

526 Design: chair for Rudolf Steiner
school,
Locarno
2005 (auction)

527 Architecture theater,
Mendrisio, CH
P 2005-2010

528 Family house,
Minusio, CH
S 2005

529 Exhibition contribution to
The 21st Century: New Museums,
Art Centre Basel
2005

35. 471
36. 517
37. 552
38. 553
39. 584

530 Car park, Piazza del Ponte,
Mendrisio, CH
P 2005

531 Design: Mirror *Mamanonmama*
For Horm 2005

532 Exhibition design
Mario Botta. Prayers of stone
RIBA Royal Institut of British Architects,
London, GB 2005

534 Residential towers,
Genova, I
S 2005

535 Urban redevelopment of former
industrial areas Oerlikon, Milan, I
S 2005

537 Exhibition design *Mantegna*,
Musei Civici agli Eremitani–Civic Museum,
Padua, I
P 2005, C 2005

538 Exhibition contribution
at AEC World Expo, Mumbai, IND
2005

539 Residential and office building,
Mendrisio, CH
P 2005, C 2011

540 Facade redesign of factory,
Rho-Milan, I
P 2005

541 Convention center at the
former general store houses,
Verona, I
P 2005/2010

542 Design: Pewter vases for Numa Design
by Roberto Zani 2005

543 Design: box and butterfly
for Riva Mobili 1920, 2005

545 Administration center and residential
building,
former Riello area,
Legnago, I
P 2005

546 State police headquarters,
Padua, I,
With arch. Gabriele Cappellato
P 2005

547 Central mosque,
Cologne, D
CP 2005

548 Residences Dogok Dong,
Seoul, ROK
P 2005

549 Shopping mall,
Forte dei Marmi, I
P 2005

550 Neri Pozza Funeral chapel,
Longara Vicenza, I
P 2005/09, C 2012

551 Design: table 01-04-43
For Riva Mobili 1920,
2005/2008

552 Agora Center,
Je Ju Island, ROK
With Samoo Architects & Engineers
P 2005, C 2008

553 Winery Château Faugères,
St. Emilion, F
Partner: arch. Serge Lansalot
P 2005-2006, C 2007-2009

2006

554 Design: table *Variabile*
for Riva Mobili 1920, 2006

555 Masterplan for a hotelcomplex,
appartments and funicular station,
Celerina, CH
P 2006

556 Redesign of a building facade,
Lugano, CH
S 2006

557 CST3 - Extension of the
Swiss National Youth Sport Center,
Tenero, CH
CP 2006/2008-2009 C 2010-2013

558 Bibliotheca Alexandrina,
Alexandria, ET
CP 2006

559 Stadium, Saint Petersburg, RUS
CP 2006

560 Urban reorganisation of Piazza Matteotti,
La Spezia, I
P 2006

561 Great Mosque,
Zarqa, HKJ
P 2006

562 Parish church of San Rocco,
San Giovanni Teatino, I,
Partner: arch. Walter Di Renzo,
Ing. Ezio Dante
P 2006, C ongoing

563 Requalification of Bracco areas,
Milan, I
S 2006

564 Bipielle bank building renovation,
Lugano, CH
S 2006

565 Churchyard redesign
St. Marienkirche, Hamburg, D
S 2006

566 Hotelcomplex,
Marina di Carrara, I
Partner: eng. Giuseppe Fruzzetti
P 2006, C ongoing

567 Palazzo del Cinema – Movietheater and
Festival convention center,
Locarno, CH
P 2006

568 Fossil museum and visitor center
Monte San Giorgio,
Meride, CH
P 2006, C 2010-2012

569 Würth cultural center,
Gaisbach, D
CP 2006

570 Exhibition design
Teatro dei sensibili di Guido Ceronetti,
Turin, I
2006

571 Urban redevelopment Isotta Fraschini
areas,
Saronno, I
P 2006

572 Building complex renovation,
Padua, I
P 2006

573 Design: Coffeemachine Hausbrandt
S 2006

574 Masterplan, I
Manazel City
S 2006

575 Apartment buildings,
Sarzana, I
P 2006

576 *Il Giardino di Marihn*
Ideas for the re-planning of *Schloss Marihn* Park,
Schwerin D
With Andreas Kippar
S 2006

577 Church of the Cross,
Nazareth, IL
S 2006

578 Urban planning
Dong Gang, ROK
CP 2006

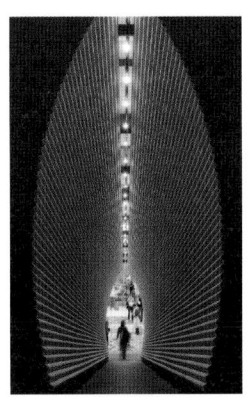

579 Urban replanning former San Paolo area,
Milan, I
P 2006

580 Residential quarter,
Trezzo sull'Adda, I
P 2006

2007

581 Church yard redesign
St. Marienkirche, Hamburg, D
Feasibility study 2007

582 Design: watches MB,
pour Pierre Junod 2007

583 Exhibition design *Ferroni*,
Palazzo della Ragione, Bergamo - Accademia
di Carrara, I
2007/2008

584 *Guscio* – Shell for Confindustria
Ceramica,
Triennale, Milan, I
P 2007, C 2007

585 XiXi Wetland Museum,
Hangzhou, CN
CP 2007

586 Winery Péby Faugères,
St. Emilion, F
P 2007/2010

587 Apartment renovation,
Via Manzoni, Milan, I
P 2007, C 2007

588 Hotel and residences, Pistoia, I
P 2007

589 Offices and residences,
Genova, I
P 2007

590 Exhibition design *Tiziano*,
Palazzo Crepadona, Belluno, I
P 2008, C 2008

591 Exhibition design *les Mythes de Dürrenmatt*
Fondation Martin Bodmer, Cologny/
Fondazione Querini Stampalia Venice/
Centre Dürrenmatt, Neuchâtel/
Benaki Museum, Athens
P 2005, C 2005-2007

592 Cloister,
Cademario, CH
CP 2007

593 Biomedical Institute,
University of Padua, I
P 2007, C 2011-2013

594 Belvedere tower,
Carate Brianza, I
S 2007

595 Masterplan, II
Manazel City UAE
S 2007

596 Masterplan new urban quarters,
Caravaggio-Bergamo, I
Feasibility study 2007

597 Residences,
Guangzhou, CN
P 2007

598 Martyr square,
Beirut, RL
S 2007

599 Bidv-tower,
Ho Chi Min, VN
CP 2007

600a/b Public thermal bath and
residences
Bäderquartier Baden, CH
P 2007/2008-2012

600c Renovation of former
hotelquarter Verenahof, Bäderquartier,
Baden, CH
S 2009

601 Urban planning - masterplan
Municipality of Sarzana, I
P 2007

602 Hotel Laorina, Sarzana I
S 2007

603 Extension Continental Hotel,
Lugano, CH
S 2007

604 Exhibition design *Giancarlo Vitali*
ANCE a Lecco, I
P 2007, C 2007

605 Mawared Corporate Center
Amman, HKJ,
Partner: Faris&Faris architects
P 2007

606 Kostantinovsky convention center,
Saint Petersburg, RUS
Feasibility study 2007

607 Holiday resort Solaria,
Davos, CH
S 2007

608 Exhibition design *Omar Galliani*,
Fondazione Querini Stampalia, Venice, I
With arch. Mario Gemin 2007

609 Park and shopping mall,
Saronno, I
P 2007

610 Mapei headquarters,
Mediglia, Milan, I
S 2007

611 Zorlu Center,
Instanbul, TR
CP 2007

612 Twleve at Hengshan road boutiquehotel,
Shanghai, CN,
Partner: ECADI East China
Architectural Design&Research Institute Co. Ltd
P 2007-2009, C 2010-2012

613 Swiss Embassy,
Moscow, RU
CP 2007

614 Swiss federal criminal court,
Bellinzona, CH
CP 2007

615 New Station,
Saronno, I
P 2007

616 Restoration and extension
of former Folonari caves,
Brescia, I
P 2007

617 Urban redevelopment of
former Terni areas Darfo Boario Terme,
Brescia, I
S 2007

618 Johor Iconic Park Competition, MAL
CP 2007

619 Tazio Nuvolari Museum,
Mantova, I
S 2007

620 Residences,
Hangzhou, CN
P 2007

621 Redesign of Piazza Roma,
Piazza Mazzini, Piazza Matteotti, Modena, I
P 2007

622 Redaelli chapel,
Sartirana, I,
With architect Ivo Redaelli
P 2007, C 2008

623 Arkade and landscape architecture
of a private House,
Porto Rotondo Sardegna, I,
with architec Ivo Redaelli
P 2007, C 2008-2009

624 Abitcoop residences
Liguria Genova,

Vado Ligure, I
P 2007

2008

625 *Fondazione Olgiati* offices, CH
Feasibility study 2008

626 Belvedere tower,
Wädenswil, CH
CP 2008

627 University museum of science and arts
(MUSA) Falck areas,
Sesto San Giovanni, I
P 2008

628 Replanning Mazzini park,
Salsomaggiore, I
P 2008

629 Hotel Resort,
Kohkrobei Island, K
S 2008

630 *Palestine Rememberance* Museum
S 2008

631 Design: Pendant R1920,
for Riva Mobili 1920,

2008

632 Masterplan of Valmadrera, I
S 2008

633 Facade remodelling, exhibition and fair center
Campo Marzio Nord, Lugano, CH
P 2008

634 Woman's hospital –
Nursery extension
S. Maria, Castellanza, I
Feasibility study 2008

635 Design of Piazza della Visitazione,
Matera, I
CP 2008

636 Shopping mall, residences and hotel complex,
Curno, Bergamo, I
S 2008

637 East Library Tshingua University,
Beijing, CN
Partner: CABR-China Academy of Building Research
P 2008, C 2011-2012

638 Extension of
National Latvian Opera,
Riga, LV
S 2008

639 Private residence and art gallery,
Meggen, CH
S 2008

640 Design table for the multipurpose room of Santo Volto parish center, Turin
With Riva Mobili 1920
P 2008, C 2008

641 The architecture theater,
Mendrisio, CH
P 2008 Project variation

642 Exhibition design
Andrea Brustolon, Palazzo Crepadona,
Belluno, I
P 2008, C 2009

643 *Korean Air* Songhyeon-Dong Residences,
Jongno-Gu, Seoul, ROK
P 2008

644 Art gallery extension,
BSI building (ex Gottardo),
Lugano, CH
S 2008

645 Masterplan Porta Mulina,
Mantua, I
Feasibility study 2008

646 Redesign of Piazza Malatesta, Rimini, I
Feasibility study 2008

647 Office building,
Curno - Bergamo, I
S 2008

648 Kindergarden,
Curno - Bergamo, I
S 2008

649 Residence building,
Lecco, I
S 2008

650 Funeral chapel,
Sesto San Giovanni, Milan I
S 2008

651 Design: Plinth for sculptures
by Federico Zeri, Bergamo
P 2008

652 Design: table Ponte
for Cleto Munari
P 2008, C 2009

653 First aid center,
Mendrisio, CH
CP 2008/2009-2010, C 2013 ongoing

653a Requalification and urban park planning,
Mendrisio, CH
S 2008

654 Design: Mug – the Mug company,
Könitz Porzellan GmbH
2008-2010

655 Design: remodelling of a ball FIGC
2008 (auction)

656 Design: heart redesign for Art4me
Milano 2008 (auction)

657 European Embankment Project
Saint Petersburg, RUS
P 2008

658 Restaurant interiors and furniture,
Lugano, CH
P 2008

2009

659 Villa Pedagna,
Arquà Tetrarca, Padua, I
S 2009

660 Design: Stool *Clessidra*
for Riva Mobili 1920, 2009

661 Guscio Installation for Confindustria Ceramica Cersaie,
Meatpacking district, New York USA
S 2009

662 Exhibition design
MarioBotta. Architetture 1960-2010,
Mart, Rovereto, I
P 2009, C 2010

663 Urban redevelopment
of former fishmarket Claudio Ponte Vetero,
Milan, I
Feasibility study 2009

664 Joinery, *Fondazione OTAF*
Lugano-Sorengo, CH
P 2009, C 2012-2013

665 Stage design *Il Barbiere di Siviglia*,
Opera, Zurich, CH
P 2009, C 2009

666 Headquarters of the Provincial offices,
Bergamo, I
With architect Emilio Pizzi
CP 2009

667 Church and parish center,
Leipzig, D
CP 2009

668 Design: Rug Anatolia 2010
With Cleto Munari for Moret
2009/2010

669 Church of the Nativity,
Culiacan, MEX
S 2009

40. 665
41. 660
42. 612

670 Exhibition design
Giancarlo Vitali at GAM,
Milan, I
P 2009

671 Furniture and altar for Sanctuary of
Church Madonna dei Miracoli,
Motta di Livenza Treviso, I
S 2009

672 Lotte Hotel and Duty Free Project,
Je Ju, ROK
Feasibility study 2009

673 Office building,
Genk, B
With Architectenburo B BVBA
P 2009, C 2011-2013

2010

674 Reuse of a building for the regional library,
Mendrisio, CH
Feasibility study 2010

675 Design: *Bricolages*
for Riva Mobili 1920,
2009/ 2010

676 Residence building,
Losone, CH
P 2009, C ongoing

677 House renovation,
Mendrisio, CH
P 2010, C ongoing

678 Design: Charity Chair – AIT for Dietiker
2010 (auction)

679 Office and residential building
Caldora, Pescara, I
P 2010

680 Parish center of the *Devine Providence*,
L'Viv, UK
P 2010-2012, C ongoing

681 Residences
Calvasina, Valmadrera, I
Feasibility study 2010

682 Reuse of the Montecolino area,
Bilzone d'Iseo, I
Feasibility study 2010

683 Requalification and redesign
of former Vismara production areas,
Vismara, Casatenova, I
Feasibility study 2010

684 Villa, Wuxi,
Shanghai, CN
S 2010

685 Tomb *Tony Scott*,
Salemi Cemetery, Sicily,
P 2010

686 Beach and bathing center Tenero, CH
CP 2010

687 Planning of new quarters,
Agno, CH
S 2010

688 Design: Logo for the Fondazione Amici
Centro Insubrico Cattaneo Varese, 2010

689 New ambo for the Cathedral,
Florence, I
CP 2010

690 Fountain for the Millenial anniversary,
St. Blaise, CH
P 2010, C 2011

691 Memorial Francesco Cabrini,
Central Station, Milan, I
P 2010, C 2010

2011

692 Replanning of Guidino Park,
Lugano-Paradiso, CH
P 2011

693 University Campus,
Lugano, CH
CP 2011

694 Multi purpose hall,
Morbio Inferiore, CH
CP 2011

695 Design: Stanza – the room,
installation for Interni Mutant Architecture
& Design,
Università degli Studi, Milan, 2011

695A Design: marble vases
with GVM Carrara
2011

696 Family house,
Montagnola, CH
S 2011

697 House renovation,
Morbio Superiore
P 2011, C 2012 ongoing

698 Headquarters of the power company
Ticino, Monte Carasso, CH
CP 2011

699 Tourist resort,
Serpiano, CH
CP 2011

700 Rhodania hotel,
Crans Montana, CH
Partner: Jean Pierre Emery
P 2011

701 Exhibition design
Andrea Martinelli,
Museo Pecci, Prato, I
P 2011, C 2011

702 Additional parking lot, family house,
Vacallo, CH.
P 2011

703 Exhibition design *Nag Arnoldi*,
Palazzo Reale, Milan 2011

704 Family house,
Sementina, CH
P 2011 C ongoing

705 Wellness center,
Savognin, CH
CP 2011

706 Design exhibition *Omar Galliani*,
Poldi-Pezzoli Museum, Milan, I
P 2011

707 Family house,
Giubiasco, CH
P 2011 C ongoing

708 Garnet chapel Penkenjoch,
Finkenberg-Zillertal, A
With architect Bernhard Stoehr
P 2011-2013 C 2013

709 *Les thermes de la Dixence* –
thermal baths and hotelcomplex,
Hérémence, CH
P 2011

710 Design: Rug *Moncucchetto*
P 2011

711 Raiffeisen Bank building,
Melano, CH
CP 2011

712 Basilica
In the shrine of our Lady of the Rosary
Namyang, Seoul – ROK
P 2011

713 Family house,
Corteglia, CH
P 2011

714 Visitor center and hotelcomplex,
Campo Marzio Nord Lugano, CH
CP 2011

715 Residential building,
Lugano-Paradiso
P 2011

43. 716
44. 747

716 New Campus Luxun Academy of Fine Arts,
Shenyang, CN
P 2011-2012

717 Apartment building,
Muggio, CH
P 2011

718 Restaurant Villa Lalique,
Wingen-sur –Moder, F
P 2011

719 Civic center, office and residential building,
Sorengo-Cortivallo, CH
CP 2011

720 Urban Replanning and building reuse,
Martinengo, Bergamo, I
S 2011

721 *Knowledge Centre*,
University of Ahmedabad
With Snehal Shah,
P 2011

722 Design: library-stool for Riva R1920,
2011

723 Residential building complex,
Losone, CH
P 2011, C ongoing

2012

724 Design exhibition *Italo Valenti*, Museo della Permanente, Milan 2012

725 Design exhibition
Mario Botta Vasi,
Galleria Antonia Jannone, Milan, I
2012

726 Restructure of an old stone house,
Semione, CH

727 Reuse of fomer Caserme Passalacqua and S.ta Marta areas for residences, Verona
PS 2012

728 Design: toy for Tobeus
S 2011

729 Refurbishment of Corso Bettini,
Rovereto, I
P 2012

730 House of Prayer and Learning,
Petriplatz,
Berlin, D
CP 2012

731 Restoration of the chancel,
Abbey of Viboldone
PS 2012

732 Theater Giuseppe Verdi,
Terni, I
PS 2012

733 University campus SUPSI,
Mendrisio, CH
CP 2012

734 University campus SUPSI –
Urban requalification railway station area north
Lugano-Massagno, CH
CP 2012

735 Refurbishment and renovation of the Swiss cultural institute Villa Maraini, Rome, I
S 2012

736 Swiss embassy residence and offices,
Seoul, ROK
CP 2012

737 Urban planning scheme
Erba city center,
Erba, I
S 2012

738 Urban requalification
former bus station areas,
Rovereto-I
CP/S 2012

739 Masterplan for requalification of former industrial areas Qingdao – CN
PS 2012

740 *Palazzo del Cinema*-Movietheater
Locarno, CH
CP 2012

741 Chinese ceramic Museum,
Nanchang, CN
P 2012

742 Urban redesign "Les Rives" quarter,
Bruxelles, B
with De Bloos,
PS 2012

743 Chapel and Clarisse convent,
Laurenzerbad
St. Laurenzen, CH
PS 2012

744 Cheese factory,
Bignasco, CH
PS 2012

745 Design exhibition
Mario Botta Zeichnungen und Modelle,
Kornfeld Art Gallery, Berne
P 2012 C 2013

746 Renovation of Cornaredo stadium and urban redevelopment for sport and event facilities, Lugano, CH
CP 2012-2013

747 Restaurant Vetta and tourist facilities
Monte Generoso, CH
P 2013

748 Design: Genes-library wooden display support,
Genes-company, Basel
P 2012 C 2013

2013

749 Residential complex,
Balerna, CH
P 2013

750 Annexe store building, Villa Turconi,
Mendrisio, CH
P 2013

751 Facade redesign of industrial building,
Contone, CH
P 2013

752 Renovation of a private House
Meride, CH
P 2013

753 *Complete works Mario Botta 1960-2013*, monographical overview by Tongji University press, Shanghai
P 2013

754 Ticino Art and crafts' school
for tailoring and dress technique, Chiasso, CH
CP 2013

755 Design: Chaise Morelato
for the MAAM Museo delle arte applicate nel mobile – Museum for applied arts in furniture, Fondazione Aldo Morelato,
Cà de lago, Cerea, I

756 Home for elderly San Rocco,
Morbio Inferiore, CH
S 2013

757 Observatory and visitor center Uecht,
Niedermuhlern-Berne, CH
S 2013

758 Design Business District,
Changchun - CN
S 2013

759 New Altar for the Rotonda of the San Vittore Prison,
Milan, I
PS 2013

760 Elementary school,
Tenero, CH
CP 2013

761 Luxury Resort
Nanxijiang Wenzhou , CN
S 2013

PERSONAL EXHIBITIONS

Mario Botta. Opere e progetti
14.11.-25.11.1977 Technische Universität Vienna, Austria
12.1979 Columbia University, New York, USA
15.10.-20.11.1979 Syracuse University, Syracuse N.Y., USA
15.12.1979-02.03.80 XVI Triennale di Milano, Milan, Italy
02. 1980 University of Virginia, Charlottesville, USA
08.03.-25.03.1980 Facoltà di architettura Università di Palermo, Italy
03.04.-24.04.1980 Blueprint: For Architecture, Seattle, Washington, USA
14.04.-05.05.1980 Istituto Nazionale di Architettura (IN/ARCH), Rome, Italy
06.06.-20.06.1980 École d'Architecture Université de Genève, Switzerland
05.11.-19.11.1980 École Polytechnique Fédérale Lausanne, Switzerland
12.1980 Technische Universität Braunschweig, Germany
01.1981 Hochschule für Gestaltende Kunst und Musik, Bremen, Germany
13.03.-10.04.1981 Stichting Architectuur Museum Amsterdam, Netherlands
25.05.-11.06.1981 Galerie Mara, Fribourg, Switzerland
09.11.-30.11.1981 Palais des Beaux-Arts, Bruxelles, Belgium
24.11.-17.12.1981 Gallery at the Old Post Office Dayton, Ohio, USA

La arquitectura de Mario Botta
09.- 10.1980 Centro de Arte y Comunicacion (CAYC), Buenos Aires, Argentina
10.08.-20.08.1981 Escola de Arquitectura da UFMG, Belo Horizonte, Brasil

Un cilindro da abitare
21.09.-23.09.1981 Studio Marconi, Milan, Italy

Architettura di Mario Botta
10.12.-24.12.1981 Casa del Movimento, Pecs, Hungary
05.03.-30.03.1982 J. Galeria (Jozsefvarosi Kiallitoterem), Budapest, Hungary

Incontro con Alberto Sartoris
27.05.1982 Centro Internazionale d'Arte, Stabio, Switzerland

Mario Botta,
02.06.-16.06.1982 Instituto de Arquitectos do Brasil, Galeria do IAB*, Rio de Janeiro, Brasil

"Prima & Seconda". Due sedie di Mario Botta
17.09.-22.09.1982 Studio Marconi Centro Culturale, Milan, Italy

Mario Botta. Dans le paysage comme un poing sur la table
07.12.1982-12.02.83 IFA Institut Français d'Architecture, Paris and Musée Savoisien, Chambéry, France

Arquiteto Mario Botta
12.03.-28.03.1983 Instituto dos Arquitectos do Brasil, San Paolo, Brasil

Mario Botta
07.05.-31.05.1983 Sala del Rettorato, Ancona, Italy

Mario Botta 1961-1982
03.09.-12.10.1983 Historisches Archiv, Köln, Germany

Preliminary studies. Mario Botta
08.09.-14.10.1984 GA Gallery, Shibuya-ku, Tokyo, Japan
17.10.-25.11.1984 Architektur - Galerie am Weissenhof, Stuttgart, Germany

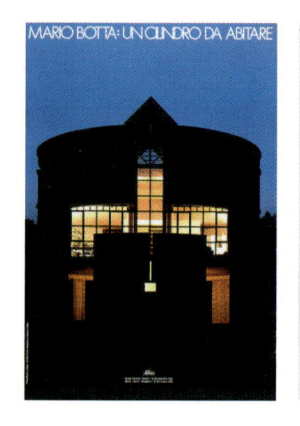

1. Poster of the exhibition *Un cilindro da abitare*, Milan, 1981
2. Poster of the exhibition at the Gallery Weissenhof in Stuttgart, 1984
3/4. Exhibition at the MoMA in New York, 1986
5. Poster of the exhibition at the Swiss Cultural Center in Paris, 1990

	Mario Botta Architecte
16.05.-24.06.1984	Musée d'Art et d'Histoire, Fribourg, Switzerland

Mario Botta. Architetture 1960-1985
Exhibition design by Mario Botta and Achille Castiglioni

12.10.-08.12.1985	Scuola di San Giovanni Evangelista, Venice, Italy
04.01.-26.01.1986	Basilica Palladiana, Vicenza, Italy
04.04.-10.05.1986	Colegio Oficial de Arquitectos, Barcelona, Spain
03.06.-18.06.1986	Colegio Oficial de Arquitectos de Baleares, Palma de Mallorca, Spain

Mario Botta

20.11.1986-10.02.87	The Museum of Modern Art, New York, USA
03.03.-17.04.1987	Farish Gallery School of Architecture, Rice University, Houston, USA
08.1987	Museum of Modern Art, San Francisco, USA

Mario Botta Architektur 1960-1985

29.11.-02.11.1987	Landesmuseum, Braunschweig, Germany
March 1987	Landeskreditbank, Baden-Württemberg, Germany
30.04.-15.05.1987	Züblinhaus, Stuttgart, Germany
23.05.-10.06.1987	Friedrichsbau, Freiburg, Germany

Mario Botta. Une architecture trois habitats

19.03.-24.04.1987	École des Arts Décoratifs, Geneva, Switzerland

Mario Botta. Parma e Torino

18.06.-25.06.1987	Ex Oratorio delle Maddalene, Padua, Italy

Mario Botta - Ein Architekt macht Möbel

01.1988	Solus, Ravensburg, Germany
06.1988	Casa Nova Galerie, Wiesbaden, Germany

Mario Botta. Proyectos y realizaciones 1972-1985

03.1988	Museo de Arte Moderno, Bogotá, Colombia
05.1988	Museo de Arte Moderno, Medellín, Colombia
10.1988	Centro Cultural di Miraflores, Lima, Perú
04.-05.1989	Centro de Arte y Comunicación (CAYC), Buenos Aires, Argentina

Villeurbanne maison du livre, de l'image et du son

08.06.-03.09.1988	IFA Institut Français d'Architecture, Paris, France

Mario Botta

30.09.-29.10.1988	Teo Jakob, Geneva, Switzerland

Adriano Heitmann: architectures de Mario Botta

07.11.-24.11.1988	Galerie de la Librairie Internationale de Photographie, Paris, France

Mario Botta. Studi preliminari per la Banca del Gottardo a Lugano

22.11.1988-18.02.89	Galleria Banca del Gottardo, Lugano, Switzerland

Mario Botta. I 53 disegni dell'agenda 1989

29.11.-07.01.1989	Galleria L'Archivolto, Milan, Italy

Mario Botta. Construire les objets

01.07.-27.08.1989	Fondation Louis Moret, Martigny, Switzerland

Mario Botta: una casa,

23.09.-15.11.1989	Museo Vela, Ligornetto, Switzerland

La chaise

14.05.-26.05.1990	Avry-Art Galerie, Avry-sur-Matran, Fribourg, Switzerland

Watari-um project in Tokyo

17.09.-18.11.1990	Watari-um, Shibuya-ku, Tokyo, Japan

Mario Botta Architectures & Design 80-90

02.02.-07.04.1991	Centre Culturel Suisse, Paris, France

Mario Botta architectures 1980-1990

20.06.-29.09.1991	Musée Rath, Musée d'Art et d'Histoire, Geneva, Switzerland
19.12.-26.01.1992	Burgkloster, Lübeck, Germany
27.02.-29.03.1992	MOPT Galeria de Exposiciones, Madrid, Spain
21.05.-21.06.1992	Fundaçao Calouste Gulbenkian, Lisbon, Portugal
09.07.-16.08.1992	Landesmuseum Volk und Wirtschaft, Düsseldorf, Germany
04.10.-21.11.1992	Volkshochschule, Reutlingen, Germany
09.03.-04.04.1993	Aristotele's University-School of Architecture, Technical Chamber of Greece, Thessaloniki, Greece
20.09.-30.09.1993	CAYC BA / 93, Centro Cultural Recoleta, Buenos Aires, Argentina
30.05.-26.06.1994	Museu de casa brasileira, San Paolo, Brasil
23.10.-30.10.1994	Bienal Internacional de Arquitectura de Brasil, Centro de Convenciones de Pernambuco Recife, Brasil
28.02.-09.04.1995	Museo de Arquitectura "Leopoldo Rother", Universidad Nacional de Colombia, Bogotá, Colombia

09.05.-30.05.1995	Museo de Arte Moderno, Quito, Ecuador		*Mario Botta Design*
17.07.-03.08.1995	Colegio de Arquitectos del Perú, Embajada Suiza, Museo de Arte, Lima, Peru	03.11.-25.12.1995	Design Museum, Thessaloniki, Greece
16.11.-08.12.1995	Pontificia Universidad Catolica de Chile, Santiago del Cile, Chile		*Mario Botta Giulio Andreolli, il museo di Rovereto*
		27.04.-05.05.1996	Galleria d'architettura, Trento, Italy
	Mario Botta architetture 1980-1990	08.05.-04.08.1996	Italian Cultural Institute, San Francisco, USA
12.12.-31.01.1993	Palazzo Strozzi, Florence, Italy		
			Mario Botta. Bauten 1980-1995.
	Mario Botta. Progetti per la chiesa di Mogno		*Eine photographische Retrospektive von Pino Musi*
15.12.-31.01.1993	Galleria SPSAS, Palazzo Morettini, Locarno, Switzerland	07.08.-14.08.1996	Faculty of Architecture, National University, Singapore
31.03.-16.05.1993	Galerie de la Grenette, Sion, Switzerland	17.09.-28.09.1996	Malaysian Institute of Architects, Pam Building, Kuala Lumpur, Malaysia
20.01.-13.02.1994	Museum Allerheiligen, Schaffhausen, Switzerland		
07.01.-05.02.1995	GSMBA Ostschweiz Katharinen, St.Gallen, Switzerland	09.11.-23.11.1996	University of Jakarta, Indonesia
		15.02.-27.02.1997	Rotunda Gallery, Seoul, South Korea
	Mario Botta	03.04.-13.04.1997	Pao Galleries 5/F, Hong Kong Arts Center, Hong Kong, China
22.07.-10.08.1994	Fuori Uso ' 94, Ex Opificio Gaslini, Pescara, Italy	17.04.-28.04.1997	The University Museum and Art Gallery Hku, Hong Kong, China
01.10.-30.11.1994	Trevi Flash Art Museum, Trevi, Italy	08.01.-31.01.1998	Artspace Gallery Woolloomooloo, Sidney, Australia
		09.02.-20.02.1998	The High Court of Australia, Canberra, Australia
	Mario Botta Enzo Cucchi, la cappella del Monte Tamaro,	09.03.-20.03.1998	Cullity Gallery, School of architecture and Fine Arts, University of Western Australia, Perth, Australia.
08.10.-06.11.1994	Museo Cantonale d'Arte, Lugano, Switzerland		
10.02 -19.03.1995	Kunsthaus, Zürich, Switzerland		
14.09.-02.12.1995	Italian Cultural Institute, Toronto, Canada	01.04.-22.04.1998	5th floor Gallery, Faculty of Architecture, Building and Planning, University, Melbourne, Australia
01.-02.1996	Italian Cultural Institute, Vancouver, Canada		
29.03.-03.05.1996	Italian Cultural Institute, Los Angeles, USA	21.01.-05.02.1999	Académie Libanaise des Beaux-Arts, Université de Balamand Sin-El-Fil, Libanon
	Mario Botta	13.02.-02.03.2000	Faculty of Architecture, University of Damascus, Damascus, Syria
18.11.-30.11.1994	Associazione Culturale Italo Francese - Alliance Française, Bologna, Italy		
		15.10.-24.10.2000	National Museum, Latakia, Syria
		11.11.-30.11.2000	Faculty of Architecture, Aleppo University, Syria
	Mario Botta. The San Francisco Museum of Modern Art project	11.02. 2001	Faculty of Architecture, Amman University, Jordanie
18.01.-25.06.1995	Museum of Modern Art, San Francisco, USA		
			Mario Botta. Cinque architetture
	Mario Botta. Bauten 1980-1990	15.09-17.11.1996	Fondazione Scientifica Querini & Stampalia, Venice, Italy
18.04.-11.07.1995	Wolfsberg Management Training Center, Schweizerische Bankgesellschaft, Ermatingen, Switzerland	13.06.-30.08.1998	Kunstmuseum Solothurn, Switzerland
			Architektur: Licht-Materie-Landschaft.
	Mario Botta in Basel.		*Mario Botta gesehen von Pino Musi*
	Ein Architekt und drei Projekte für die Stadt	10.01.-09.02.1997	Städtisches Museum Schloss Morsbroich, Leverkusen, Germany
10.06.-20.08.1995	Architekturmuseum, Basel, Switzerland		
			Mario Botta. Emozioni di pietra.
	I musei di Mario Botta		*Un percorso fra le architetture pubbliche*
8.07.-22.07.1995	Ex Chiesa della Maddalena, Pesaro, Italy	30.06.-28.09.1997	Palazzo Reale, Sala Dorica-Cortile delle Carrozze, Naple, Italy
		27.06.-27.09.1998	Bonnefantenmuseum Maastricht, Netherlands

6. Exhibition at Musée Rath in Geneve, 1991
7. Exhibition *Mario Botta. Cinque architetture* at the Querini Stampalia Foundation in Venice, 1996
8. Exhibition at the DAZ-Deutsches Achitektur Zentrum Berlin, 1999
9. Exhibition Mario Botta Light and Gravity, Palazzo della Ragione in Padua, 2003
10. Exhibition *Mario Botta. Preghiere di pietra - prayers in stone,* Plaster casts gallery, State Institute of Art, Florence, 2005

	Mario Botta. Museum Jean Tinguely		*Mostra del libro di architettura*
09.01.97- 19.04.1998	Museum Jean Tinguely, Basel, Switzerland	15.03.-15.04.2007	Libreria Bernardelli SNC, Centro Einaudi Ragazzi-Galleria Einaudi, Mantova, Italy.
	Mario Botta Sinagoga Cymbalista a Tel-Aviv		[for the presentation of: Mario Botta, Dario Fertilio, *La lingua degli angeli per principianti*, Skira, Milan 2006].
24.09.-28.09.1998	Mostra Internazionale di Marmi Pietre e Tecnologie Verona Fiere, Verona, Italy		
	Licht und Materie. Mario Botta 1990-2000		*Mario Botta. Tredici vasi. Limited Edition Collections*
12.11.1999-15.01.00	DAZ Deutsches Architektur Zentrum, Berlin, Germany	17.11.-25.11.2007	The Gallery, Bruxelles, Belgium
	Mario Botta. Bühnenarchitektur. Entwürfe und Fotografien		*Mario Botta Architetture 1960-2010*
13.12.1999-14.01.00	Graphisches Kabinett, Saarland Museum, Saarbrücken, Germany	25.09.10-23.01.2011	Mart Museo di arte moderna e contemporanea di Trento e Rovereto, Italy
	Mario Botta. Modelli di architettura		
19.05.-02.07.2000	OIKOS Bologna 2000, Padiglione dell'Esprit Nouveau, Bologna, Italy		*Mario Botta Architecture et mémoire / Architektur und Gedächtnis*
		02.04.-15.08.2011	Centre Dürrenmatt, Neuchâtel, Switzerland
	Mario Botta, legni e ceramiche		
25.05.-25.06.2001	Università Cattolica, Sala Chizzolini, Brescia, Italy		*Mario Botta*
	Mario Botta: designing a synagogue		*12 oeuvres uniques en marbre de Carrara*
05.-06.2001	Beth Hatefutsoth, The Nahum Goldmann Museum of the Jewish Diaspora, Tel Aviv, Israel	25.05.-25.07.2011	White Moon Gallery, Paris, France
	Mario Botta. 13 Vasen Skizzen Holz Keramik		*Mario Botta "Tredicivasi"*
31.08.-29.09.2001	Galerie Stuker, Zürich, Switzerland		(A collection of 13 large vases in pewter produced by NUMA* in a limited and numbered edition of 33)
	Mario Botta. Luce e gravità. Architetture 1993-2003	23.09.-09.10.2011	The Gallery, Bruxelles, Belgio
12.12.03- 21.03.2004	Palazzo della Ragione, Padua, Italy		
	La ristrutturazione architettonica e la nuova macchina scenica del Teatro alla Scala		*Mario Botta "Vasi"*
08.03.-31.05.2005	Teatro alla Scala, Ridotto dei palchi "Arturo Toscanini", Milan, Italy	08.05.-09.06.2012	Antonia Jannone Disegni di Architettura, Milan, Italy
	Mario Botta. Architetture del sacro. Preghiere di pietra	12.01.-02.03.2013	*Mario Botta Skizzen Zeichnungen Modelle*
30.04.-30.07.2005	Gipsoteca dell'Istituto Statale d'Arte, Florence, Italy		Galerie Kornfeld, Bern, Switzerland
23.11.2005-14.01.06	RIBA The Royal Institute of British Architects, London, United Kingdom		
	Il teatro alla Scala e le architetture del sacro		
08.10.-30.10.2005	Chiesa di San Giuseppe, Alba, Italy		

GROUP EXHIBITIONS

	Tendenzen neuere Architektur im Tessin, Switzerland		*Construire aujourd'hui dans la ville d'hier*
20.11.1974 -12.12.75	Eidgenössische Technische Hochschule Zurich, Switzerland	26.05.-12.06. 1981	Halle de l'Ile Geneva, curated by architects SIA Geneva section, Geneva, Switzerland
05.-06.1976	Technische Hochschule, Darmstadt, Germany		
28.10.-28.11.1976	Fakultät für Architektur Universität (TH), Karlsruhe, Germany		*Dopo l'architettura post-moderna*
		04.09.-05.09. 1981	Centre International d'Expérimentation Artistique Marie-Louise Jeanneret, Boissano, Italy
	Transformations in modern architecture,		
21.02.-24.04.1979	The Museum of Modern Art, New York, USA	10.12. 1981	Laboratorio Architettura Contemporanea, Rome, Italy,
	Neues Bauen in Alter Umgebung,		*Dokumente, Skizzen und Projekte für die IBA 1984*
03.03.-10.03. 1979	BSA Bund Schweizer Architekten Ortsgruppe Zurich and editor of Werk-Archithese, Chur, Switzerland.	20.10.-25.11.1981	Akademie der bildenden Künste, Vienna, Austria
			Disegni di architettura
	Tien Tessiner Architekten	23.04. 1982	Università degli Studi di Venezia, Facoltà di lettere e filosofia, Istituto di Discipline Artistiche, Venice, Italy
26.03.-06.04. 1979	Techniese Hogeschool Delft, Netherlands		
	Autonomous Architecture:		*Concours pour la maison de la culture de Chambéry et de la Savoie*
	The Work of Eight Contemporary,		
02.12.1980- 18.01.81	Fogg Art Museum, Harvard University, Cambridge Mass., USA	05.1982	IFA Institut Français d'Architecture, Paris, France
			Vergangenheit - Gegenwart Zukunft
	Am Rand des Reissbretts. 10 Schweizer Architekten. Skizzen, Zeichnungen, Grafik, Bilder.	26.05.-22.08.1982	Württembergischer Kunstverein, Stuttgart, Germany
06.12.-30.12.1980	Galleria Studio 10, Chur, Switzerland		*Maquettes d'architectes*
		04.06.-20.07.1982	Centre d'Art Contemporain, Geneve, Switzerland
	Panorama Van de Avant-gardes Kaa/Aarchitectuur 1981,	16.09.-31.10.1982	Le Nouveau Musée, Villeurbanne, France
23.01.-02.03.1981	Akademie voor Beeldende Kunsten Arnheim, Netherlands		
			Zwiterse Avant-garde
	Architecture 70/80 in Switzerland	10.07.-28.08.1982	Galerie Nouvelles Images, Den Haag, Netherlands
15.03.-26.04. 1981	Kunsthalle Basel, Switzerland		
29.04.-22.05.1981	Hochschule für angewandte Kunst, Vienna, Austria		*Ten new buildings*
13.01.-04.02.1982	Palazzo delle Esposizioni, Sale di Via Milano, Rome, Italy	19.01.-20.02.1983	Ica Gallery Institute of Contemporary Arts, London, United Kingdom
04.09.1982	Civica Galleria, Padua, Italy		
15.09.1982	Centre de Création et de Diffusion en Design, Pavillon Arts IV-Design, Montréal, Canada		*Architettura Switzerland*
15.10.-06.11.1982	Facoltà di Architettura, Castello del Valentino, Turin, Italy	20.04.-29.05.1983	Finlands Architekturmuseum, Helsinki, Finnland
	Internationale Bauausstellung Berlin 1984		*Architectures en France. Modernité-post modernité*
22.04.-15.05.1981	Museum am Ostwall, Dortmund, Germany	18.11.-06.02.1984	IFA Institut Français d'Architecture, Paris, France
		11.01.-10.02.1984	Architectural Association School of Architecture, London, United Kingdom
	Architettura: oltre il razionalismo verso l'eclettismo		
23.05.-25.05.1981	Pinacoteca Comunale Loggetta Lombardesca, Ravenna, Italy	25.04.-26.05.1984	Philippe Bonnafont Gallery, San Francisco, California, USA

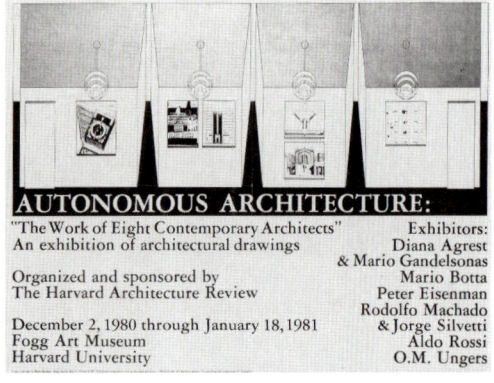

1. Exhibition poster Delft, 1979
2. Exhibition poster Fogg Art Museum, Cambridge Mass., 1981
3. Poster of the exhibition on Swiss architecture in Montréal, 1982
4. Exhibition poster, Helsinki, 1983

21.02.-22.04.1985	*Nouveaux Plaisirs d'Architectures* Centre Georges Pompidou, Galerie du CCI, Paris, France	20.02.1987	*Progetti per Napoli* Facoltà di Architettura, Università degli Studi, Naple, Italy
23.02.-31.03.1985	*Affinità elettive, 17ma Triennale di Milano* Palazzo della Triennale Milano, Italy	03.03.-21.03.1987	*Exposicio sobre la consulta internacional d'ideas de l'Illa Diagonal* Demarcacio de Barcelona del Collegi d'Arquitectes de Catalunya, Barcelona, Spain
21.03.1985	*XIII Biennale de Paris* Grande Halle du Parc de la Villette, Paris	21.03.-28.05.1987	*750 Years of Architecture and Urban planning* Berlin National Gallery, Berlin, Germany
03.06.-15.06.1985	*Architecture en Rhône-Alpes Septen* Quartier du Tonkin, Villeurbanne, France	09.04.-03.05.1987	*Der Wettbewerb SBG in Basel* Architektur Forum Zurich, Switzerland
06.07.-15.09.1985	*Homo Decorans – Decorating Man* Louisiana Museum of Modern Art, Humlebaek, Denmark	25.04.-31.05.1987	*GA International 87* GA Gallery, Tokyo, Japan
10.09.1985	*Contemporary landscape from the horizon of postmodern design* Kyoto Municipal Art Museum, Okazaki- Kôen (Park), Sayko-ku, Kyoto, Japan	20.01.1988	*Scenografia Alias* Galerie Zwirner, Köln, Germany
19.09.-27.10.1985	*La chaise: un objet de design ou d'architecture?* Centre de Création et diffusion en Design 200, Montréal, Canada	21.03.-16.04.1988	*Dessins* Galerie Jean-François Dumont, Bordeaux, France
04.03.-19.04.1986	*Modern redux: critical alternatives for architecture in the next decade* Grey Art Gallery and Study Center, New York University, New York, USA	21.10.-23.10.1988	*Sotto Napoli. Idee per la città sotterranea* Castel dell'Ovo, Naple, Italy
		23.10.-04.12.1988	*De collectie* Kunsthal, Rotterdam, Netherlands
15.04.-21.05.1986 04.06.-20.07.1986 23.09.-09.11.1986	*Mobilier suisse création de 1927-1984* Musée des Arts Décoratifs, Lausanne, Switzerland Museum für Gestaltung Kunstgewerbemuseum, Zurich, Switzerland Gewerbemuseum Museum für Gestaltung, Basel, Switzerland	15.04.-28.05.1989	*GA International '89* Sendagaya, Shibuya-ku Tokyo, Japan
		03.06.-13.08.1989	*New York architektur 1970-1990* Deutsches Architekturmuseum, Frankfurt, Germany
14.06.-28.09.1986	*Il luogo del lavoro* Triennale di Milano, Milan, Italy	03.10.-28.10.1989	*Bibliothèque de France* IFA Institut Français d'Architecture, Paris, France
04.10.-30.11.1986	Internationale Bauaustellung Berlin 1987 Deutsches Architekturmuseum, Frankfurt, Germany	10.1989 14.11.-29.01.1990	*Grands projets culturels en France* Bibliothèque Corderie Royale, Rochefort-sur-mer, France Espace Pierre Mendès, Poitiers, France
10.-11.1986	*Ridisegnare Venezia* Ateneo S. Basso, Piazza San Marco, Venice, Italy	05.05.-01.06.1990	*Kunsten a tegne the art of drawing* Kunsternernes Hus, Oslo, Norway
16.01.-01.03.1987	*Architects' drawings from the collection of Barbara Pine* Leigh and Block Gallery Northwestern University, Evanston Illinois, USA	05.12.-16.01.1991	*Welches Bild der Schweiz?* *Projekte für CH 91 und Sevilla 1991* Architektur Forum, Zurich, Switzerland

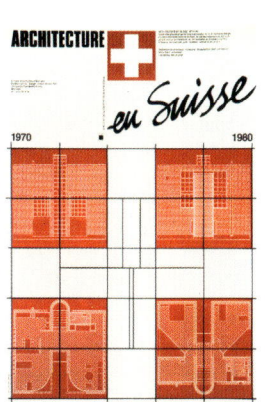

	Dessin de ville		Schweizer Kunstmuseen.
07.11.-01.12.1991	Aire-Libre Art Contemporain, Agora, Évry Essonnes, France		*Bauten und Projekte von 1980-1994,*
		05.11.-08.01.1995	Architektur-Forum, Centre PasquArt, Bienne, Switzerland
	Frammenti Interfacce Intervalli.	22.05.-09.06.1995	Theater Casino, Zug, Switzerland
	Paradigmi della frammentazione nell'arte svizzera		
08.04.-28.06.1992	Museo d'Arte Contemporanea, Villa Croce, Genova, Italy		*Un lugar cuatro arquitectos*
		11.1995-02.1996	Museo de Bellas Artes, Caracas, Venezuela,
	Nara Convention Hall International design competition	19.06.-31.08.1996	Museo Nacional de Arquitectura Palacio de Bellas Artes, Ciudad de Mexico, Mexiko
16.05.-14.06.1992	Nara Provincial Museum, Nara, Japan	12.1996	Museo Nacional de Bellas Artes, Buenos Aires, Argentina
	Modern design and architecture		*Design and Identity.*
14.06.-19.06.1992	Aspen Art Museum, Aspen, Colorado, USA		*Aspects of European Design Louisiana*
		09.02.1996	Louisiana Museum of Modern Art, Humlebaek, Denmark
	Sonderfall?		
	Die Schweiz zwischen Reduit und Europa		*Architektur im Bühnenraum.*
19.08.-15.11.1992	Schweizerisches Landesmuseum, Zurich, Switzerland		*Mario Botta, Jean Nouvel, Renzo Piano, Aldo Rossi*
		01.06.-13.07.1996	Galerie Marie-Louise Wirth, Zurich, Switzerland
	Licht und Architektur		
11.09.-04.10.1992	Turm Triva, Landesgartenschau, Ingolstadt, Germany		*Kolonihaven. The International Challenge*
		20.07.-01.09.1996	Arken Museum for Moderne Kunst, Ishoj, Denmark
	Museo d'arte e Architettura	20.07.-08.09.1996	Kunstmuseet Koge Skitsesamling, Koge, Denmark
20.09.-22.11.1992	Museo Cantonale d'Arte, Lugano, Switzerland		
			Between sea and city. Eight piers for Thessaloniki
	Contemporary architectural freehand drawing	17.12.-16.02.1997	Netherlands Architecture Institute, Rotterdam, Netherlands
24.10.-15.11.1992	GA Gallery, Tokyo, Japan		
			Zukunftsweisende Bibliotheksbauten
	Architetture cosmpolite		*in Nordrhein-Westfalen,*
25.10.-09.11.1992	Fondazione Tetraktis, Nuovo Museo Archeologico, Teramo, Italy	20.05.-24.05.1997	"Bibliotheka 1997", Messezentrum Westfalenhallen, Dortmund, Germany
	Nara Convention Hall international design competition		*Sotto il cielo della cupola.*
20.11.-07.03.1993	The Museum of Modern Art, New York, USA		*Il coro di S. Maria del Fiore dal rinascimento al 2000*
		19.06.-21.09.1997	Sala D'Arme di Palazzo Vecchio, Florence, Italy
	Architettura e spazio sacro nella modernità		
04.12.-06.01.1993	Antichi Granai della Giudecca, Biennale di Venezia, Italy		*Architekten als Designer*
		26.06.-30.08.1998	Museum für Gegenwart, Hamburger Bahnhof, Berlin, Germany
	GA International '93		
17.04.-30.05.1993	GA Gallery, Tokyo, Japan		*Architektur im 20. Jahrhundert: Schweiz*
12.06.-11.07.1993	K2 Gallery, Osaka, Japan	26.09.-29.11.1998	Deutsches Architekturmuseum, Frankfurt, Germany
	Das geordnete Labyrinth: neue Bibliotheken und ihre Architektur		*Licht-Zeichen. Sakrale Architektur und Symbole im Zeichen einer religiösen Sprache*
25.08.-15.10.1993	Schweizerische Landesbibliothek, Berne, Switzerland	20.11.-02.12.1999	Akademie für Gestaltung und Denkmalpflege, Ebern, Germany
	Ticino en Madrid. La esencia de habitar		
13.09.-30.10.1993	Museo Español de Arte Contemporáneo, Madrid, Spain		*Cantico 2000. A misura di ambiente*
		26.04.-25.05.2000	Museo della Permanente, Milan, Italy
	Ergebnisse des Stadtbaulichen Ideenwettbewerbs Alexanderplatz		
09.10.-09.11.1993	Berolinahaus am Alexanderplatz, Berlin, Germany		

5. Poster of the exhibition of the projects for Sotto Napoli (Naple underground), 1988
6. Poster GA International '93, Toyko and Osaka, 1993
7. Catalog *Between Sea and City, Eight Piers for Thessaloniki*, 1997
8. Catalog cover *Sotto il cielo della Cupola*. Milan, 1997

	Museums for a new millennium: concepts, projects, buildings		*Dinner for architects.*
04.02.-30.04.2000	Hessenhuis, Antwerpen, Belgum		*Serviettenskizzen für das Architekturmuseum*
30.05.-10.09.2000	Deichtorhallen, Hamburg, Germany	10.04.-18.05.2003	Architekturmuseum der Technischen Universität, Munich, Germany
03.10.2000-07.01.01	Kunsthaus, Bregenz, Germany		
01.02.-29.04.2001	Centro Cultural de Belém, Lisbon, Portugal		
30.05.-26.08.2001	Castello di Rivoli, Rivoli Turin, Italy		*Die erste Skizze / The first sketch*
21.09.-06.01.2002	Galerie der Stadt Stuttgart, Stuttgart, Germany	18.04.-25.05.2003	Evangelische Kirche, Birkenfeld, Germany
09.02.-14.04.2002	Modern Art Museum, Forth Worth, Texas, USA,	04.07.-24.08.2003	Galleria Aedes West, Berlin, Germany
10.05.-04.08.2002	Art Museum, Milwaukee, Wisconsin, USA,		
30.08.-24.11.2002	The Columbus Museum of Art, Columbus, Ohio, USA,		*Visionen und Utopien.*
20.12.2002-02.02.03	Museu de Arte Moderna, Rio de Janeiro, Brasil		*Architekturzeichnungen aus dem Museum of Modern Art New York*
28.02.-20.07.2003	MARCO Museo de Arte Contemporaneo, Monterrey, Mexiko	29.04.-03.08.2003	Schirn Kunsthalle, Frankfurt, Germany
18.09.-29.11.2003	Miami Art Museum, Miami, Florida, USA		
03.10.-18.01.2004	Miami Art Museum, Miami, Florida, USA		*Disegni e progetti per quattro fontane in pietra trentina:*
			Mario Botta, Pierluigi Cerri, Alessandro Guerriero,
	30 years after, Architecture and Art		*Ettore Sottsass jr.*
26.10.2000	Kévés Studio Gallery, Budapest, Hungary	31.07.-31.08.2003	MART-Museo di Arte Moderna e Contemporanea, Trento Rovereto, Italy
	Il progetto della luce lungo i percorsi del Premio Compasso d'Oro ADI	02.10.-05.10.2003	MARMOMACC 2003 Veronafiere, Verona, Italy
12.12.-25.12.2000	Manezh, Moscow, Russia,		
21.02.-25.02.2001	Fidexpò, San Petersburg, Russia		*Yibaneh! Jewish Identity in Contemporary Architecture*
		26.03.-29.08.2004	Jewish Historical Museum, Amsterdam, Netherlands
	20 siècles en cathédrales	19.09.-14.11.2004	Felix-Nussbaum-Haus, Osnabruck, Germany
29.06.-04.11.2001	Palais du Tau, Reims, France	05.01.-20.02.2005	Museum of the History of Polish Jews, Varsavia, Poland
		04.03.-29.05.2005	Jüdisches Museum Berlin, Berlin, Germany
	30 años después. El futuro del pasado	21.06.-04.09.2005	Jüdisches Museum, Vienna, Austria
27.09. 2001	Sala Ixca Farias, Museo Regional de Guadalajara, Guadalajara, Mexiko	04.11.-05.02.2006	München Stadtmuseum, Munich, Germany
		16.04.-18.06.2006	The London Jewish Museum of Art, London, United Kingdom
	Das Geheimnis des Schattens.		
	Licht und Schatten in der Architektur		*USD. Urban Stone Design. Antichi e nuovi percorsi della Pietra*
23.03.-16.06.2002	Deutsches Architektur Museum DAM, Frankfurt, Germany		*Trentino / Old and new uses of Trentino stone*
		14.04.-19.04.2004	Salone del Mobile di Milano, Fondazione Piero Portaluppi, Milan, Italy
	Nuova architettura di pietra in Italia	07.-09.2004	Parco Giardino Sigurtà, Valeggio sul Mincio, Verona, Italy
03.10.-06.10.2002	Veronafiere -37a MARMOMACC, Verona, Italy		
			The International Highrise Award 2004 / Internationaler
	Drôles de trames, tapisseries médiévales et contemporaines		*Hochhaus Preis 2004,*
16.11.-23.02.2003	Musée des Beaux Arts, Beaune, France	12.06.-11.07.2004	Deutsches Architektur Museum DAM, Frankfurt, Germany
	Year of the bible 2003		*Johan Rudolf Rahn 1841-1912. Geografia e monumenti*
02.02.-30.03.2003	Künstlergilde Buslat, Schloss Bauschlott, Neulingen, Germany	11.09.-31.10.2004	Museo d'arte, Mendrisio, Switzerland
	Architetture ticinesi nel mondo.		*Costruzioni Federali.*
	Capisaldi e protagonisti 1970-2003		*Architetture 1988-1998. Circondario 2*
27.02.-26.03.2003	CCS-Centro Culturale Svizzero, Milan, Italy	16.09.-16.10.2004	Spazio Culturale Svizzero, Palazzo Trevisan degli Ulivi, Campo S. Agnese, Venice, Italy
16.06.-04.07.2003	Palazzo Reale, Naple, Italy		
01.12.2003-16.01.04	Accademia di architettura di Mendrisio, Palazzo Canavée, Mendrisio, Switzerland	28.04.-29.05.2005	Istituto Svizzero, Rome, Italy
24.09.-24.10.2004	Galleria del Design e dell'Arredamento, Cantù, Italy		

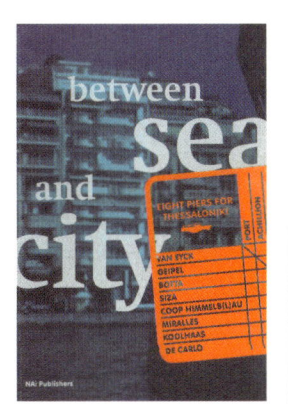

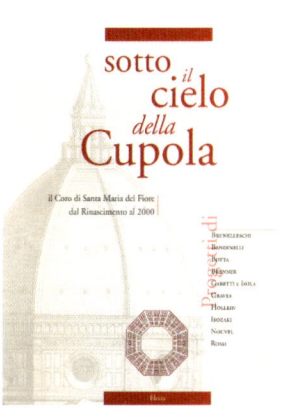

09.06.-08.07.2005	SUPSI, Blocco A, Trevano-Canobbio, Switzerland
09.09.-08.10.2005	Galleria Studio 10, Chur, Switzerland

Arti & Architettura
02.10.-13.02.2005	Salone del Maggior Consiglio, Palazzo Ducale, Genova, Italy

Archiskulptur.
Modelle, Skulpturen und Gemälde
03.10.-30.01.2005	Fondation Beyeler, Riehen, Basel, Switzerland

Ticinese architecture in the world: milestones and protagonists 1970-2003
11.10.-07.11.2004	Taipei Museum of Fine Arts, Taipei, Taiwan
03.12. 2004	Kaohsiung, Taiwan
12.04.-24.04.2005	Museum of Arts and Crafts, Zagreb, Croatia
25.02.-12.03.2006	Virginia Tech's Washington, Alexandria Architecture Center, Virginia, USA
01.12.-02.12.2006	Università di Coimbra, Portugal

Muse-um? Companionship of plurality
15.10.-09.04.2005	Black Box, Samsung Child Education & Culture Center, Seoul, Korea

Culture Design
20.10.2004- 16.01.05	Palais de la Porte Dorée, Paris, France

Mario Carrieri. Amata luce
21.10.-18.12.2004	Palazzo delle Stelline, Sala del Collezionista, Milan, Italy

Milano e Lombardia. La rinascita del futuro
27.10.-07.11.2004	Pavillon de l'Arsenal, Paris, France

Fare turismo a Salerno. Piani e progetti per un nuovo modello turistico del mezzogiorno
07.04.-10.04.2005	Tempio di Pomona, Salerno, Italy

La porta del cielo
08.05.-28.05.2005	Palazzo Comunale, Sala Espositiva "Virgilio Carbonari", Seriate-Bergamo, Italy

Arte e cinema 2005
Le sedie di piazza grande interpretate dagli artisti. Asta finale
12.08. 2005	Rotonda del Festival, Locarno, Switzerland

Auktion mit Originalzeichnungen Originalskizzen und Modellen internationaler Architekten
24.09. 2005	DAM Deutsches Architektur Museum, Frankfurt, Germany

Archisculpture: dialogues between architecture and sculpture from the 18th century to the present day
28.10.2005-26.02.06	Museo Guggenheim, Bilbao, Spain
30.03.-02.07.2006	Kunstmuseum, Wolfsburg, Germany

Werdende Wahrzeichen Architektur-und Landschaftsprojekte für Graubünden
18.12.2005-23.04.06	Das Gelbe Haus, Flims, Switzerland
28.09.-08.11.2006	ARchENA + Architekturfoyer Hönggerberg ETH, Zurich, Switzerland

Photography and video by Silvio Wolf
15.02.-06.05.2006	Galleria Gottardo, Lugano, Switzerland

L[ES] ETRANGER[ES] 1995/2005.
Esperienze progettuali di architetti stranieri in Italia
18.02.-11.03.2006	Museo Diocesano, Brescia, Italy
04.2006	MAXXI Museo Internazionale delle arti del XXI secolo, Rome, Italy

Silvio Wolf thresholds
02.03.-22.04.2006	Robert Mann Gallery, New York, USA

Museen im 21. Jahrhundert:
Ideen, Projekte, Bauten / Museums in the 21st century
01.04.-25.06.2006	K20 Kunstsammlung Nordrhein-Westfalen, Düsseldorf, Germany
21.09.-29.10.2006	MAXXI-Museo Nazionale delle Arti del XXI° secolo, Rome, Italy
24.11.2006-18.02.07	Lentos Kunstmuseum, Linz, Austria
18.06.-14.09.2008	Louisiana Museum of Modern Art, Humlebaek, Denmark
10.10.2008-11.01.09	The National Museum Architecture and The Art Hall at Tullinløkka, Oslo, Norway
28.03.-03.05.2009	University of Michigan Museum of Art, Ann Arbor, Michigan, USA, Art Gallery of Alberta, Edmonton Canada
2009	BMW Museum, Munich, Germany
20.01.2010	New Mexico Museum of Art, Santa Fe, New Mexico

Laboratorio Ialia [Rome 2006]: 200 architetti italiani + 50 architetti stranieri
06.05.-04.06.2006	Ex Casa di correzione del San Michele, Rome, Italy

La bellezza
06.05.-04.06.2006	Museo della Permanente, Milan, Italy

Mostra dei progetti premiati e segnalati in occasione del premio internazionale Dedalo Minosse
30.06.-03.09.2006	Basilica Palladiana, Vicenza, Italy

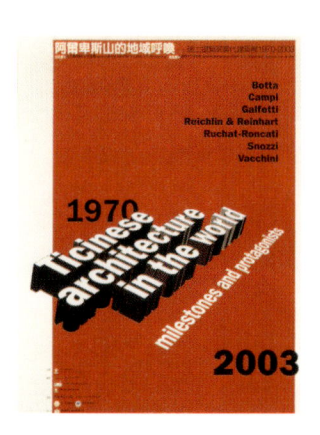

9. Poster of the exhibition *Ticinese architecture in the world, milestones and protagonists 1970-2003*

10.09.-19.11.2006	*Verso il terzo Veneto* Padiglione Italia, Giardini della Biennale di Venice, Italy	30.05.-24.08. 2008	*Mostra dei progetti premiati e segnalati in occasione della VII edizione del Premio Internazionale Dedalo Minosse* Palazzo Valmarana Braga, Vicenza, Italy
16.11.2006-10.01.07 28.06.-20.07.2007 13.09.-05.10.2007 23.10.-10.11.2007	*New World Architecture, International Architecture Award The Chicago Athenaeum* Royal Institute of Irish Architects, Dublin, Ireland Knoll International, London, United Kingdom Knoll International, Tour & Taxis, Bruxelles, Belgium Knoll International, Elzenga Project B.V., Eindhoven, Netherlands	06.06.-06.07.2008	*Art on football field* Swatch Group, Cité du Temps, Geneva, Switzerland
		25.06.-20.07.2008	*Fabrizio Musa. Santo Volto. Testi, dipinti, grafiche, wall paint con disegni inediti di Mario Botta* Transport + 500 Art Garage, Turin, Italy
17.01.-23.02.2007	*La belle voisine. La création contemporaine suisse à Lyon et en Rhône-Alpes* Maison de l'architecture Rhône-Alpes, Lyon, France	04.10. 2008-11.11.09	*Omaggio a Palladio. 18 allestimenti per la Basilica Palladiana. Mario Botta. Architetture 1960-85* Villa Caldogno, Vicenza, Italy
19.03.-27.04.2007	*Architectures tessinoises dans le monde 1970-2003* École Nationale Supérieure d'Architecture, Saint Etienne, France	15.10.-18.10.2008	*SAIE Fare Futuro* SAIE 2008, Bologna Fiere, Bologna, Italy
11.04.-30.04.2007	*"I Creativii". Cristina Pica* Spazio Eventi Sagsa, Milan, Italy	21.11.2008-31.03.09	*Tracce del vuoto. 6 traiettorie italiane verso una scena essenziale. Gastone Novelli, Mimmo Paladino, Mario Botta, Mimmo Jodice, Andrea Fogli, Lino Fiorito* Studio Angeletti, Rome, Italy
18.04.-23.04. 2007	*Mario Botta: Guscio – sit down – please* Cersaie, Triennale di Milano, Salone del Mobile 2007, Milan, Italy	13.12.2008-18.10.09	*Wie es dem Gast gefällt. Hotelarchitektur einst und heute* Gelbe Haus, Flims, Switzerland
21.04.-14.10. 2007	*Draft or Dream on Intuitive Architecture* Dr. Guislain Museum, Gent, Belgium	20.12.2008-30.06.09	*L'Accademia Nazionale di San Luca per una collezione del Disegno Contemporaneo* Accademia Nazionale di San Luca, Rome, Italy
24.10.-28.10.2007 05.02.-09.02.2008	*Stand by me* SAIE 2007, Bologna Fiere, Bologna, Italy Fiera Milano International, Milan, Italy	26.03.-26.07.2009	*Il cotto dell'Impruneta. Maestri del Rinascimento e le fornaci di oggi* Basilica e Chiostri di Santa Maria, Loggiati del Pellegrino, Impruneta, Italy
01.12.-24.02.2008 19.04.-11.05.2008	*99 Icone. Da segno a sogno* GAMeC, Galleria d'Arte Moderna e Contemporanea-Accademia di Carrara, Bergamo, Italy GAMeC, Palazzo Reale, Milan, Italy	21.04.-07.06.2009	*Ballo+Ballo. Il linguaggio dell'oggetto attraverso le fotografie di Aldo Ballo e Marirosa Toscani Ballo* PAC Padiglione d'Arte Contemporanea, Milan, Italy
08.12.-31.12.2007	*Trento ieri, oggi, domani. Uno sguardo sulla città. La storia, i luoghi, i progetti* Facoltà di Giurisprudenza e Biblioteca dell'Università degli Studi di Trento, Torre Mirana, Trento, Italy	22.04.-27.04.2009 18.04.-10.05.2009	*La mano dell'architetto* FAI Fondo per l'Ambiente Italiano e Alterstudio Partners, i Saloni, Milan, Italy Villa Necchi Campiglio, Triennale Bovisa, Abitare, Milan, Italy
08.02.-08.06.2008	*Cut: Revealing the Section* San Francisco Museum of Modern Art, San Francisco, USA	23.04.-02.06.2009	*Piazza della Visitazione Matera. Mostra dei progetti del concorso* Ex stazione ferroviaria, Piazza Matteotti, Matera, Italy
19.04.-21.06.2008	*Immagini dell'invisibile Jean Odermatt-Silvio Wolf* ISR Istituto Svizzero di Rome, Italy		

08.05.-05.06.2009	*Gli strumenti da disegno prima del computer* SUPSI-Scuola universitaria professionale della Svizzera Italiana, Cannobio, Switzerland		*L'architettura che ti piace © / The architecture you like ©* a cura di GIZMO
10.05.-04.06.2010	ANCE, Como, Italy	24.02.-10.04.2011	MAXXI Museo nazionale delle arti del XXI secolo, Rome, Italy
26.05.-30.05.2009	*Urban solutions* LivinLuce ed EnerMotive, Fieramilano, Milan, Italy	11.04.-23.04.2011	*Interni Mutant Architecture & Design* Progetto Stanza – the room project Installation Cortile d'Onore with GVM Marmi, Mapei, Riva 1920 Università degli Studi di Milano, Ca' Granda, Milan, Italy
23.06.-31.12.2009	*Highlights from the modern design collection 1900-2006* The Metropolitan Museum of Art, New York, USA		
24.06.-31.07.2009	*I feel good!* Spazio FMG, Milan, Italy	08.05.-10.07.2011	*Baden* Museum Langmatt, Baden, Switzerland
29.09.-03.10.2009	*Cersaie* Salone Internazionale della ceramica per l'architettura, Bologna, Italy	05.07.-04.09.2011	*Lo Splendore della Verità* *La Bellezza della Carità* Artists' tribute to the 60th anniversary of Pope Benedict XVI's Ordination Atrio Aula Paolo VI, Vaticano, Rome, Italy
24.10.-01.11.2009	*Neue Räume 09* Internationale Wohn- und Möbelausstellung, Zurich-Oerlikon, Switzerland	06.09.-29.10.2011	*The 43 Uses of Drawing* Rugby Art Gallery and Museum, Rugby UK
04.02.-04.04.2010	*Sitting Pretty* Glynn Vivian Art Gallery, Swansea, UK	29.10.-13.11.2011	*Francesco De Rocchi – Mario Botta Angeli* Centro Studi sul Chiarismo Francesco De Rocchi, Saronno, Italy
14.04.-19.04.2010 12.04.-17.04.2011 06.05.-30.06.2011 18.01.-13.03.2011	*Tra le Briccole di Venezia* "Bricolages" Riva 1920 Triennale di Milano, Italy Salone Internazionale del Mobile, Milan, Italy Seipp Wohnen, Waldshut, Germany Museum für Angewandte Kunst, Köln, Germany	19.11.2011-15.01.12	*Eminent architects Seen by Ingrid von Kruse* DAM Deutsches Architekturmuseum, Frankfurt am Main, Germany
		17.12.2011-15.04.12	*Judaism – A World of Stories* The Nieuwe Kerk Amsterdam, Netherlands
10.04.-09.05.2010	*La mano del Designer / The Hand of the Designer* FAI Fondo Ambiente Italiano, Villa Necchi Campiglio, Milan, Italy	06.07.-28.10.2012	*Postmodernism. Style and Subversion 1970-1990* Landesmuseum, Zurich, Switzerland
11.06.-24.06.2010 09.12.2010	*Charity Chair* AIT-Architektursalon, Munich, Germany Laurenskerk, Rotterdam, Netherlands BC Design Center, Copenhagen, Denmark St. Johannes-Evangelist-Kirche, Berlin, Germany	08.12.-01.04.2013	*Bildbau. Schweizer Architektur im Fokus der Fotografie / Buiding Images. Photography focusing on Swiss Architecture* S AM Schweizerisches Architekturmuseum, Basel, Switzerland
09.06.-28.11.2010	*ARCHI & BD La ville dessinée* Cité de l'Architecture & du Patrimoine, Paris, France	19.10.-09.11.2013	*Design Landscape* Ueli Frauchiger Design, Zofingen, Switzerland

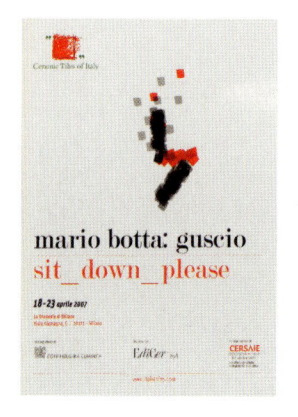

10. Pamphlet of the exhibition *Mario Botta: guscio-sit down please*, La Triennale di Milano, 2007

MONOGRAPHIC BIBLIOGRAPHY
BY MERCEDES DAGUERRE

1979

AA.VV., *Mario Botta. Architettura e progetti negli anni '70 / Architecture and Projects in the '70*, exhibition catalog by Italo Rota, Electa, Milan 1979 [Italian/English edition].
Kenneth Frampton, *La tendenza a costruire / The will to build*, pp. 7-13.
Emilio Battisti, *Esperienze di architettura / Architectural experience*, pp. 15-28.
Photography: Alo Zanetta, Archivio Mario Botta
The bilingual catalog presents for the first time Botta's work to an international public.

1980

Jorge Glusberg, *Mario Botta*, catalog, CAYC-Centro de Arte y Comunicación, Buenos Aires 1980.
Gaspar Bodmer, *Prefacio*, p. 3.
Jorge Glusberg, *La arquitectura de Mario Botta entre la historia y la memoria: el pasado como amigo*, pp. 4-16.
The exhibition introduces Botta's work in the architectural debate in Argentina and South America.

1982

AA.VV., *Mario Botta. La casa rotonda*, edited by Robert Trevisiol, L'Erba Voglio, Milan 1982 [Italian/English ed.; French ed.: *Mario Botta. La maison ronde*, l'Equerre, Paris 1982; Spanish ed.: *Mario Botta, la casa redonda*, Editorial Gustavo Gili, Barcelona 1983].
Edoardo Sanguineti, *ab edendo*, p. 7.
Robert Trevisiol, *La casa rotonda / The round house*, pp.81-83; *Sull'architettura di Mario Botta / Notes on the architecture of M.B.*, pp. 98-103.
Alberto Sartoris, *Mario Botta, trasfiguratore della geometria / Mario Botta, transfigurer of geometry*, pp. 84-85.
Pierluigi Nicolin, *Il cerchio domato / The tamed circle*, pp. 86-87.
Rob Krier, *Caro Mario / Dear Mario*, pp. 88-89.
Mario Botta, *Nota / Note*, pp. 90-91.
Jean Marc Reiser, *La maison ronde*, pp. 92-93.
Photography: Gabriele Basilico.
The monograph documents exhaustively the different phases of the design process and construction of the famous round house (built in Stabio in 1980-81) and offers different critical and cultural considerations.

Pierluigi Nicolin, François Chaslin, *Mario Botta, 1978-1982. Laboratoire d'architecture*, catalogue, Electa Moniteur, Paris 1982 [Italian ed.: *Mario Botta 1978-1982. Il laboratorio d'architettura*, Milano 1982].
Pierluigi Nicolin, *Nota per il secondo volume dell'opera di Mario Botta*, pp. 7-12.
François Chaslin, *Nel paesaggio come un pugno sul tavolo*, pp. 13-16.
Mario Botta, *Architettura e ambiente, Note per una conferenza*, pp. 115-116.
Photography: Archivio Mario Botta, Alo Zanetta.
The book presents the consistent architectural work of Botta's research, from the family houses in Ticino built in 1979-82, to the first significant buildings under construction in Lugano, Fribourg, Chambéry as well as urban scale projects and first experiences in design.

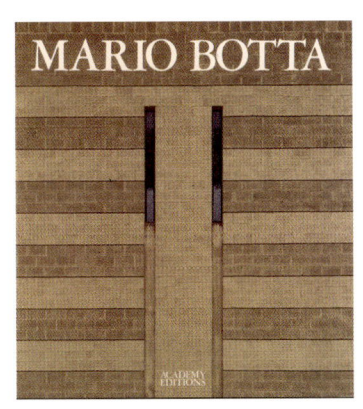

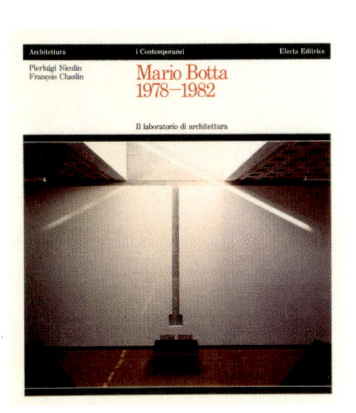

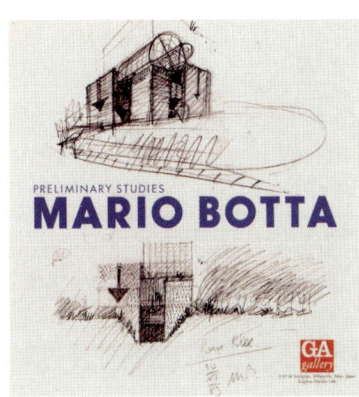

1984

Mario Botta, *Preliminary Studies*, exhibition catalog, GA Global Architecture Gallery, Tokyo 1984 [English/Japanese ed.].
Alberto Sartoris, *On the Architectural Drawing by Mario Botta*, n.pag.
Alberto Sartoris essay introduces to a book that highlights the importance of the preliminary sketches in Botta's project design.

Yukio Futagawa (editor), 'Mario Botta', *GA Global Architecture Architect*, 1984, 3.
Christian Norberg-Schulz, *Introduction*, pp. 8-21.
Mirko Zardini, *Works*, pp. 22-228.
Photography: Yukio Futagawa [et al.]
The famous japanese magazine dedicates a monographic issue to the main works of Mario Botta, with an introduction by Christian Norberg-Schulz and descriptions by Mirko Zardini. The edition evidences the rising interest in Japan in Botta's architectural research.

Virgilio Gilardoni, 'Gli spazi dell'uomo nell'architettura di Mario Botta. Note sulla biblioteca luganese dei Frati', *Archivio Storico Ticinese* (Bellinzona), 100, 1984, dicembre, pp. 219-244.
The essay presents the Capuchin library in Lugano and introduces to the written report of the convention on the new Swiss "historiography" (held at the same library on October 14-15, 1983). Furthermore the text offers an artistic and cultural profile of the architect.

Pierluigi Nicolin (hrsg.), *Mario Botta Bauten und Projekte 1961-1982*, DVA Deutsche Verlags-Anstalt, Stuttgart 1984 [English ed.: *Mario Botta Buildings and Projects 1961-1982*, Electa-Rizzoli, New York 1984; Spanish ed.: *Mario Botta Construcciones y Proyectos*, Editorial Gustavo Gili, Barcelona 1984].
Pierluigi Nicolin, *Anmerkungen zum Werk von Mario Botta*, pp. 7-11.
Mario Botta, *Die Bedeutung des Ortes in der Architektur*, pp. 13-15.
Photography: Archivio Mario Botta, Alo Zanetta.
Pierluigi Nicolin presents the first twenty years of the architect's production to a European and American public.

1985

AA.VV., *Mario Botta. Architetture 1960-1985*, a cura di Francesco Dal Co, Electa, Milano 1985 [French ed.: *Mario Botta. Architectures 1960-1985*, Electa-Moniteur, Paris 1985; English ed.: *Mario Botta. Architectures 1960-1985*, Electa-Rizzoli, New York 1986].
Francesco Dal Co, *La pazienza delle cose*, pp. 7-45.
Mirko Zardini, *Quattro temi. Il luogo, il muro, le aperture, la luce*, pp. 47-93.
Mercedes Daguerre, *catalogo delle opere*, pp. 95-267.
Sergio Polano (a cura di), *Antologia critica* [essays by Giuseppe Mazzariol, Emilio Battisti, Martin Steinmann, Alberto Sartoris, Pierluigi Nicolin, François Chaslin, Livio Dimitriu, Tita Carloni, Giovanni Pozzi, Virgilio Gilardoni, Kenneth Frampton, Benedetto Gravagnuolo, Mario Botta], pp. 269-276.
Photography: Sergio Anelli, Aldo Ballo, Gabriele Basilico, Lorenzo Bianda, Dida Biggi, Arno Carpi, Mario Carrieri, Alberto Flammer, Gilbert Fleury, Adriano Heitmann, Leo Hilber, Daniel Leugeurlier, Nicolas Monkewitz, Alo Zanetta, Archivio Mario Botta [et al.].
The result of a first systematic cataloguing of the architect's archive and of a rigorous critical lecture on the architectural production of this period. The book goes together with the exhibition opened at the Scuola di San Giovanni Evangelista in Venice on October 12, 1985; an exhibition designed by Mario Botta together with Achille Castiglioni.

1986

AA.VV., 'Mario Botta', edited by Toshio Nakamura, *A+U Architecture and Urbanism*, 1986, 9, September [Japanese/English ed.].
Toshio Nakamura, *Building the Site*, p. 5.
Mario Botta, *The Archaicity of the New*, pp. 9-16.
Sergio Polano, *Mario Botta: Ten Works*, pp. 17-176.
Francesco Dal Co, *Architecture of Mario Botta*, pp. 177-206.
Takamitsu Azuma, *Creation of a Sense of Place*, pp. 258-59.
Takefumi Aida, *Something Hard*, pp. 260-61.
Tadao Ando, *Poetic Geometry*, pp. 262-63.
Photography: Antonio Martinelli.
An analyse of Botta's work by well-known critics and architects published by one of the most important Japanese magazines confirms the growing interest worldwide.

Stuart Wrede, *Mario Botta*, exhibition catalog, The Museum of Modern Art, New York 1986.
Stuart Wrede, *Mario Botta and the Modernist Tradition*, pp. 8-21.
Stuart Wrede (by), *Interview with Mario Botta*, pp. 64-69.
Photography: Adriano Heitmann.
A great opportunity for the young Ticino architect to show his work at the MoMA in New York.

1987

AA.VV., *Mario Botta. Une architecture trois habitats*, catalogue d'exposition, École des Arts Décoratifs, Genève 1987.

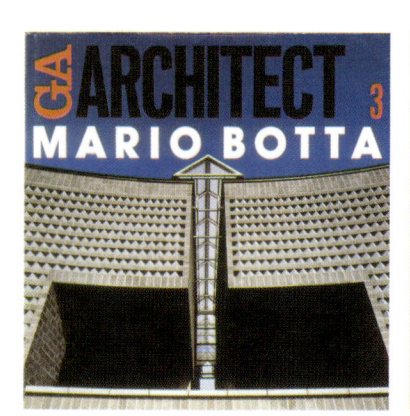

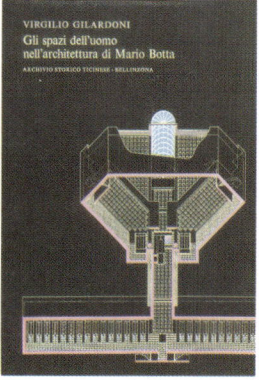

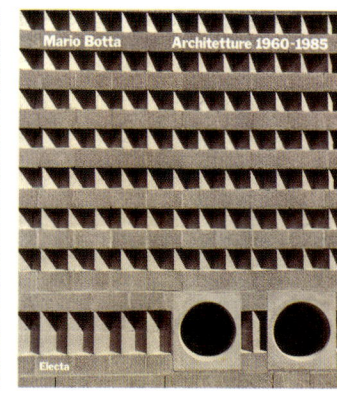

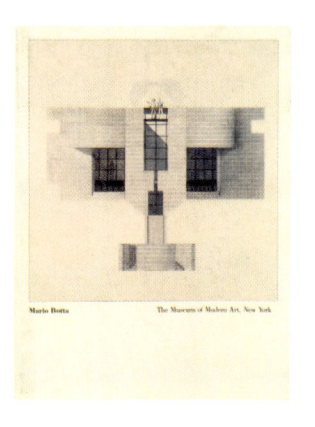

Mario Botta, *Avant-propos*, p. 5.
Claude Ritschard, Jerôme Baratelli, *Entretien avec Mario Botta*, pp. 6-12.
Jacques Gubler, *Sur quelques "ismes" de l'architecture moderne*, pp. 13-14.
Philippe Thomé, *Maison à Breganzona 1983-1987*, pp. 16-21.
Vincent Mangeat, *"Vues de l'intérieur". Essais sur le mode d'assemblage*, pp. 38-40.
Alberto Sartoris, *Quartier d'habitation à Turin 1985-1986*, p. 56.
Bernard Zumthor, *Lecture d'un plan*, pp. 57-64.
The book is published for an exhibition at the School for Applied Arts in Geneva (March - April, 1987). The show presents three housing projects (the family house in Breganzona 1983-87, projects for row houses in Pregassona 1985-1986 and for a housing quarter in Turin (1985-1986)), an interview and four critical essays on theoretical considerations and aspects of the design research.

Peter Pfeiffer (a cura di), *Mario Botta Designer*, Corus, Wohlen-Milano 1987.
Hanna Zurlinden, *Conversazione con Mario Botta, Lugano, 24 maggio 1987*, pp. 4-5.
Design starts to be a productive field to explore within the architectural research.

1988

AA.VV., 'Mario Botta', *Techniques & Architecture*, 1988, 377, avril-mai [numéro monographique].
Alain Pélissier, *L'éthique constructive*, pp. 50-53; *Force d'inscription*, pp. 58-61; *Des volumétries urbaines*, pp. 82-91; *Quêtes d'identité*, pp. 92-97; *Un jeu entre l'espace et le lieu. Entretien avec Mario Botta*, pp. 134-137. Jean-François Pousse, *Un itinéraire singulier*, pp. 54-57; *A l'origine, les maisons*, pp. 112-121; *Prégnance des églises*, pp. 122-123.
Marie-Christine Loriers, *La quadrature du cercle*, pp. 70-79; *Les temps court*, pp. 128-133.
Françoise-Hélène Jourda, Gilles Perraudin, *Un art du temps*, pp. 80-81.
Photography: Stéphane Couturier, Lorenzo Bianda, Adriano Heitmann, Mauro Cassina, Elliot Kaufman.
A richly illustrated monographic magazine introduces to French readers the library in Villeurbanne, the theater in Chambéry, the Ransila 1 building in Lugano, various family houses and first church projects, and shows among different aspects the evolution of Botta's architectural language.

Benedetto Gravagnuolo (a cura di), *Mario Botta, Studi preliminari per la Banca del Gottardo a Lugano*, catalogo, Edizioni A. Salvioni, Bellinzona 1988.
Mario Botta, *Il disegno dell'architetto e l'opera di architettura*, pp. s.n.
Benedetto Gravagnuolo, *I disegni della Banca del Gottardo*, pp. s.n.

The Gottardo Gallery hosts in the building of the new bank and for its opening the exhibition of a wide selection of sketches that reveal the detailed studies of the whole design process for the building.

1989

Francesco Dal Co (a cura di), *Mario Botta. Una casa,* catalogo, Electa, Milano 1989.
Vittorio Fagone, *In forma di freccia: il disegno e l'architettura della casa a Breganzona*, pp. 7-10.
Mario Botta e Francesco Dal Co, *Una conversazione intorno all'architettura (1989)*, pp. 81-87.
Photography: Pino Musi.
A paradigmatic work of Botta's production undergoes a detailed examination from a critical and architectural point of view.

Jean-Paul Felley, Olivier Kaeser, *Mario Botta construire les objets. Oeuvre design 1982-1989*, catalogue d'exposition, Fondation Louis Moret, Martigny 1989.
Mario Botta, *La construction des objets*, p. 7; *Objets récents* (conférence), pp. 62-65; *Entretien avec Mario Botta*, pp. 66-69.
Jean-Paul Felley, Olivier Kaeser, *Introduction*, p. 9.
Benedetto Gravagnuolo, *La mesure du rêve*, pp. 70-72.
Photography: Ballo & Ballo, Lorenzo Bianda, Mauro Cassina, Michel Darbellay, Gitty Darugar, Felley & Kaeser, Adriano Heitmann, Marcel Imsand, Antonio Martinelli, Jean-Marie Monthiers, Pino Musi, Archivio Mario Botta [et al.].
A show presented by two young curators at the Fondation Moret in Martigny, from July 1 to August 27, 1989, focuses on the items designed in the 80's.

Mirko Zardini (edited by), 'The latest Works of Mario Botta', *A+U Architecture and Urbanism*, 1989, 220, January.
Mirko Zardini, *New Myths*, pp. 56-61; *Interview with Mario Botta*, pp. 111-121.
Photography: Antonio Martinelli, Stephane Couturier.
An update of Botta's most important work realised in the 80's and published by the Japanese magazine with an excellent photographic service.

1990

AA.VV., *Mario Botta. Watari-um Project in Tokyo 1985-1990*, catalog edited by Etsuko Watari, Watari-um, Tokyo 1990.
Mario Botta, *"Dear Mrs. Watari"*, pp. 6-9.
Shizuko Watari, *Foreword*, pp. 10-11.
Harald Szeemann, *"A Sounding Triangle"*, pp. 37-39.
Enrico Mantero, *"Migrating Architectural Foundations"*, pp. 40-42.
Nam June Paik + Mario Botta, *Conversation*, pp. 109-112.

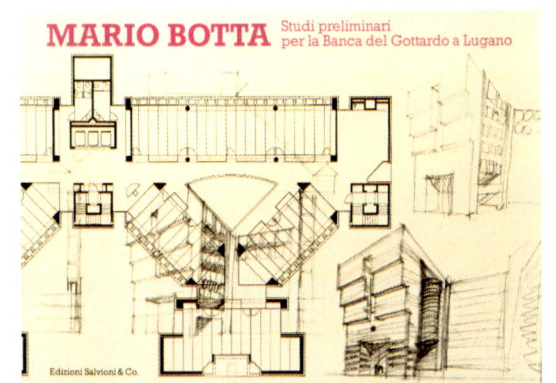

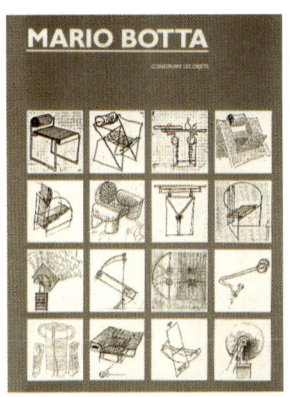

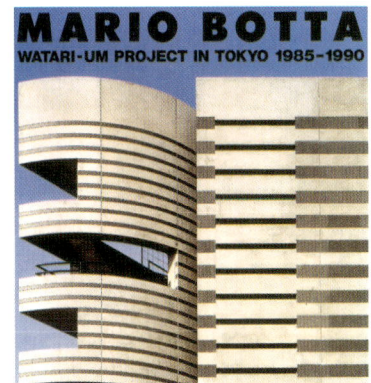

Photography: Pino Musi, Gantame, Shigeru Ohno, Masataka Nakano, Yasuyuki Ogura, Kikuo Kitabayashi, Atsuo Furuta, Shinjiro Kamiyama, Kokudo-chirin.
The opening of the Watari-Um art gallery and the exhibition of the whole design process for the homonymous building marks Botta's presence in the Japanese capital.

Peter Disch (a cura di), *Mario Botta. La ricerca negli anni ottanta*, ADV, Lugano 1990.
Mario Botta, *Grazie a Peter Disch*, p. 5.
Peter Disch, *Uno sguardo retrospettivo*, pp. 7-8.
Mario Botta, Stanislaus von Moos, Tita Carloni, *Dibattito sulla ricerca*, pp. 9-18.
Peter Disch, Claudio Negrini (a cura di), *Colloquio con Mario Botta*, pp. 19-24.
Margherita Snider-Noseda (a cura di), *"Il dissenso è tempestivo, il consenso arriva tardi"* (intervista con Mario Botta), pp. 25-27.
Photography: various
A selection of abstracts published in the 80's in the *Rivista tecnica*, a Swiss italian monthly magazine, are gathered in a book by the same author.
The essays reflect on themes that characterise Botta's architectural activity in this period.

Jean Claude Garcias, 'La cathédrale du XXIème siècle', *Art Sacré, Le Renouveau*, [numéro spécial de *Beaux Arts*], Paris 1990.
Jean Claude Garcias, *La cathédrale du XXIème siècle*, pp. 5-13.
Philippe Dufour, *Art Sacré, le renouveau*, pp. 15-33.
Photography: Dominique Planquette, Daniel Giraudon, Roger Viollet, René Percheron [et al.].
The project for the cathedral in Evry and the distinctiveness of the theme attracts the interest of the architectural press.

Giovanni Pozzi, *Mario Botta, at the crossroads of culture*, «approach» (Osaka), winter 1990 [Japanese/English ed.].
Giovanni Pozzi, *"Novantiqua" for Mario Botta*, pp. 12-17.
Photography: René Burri, Pino Musi.
The thoughts and considerations of the Ticino philosopher and philologist are fundamental references.

1991
AA.VV., *La tenda / La Tente / Das Zelt*, Edizioni Casagrande-Verlag für Architektur, Bellinzona 1991 [Italian/German/French edition].
Tita Carloni, *Topos, città, anti-città*, p. 9; *Alla ricerca degli antenati*, pp. 14-18; *... ma quale tecnologia*, pp. 19-23.
Jacques Pilet, *Il trabocchetto di Botta*, pp. 45-47.

Harald Szeemann, *Il miracolo di Castel Grande*, pp. 56-60.
Mario Botta, *Postscriptum*, pp. 70-72.
Photography: Pino Musi.
Trilingual edition dedicated to the happy event of the tent designed by Botta for the 700th anniversary of the Swiss Confederation.

Mario Botta – Schizzi di studio per l'edificio in Via Nizzola a Bellinzona, Spazio XXI - Arti Grafiche A. Salvioni, Bellinzona 1991.
Photography: Pino Brioschi, Marco D'Anna.
The booklet presents twelve sketches as fragments of a wide puzzle of drawings that define the project development "from the first notes to the final details".

Pippo Ciorra (a cura di), *Botta, Eisenmann, Gregotti, Hollein: musei*, Electa, Milano 1991, pp. 39-64 [Atti del convegno "Progettare musei oggi", Bologna, 5 ottobre 1990].
Pippo Ciorra, *Dalla "città-museo" al "museo-città"*, p. 7.
Mario Botta, *Museo privato Watari-um a Tokio e Museo di arte contemporanea a San Francisco*, pp. 39-63.
[et al.]
Two buildings presented during a workshop about designing contemporary museums, were later published in a a book.

Emilio Pizzi (a cura di), *Mario Botta. Architectures 1980-1990*, catalogue d'exposition, Editorial Gustavo Gili, Barcelona 1991 [German ed.: *Mario Botta 1980-1990*, Verlag für Architektur-Artemis & Winkler Verlag, Zürich-München 1991; Portuguese ed.: *Mario Botta. Arquitecturas 1980-1990*, Editorial Gustavo Gili-Fundaçao Calouste Gulbenkian, Barcelona-Lisboa, 1992].
Werner Oechslin, *Introduction*, pp. 8-19. Pier Luigi Nicolin, *Propos sur l'architecture des années 80* [interview], pp. 20-31.
Photography: Aldo Ballo, Lorenzo Bianda, Alberto Flammer, Adriano Heitmann, Pino Musi, Maurizio Pelli, Roberto Sellito, Alo Zanetta.
The catalog of the exhibition at the Swiss Cultural Center in Paris, from February 2 to April 7 1991, and at the Musée Rath in Geneva, from June 20 to September 29, 1991 (and later on presented in several other European cities), offers a good occasion to review Botta's architectural work of the last ten years and involves important figures of the Swiss and Italian cultural debate.

Emilio Pizzi (edited by), *Mario Botta. Obras y Proyectos/Works and Projects*, Editorial Gustavo Gili, Barcelona 1991 [Spanish/English updated reprint 1998; German/French ed.; *Mario Botta*, Verlag für Architektur/Les Editions d'Architecture-Artemis & Winkler Verlag, Zürich-München 1991, re-edited 1998;

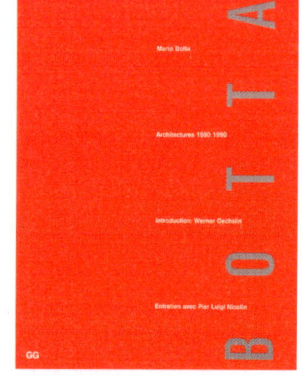

Italian ed. *Mario Botta*, Zanichelli, Bologna 1991; Portuguese ed.: *ibidem*, Martins Fontes Editora, Sao Paulo 1994; Chinese ed.: *ibidem*, Lnkj Edition, Cina 2005].
Emilio Pizzi, *Introducción / introduction*, p. 9; *Viviendas unifamiliares / Private houses*, pp. 13-14; *Edificios residenciales / Residential buildings*, pp. 55-56; *Edificios de culto / Religious buildings*, pp. 91-92; *Edificios administrativos / Administrative buildings*, pp. 105-106; *Edificios públicos / Public buildings*,
pp. 145-147; *Proyectos para la ciudad / Urban design projects*, pp. 191-193; *Diseño / Design*, p. 225.
Photography: Aldo Ballo, Lorenzo Bianda, Pino Brioschi, Mauro Cassina, Michel Darbellay, Alberto Flammer, Adriano Heitmann, Marcel Imsand, Pino Musi, Paolo Pedroli, Alo Zanetta.
The first popular paper book edited in different languages offers a complete summary of Botta's work.

1992

Rolando Bellini, 'Mario Botta, The Museum of Modern Art, San Francisco', *Critica d'Arte*, 1992, 8, [printed extract], pp. 1-16.
Rolando Bellini, *Note per una architettura liberatrice*, pp. 1-16.
The article on the Museum of Modern Art in San Francisco as pretext for a more complex reflection on Botta's architecture.

Rolando Bellini (a cura di), *Mario Botta Architetture 1980-1990*, catalogo della mostra, Artificio Edizioni, Firenze 1992.
Adolfo Natalini, *Mario Botta (testimonianza per)*, pp. 10-11.
Rolando Bellini, *Sul disegno di architettura*, pp. 12-22.
Vittorio Savi, *Postfazione*, pp.164-166.
Schede critiche a cura di Mario Gemin.
Photography: Aldo Ballo, Giasco Bertoli, Lorenzo Bianda, Mauro Cassina, Giovanni Chiaramonte, Marco D'Anna, Michel Darbellay, Alberto Flammer, Adriano Heitmann, Marcel Imsand, Pino Musi, Urs Tschopp, Alo Zanetta.
Exhibition catalog of the show presented at Palazzo Strozzi in Florence, December through January 1993.

Giasco Bertoli, *Studi su Mario Botta: una ricerca fotografica*, Istituto Europeo di Design, Idea Books, Milano 1992.
Edward Rozzo, *Insegnare a fotografare*, pp. 7-9.
Mario Botta, *Incontro con Giasco Bertoli*, p. 10.
Photography: Giasco Bertoli.
Mario Botta's architecture seen from the lens of the photographer Giasco Bertoli.

Jean Petit (a cura di), *Mario Botta progetto per una chiesa a Mogno*, catalogo della mostra, Collection Forces Vives-Fidia Edizioni d'Arte, Lugano 1992 [Italian/French ed.; id. English/German ed.].
Jean Petit, *Spazio e forma dell'invisibile*, pp. 8-9.
Mario Botta, *Per Jean Petit*, pp. 17-18; *A proposito di Mogno*, pp. 33-35; *Preghiere di pietra*, pp. 122-127.
Giovanni Pozzi, *Evocando uno sconcerto*, pp. 39-41.
Photography: Robert Doisneau [et al.].
The book with the graphic touch of the famous publisher documents one of the architect's favourite works.

1993

Raffaella Baraldi, Marco Fiorucci, *Mario Botta architettura e tecnica*, Clean Edizioni, Napoli 1993.
Benito De Sivo, *Presentazione*, p. 7.
Raffaella Baraldi, Marco Fiorucci, *Premessa*, p. 8.
Raffaella Baraldi, *Le matrici culturali e il rapporto con l'architettura contemporanea*, pp. 16-19; *Direttrici progettuali e segni ricorrenti nell'architettura di Mario Botta*, pp. 20-35; *Casa unifamiliare a Stabio*, pp. 36-43; *Casa unifamiliare a Vacallo*, pp. 49-55; *Edificio per residenze e uffici a Via Ciani a Lugano*, pp. 80-89.
Marco Fiorucci, *Biografia*, pp. 9-15; *Casa unifamiliare a Morbio Superiore*, pp. 44-48; *Casa unifamiliare a Daro*, pp. 56-63; *Edificio amministrativo e residenziale a Bellinzona*, pp. 71-79; *Edificio residenziale e commerciale in località Paradiso a Lugano*, pp. 90-97; *La progettazione degli elementi costruttivi*, pp. 98-117.
Photography: Gabriele Basilico, Lorenzo Bianda, Enrico Cano, Mario Carrieri, Marco D'Anna, Benito De Sivo, Alberto Flammer, Adriano Heitmann, Marcel Imsand, Pino Musi, Roberto Sellito, Alo Zanetta [et al.].
A detailed approach by different authors to analyze the characteristics in Botta's architecture.

Toshio Nakamura (edited by), 'Recent Ten Works by Mario Botta', *A+U Architecture and Urbanism*, 1993, 279.
Sergio Polano, *Under the Sign of Aries: New Directions in Mario Botta's Architectural Research*, pp. 8-13.
Photography: Pino Musi.
An important essay introduces this monographic issue that documents the most recent works.

Emilio Pizzi (hrsg.), *Mario Botta, Das Gesamtwerk, Band 1, 1960-1985*, Birkhäuser Verlag für Architektur, Basel-Boston-Berlin 1993 [Italian ed.: *Mario Botta, Opere complete, Volume 1, 1960-1985*, Federico Motta Editore, Milano 1993; English ed.:

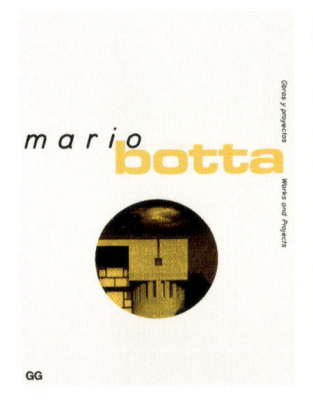

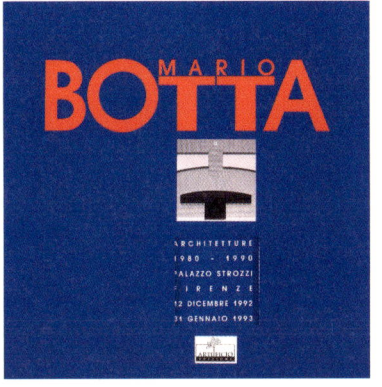

Mario Botta, The complete works, Volume 1 1960-1985, London 1993].
Tita Carloni, *Prefazione*, pp. 7-8.
Photography: Archivio Botta [et al.].
The first volume of the complete works edited at the same time in German, Italian and English confirms the importance of Botta's work within the contemporary architectural debate. The next volumes will be published in 1994 and 1998.

1994

AA.VV., *Mario Botta, Enzo Cucchi. La cappella del Monte Tamaro*, catalogo della mostra, Museo Cantonale di Lugano, Umberto Allemandi, Torino 1994 [Italian/English ed., updated reprint 1996].
Manuela Kahn Rossi, *Prefazione*, pp. 7-11; *Pietre e Angeli* (colloquio con Mario Botta ed Enzo Cucchi), pp. 13-27.
Fulvio Irace, *Un chiodo di pietra*, pp. 29-54.
Ursula Perucchi-Petri, *Enzo Cucchi sul Monte Tamaro*, p. 55-81.
Giovanni Pozzi, *Una litania dipinta*, pp. 99-115.
Photography: Andrea Cometta, Alberto Flammer, Vincenzo Vicari
The result of the art and design experience that Mario Botta shared with Enzo Cucchi for the chapel on Mount Tamaro is the *Leitmotiv* of this book published for the exhibition at the Museo Cantonale di Arte in Lugano, October 8 to November 6, 1994.

Pietro Bellasi e Danielle Londei, *Mario Botta*, catalogo della mostra, Danilo Montanari Editore, Ravenna 1994.
Pietro Bellasi, Danielle Londei, *Botta a Bologna*, n.pag.
Giuliano Gresleri, *Mario Botta: Homo ad circulum*, n. pag. [text Italian/French]
Photography: Marco d'Anna, Robert Canfield.
Botta's presence in Bologna for the exhibition organized by the Italian-French cultural association offers Giuliano Gresleri the occasion to analyze the architects work referred to geometry and in particular to the circular form.

Cesare Manzo (a cura di), *Mario Botta. Fuori Uso*, catalogo della mostra, Edizioni Arte Nova, Pescara 1994 [limited ed. republished by Giancarlo Politi Editore, Milano 1994].
L'allestimento [a cura di Sabina De Deo], n. pag.
I progetti, n.pag.
Photography: Aldo Ballo, Enrico Cano, Marco D'Anna, Pino Musi, Alo Zanetta.
Limited edition catalog for the exhibition realized at the former Opficio Gaslini of Pescara, July 22 to August 1994.

Jean Petit, *Traces d'architecture-Botta*, Fidia Edizioni d'Arte/ Bibliothèque des Arts, Lugano-Paris 1994.

Jean Petit, *Salut l'artiste*, pp. 6-9; *Mario Botta: faire son métier*, pp. 268-269; *Récit*, pp. 291-299; *Questions. Un interrogatoire*, pp. 302-307; *Une correspondance*, pp. 308-311; *Envoi*, p. 413.
Mario Botta vu par Robert Doisneau, pp. 10-17.
Itinéraire, pp. 21-63.
Espaces d'architecture, pp. 69-229.
Espaces de vie, pp. 247-261.
Botta vu par Clargue, pp. 270-271.
Le petit Botta illustré (fotografie biografiche e contributo di Jean Marc Reiser), pp. 273-290.
Pièces à convictions. Réponds a des journalistes, pp. 316-320.
Lettres, pp. 322-323.
Temoignages: Tita Carloni, *Le débuts de Mario Botta*, p. 325; Aurelio Galfetti, *Un portrait de Mario*, p. 326.
Dits et écrits [testi di Mario Botta: *On ne nait pas architecte; Travail d'architecte; Architecture et transformation; Valeur urbaine; Present et passé; Confrontation; Imaginaire et realité; Conscience de l'après; Probleme de langage; Discussion; Le passé comme ami; Le Mouvement Moderne; Maison individuelle; L'Architecte Aujourd'hui; Enseignement et école; Crise de la pianification urbaine; Le plans regulateurs, instruments ne fastes; La ville, le profane et le sacre; Architecture et environnement; L'Arbre; Valeurs; L'Oeuvre architectural, Dessin d'architecte et architecture; Dessin, lieu et projet; Design: une chaise; Objets; Écrire sur l'architecture, Giuseppe Mazzariol et Venise; Giacometti; Al'interieur du dessin de Moore; Louis Kahn; Le mur et la lumière: Tadao Ando; Cinema; Suisse-Europe, Drapeau, Mecene; Transformation; Conscience; La Suisse, une prison?*], pp. 329-352.
Le dossier Botta (annexes), pp. 355-404.
Photography: Pino Musi [et al.].
The author takes the chance to concentrate on Bottas person and biography; he follows the architect in his daily activities to seize the main features of his personality.

Giacinto Di Pietrantonio (a cura di), *Mario Botta*. catalogo della mostra, Trevi Flash Art Museum of Contemporary Art, Giancarlo Politi Editore, Milano 1994.
Mario Botta e Giacinto Di Pietrantonio, *Il dialogo*, p. s.n.
Photography: Aldo Ballo, Enrico Cano, Marco D'Anna, Pino Musi, Alo Zanetta.
A simple catalog edited for the exhibition at Trevi Flash Art Museum, October 1 to November 30, 1994.

Emilio Pizzi (hrsg.), *Mario Botta. Das Gesamtwerk, Band 2, 1985-1990*, Birkhäuser Verlag für Architektur, Basel-Boston-Berlin 1994 [Italian ed. *Mario Botta Opere complete, Volume 2, 1985-1990*, Federico Motta Editore, Milano 1994; English ed., *Mario Botta The complete works, Volume 2, 1985-1990*, London 1994].

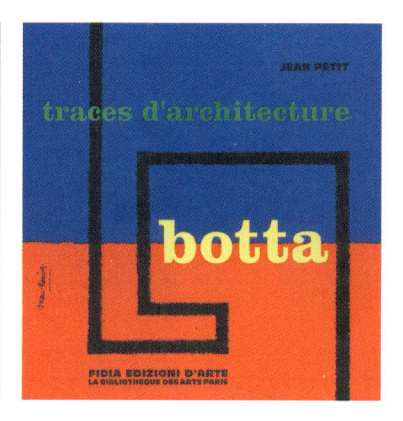

Jacques Gubler, *Cantieri*, pp. 6-8.
Photography: Archivio Mario Botta [et al.].
The well-known Swiss critic opens the second volume of the complete works that covers the activity and production of the second half of the 80's.

1995

AA.VV., *Il museo di Arte Moderna e Contemporanea di Trento e Rovereto*, Skira, Milano 1995.
Gabriella Belli, *Progetto culturale*, pp. 9-21.
Effetto Museo: dialogo tra Fulvio Irace e Mario Botta, pp. 22-26.
Photography: Marco D'Anna, Carlo Baroni, Mauro Cassina [et al.].
A monograph on the Mart in Rovereto featuring an interview with the architect and considerations on the cultural role of the new museum within the Italian panorama.

AA.VV., *Un lugar cuatro arquitectos: Botta, Galfetti, Snozzi, Vacchini en el Ticino*, catálogo de exposición, Museo de Bellas Artes, Caracas 1995.
Nydia Gutiérrez, *Presentación*, p. 6.
Fabiola López Durán, *Cuatro temas para cuatro maneras de hacer arquitectura*, pp. 40-69.
Giovanna Rosso, *Por una exposición in controtendenza*, pp. 184-85.
Luca Gazzaniga, *El lugar del Ticino*, pp. 186-88.
Josep M. Montaner, *Tradición y lugar: de la influencia de Kahn al minimalismo*, pp. 190-92.
Eligia Calderón, *Restaurar: otra forma de hacer arquitectura*, pp. 194-96.
Photography:: Gianna Guerra, Corinna Ceruti, Fabiola López Durán, Stefania Beretta, Enrico Cano, Arno Carpi, Alberto Flammer, Adriano Heitmann, Eduard Hueber, J. Kurtz, Pino Musi, Filippo Simonetti, Alo Zanetta, Archivio Mario Botta, Galfetti, Snozzi, Vacchini.
The catalog published for the exhibition at the Museo de Bellas Artes in Caracas is dedicated to the Ticino architecture and its most important exponents.

Sergio Grandini, *Una profezia su Mario Botta*, Natale Mazzuconi, Lugano 1995.
Sergio Grandini, *Una profezia su Mario Botta*, pp. 7-27.
A private and limited essay edition illustrated with preliminary sketches of five different architectural works (from the MoMA of San Francisco to the tent for the 700th year anniversary of the Swiss Confederation).

Vera Isler, Markus Mäder, *Mario Botta - Bank am Aeschenplatz, Basel*, Birkhäuser Verlag, Basel-Boston-Berlin 1995.
Markus Mäder (Text).
Photography: Vera Isler.
The book of the bank building in Basel offers an interesting photographic report.

1996

AA.VV., *Mario Botta. Cinque Architetture*, catalogo della mostra a cura di Mario Gemin, Skira, Milano 1996.
Mario Gemin, *Introduzione*, pp. 11-12; *La nuova chiesa di San Giovanni Battista a Mogno*, p. 29; *Chiesa parrocchiale Beato Odorico da Pordenone*, p. 53; *Chiesa di San Pietro Apostolo a Sartirana di Merate*, p. 77; *Cattedrale della Resurrezione a Évry*, p. 101; *Cappella di Santa Maria degli Angeli al Monte Tamaro*, p. 125
Christian Norberg-Schulz, *Luoghi tra cielo e terra*, pp. 13-16.
Giovanni Pozzi, *La chiesa in cinque chiese*, pp. 17-21.
Gabriele Cappellato, *Muri e terra*, pp. 23-28; *Geometrie per il sacro*, pp. 54-60.
Rudolf Arnheim, *Note a proposito dell'architettura religiosa*, pp. 30-36.
Emilio Pizzi, *La chiesa di San Pietro Apostolo a Sartirana di Merate*, pp. 78-84.
Giorgio Busetto, *Dentro lo spazio*, pp. 102-108.
Werner Oechslin, *Mario Botta: l'architettura sacra, l'espressione e la pietra*, pp. 126-130.
Virginia Baradel, *L'opera di Cucchi nella Cappella del Monte Tamaro*, pp. 149-152.
Mario Botta, *Cinque architetture*, pp. 153-154.
Claudio Nembrini (a cura di), *Colloquio con Mario Botta*, pp. 155-158.
Photography: Alberto Flammer.
The critical writings as well as the important documentation of five sacred buildings presented at the Querini Stampalia Foundation in Venice, from September 15 to November 17, 1996 constitute an essential reference for who wants to learn more about this architectural theme.

Cristina Bechtler (hrsg.), *Mario Botta - Mario Merz: Im Gespräch Mit Marlies Grüterich*, Kunsthaus Bregenz, Cantz Verlag, Ostfildern-Ruit, Stuttgart 1996.
Marlies Grüterich, *Warum ein Gespräch Zwischen Mario Botta und Mario Merz? Oder Wie kommen Architektur und Kunst aus der Utopie in unsere Topographie?*, pp. 7-9; *Resonanzarchitektur im Welthaus bauen und Wachsen lassen*, pp. 35-61.
Mario Botta, Mario Merz, Marlies Grüterich, *Gespräch vom 24. August 1994 in Lugano*, pp. 11-34.
The book shows Botta's interest to create new occasion for collaborations between architecture and art. The author takes the two protagonists into a reflection regarding common roots and references in the cultural field, the origins of the artistic creation and the way to conserve it through the modern world. A dialogue that evokes the archetypal-religious and pragmatic aspects in Botta's and Merz's work.

Benedetto Gravagnuolo (a cura di), *Mario Botta. Etica del costruire*, Laterza, Roma-Bari 1996 [German/English ed.: *Mario Botta Ethik des Bauens-Ethics of building*, Birkhäuser Verlag, Basel-Boston-Berlin 1997; Portuguese ed., *ibidem*, Ediçoes 70, Lisboa 1998; Japanese ed., *ibidem*, Kajima Institute-Laterza, Bari 1999; French ed., *ibidem*, Editions Parenthèses, Marseille 2005].
Benedetto Gravagnuolo, *Verso un'architettura millenaria*, pp. IX-XXII.
Mario Botta, *Pensieri costruiti*, p. 4-74; *La città nei limiti del progetto*, p. 75-86; *Tre progetti*, pp. 87-97; *L'oggetto e la sua forma plausibile*, p. 99-127; *Dialogo in appendice*, p. 129-147; *Nota autobiografica*, pp. 149-150.
The book offers the possibility to seize the theoretical fundamentals of the architect's research through a collection of some of his most significant writings.

Philip Jodidio (par), 'Musée Jean Tinguely', *Connaissance des Arts*, 1996, 98 [numéro monographique].
Fritz Gerber, *Préface*, pp. 4-6.
Philip Jodidio, *Pour un musée (entretien avec Mario Botta)*, p. 8-17.
Margrit Hahnloser, *Le démiurge*, pp. 18-44.
Jean-Louis Andral (par), *Mise en scène (entretien avec Pontus Hulten)*, pp. 46-58.
Andres Pardey, *Biographie*, pp. 60-65.
Arnaud Carpentier, *Guide pratique*, p. 66.
Photography: Roger Guillemot/Bernard Saint-Genés, Arnaud Carpentier, Pino Musi, Christian Baur, Martha Rocher, Leonardo Bezzola [et al.].
The new Tinguely museum arouses the interest of the famous French art magazine that dedicates a monographic to the artistic event of that moment.

Mario Botta gesehen von/vu par/seen by Pino Musi, Daco-Verlag, Stuttgart 1996 [French/English/German ed.].
Mario Botta, *Les architectures remercient*, p. s.n.
Fulvio Irace, *Pas de deux*, p. s.n.
Photography: Pino Musi.
Pino Musi's trained look qualifies once more Botta's work in a trilingual edition with an introduction by the architect himself.

Nicolas Westphal, Denyse Bertoni, *Mario Botta. La cathédrale d'Évry*, Skira, Milano 1996 [updated reprint 1999].
Nicolas Westphal, *Entrées pour une cathédrale nouvelle*, pp. 7-10.
Denyse Bertoni, *Mario Botta. L'architecture en héritage*, pp. 11-12.
Mario Botta, *Une cathédrale à Évry* e *Pour Évry*, p. 13.
Photography: Pino Musi.
Sketches, drawings and photographs documents the new cathedral in Evry.

1997

AA.VV., *Mario Botta. Architecture 1980-1995. A photographic Retrospective by Pino Musi*, Department of Architecture, University of Hong Kong, Hong Kong 1997.
Patrick Lau, Foreword, p. s.n.
Eric K-C-Lye, Introduction, p. s.n.
Rolf Bodenmüller, Foreword, p. s.n.
Photography: Pino Musi.
Exibition catalog published on occasion of a show presented at the Pao Galleries, Hong Kong Art Center (April 3-1, 1997) and at the University Museum and Art Gallery, HKU (April 17-28, 1997), with photographs by Pino Musi.

AA.VV., *Mario Botta. Emozioni di pietra. Un percorso fra le architetture pubbliche*, catalogo della mostra a cura di Luca Molinari, Skira, Milano 1997 [English ed.: *Mario Botta. Public Buildings 1980-1990*, Thames and Hudson, London 1998; Spanish ed.: *Mario Botta. Edificios públicos 1990-1998*, Editorial Gustavo Gili, Barcelona 1998; French ed.: *Mario Botta Bâtiments publics 1990-1998*, Skira/Seuil, Paris 1998].
Benedetto Gravagnuolo, *Sacro e profano*, pp. 13-16.
Cesare De Seta, *Mater Tellus*, pp. 17-21.
Aldo Masullo, *Emozioni di pietra*, pp. 23-25.
Werner Oechslin, *La vocazione di Mario Botta per il sacro ed il monumentale*, pp. 26-30.
Gabriele Cappellato, *Simboli e immagini*, pp. 31-33; *Il senso umano delle cose*, pp. 205-211.
Mario Botta, *Una mostra di architettura*, pp. 34-36.
Progetto grafico: Werner Jeker
Photography: Pino Musi (architectures), Marco D'Anna (models).
An essential book that expresses by means of different critical approaches various themes through Botta's design research (the relation with the city, the notion of monumentality, the significance of public architecture).

AA.VV., *Mario Botta Museum Jean Tinguely*, Museum Jean Tinguely, Benteli Verlag, Bern 1997 [English/French/German ed.].
Margrit Hahnloser, *Foreword*, pp. 6-7.
Niki de Saint Phalle, *I'm truly fond of Mario*, pp. 8-12.
Richard Ingersoll, *A Home for Entropy*, pp. 15-32.
Sergio Polano, *Contemporaries Mario Botta and Jean Tinguely*, pp. 44-53.
Lutz Windhöfel, *The Building, the City and the Public*, pp. 60-63.
Ulrike Jehle-Schulte Strathaus, *The language of Mario Botta*, pp. 66-70.
Jean-Yes Mock, *Tinguely and the Museums*, pp. 75-78.
Mario Botta, *Art and Architecture*, pp. 105-108.
Photography: Thomas Dix [et al.].
The importance of the critical essays and the complete documentation make this book an essential bibliographic reference.

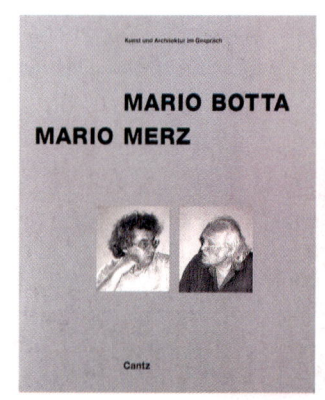

AA.VV., *Évry: moments de vie, histoires, architectures*, a Jacques Longuet, Acatos, Lausanne 1997.

Jacques Guyard, *Préface*, p. 5.

Dominique Lemaire, *Sur le banc*, pp. 9-13.

Jacques Longuet, *Petite chronique d'un village en quinze tableaux*, pp. 15-53; *Les lieux phares*, pp. 95-119; *Vivre sa ville au pluriel*, pp. 169-189; *Conclusion*, pp. 191-92.

Yves Damoiseau, *Gestation et naissance d'une ville*, pp. 55-71.

André Darmagnac, *Une architecture évolutive*, pp. 73-93.

Charlotte Hug, *Une tour de Babel enfin terminée*, pp. 120-135; *Entretien avec Mario Botta*, pp. 137-140.

Henri Jarrige, *De l'art en ville nouvelle*, pp. 143-167.

Photography: Dominique Planquette, Alain Bettey.

The cathedral in Evry is lived as an exceptional and important event in the historic-cultural context of the place.

Jean Petit, *Botta, parole di un architetto*, Fidia Edizioni d'Arte, Lugano 1997.

Photography: Pino Musi.

A booklet edited by *Carnets Forces Vives* realised and design by Jean Petit collects thoughts and reflections by Mario Botta, illustrated with sketches and photographs.

1998

AA.VV., *Banque et Architecture. Banque Bruxelles Lambert – Genève, Mario Botta – Architecte*, Electa-Banque Bruxelles Lambert, Milano-Genève 1998 [French/English ed.; reprint 2003].

Terence Riley, *Introduction*, p. 3.

Daniel Abramson, *Une histoire de l'architecture bancaire – la Maison, le Hall, le Temple, la Voûte et le Bureau*, pp. 4-15.

Vincent Scully, *L'Immeuble de la Banque Bruxelles Lambert (Suisse), Genève, dans son contexte*, pp. 16-27.

Francesco Dal Co, *Les outils du métier. Considérations sur la réalisation, par Mario Botta, du Siège de la Banque Bruxelles Lambert (Suisse) à Genève*, pp. 28-34.

Enrico Cano, *De l'extérieur à l'intérieur de la Banque Bruxelles Lambert (Suisse), Genève. Une promenade photographique*, pp. 35-63.

Photography: Enrico Cano, Pino Musi, Marco D'Anna [et al.].

The volume is entirely dedicated to the Bank Bruxelles Lambert and offers richly illustrated critical essays regarding all aspects of the bank building in Geneva.

Alessandra Gargiulo (a cura di), *Saper credere in architettura/7. Quarantaquattro domande a Mario Botta*, Clean Edizioni, Napoli 1998.

Alessandra Gargiulo, *Nota del curatore*, p. 5.

Photography: Pino Musi, Roberto Sellito, Lorenzo Bianda, Bruno De Sivo.

A useful interview conceived for the student-reader that allows seizing directly some aspects of the Botta's thoughts and his didactic approach to architecture.

Emilio Pizzi (hrsg), *Mario Botta. Das Gesamtwerk, Band 3 1990-1997*, Birkhäuser Verlag für Architektur, Basel-Boston-Berlin 1998 [Italian ed.: *Mario Botta Opere complete, Volume 3, 1990-1997*, Federico Motta Editore, Milano 1998; English ed.: *Mario Botta. The complete works 1990-1997*, London 1998].

Benedikt Loderer, *Mit modernen Formen römisch / Romano dalle forme moderne / Roman with modern forms*, pp. 6-7.

Photography: Archivio Mario Botta [et al.].

The third and last volume of the complete works with an introduction by the Swiss german critic Benedikt Loderer documents the work production of the 90's.

1999

AA.VV., *Borromini sul Lago. Mario Botta, la rappresentazione lignea del San Carlo alle Quattro Fontane a Lugano*, catalogo della mostra a cura di Gabriele Cappellato, Accademia di architettura USI-Skira, Mendrisio-Milano 1999.

Edoardo Sanguineti, *guardami, me: ti scopri un postcarlino*, p. 11.

Mario Botta, *Appunti sulla rappresentazione lignea del San Carlino a Lugano*, pp. 13-19.

Carlo Bertelli, *Francesco Maria "Bottomini" ovvero Borromini sul lago*, pp. 21-23.

Giuseppe Panza di Biumo, *Lo spaccato di San Carlino alle Quattro Fontane di Roma a Lugano*, p. 25-26.

Arduino Cantafora, *Se con l'arte vostra*, pp. 27-31.

Stanislaus von Moos, *Urbanistica virtuale. Due quasi-monumenti di Mario Botta*, pp. 33-38.

Nicola Emery, *Volontà d'arte*, pp. 39-44.

Georges Abou-Jaoudé, *Cattedrale di carta*, pp. 45-49.

Aurelio Muttoni, Franco Lurati, Marco Tajana, *La struttura portante*, pp. 249-251.

Gabriele Cappellato, *Atelier. Officina. Cantiere*, pp. 253-54.

Photography: Pino Musi, Fabrizio Arena.

The catalog of the exhibition at the Architecture Academy in Mendrisio dedicated to the wooden model of the San Carlo alle Quattro Fontane temporarily anchored on the shore of the lakefront Lugano, is characterized by the many critical essays on this event.

AA.VV., *La chiesa di San Giovanni Battista a Mogno*, Associazione Ricostruzione Chiesa di Mogno, Skira Ginevra-Milano 1999.

Mario Botta, *Per Mogno*, pp. 9-10.

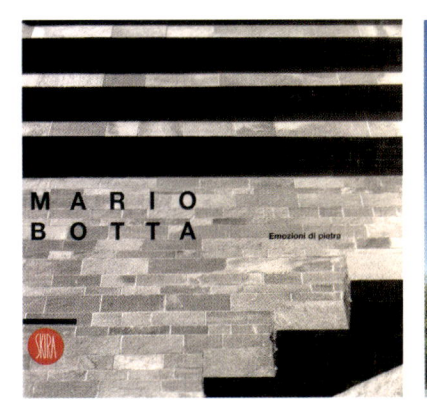

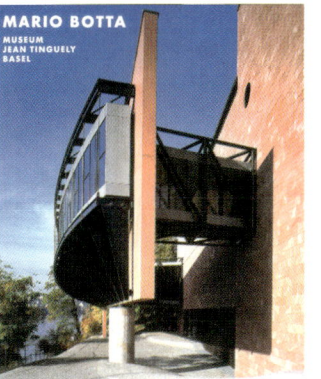

Giovan Luigi Dazio, *Una chiesa come dono*, pp. 11-15.
Antologia critica, pp. 131-144 [text by Giovanni Pozzi, Francesco Dal Co, Rudolf Arnheim, Gabriele Cappellato, Pia Serena, Ueli Pfammatter, Anthony Tischhauser (interview)].
Giorgio Cheda, *Un cristallo per contemplare l'aquila reale*, pp. 149-214.
Photography: Pino Musi.
The book released by the association for the reconstruction of the Mogno church illustrates the project with an essay of the Ticino historian Giorgio Cheda and offers an interesting critical anthology.

Philip Jodidio, *Mario Botta*, Taschen Verlag, Köln 1999. [English/French/German ed.; updated Spanish/Italian/Portuguese and English/French/German ed., Taschen, Köln 2003].
Philip Jodidio, *Pietra, luce e ragione*, pp. 6-17.
Photography: Aldo Ballo, Lorenzo Bianda, Enrico Cano, Mario carrieri, Marco D'Anna, Michel Darbelley, Alberto Flammer, Jean Paul Lüthy, Pino Musi, Paolo Rosselli, Roberto Sellito, Alo Zanetta [et al.].
A popular monographic book edited in three languages.

2000

AA.VV., *Mario Botta Centre Dürrenmatt Neuchâtel*, a cura di Peter Edwin Erismann/Archivio svizzero di letteratura, Birkhäuser Verlag, Basel-Boston-Berlin 2000 [Italian/English ed. and French/German ed.].
Kaspar Villiger, *Una porta aperta sull'opera di Dürrenmatt*, p. 7.
Peter Edwin Erismann, *Introduzione / Introduction*, p. 11.
Friedrich Dürrenmatt, *Vallon de l'Ermitage*, p. 46.
Roman Hollenstein, *Una torre e un ventre / A Tower and a Belly*, p. 79.
Charlotte Kerr Dürrenmatt, *Sta volando un albero!*, p. 151.
Stephan Stadler, *Un'opera ineguagliabile*, p. 158.
Blaise Duport, *Rendere omaggio a un contestatore senza recuperarlo*, p. 161.
Thierry Béguin, *Paradosso*, p. 163.
Laurent Gioria, *Il Centre Dürrenmatt – Missione Speciale*, p. 166.
Photography: Thomas Flechtner.
The curator Peter Erismann develops an interesting approach in connecting the architectural oeuvre of Mario Botta to the literary oeuvre of Friedrich Dürrenmatt.

Rolando Bellini, Fabio Minazzi, *Mario Botta per Borromini: il San Carlino sul lago di Lugano*, Edizioni Agorà, Varese 2000.
Rolando Bellini, Fabio Minazzi, *Premessa*, p. 9.
Rolando Bellini, *Ifetecne del San Carlino sul lago di Lugano*, pp. 11-49.
Fabio Minazzi, *Una lettura epistemologica del San Carlino di Mario Botta*, pp. 51-87.
Photography: Pino Musi.
Il volume affronta l'episodio del San Carlino di Botta in quanto omaggio architettonico borrominiano, diventando inoltre testimonianza della sua fugace presenza luganese.
The books concentrates on the temporary event of Botta's San Carlino created as an architectural tribute to Borromini.

Mario Botta, Charlotte Kerr Dürrenmatt, *Dürrenmatt Botta*, Skira, Milano 2000.
Mario Botta, *Il Centro Dürrenmatt a Neuchâtel*, p. s.n. [Italian/French ed].
Charlotte Kerr Dürrenmatt, *Une vision prend corp*, p. s.n. [French/German ed].
Photography: Pino Musi.
The folder published on occasion of the opening of the Centre Dürrenmatt in Neuchâtel stands for a fruitful collaboration between the architect and the client and witnesses a particular happy event.

Mario Botta, PA Pro Architect [Korea], 2000, 20, October [Korean/English ed.].
Mario Botta, 'The architect-figure today', pp. 6-11 [translation of Mario Botta, 'La figura dell'architetto oggi', *Domus*, 1994, 762, luglio-agosto, pp. 78-80]; 'The Past in Present Terms: An Architect's View', pp. 12-17 [from *Wordlink*, 1988, march, pp. 98-99]; *Thoughts on Building*, pp. 18-23 [from Benedetto Gravagnuolo (by), *Mario Botta. Etica del costruire*, Laterza, Roma-Bari 1996; German/English ed.: *Mario Botta Ethik des Bauens-Ethics of building*, Birkhäuser Verlag, Basel-Boston-Berlin 1997].
Photography: Marco D'Anna, Pino Musi, Enrico Cano, Robert Canfield, Nicola Eccher, Ralph Richter, Cornelia Suhan, Remy Steinegger.
Botta's work is introduced to a South-Korean public with a selection of his essays.

Mario Botta Centro Swisscom a Bellinzona, Skira, Ginevra-Milano 2000 [Italian/English ed.].
Mario Pisani, *La sede di Swisscom a Bellinzona*, pp. 7-9.
Photography: Enrico Cano.
A complete documentation of the Swisscom center built in Bellinzona in the 90's.

Luisella Gelsomino (a cura di), *Mario Botta. Modelli di architettura*, catalogo della mostra, Centro studi dell'abitare OIKOS-Alinea Editrice, Firenze 2000 [Italiana/English ed.].
Werner Oechslin, *"Portato dalla ragione & dalle linee…" Modelli e vasi – Mario Botta alla ricerca del corpo e della forma*, pp. 7-12.
Mario Botta, *Modelli lignei come personaggi nello spazio domestico*, pp. 13-14.
Photography: Pino Musi, Marco D'Anna.
Models: Simone Salvadé, Roberto Vismara, Stefano Vismara.
Catalog released for the exhibition at the Esprit Nouveau Pavilion in Bologna, May 19 – July 2, 2000.

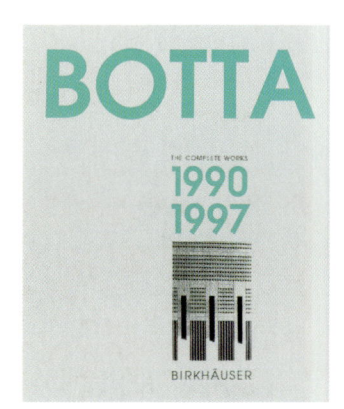

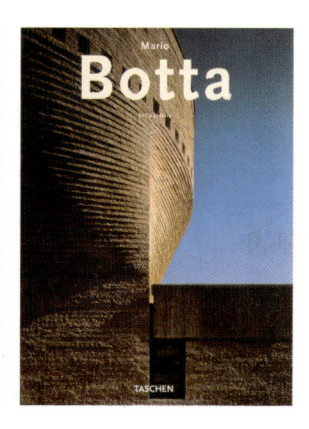

Emma Lavigne, *La cathédrale de la résurrection d'Évry*, Centre de Monuments Nationaux / Éditions du Patrimoine, Paris 2000.
Histoire: Une nouvelle cathédrale à l'aube du XXIe siècle, p. 7; *De la maison à la cathédrale*, p. 9; *Les sources architecturales*, p. 10.
Extérieur: L'environnement urbain, p. 15; *Un cylindre tronqué, couronné d'arbres*, p. 17; *Une enveloppe de brique*, p. 21; *Les vues nor-ovest et sud-ovest, l'entreé*, p. 23.
Intérieur: Le plan circulaire, p. 31; *La lumière zénithale*, p. 39; *La galerie-dèambulatoire*, p. 41; *Le choeur*, p. 45; *La nef*, p. 51; *La chapelle du jour dite "du Saint-Sacrement"*, p. 55; *La crypte*, p. 57.
Photography: Jean Luc Paillé / Centre des Monuments Nationaux [et al.].
A small guide-book offers all historical and architectural aspects of the project for the Evry cathedral.

Irena Sakellaridou, *Mario Botta Poetica dell'architettura*, Rizzoli, Milano 2000 [English ed.: *Mario Botta Architectural Poetics*, Rizzoli, New York 2000; reprint Rizzoli/Skira, Milano 2002; Thames & Hudson, London 2001].
Irena Sakellaridou, *Logica della forma, ricchezza del significato* (introduzione), pp. 6-11; *Alla ricerca dell'ordine* (capitolo uno), pp. 13-29; *Mezzi di creatività* (capitolo due),
pp. 30-97; *Forma e significato* (capitolo tre), pp. 98-167; *Una questione di scala* (capitolo quattro), pp. 168-211, *Un mondo di immaginazione e di oggetti* (capitolo cinque), pp. 220-225.
Anne-Marie Werner, *Le scenografie*, pp. 214-219.
Photography: Lorenzo Bianda, Robert Canfield, Enrico Cano, Stephan Couturier, Marco D'Anna, Nicola Eccher, Alberto Flammer, Adriano Heitmann, Jean Paul Lüthy, Pino Musi, Ralph Richter, Paolo Rosselli, Roberto Sellito, Arjen Schmitz, Filippo Simonetti, Cornelia Suhan, Alo Zanetta.
A closer look on Botta's architectural language in its various forms.

Ugur Tanyeli, Boyut Kitaplari (by), *Mario Botta*, Eylül 2000 [Turkish ed.].
Ugur Tanyeli, *Mario Botta ya da Aslolan Biçimdir*, pp. 8-21.
The presentation of Botta's work to Turkish readers.

Janet Wilson (by), *San Francisco Museum of Modern Art*, San Francisco Museum of Modern Art-Marquand Books, Seattle 2000.
David A. Ross, *When the San Francisco Museum of Modern Art's new building*, p. 11.
Mario Botta, *I think a relationship based on dialogue is imperative between the…*, p. 13.
Justin Henderson, *In 1995 The San Francisco Museum of Modern Art (SF.MOMA)*, p. 16.
Photography: Richard Barnes [et al.].
The MoMa of San Francisco presents itself with a collection of interesting and valuable considerations.

2001

AA.VV., *Mario Botta The Cymbalista Synagogue and Jewish Heritage Center*, Skira, Ginevra-Milano 2001.
Norbert Cymbalista, *Why Did I Want to Build a Synagogue?*, pp. 7-13.
Aron Dotan, *A Citadel of Dialogue. Understanding and Hope*, pp. 15-23.
Roman Hollenstein, *Citadel of Faith*, pp. 25-35.
Mario Botta, *The Cimbalista Synagogue*, p. 37.
Photography: Pino Musi [et al.].
Motivations and thoughts on the particular occasion to built a synagogue as a place for peace and cultural exchange.

AA.VV., *Mario Botta Legni e ceramiche*, catalogo della mostra, Dams Laborart 2001 - Università Cattolica del Sacro Cuore, Brescia 2001.
Dams Laborart 2001, *Presentazione*, p. 7.
Francesco Tedeschi, *Il lavoro sulla forma*, pp. 8-11.
Tino Bino, *Qualche cosa che emoziona*, pp. 60-61.
Werner Oechslin, *Tra il corpo e la forma*, pp. 62-63.
Roberto Consolandi, *Vas insigne devotionis (olla oggetto d'insigne devozione)*, pp. 64-65.
Photography: Basilio, Matteo e Stefano Rodella.
Another evidence of the multiple activities in Botta's research.

Mario Botta 13 Vasen - Skizzen Holz Keramik, catalogo della mostra, Galerie Stuker Zürich, Ostfildern 2001. [German/English ed.]
Werner Oechslin, *"Portato dalla ragione & dalle linee…" Modelle und Vasen — Mario Botta auf der Suche nach dem Körper und nach der Form*, pp. 5-11.
Mario Botta, *Vorwort*, p. 13.
Photography: Marco D'Anna.
Models: Simone Salvadé, Roberto e Stefano Vismara.
A small catalog for the exhibition held at the Stuker Gallery in Zurich, from August 31 to September 29, 2001 highlights the way to experiment form and geometry through the ceramic works.

'Mario Botta', *World Architecture* [China], 2001, 9.
red., *Architect Mario Botta*, p. 16.
Brian Chang, Brenda Yao, *Basic geometry and meaning in Architecture: Mario Botta and the tradition of simbolic Geometry in western Architecture*, pp. 18-22.
Gabriele Cappellato, *Sign, Form, Design*, p. 23.
Mario Botta, *Thoughts and writing by Mario Botta*, pp. 24-27.
Zhi Wen Jun, Guo Dandan, *Building Sites – The sacred buildings by Mario Botta*, pp. 28-31.
A volume that evidences the Chinese growing interest in Botta's work.

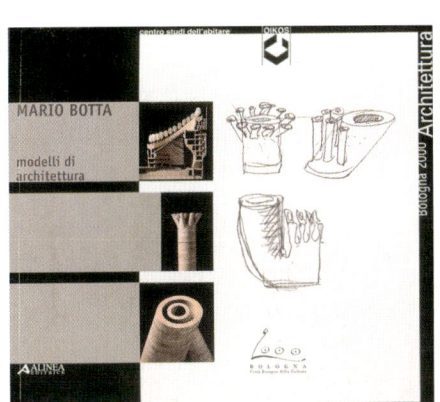

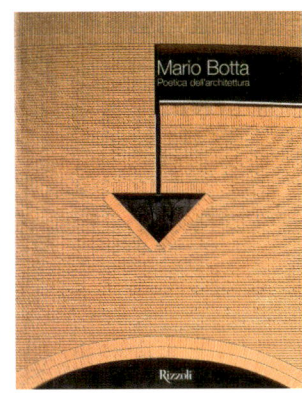

Giovanni Pozzi, *Mario Botta Santa Maria degli Angeli sul Monte Tamaro*, Edizioni Casagrande, Bellinzona 2001 [id. German/French ed.].
Mario Botta, *Il monte e la cappella*, pp. 5-6.
Giovanni Pozzi, *L'origine della chiesa*, p. 9; *Il titolo: Santa Maria degli Angeli*, p. 10; *La fabbrica*, p. 11; *Un'idea di chiesa*, pp. 12-13; *L'architettura*, p. 16; *l'iconografia*, p. 18; *L'incontro dell'architettura con l'iconografia*, p. 20
Photography: Enrico Cano, Alberto Flammer, Marco D'Anna, Andrea Cometta [et al.].
With thoughts written by the Swiss Italian philologist and essay by the architect, the booklet guides through a lecture of the project, its site and the suggestive relation the chapel establishes with its surroundings.

Emanuele Saurwein (a cura di), *Un mantello tinto d'inchiostro: note sul ligneo San Carlino di Lugano di Mario Botta*, Gabriele Capelli Editore, Mendrisio 2001 [German ed.: *Der düstrer Mantel: über den aus Holz gebauten San Carlino con Lugano von Mario Botta*; English ed.: *My inky cloak: notes on the wooden model of the San Carlino in Lugano by Mario Botta*].
Emanuele Saurwein, *Ombre*, pp. 3-11.
Photography: Pino Musi.
Considerations on the unusual presence that characterized the Lugano lakefront for a couple of years.

2002

AA.VV., *Per un'architettura vivente*, a cura di Fabio Minazzi, Accademia di architettura-USI, Mendrisio 2002.
Fabio Minazzi, *Premessa*, pp. 7-10; *Per una nuova lettura del progetto architettonico*, pp. 77-89.
Fulvio Papi, *La genealogia del San Carlino bottiano e il suo senso*, pp. 13-26.
Stanislaus von Moos, *"Ceci n'est pas un Borromini"*, pp. 27-36.
Mario Botta, *La struttura stratificata del San Carlino luganese*, pp. 37-61.
Rolando Bellini, *La sfida architettonica neoilluminista di Botta*, pp. 63-74.
Photography: Archivio Mario Botta.
Botta's San Carlino as an example for considerations on the relation between project and history.

Mario Botta, PLUS Korean Architecture+Interior Design [Seoul], 2002, 6, pp. 36-73.
red., *A current View*, pp. 36-37.
Opere, pp. 38-73.
A famous architectural magazine from South Korea presents an accurate report on different buildings realized between 2000-01 (for cultural, office and sport facilities).

2003

AA.VV., *Mario Botta, Luce e Gravità. Architetture 1993-2003*, catalogo della mostra a cura di Gabriele Cappellato, Editrice Compositori, Bologna 2003 [English ed.: *Mario Botta Light and Gravity: Architecture 1993-2003*, Prestel Publishing, Munich-Berlin-London-New York 2004; updated reprint: *Mario Botta, Luce e Gravità: Architetture 1993-2007*, Editrice Compositori, Bologna 2008].
Giuseppe Cappochin, *Presentazione*, p. 6 [in the first edition only].
Giustina Mistrello Destro, *Presentazione*, p. 7 [in the first edition only].
Mario Botta, *Luce e gravità*, pp. 8-11.
Giuliano Gresleri, *"Bottiana"*, pp. 12-25.
Lionello Puppi, *Lo spazio, la geometria e la luce*, pp. 26-33.
Heinrich Thelen, *I disegni di Mario Botta*, pp. 34-37.
Photography: Fabrizio Arena, Lorenzo Bianda, Enrico Cano, Young Chea Park Seoul, Alberto Flammer, Rainer Hofman, Urs Homberger, Horm, Thomas Jantscher, Pino Musi, Charles Page, Ralph Richter, Pietro Savorelli, Cornelia Suhan, Alo Zanetta; Photography of models modelli: Mauro Cassina, Marco D'Anna, Nicola Eccher, Archivio Mario Botta.
models: Ivan Kunz, Mauro Mauri, Simone Salvadé, Studio Snehal Shah, Roberto Vismara, Stefano Vismara, Archivio Mario Botta.
From the Tinguely museum in Basel to the "Bergoase" of Arosa the catalog of the exhibition at the Palazzo della Ragione in Padova (December 12, 2003 to March 21, 2004) presents an overview of themes faced during the last fifteen years.

AA.VV., *La chiesa di Sartirana... perché nulla vada perduto*, a cura di Gabriele Cappellato, Editrice Compositori, Bologna 2003.
Gianfranco Ravasi, *Quattro emozioni*, pp. 9-10.
Emilio Pizzi, *I semi di una cultura architettonica perduta*, pp. 11-13.
Fabiano Redaelli, *Nota tecnica*, p. 14.
Gabriele Cappellato, *Il progetto: considerazioni*, p. 15.
Rassegna stampa, pp. 82-88.
Documenti critici, pp. 89-95 [texts by di Mario Botta, Giovanni Pozzi, Emilio Pizzi, Lorenzo Spagnoli, Andrea Colombo Giuseppe Arosio].

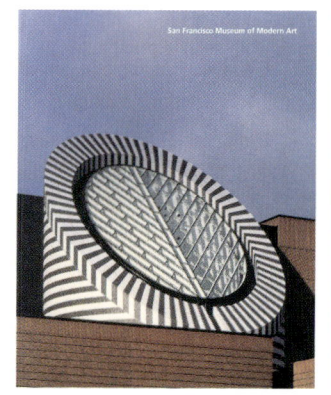

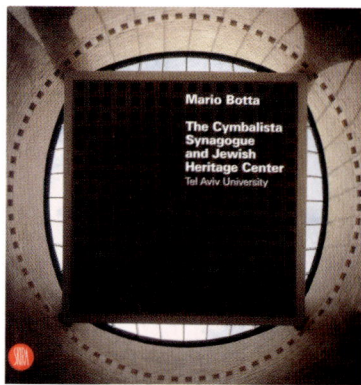

Photography: Enrico Cano, Pino Musi, Pierantonio Sala.
The book on the church in Sartirana presents the reasons and motivations of this project and proposes an important critical anthology.

Tino Bino (a cura di), Mario Botta, *La cantina di Suvereto*, La Quadra Editrice, Brescia 2003.
Tino Bino, *Introduzione*, p. 7-11.
Mario Botta, *Una cantina a Suvereto*, pp. 13-17; *Frammenti*, pp. 63-76 [opinioni, riflessioni, pensieri, pubblicati in appendice nel volume *Mario Botta. Quasi un diario*, Le Lettere, Firenze 2003, pp. 258-269].
Photography Guglielmo De Micheli, Pino Musi.
An architectural theme that has marked the last decade finds in Botta's architectural language a new interpretation.

Mario Botta, Giulio Andreolli, *Il Museo di Arte Moderna e Contemporanea di Trento e Rovereto*, Skira, Milano 2003 [id. French/English ed.].
Gabriella Belli, *Mart- Museo di Arte Moderna e Contemporanea di Trento e Rovereto*, pp. 6-8.
Mario Botta, *Mart a Rovereto*, pp. 9-13; *Il Museo di Arte Moderna e Contemporanea a Rovereto*, p. 15.
Luca Molinari, *Un marziano a Rovereto*, pp. 17-19.
Mario Botta, Giulio Andreolli, *Nota al progetto*, pp. 21-23.
Photography: Enrico Cano, Pino Musi.
The volume documents with plenty of details and great pictures the project and complex of the museum in Rovereto.

Gabriele Cappellato (a cura di), 'Mario Botta Mart Museo di Arte Moderna e Contemporanea di Trento e Rovereto', *OP/1 – Opera progetto Rivista Internazionale di Architettura Contemporanea*, Editrice Compositori, Bologna 2003 [numero monografico; Italian/English ed.].
Gillo Dorfles, *Introduzione*, p. 5.
Giulio Andreolli, *Genesi della città*, pp. 13-21.
Gabriele Cappellato, *Dialogo con Mario Botta*, p. 27.
Nicola Marzot (a cura di), *Colloquio con il direttore*, pp. 88-99.
Pierluigi Cerri, *Spedizione su Mart*, p. 100.
Photography: Enrico Cano, Pino Musi.
A monographic issue on the Mart museum, richly illustrated and proposing some reviewer's considerations.

Rocco Cerone (a cura di), *Rovereto e il nuovo polo culturale*, Nicolodi Editore, Rovereto 2003 [Italian/English ed.].

Rocco Cerone, *Introduzione*, pp. 7-12.
Diego Quaglioni, *Le radici storiche di una città-frontiera della cultura*, pp. 13-26.
Franco de Battaglia, *La grotta di Prospero. La nascita del Mart a Rovereto*, pp. 27-40.
Carlo Martinelli, *Al centro della luce*, pp. 41-48.
Pino Musi, *Spazi d'ombra*, pp. 49-86 [saggio fotografico].
Fabrizio Rasera, *Le vie del Mart*, pp. 87-100.
Livio Caffieri, *Le sinergie*, pp. 101-107.
fotografie: Pino Musi.
La genealogia storico-culturale del Mart di Rovereto segna l'approccio di una pubblicazione ricca e variegata.
The historic-cultural geneology of the Mart in Rovereto marks the approach of a rich and diversified publication.

Stefano Crespi (a cura di), Mario Botta, *Quasi un diario: frammenti intorno all'architettura*, Le Lettere, Firenze 2003 [riprint 2004].
Architettura e "contesto", p. 9; *Il disegno degli architetti*, p. 14; *Venezia-Le Corbusier, l'ultimo progetto*, p.16; *Picasso: Guernica*, p. 25; *L'albero anomalo*, p. 28; *Tadao Ando (1981)*, p. 31; *Alvaro Siza, uno specchio*, p. 32; *La Casa rotonda*, p. 33; *Disegnare una sedia*, p. 37; *Emilio Ambasz*, p. 39; *Virgilio Gilardoni*, p. 40; *Castelgrande a Bellinzona*, p. 47; *James Stirling a Stoccarda*, p. 53; *La chiesa di Mogno*, p. 59; *Le corbusier: viaggio d'Oriente*, p. 63; *Il sacro e il profano: Locarno e il suo festival*, p. 66; *Sottonapoli*, p. 71; *Il percorso del progetto*, p. 74; *Architettura come trasformazione*, p. 77; *Aurelio Galfetti*, p. 81; *Disegnare gli oggetti*, p. 84; *Cara signora Watari*, p. 86; *La tenda*, p. 90; *Postscriptum tenda*, p. 91; *Tadao Ando (1990)*, p. 94; *Giuseppe Mazzariol (1991)*, p. 99; *Sculture lignee*, p. 105; *Luigi Snozzi*, p. 106; *Alberto Giacometti*, p. 109; *Accademia di Architettura*, p. 109; *Cattedrale di Evry*, p. 113; *Questa mia terra*, p. 114; *Preghiere di pietra*, p. 118; *Rino Tami*, p. 123; *Giuseppe Mazzariol (1992)*, p. 124; *Henry Moore*, p. 126; *Hans Bernoulli*, p. 128; *Mogno per Jean Petit*, p. 131; *Svizzera*, p. 133; *La zattera di pietra*, p. 136; *Costruire*, p. 137; *Casabrutta*, p. 138; *Atelier Giacometti*, p. 148; *Vittoriano Viganò*, p. 148; *Azuma a Mendrisio*, p. 151; *Lettera a un fotografo*, p. 152; *Museo di San Francisco*, p. 153; *Memoria e architettura*, p. 155; *Bruno Delamain*, p. 155; *Cinque architetture*, p. 157; *La casa e le aggregazioni*, p. 159; *Ignazio Gardella*, p. 162; *Pino Musi*, p. 163; *Jean Tinguely*, p. 164; *Primo giorno all'Accademia*, p. 166; *Un cubo sul mare*, p. 170; *La casa di Dio*, p. 172; *Niki de Saint Phalle: Giardino dei Tarocchi*, p. 174; *Pierre Zoelly*, p. 176; *L'Arca di Noè*, p. 178; *Una sinagoga*, p. 180; *Cultura e politica*, p. 182; *Lo spazio sacro*, p. 187; *Louis Kahn*, p. 192; *San Carlino a Lugano*, p. 197; *Ancora Mogno*, p. 208; *La città dipinta*, p. 211; *Modelli come personaggi*, p. 211; *Abitare*, p. 213; *Max Frisch*, p. 215; *Dürrenmatt a Neuchâtel*, p. 216; *Architettura e spazio sacro*, p. 219; *Expo 2002*, p. 221; *Un allievo del Bauhaus*, p. 225; *Le polveri e le ceneri*, p. 227; *Luoghi dell'infinito*, p. 231; *Visita a uno scultore*, p. 231; *Solo la bellezza potrà salvare il mondo*, p. 233; *Sulla matita*, p. 235; *Giuliano Vangi*, p. 237; *Mart a Rovereto*, p. 240; *Caro signor Shin*, p. 241; *Cantiere*, p.

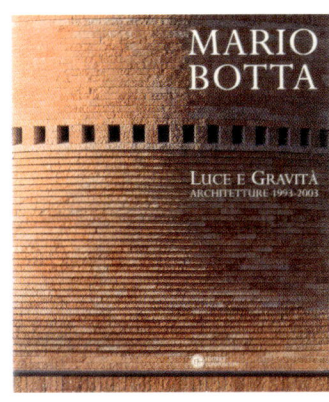

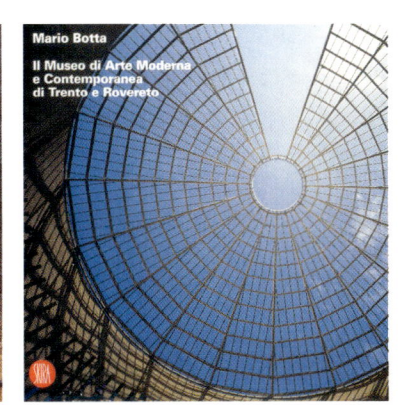

243; *Paolo Soleri*, p. 245; *Visite al cantiere della Scala*, p. 247; *Mumbai*, p. 250; *Hyderabad*, p. 252; *New Delhi*, p. 254; *La verità fugge dai vincitori*, p. 257; *Frammenti*, p. 258.
A collection of fragments as a "written" diary of a mainly "drawn" itinerary; notes revealing thoughts that mark a still ongoing research.

Aurora Cuito (a cura di), *Mario Botta*, TeNeues Loft, Düsseldorf-New York-West Byfleet-Paris 2003 [Italian/French/English/Germand ed.; Chinese ed. 2008].
Aurora Cuito, *Introduzione*, pp. 6-7.
Opere, pp. 8-77.
Photography: Pino Musi, Robert Canfield, Enrico Cano, Markus Steur, Cornelia Suhan, Ralph Richter, Rainer Hofmann.
The multilingual edition proves once more the international diffusion of Botta's work.

Zhi Wenjun e Zhu Guangyu (by), *Mario Botta*, Dalian Science and Technology University Press, Dalian 2003 [English/Chinese ed.].
Mario Botta, *Preface*, pp. 9-10.
red., *Critical Regionalism Architect – Mario Botta*, p. 12.
Photography: Aldo Ballo, Robert Canfield, Enrico Cano, Marco D'Anna, Alberto Flammer, Rainer Hofmann, Pino Musi, Arjen Schmitz, Cornelia Suhan, Ralph Richter, Alo Zanetta [et al.].
A bilingual University press edition introducing Mario Botta's complete architectural work in China.

Kyobo Tower, Symbol of success for the next 50 years, Kyobo Seoul 2003.
Chang Jae Shin, *Introduction*
Mario Botta, *Insights from the creator, Mario Botta*.
Photography: Young Chea Park
The book has been released by Kyobo Life Ins. for the opening of their new headquarters in Seoul.

2004

Annalisa Cima, *Segno del domani. Schizzi di Mario Botta*, Dîvân, Josef Weiss Edizioni, Mendrisio 2004 [limited ed.].
Annalisa Cima, *Segno del domani (per M.B.)*, n. pag.
A small folderbook with sketches of the Tel Aviv Synagogue printed in a limited edition of 33 copies for the collection Dîvân.

Yoshio Futagawa (by), 'Leeum, Samsung Museum of Art Seoul', Korea, *GA Global Architecture Document*, 2004, 83, December, pp. 8-59.
OMA, Jean Nouvel, Mario Botta, Leeum, Samsung Museum of Art, Seoul, Korea (1994-2004), pp. 8-59.
Gibson G. Rhie / Samoo Architects & Engineers, *Mario Botta. Museum of Traditional Art*, pp. 46-59.
Photography: Yukio Futagawa.
The internationally well-known magazine presents the projects of the three architects Botta, Kolhaas and Nouvel for the new Leeum-Samsung museum of art in Seoul.

Luca Molinari (a cura di), *Mario Botta Chiesa a Seriate*, Centro Pastorale Giovanni XXIII, Skira, Milano 2004.
Gianni Contessi, *La consacrazione della casa*, pp. 9-19.
Mario Botta, *Costruire una chiesa*, pp. 21-24; *Di fronte a una scultura*, pp. 115-126.
Photography: Pino Musi.
The book is part of a monographic collection on churches and documents the project and realization of the church in Seriate.

2005

AA.VV., *Mario Botta. Architetture del Sacro. Preghiere di Pietra*, catalogo della mostra a cura di Gabriele Cappellato, Editrice Compositori, Bologna 2005 [English ed.: *Mario Botta Architetture del Sacro. Prayers in Stone*, Editrice Compositori, Bologna 2005].
Mario Botta, *Lo spazio del sacro*, pp. 3-5.
Timothy Verdon, *Mario Botta e lo spazio del sacro a Firenze*, pp. 6-15.
Aldo Colonetti, *L'architettura come non-ancora*, pp. 16-20.
Alda Merini, *All'architetto Mario Botta*, p. 21.
Photography: Enrico Cano, Pino Musi, Paolo Mazzo, Alberto Flammer, Paolo Rosselli, Marco D'Anna.
models: Ivan Kunz, Simone Salvadé, Roberto Vismara.
Catalog of the exhibition at the Plaster casts gallery of the State Institute of Art in Florence, April 30 to July 30, 2005 and later on presented at the RIBA Royal Institute of British Architects in London, November 21, 2005 to January 14, 2006.

AA.VV., *Il Teatro alla Scala, Restauro e ristrutturazione*, a cura di Luca Molinari, Skira, Milano-Ginevra 2005.
Gillo Dorfles, *La riconversione della Scala*, p. 7.
Mario Botta, *Ristrutturazione del Teatro alla Scala di Milano*, pp. 19-23; *Il modello del Teatro alla Scala*, p. 41-45; *Note al progetto*, p. 139.
Emilio Pizzi, *I temi del progetto*, pp. 52-86.

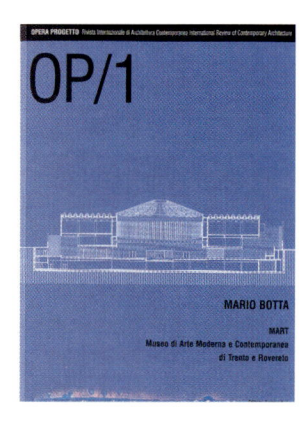

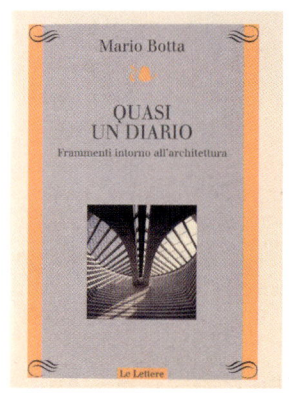

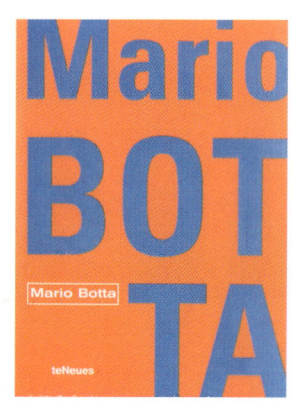

Elisabetta Fabbri, *Il restauro conservativo del Teatro alla Scala*, pp. 87-94.
Franco Malgrande, *Meccanica di scena*, pp. 95-99.
Alda Merini, *Per la Scala e Mario Botta*, p. 143.
Photography: Pino Musi, Enrico Lonati.
The publication presents the successful architectural work of the restructuring and offers considerations on interventions and restoration of historical building.

Brigitte Labs-Ehlert (hrsg.), *Mario Botta Architektur und Gedächtnis,* Wege zur Architektur 2, FSB Franz Schneider, Brakel 2005 [German/Italian ed.].
Brigitte Labs-Ehlert, *Gebaute Gedanken/Pensieri costruiti*, pp. 9-11.
Photography: Pino Musi.
Thoughts on the relation that Botta's architecture establishes with memory.

'Leeum Samsung museum of art', *Space* [Seoul], 2005, 446, January, pp. 48-155 [English/Korean ed.].
Museum 1 [Mario Botta], pp. 66-89.
Museum 2 [Jean Nouvel], pp. 90-113.
Child Education & Culture Center [Rem Koolhaas], pp. 114-133.
Deck [Alexander Calder, artsworks: Grand Crinkly (1971); Untitled (Swiss Cheese) (1976)], pp. 134-141.
Chang, Soo Hyun, *From the fractal phenomenon to a dramatic space*, pp. 50-51.
Choi, Jini, *a 21 st. century museum*, pp. 54-55.
Park, KilYong, *The three different colors of Leeum*, pp. 63-65.
Museum 1, Mario Botta + Samoo, pp. 66-89.
Mario Botta, *A design that constructs a visual impression*, p. 69.
Photography: Leeum Samsung Museum of Art.
The bilingual edition presents a detailed report on the different buildings designed by three famous European architects for the new culture complex of Leeum Samsung museum of Art in Seoul.

Seong Tae Park (by), *Leeum Samsung Museum of Modern Art*, Samsung Museum of Art, Seoul 2005, pp. 16-57 [English/Korean ed.].
Ra Hee Hong Lee, *Director's Foreword*, p. 15.
Mario Botta, *Architecture is the matrix of all arts / Museum 1 by Mario Botta: Traditional Art*, pp. 16-57.
Jean Nouvel, *I put the art in the architecture and put the architecture in the city / Museum 2 by Jean Nouvel: Modern Art*, pp. 58-99.
Rem Koolhaas, *I like to express the concealed architecture / Samsung Child Education & Culture Center*, pp. 100-143.
O Young Lee, *Poetics of Leeum, Samsung Museum of Art*, pp. 146-151.
Won Kim, *Leeum, Samsung Museum of Art; One Masterpiece of Three Architects*, pp. 152-56.

Sohn Joo Minn, *Gateway to the Imagination, Transgression of Time and Space*, pp. 158-168.
Photography: Hankoo Lee, Yongkwan Kim, SeungHoon Yum, Philippe Ruaurt.
The official catalog of Samsung Museum of Art in Seoul to present its new quarters, richliy illustrated and with considerations of the architects in charge of the project design.

Timothy Verdon (a cura di), *Di fronte all'altissimo. La cappella di Mario Botta e Giuliano Vangi ad Azzano di Seravezza*, Electa, Milano 2005 [Italian/English ed.].
Timothy Verdon, *Di fronte all'altissimo La cappella di Mario Botta e Giuliano Vangi ad Azzano di Seravezza*, pp. 6-63.
Mario Botta, *Giuliano Vangi*, pp. 64-69.
Danilo D'Angiolo, *Il Giobbe di Giuliano Vangi. L'attualità del dramma esistenziale*, pp. 70-79.
Filippo Rossi, *Il filo della memoria*, pp. 80-85.
Il libro di Giobbe (dalla Bibbia di Gerusalemme a cura della Conferenza Episcopale Italiana).
Nuova opportunità per l'architetto di misurarsi con la dimensione sacra attraverso la collaborazione artistica tra architettura e scultura.
A new opportunity for the architect to confront himself with the dimension of the Sacre through an artistic collaboration between architecture and sulpture.

2006

Mario Botta e Dario Fertilio, *La lingua degli angeli per principianti*, Skira, Milano 2006.
Dario Fertilio, *Angeli e parole*, pp. 68-69.
Mario Botta, *Angeli e architetture*, pp. 70-71.
Il tema angelico affrontato con testi e immagini vicini alla dimensione poetica.
The angelic theme approached with essays and pictures close to a poetic dimension.

Giuseppe Zois (a cura di), *La chiesa che catturò il cielo*, Associazione Ricostruzione Chiesa di Mogno, Società Editrice Corriere del Ticino, Lugano 2006.
Vesc. Pier Giacomo Grampa, *La porta verso il cielo*, p. 11; *Dopo la gran tempesta di vento*, pp. 135-36; *Speranza, slancio verso il futuro*, p. 147.
G.Z. (Giuseppe Zois), *Il coraggio della modernità*, pp. 13-15; *Un gesto di luce avvolto d'azzurro*, p. 17; *La storia*, pp. 20-22 [*La luce di un faro di pietra*, pp. 23-24; *Tutti i 6 di Mogno*, pp. 25-30; *Il villaggio nei secoli*, pp. 31-35]; *Il ricordo*, p. 38 [*Il giorno della valanga*, pp. 39-62]; *Le interviste*, p. 63 [*Come un'inmensa sciarpa nera* (intervista a Giovanni Luigi Dazio), pp. 65-81; *Il signore del cantiere*, pp. 83-92; *Tra passato e futuro* (intervista a Mario Botta), pp. 93-111]; *Memoria e ricostruzione*, pp. 129-134; *Segni della religiosità nelle nostre valli*, pp. 137-138; *Ogni giorno una presa d'immenso*, p. 171.
Vesc. Giuseppe Torti, *E come prospettiva, l'infinito*, pp. 115-16; *"Qui diventiamo pietre vive"*, pp. 117-18.

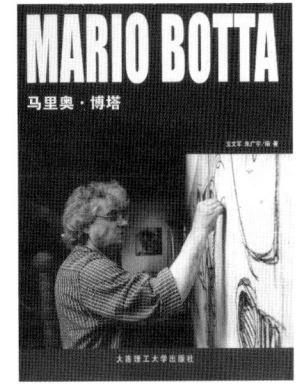

Giovanni Luigi Dazio, *Guidati da un codice invisibile*, pp. 119-120; *Abbiamo fatto fiorire il domani*, pp. 140-42.

Pietro Martinelli, *I riflessi di un gioiello*, p. 121.

Kaspar Villiger, *La vitalità dopo la festa*, pp. 123-24.

Mario Botta, *Quando finisce un cantiere*, pp. 125-26; *Lasciai un edificio, ho trovato un territorio*, pp. 150-51.

Michele Rolanzi, *Simbolo forte della comunità*, p. 139.

Luigi Pedrazzini, *Simbolo sulla strada dell'innovazione*, pp. 144-46.

Bruno Lepori, *Il sogno realizzato*, p. 148.

Teresio Valsesia, *Grandi silenzi sotto cieli di stelle*, pp. 155-56.

Claudio Suter, *La scommessa di continuare a crederci*, pp. 159-60.

don Italo Molinari, *L'altra cattedrale del Ticino*, pp. 161-65.

don Sandro Vitalini, *Una chiesa… non finita*, pp. 167-68.

Marianne Bockerhoff, *Die kirche die den Himmel einfing*, pp. 173-78.

Simona De Stefani, *L'église qui captura le ciel*, pp. 179-184.

Reno Gwaltney, *The church that captured the heavens*, pp. 185-89.

Photography Jo Locatelli [et al.].

The book talks about the involvement of an entire community in the reconstruction of its own church which was destroyed by an avalanche.

2007

Mario Botta (a cura di), *La chiesa del Santo Volto a Torino*, Skira, Ginevra-Milano 2007.

Card. Severino Poletto, *Presentazione*, p. s.n.

Sergio Pace, *Dopo il tempo del lavoro, lo spazio della domenica*, pp. 20-23.

Mario Botta, *Lo spazio del sacro*, pp. 24-29; *Riflessioni progettuali* ["*Mi costruisca una chiesa bella!*"; *Disegnare una chiesa; La recente urbanizzazione; Il progetto come articolazione; La ciminiera come memoria; L'impianto distributivo; Una geometria nel disordine urbano; La pianta centrale e l'ettagono; I materiali; Il volto della Sindone; Il sacro è nell'animo dell'uomo; Il territorio della memoria*], pp. 64-86.

Photography: Enrico Cano [et al.].

A selection of the architect's writings on the theme of the project illustrated with an interesting documentation of the building.

Architects & Design: Mario Botta, edited by Jeong, Ji-Seong, CA Press Co. Ltd. Seoul, Korea. 2007.

Mario Botta, *Light and Gravity*, pp. 6-7

Photography: Enrico Cano, Pino Musi, Alo Zanetta, Alberto Flammer [et al.].

The monographic Korean publication shows in detail a wide selection of recent buildings.

Mario Botta, Paolo Crepet, Giuseppe Zois, *Dove abitano le emozioni. La felicità e i luoghi in cui viviamo*, Einaudi, Torino 2007.

Giuseppe Zois, *Progettare emozioni: un viaggio a due voci*, pp. V-VII.

Dove abitano le emozioni [colloquio fra Mario Botta, Paolo Crepet e Giuseppe Zois], pp. 3-132.

A dialogue that reveals the discomfort and the hopes in the contemporary living.

Mario Botta. World Great Architects, Cepp Edition 2007 [Chinese ed.; reprint 2008].

A visual inventory of recent works directed to a Chinese public.

Alessandra Coppa (a cura di), *Mario Botta*, Motta Architettura, Milano 2007 [updated ed. 2009; paperback ed.: *Mario Botta, L'architettura I protagonisti*, Motta Architettura, Milano 2007, La Biblioteca di Repubblica-L'Espresso, Milano 2007, Vol. 9; Chinese ed.: Motta Architettura, Milano 2008; French ed.: Actes Sud, Arles 2009].

Mario Botta. La memoria nel muro, pp. 21-28.

Il pensiero. Frammenti [*L'architettura è una scommessa; Abitare, maggio 2000; Luce e gravità; Storia e memoria; L'architettura del sacro*], pp. 88-91.

La critica. Territorio, città e geometria [antologia critica: testi di Giovanni Pozzi, Jacques Gubler, Benedikt Loderer, Rudolf Arnheim; Lionello Puppi; Heinrich Thelen, Fulvio Irace], pp. 112-118.

Photography: Gabriele Basilico, Enrico Cano, Mario Carrieri, Alberto Flammer, Pino Musi, Robert Frank.

A great popular edition presents Botta's recent works and focuses on three principal objectives: the thought, the critic and the work.

Yun Sung-Chul (by), 'Mario Botta', *CA. Contemporary Architecture* [Seoul], 2007, Vol. 67, January [English/Korean ed.].

Mario Botta, *Light and Gravity*, pp. 6-7.

The architect's essay introduces an overview of recent works addressed to a South Korean public.

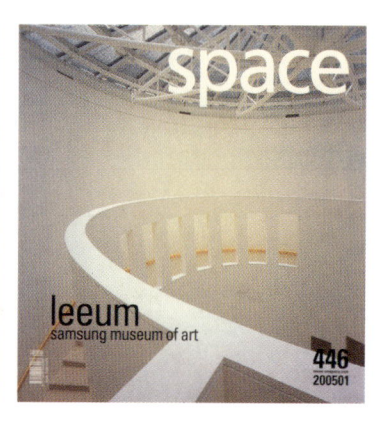

2008

Krassimira Yavasheva, Nikolina Stoykova (a cura di), 'Mario Botta', *WAM World Architecture Masters* [Sofia], International Academy of Architecture, 2008, 6, pp. 5-88.
A Bulgarian academic edition presenting Botta's recent works.

2009

AA.VV., *Mario Botta Riflessioni*, a cura di +xm Plusform (Simona De Giuli, Maria Francesca Faro, Francesco Messina, Daniele Vacca, Clara Stella Vicari Aversa), Dialoghi di architettura/05, Iiriti Editore, Reggio Calabria 2009.
Giuliano Gresleri, *Mario Botta parla*, pp. 9-22.
Clara Stella Vicari Aversa, *Luce, geometria e rigore*, pp. 23-32.
+xm plusform, *Dialogo con Mario Botta*, pp. 33-178.
Simona De Giuli, *Una amorevole invidia*, pp. 179-183.
The aim of the collection *Dialoghi di architettura* – dialogues in architecture – is to investigate, through the participation of great architects, on central themes of the contemporary architectural debate, comparing different protagonists, cultures and generations.

2010

Mario Botta, I maestri dell'Architettura, a cura di Grazia Massone, Hachette Fascicoli – Milano 2010.
Grazia Massone, *La vita e le opere*, pp. 5-13; *Costruire il sito, costruire cultura – scuola media* pp .16-19;
Un ambiente di famiglia – casa unifamiliare pp. 20-23; *Geometria regolare di un lotto triangolare – Galleria d'arte contemporanea Watari-um* pp.24-27; *Un occasione di riflessione e di preghiera – Cattedrale della Resurrezione* pp. 28-31;
Un edificio che ha messo radici – SFMoMA, museo d'arte moderna pp. 32-37; *Un passo verso l'infinito – Cappella Santa Maria degli Angeli* pp. 36-39; *Una presenza di richiamo- Museo Leeum* pp. 40-43; *Un punto di incontro fra religione e cultura - Sinagoga Cymbalista e centro dell'eredità ebraica* pp. 44-45, *Una presenza fisica fra terra e cielo – Chiesa del Santo Volto* pp. 46-49; *Un'architettura dal forte impatto visivo – Centro Benessere Tschuggen Berg Oase* pp. 50-53; *Analisi di un'opera, Opere d'arte protagoniste degli interni- Museo MART* pp. 54-67
The book is part of a monographic collection of masters in architecture. The collection proposes a look into the artistic and professional path of the architect through a detailed biography, an overview of the works as well as a closer analyze of a single project.

Mario Botta, *Räume des Übergangs* in Mario Botta, Gottfried Böhm-Peter Böhm, Rafael Moneo, *Sakralität und Aura in der Architektur*, Vorwort Andreas Tönnesmann, Architketurvorträge der ETH Zürich, Heft 8, DARCH GTA Verlag 2010, pp. 10-51, 106-107.

Mario Botta, *Räume des Übergangs*, pp. 10-54
Gottfried Böhm, Peter Böhm, *Das Sakrale in der Architektur*, pp. 52-83
Rafael Moneo, *Cathedral of Our Lady of the Angels Los Angeles, CA, 1996–2002*, pp. 84 - 105.
Four lecturers invited by the GTA – Institute for History and Theory in Architecture in Zurich are asked to talk about their considerations and creative experience regarding the question of the sacred and the aura in architecture.

Roman Hollenstein, *Switzerlarch:Banca e bastione/Bank and bastion/Bank und Bollwerk, BSI Lugano / Palazzo Botta*, BSI – JRP I Ringier 2010.
Roman Hollenstein, *Palazzo Botta di Mario Botta Lugano*, pp. 25-27; Un palazzo bancario innovativo, pp. 41-46, La quintessenza dell'opera giovanile, pp. 61-66; Una visione metropolitana, pp. 79-89; Lo sviluppo del progetto, pp. 105-110; Una cinta muraria munita di torri, pp. 127-134; Un interno polifunzionale, pp. 155-166; Trasformazione dell'immagine della città, pp. 179-183; Un capolavoro di architettura bancaria, pp. 197-206.
Photography: Enrico Cano
The booklet edited in three languages presents the building "Palazzo Botta" in Lugano with new photographs and interesting details in relation to other works realized by Botta. The publication is part of a collection produced by the BSI bank within the architectural and artistic field.

Mario Botta. Architetture 1960-2010, catalogo della mostra, Museo di Arte Moderna e Contemporanea di Trento e Rovereto, Silvana Editoriale, Cinisello Balsamo-Milan 2010 [Parts published as French/German ed. : *Mario Botta, Architecture et mémoire/Architektur und Gedächtnis*,CDN Neuchâtel-Silvana Editoriale, Cinisello Balsamo, 2011 with introductions by Didier Burkhalter,
Marie-Christine Doffey, Janine Perret Sgualdo, Charlotte Kerr Dürrenmatt, Peter Erismann, Mario Botta].
Introduzione: testi di Jean Frédéric Jauslin, Franco Bernabé, Gabriella Belli, Pius Knüsel.
Gillo Dorfles, Aldo Colonetti, Mario Botta, *Dal cucchiaio alla città* [colloquio] pp. 20-31.
Carlo Bertelli, *Il passato presente*, pp. 36-38.
Mario Botta, *Incontri* pp. 40-81; *Spazi dell'abitare* pp. 162-197; *Spazi dell'abitare collettivo*, pp. 198-205; *Spazi del lavoro*, pp. 206-233; *Spazi della scuola e del tempo libero*, pp. 234-247; *Cantine vinicole*, pp. 248-255; *Dentro il tessuto della città*, pp. 256-267; *Biblioteche*, pp. 268-279; *Musei*, pp. 280-297; *Teatri*, pp. 298-305; *Lo spazio del sacro*, pp. 306-331; *Interni*, pp. 332-341; *Scenografie*, pp. 342-343, 350-357; *Allestimenti*, pp. 358-381; *Design*, pp. 384-385, pp. 396-431; *Postfazione*, pp. 434-439.

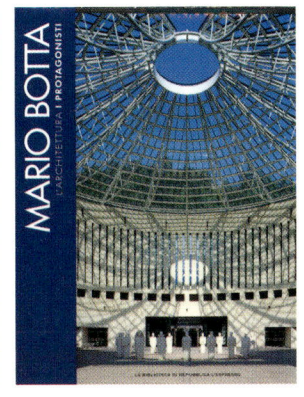

Lionello Puppi, *Geometria della luce e del colore; nel tempo*, pp. 84-92.
Roman Hollenstein, *Mario Botta e la Svizzera*, pp. 94-102.
Giuliano Gresleri, *Le opere sono le parole del maestro*, pp. 106-121.
Benedetto Gravagnuolo, *La nuova arcaicità del fluire del tempo*, pp.122-128.
Jacques Gubler, *Dal paese alla città*, pp. 130-139.
Diego Peverelli, *Appunti sul processo creativo di Mario Botta*, p. 140-146.
Gabriele Cappellato, *Le ragioni del cerchio*, pp. 148-158
Anne Marie Werner, *Mario Botta e "la magia del teatro"*, pp. 344-349.
Alessandra Coppa, *Allestimenti e Design*, pp. 386-395.
Antologia critica [testi di: Giuseppe Mazzariol, Emilio Battisti, Pier Carlo Santini, Alberto Sartoris, François Chaslin, Christian Norberg-Schulz, Kenneth Frampton, Virgilio Gilardoni, William Curtis, Francesco Dal Co, Tadao Ando, Stuart Wrede, Joseph Rykwert, Paolo Fumagalli, Vittorio Fagone, Paul Goldberger, Harald Szeeman, Rudolf Arnheim, Jean Petit, Allan Temko, Fulvio Irace, Cesare de Seta, Werner Oechslin, Benedikt Loderer, Giovanni Pozzi, Stanislaus von Moos, Irena Sakellaridou, Paolo Portoghesi], pp. 492-505.
Photography: Enrico Cano, Alberto Flammer, Alo Zanetta, Pino Musi, Paolo Pedroli, Robert Canfield, Rainer Hofmann, Joël Lassiter, Ralph Richter, Marco D'Anna [et al.].
The volume edited for the exhibition at the Mart in Rovereto in 2010, documents the most significant built works by Mario Botta in fifty years of activity (1960-2010). From the first family houses – protagonists of the Ticino school – to the large public buildings, libraries, theaters, museums and sacred buildings realized all over the world. A particular attention is given to less known themes as the stage design, exhibitions and design items. The book opens with a personal consideration on suggestions, artist's work and events that left a strong influence in Botta's education as a human being and architect.
The French/German catalog edited for the exhibition presented at Centre Dürrenmatt concentrates on four themes only: the libraries, the museums, the theaters and the sacred buildings. Themes, that express in their particular way the idea of "spaces of memory".

Mario Botta San Carlino a Lugano, Nota di Roberto Fregna, Ogni uomo è tutti gli uomini Edizioni, Bologna [dicembre] 2010.
Mario Botta, San Carlino a Lugano, pp. 5-34.
Roberto Fregna, Nota Tappeti volanti, pp. 35-36.
Photography: Pino Musi.
A booklet offering once again Botta's approach, thoughts and motivation to propose in Lugano, in Borromini's native land, a real size wooden model of the arist's and architect's famous San Carlo alle Quattro Fontane in Rome.

Urban Environment Design, Mario Botta 2004-2010 , 051, 2011-3, Urban Environment Design Press, Beijing 2011[Northern United Publishing&Media Group Company Limited].
Photography: Enrico Cano, Pino Musi, Urs Homberger, Joël Lassiter [et al.]
The Chinese magazine publishes a richly illustrated monographic issue with attention to Botta's recent work and proposes some of Botta's major essays on architecture and memory, the designing of sacred spaces, architecture and urband context.
[all text in Chinese language].

Mario Botta. La scuola, l'architettura, la città, a cura di Nicola Delledonne e Barbara Stasi, con un testo di Massimo Fagioli, Aión Edizioni, Industria Grafica Valdarnese, San Giovanni Valdarno (AR), luglio 2011.
Massimo Fagioli, *Della Perennità. Su Mario Botta e l'arcaic*, pp. 5-11
Nicola Delledonne, Barbara Stasi, *Nota dei curatori*, pp. 12-13
Mario Botta, Nicola Delledonne, Barbara Stasi, [*La scuola. l'architettura, la città*], pp.14-77.
Photography: Enrico Cano, Urs Homberger, Joël Lassiter, Pino Musi, Alo Zanetta.
Out of the need to talk about fundamental questions of architecture in a historic moment of the present where the architectural production seems rather to search for extemporality, the interview starts on some autobiographical aspects that reveal the possible artistic and critical geneology of the architect and leads into themes as the learning of architecture, the relation between theory and project, and the changing of the urban context.

2012

Mario Botta Architektur leben, Ein Gespräch mit Marco Alloni, Stämpfli Verlag AG, Bern 2012; Italian ed.: *Mario Botta Vivere l'architettura*, Conversazione con Marco Alloni, Edizioni Casagrande, Bellinzona Marzo 2012 [reprint June 2012].
Photography: Mario Botta Archive, Enrico Cano, Pino Musi, Alo Zanetta [et al.]
Memories of Botta's childness, his youth passion for the drawing, the artistic and intellectual education, the encounters with his masters Le Corbusier, Kahn Scarpa, the ambivalent relation to his homeland, his ambitions, disappointments and success are revealed in an engaging conversation conducted by the journalist and author Marco Alloni.

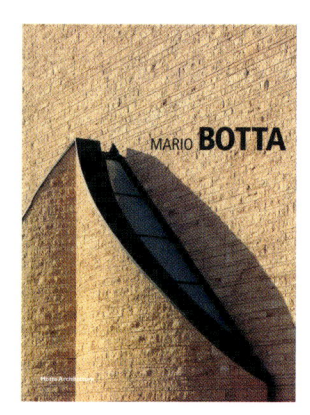

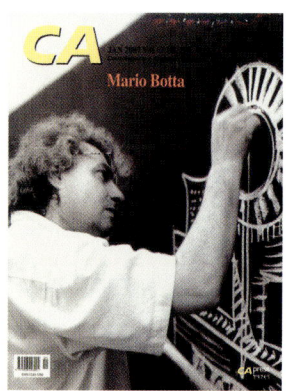

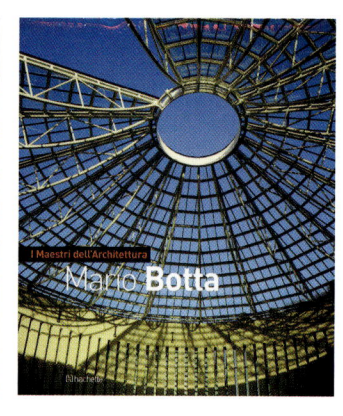

CRITICAL ANTHOLOGY

GIUSEPPE MAZZARIOL

Un giovane ticinese è da pochi mesi a Venezia per studiare architettura, mentre Le Corbusier sta disegnando il suo ultimo progetto: il nuovo ospedale per Venezia.
Mario Botta mi chiede di poter andare a Parigi [...]. Nell'estate di quel 1965, proprio nei mesi ultimi di Le Corbusier, Mario Botta lavora vicino a Jullian e a Oubrerie al progetto dell'ospedale, in uno studio improvvisato dentro alla Scuola di San Marco. Poi, subito dopo il 27 agosto, morte del Maestro, il giovane ticinese lascia Venezia per Parigi [...]. Mario Botta ha lavorato per Le Corbusier senza avergli mai parlato. La sua lezione, quella che cercava con determinazione quasi testarda, l'ha trovata nelle parole dei diretti collaboratori di Corbu, nell'ambiente, negli appunti, nei libri del Maestro durante i mesi silenziosi di quel lungo autunno parigino, colmo di tristezze e di attese. Questa casa di Stabio è, a distanza di due anni, la testimonianza di un'autentica esperienza di vita e di cultura; il segno profondo in una memoria spirituale, che per un giovane architetto non poteva diversamente esprimersi dalla realtà architettonica; un fiore semplice sulla pianura del Mendrisiotto, che il grande e superbo Le Corbusier avrebbe accolto con un sorriso commosso e una rapida bordata di domande, tutte di tono contestativo sulla legittimità dell'omaggio [...]. Questo ritrovarsi dentro lo spazio come forma dell'uomo, che l'uomo commisura per sé e non ricava occasionalmente dalla natura, questo definire la natura come altro da sé, costituisce l'imprestito più vero, ma anche più fecondo quanto segreto, della fondamentale lezione di Le Corbusier. In questa direzione Mario Botta, giovane ticinese di sicura vocazione architettonica, muove le proprie intenzioni critiche ed esprime le proprie aspirazioni poetiche, mostrando di credere nell'architettura come in una delle possibili dimensioni della moralità, della conoscenza, della fantasia [...].

Giuseppe Mazzariol,
'Un fiore per Le Corbusier',
in *Werk*, 1969, 4, p. 227.

EMILIO BATTISTI

[...] Ognuno di questi eventi, capolavori nel suo curriculum di progetti ed opere, è preparato, annunciato e prefigurato con estrema evidenza e precisione, ma proprio per questo motivo il loro apparire sulla scena delle cose compiute e concrete, risulta ancora più sorprendente. [...] In questa casa di Ligornetto, meglio conosciuta come "la casa a strisce" gli elementi che la compongono erano già stati tutti sperimentati [...]: il parametro continuo di blocchetti di cemento, il ritaglio delle grandi aperture in facciata, lo straniamento dei pochi elementi-finestra ridotti a semplici, piccole forature circolari o quadrate ed anche l'uso del colore con spregiudicatezza antimateria. [...]. Una volontà espressiva che riduce la propria componente edilizia e tecnica per farsi senz'altro completamente architettonica e simbolica, caratterizza il grande decoro di questo edificio [...]. La sua spazialità diventa dinamica e dialettica e mette in risonanza lo spazio che la circonda, quando più ci si lascia captare e comprendere dal suo dispositivo interno. La sua forma allungata, la sproporzione dimensionale del suo quadrilatero di base, fa sì che essa non occupi semplicemente lo spazio, ma lo "divida"; il microclima che si crea all'interno della grande apertura, abbraccia ed introietta lo spazio circostante, rimisurandolo secondo rapporti di scala e scenografici del tutto imprevedibili [...]. La concatenazione delle porzioni di spazio interno deputate alle diverse funzioni non ha alcuna cesura o intersezione: un unico sistema li integra ed aggrega in un fluido ordine senza priorità e gerarchie con una straordinaria evidenza delle connessioni, disvelamento dei rapporti, esplicitazione dei nessi. Io credo che in questa assenza di riservatezza, in questa volontà di rivelazione di ogni recondito risvolto spaziale, in questo sviscieramento dello spazio interno, tutto basato sull'applicazione di un codice anticlassico, ci sia proprio l'antitesi della principale sublimazione formale di questa architettura, ci sia la negazione del "decoro" [...].

Emilio Battisti,
La misura del decoro.
'Un parametro alla natura',
in *Gran Baazar*, 1979, 3,
pp. 74-78.

PIER CARLO SANTINI

[…] Una radice geometrica costante ma non rigida si determina come una sorta di griglia più o meno elementare o complessa, atta a regolare il comporsi, il dislocarsi e il connettersi dei temi e degli elementi basici dell'edificio. Non c'è soggezione a un sistema aprioristicamente stabilito, che darebbe luogo a organismi "astratti", ma piuttosto ricorso a principi ordinatori operanti sulle forme primarie. […]. Solo visitando i luoghi di questo Ticino, italianamente piuttosto devastato e caotico, al pari di Lugano del resto, ho potuto rendermi conto del rapporto che Botta ha cercato e trovato con l'ambiente. […]. egli non si accontenta di non deteriorare ulteriormente situazioni già compromesse, o di non nuocere mediante mimetismi rinunciatari, ma intende operare puntando sul valore positivo dell'architettura nel conformare le sedi umane, o nel riscattarle dal degrado e dal disordine, recuperandole a più civili esistenze. Per svolgere questo ruolo, l'architettura deve emergere, introdurre temi e motivi autentici, cioè linguisticamente originali, spiccare come termine attivo di un rapporto che poco o tanto varrà a cambiare il volto dell'ambiente […]. Ma oltre i dati fisici, c'è da tener conto della storia. […]. E qui il discorso si fa più sottile e l'analisi più difficile, perché i caratteri debbono essere astratti e ricavati da mille segni labili e spesse volte segreti. In tal senso appare di primaria importanza quel certo radicamento nella propria terra che consente di intenderne l'ethos dominante e profondo. E mi pare che Botta proprio di questo suo esser ticinese abbia fatto tesoro. […] i risultati hanno tale carattere di autografia, e sono così assoluti nella logica conseguenza dei rapporti, da far credere che ogni eventuale deviazione o modifica riguardi qualche dettaglio, o sia stata ricondotta alla misura e alla forma previste e volute […].

Pier Carlo Santini,
'Mario Botta architetto ticinese',
in *Ottagono*, 1980, 58,
pp. 20-29.

ALBERTO SARTORIS

Analizzando senza pregiudizi le opere di Mario Botta, se ne può facilmente dedurre che alcuni grandi interrogativi posti dall'architettura del presente e del divenire non sono rimasti senza risposta. […] L'opera di Mario Botta va collocata nel quadro di una creatività le cui maggiori espressioni sfuggono agli schemi frustranti delle incorniciature fallaci e delle lottizzazioni anonime. Il suo ideografico cilindro da abitare si ravvolge infatti nei valori cosmici, spaziali e paesaggistici di un circondamento dal quale trae la propria origine e la distinta natura, e al quale offre le ricchezze di una nuova identità terrena. […] Con la casa rotonda di Stabio, Botta non insegue solo un sogno legittimo, ma attualizza un volume abitabile la cui trama d'immagine è altrettanto perfetta all'interno che all'esterno. Sotto il suo impulso generatore, la geometria si trasforma in lirismo e, mediante la costruzione, sorge dall'ombra un'armonia esaltata da piani circolari a convergenze centrali. Questo cilindro, che Botta taglia verticalmente e trasversalmente sul suo asse, per introdurvi una maggiore luminosità e farvi penetrare il cielo […], accoglie anche il brillìo e la lucentezza di una atmosfera singolare, il calore e i segreti dell'intimità. Gli edifici di Mario Botta, concepiti per essere imperniati sullo scrigno formato dal paesaggio e dal territorio, non sono soltanto manifestazioni evidenti e visibili di una intransigenza estetica, plastica, quanto scientifica, ma corpi viventi e volti d'architettura costruiti anche con lo scopo prefisso di personificare l'ambiente naturale. […] Nella rotonda Medici di Stabio, si può leggere che uno dei lati più splendidi del grado di maturità architettonica di Mario Botta sta nel fatto che le sue doti primigenie si trasformano, senza rimpianti, nei richiami evocatori di uno stile che consuona per natura con il senso della continuità. […]

Alberto Sartoris,
'Mario Botta, trasfiguratore della geometria', in
Futurismo-Oggi, 1981, 9-10,
pp. 3-4.

FRANÇOIS CHASLIN

[…] Les poings fermés face à face, coudes levés dans un lent mouvement, mâchoire crispée, sérieux, tendu, les reins calés, il se fige un instant, et semble vivre dans son corps les tensions qui traversent ses constructions. Des poings aux coudes, et des coudes aux épaules, ses muscles bandés expriment des lignes de force, soutiennent l'édifice et le soudent à la terre, les jeux spatiaux qui s'y déploient. L'attitude exprime l'ineffable; le corps vit les drames de la forme. Botta est compact, souple et solide, tout d'un pièce, authentique. Il ressemble à son architecture. […] Aucune préciosité, aucun raffinement pédant, aucune sophistication apparente: sa rhétorique est équilibrée, modeste, jamais contournée. On ne peut pas être moins littéraire; ses constructions disent peu mais avec une force d'évocation parfaite. […] lorsqu'il est le meilleur […] il atteint à l'essence des choses. Les métaphores y sont alors puissantes quoique à demi masquées; l'expressivité y paraît naturelle. Ses plus belles constructions sont à l'exact mi-chemin entre l'insolite et le familier, entre la froide rationalité et l'émotion lyrique, entre les héritages modernes et la tentation classique. […] Mais le grand talent de Mario Botta reste peut-être son sens de l'implantation. Comme nul autre, il sait se poser fermement, avec sûreté, sur les sites les plus pentus. Il sait aussi ne pas "s'intégrer", au sens timide du mot, mais s'affirmer, réagir à l'environnement. Son architecture est irruptive; compacte, calme, bien assise quand il le faut, dynamique ailleurs, contradictoire si nécessaire. Il sait taper un grand coup, écraser de sa force la médiocrité ambiante. Il sait constituer des pivots qui réordonnent les paysages. Il sait respecter un lieu, prolonger une configuration ancienne, mail il sait aussi ne pas avoir forcément le dessous dans le dialogue avec l'histoire.

François Chaslin,
Dans le paysage comme un poing sur la table,
in *Mario Botta 1978-1982. Laboratoire d'architecture*,
Electa-Moniteur, Milano-Paris
1982, pp. 13-16.

CHRISTIAN NORBERG-SCHULZ

Mario Botta's buildings are distinguished by a singular image quality. Like powerful "things" they stand forth in our confused present-day environment and create order and meaning. They are easily comprehended and remembered, and satisfy man's need for orientation and identification. Botta's success as an architect is undoubtedly due to this image quality. Thus his works prove that we are no longer satisfied with an architecture which is merely "functional" but want that the buildings should tell us *where we are*, and hence "explain" the world to us. Botta's houses and large-scale buildings in fact appear as such explanations. With self-assurance they stand on the ground, and rise up in space to form a distinct "figure". At the same time they communicate with the environment to which they belong; a dialectical relationship is created which reveals the landscape as what it is. […]. What Botta proposes is a return to *architecture*. […] what Botta wants is a concrete "establishment of a rapport between man and the elements of nature, of the countryside, of the different seasons, the values of the cosmos, the values of the sky". His works demonstrate that this rapport does not imply passive adaptation. Rather it means a promotion and reinterpretation of the environmental values. […]. The characteristics of the Ticinese vernacular reappear in the works of Mario Botta. […] his one-family houses recall the traditional values without making use of superficial, nostalgic imitation. […] Botta is concerned about reinterpretation rather than nostalgic protection, and in fact he above all considers himself a *modern* architect. His modernism is however different from the abstract utilitarianism of late-modern architecture. […]. Botta's interest in the past is therefore guided towards the order of things rather than the sentimental motif, and as a consequence he refuses those "post-modern" currents which return to superficial historicism. From what has been said above, we may conclude that Botta's world is local as well as general, ancient as well as modern.

Christian Norberg-Schulz,
Introduction,
in Yukio Futagawa (edited by),
'Mario Botta',
GA Global Architecture Architect, 3, 1984, pp. 8-20.

KENNETH FRAMPTON

VIRGILIO GILARDONI

Influenced by Louis Kahn's concept of the "house-within-the-house" […] Botta's domestic model has crystallized over the years around the ideal format of a symmetrical cubic volume. […] Deriving from the spectacularly contoured topography of the Ticino region, the belvedere theme first appeared in Botta's work with the asymmetric tower house he built in Riva San Vitale in 1973. The axial rearrangement of this paradigm emerged with the Pregassona house of 1979, and therefore almost all of Botta's houses have been predicated on a centralized scheme. Despite this formality, Botta's later houses still adhere to the policy of framing the landscape. The perimeter walls are arranged in such a way as to reveal and conceal the irreducible features of the site; […]. In this regard Botta has remained faithful to the principle of "building the site" […] the Origlio and Morbio Superiore houses elaborate the bunker theme, which is the other alien "figure" informing Botta's domestic work. […] This cavernous motif has become increasingly elaborated over the years, with Botta departing from the expansive and limpid volumes of the Pregassona house to create houses whose volumetric configurations border on the "baroque". Such spatial elaboration seems to have been accompanied by an increasingly emblematic attitude towards the overall appearance of the structure. […] The houses at Massagno, Viganello and Morbio Superiore concentrate most of their plastic energy on the superficial elaboration of their belvedere façades. Unlike Botta's previous domestic work, these fronts seem to be on the verge of becoming deliberately divorced from their tectonic substance […]. Despite a tendency to degenerate into formalism, this remarkably consistent typological elaboration is ultimately sustained by Botta's superb craftsmanship and tectonic mastery – a level of *techne* which is becoming increasingly rare […].

[…] L'idea e la costruzione (1976-79) della Biblioteca dei Frati, per la molteplicità stessa dei problemi tecnici e formali (l'eticità del progetto quale figura architettonica) da risolvere, furono uno stimolo salutare all'attività inventiva ed operativa di Mario Botta. […] l'architetto immagina subito l'ampio squarcio zenitale […] per inondare di luce la sala di lettura attraverso la volta a botte vetrata che diventerà uno dei leitmotiv di quasi tutte le sue case di poi e di molti altri progetti; né sarà certo soltanto una trovata tecnica, funzionale, ma, come sempre nel disegno delle "figure" di questo felice inventore di metafore plastiche, un elemento chiave di una ben precisa concezione della casa e del destino storico e metastorico dell'uomo. […]. L'idea dell'officina e del laboratorio artigianale che l'architetto rimugina dentro di sé come una delle sue "immagini germinali" […] e che non trova modo di sperimentare in una vera fabbrica prende corpo ora in certe parti della Biblioteca. […]. La Biblioteca dei Frati rivela in più di un elemento l'inizio della piena maturità "classica" […] dell'architetto quale si manifesta in tanta parte della sua produzione degli anni di poi; la "classicità" senza orpelli che segna per lui il pieno recupero di un'etica legata alla costruzione come "immagine grande", di poesia, che si contrappone alla "langue" quotidiana della funzionalità materiale, che è solo apparentemente razionale […], essendo un'immagine innamorata dei sensi delle cose […] in ogni dato, fatto, elemento costruttivo. […]. Con questa sensibilità che è abito anche di cultura – di una cultura che è anzitutto scelta critica di campo, "etica prima che estetica" – Mario Botta ha costruito la Biblioteca luganese […].

Kenneth Frampton,
'Botta's paradigm',
in *Progressive Architecture*,
1984, 12, pp. 82-90.

Virgilio Gilardoni,
Gli spazi dell'uomo nell'architettura di Mario Botta. Note sulla Biblioteca Luganese dei Frati,
Archivio Storico Ticinese,
Bellinzona 1984, pp. 219-242.

WILLIAM CURTIS

[…] Botta has never pretended to be anything other than a "modern architect" […]. Indeed Botta has a better claim to the title than most since he was apprenticed briefly to both Kahn and Le Corbusier. […] Botta has explored the correspondences between these two mentors and has sought to link the dual inheritance to regional concerns but without recourse to a superficial regionalism […]. In his case, abstraction has served to blend and to compound historical precedents rather than to exclude them. This is also the level on which he has understood Le Corbusier and Kahn: as a way back to the past rather than away from it. The Casa Rotonda (1980-81) is surely one of the most bizarre of Botta's creations to date. This semi-suburban house is transformed into a solid monument that defies the recent urban sprawl and invokes a return to archaic, rural values. Its plan contains an elemental gesture: an axis across a circle. This aligns the cylinder and cuts it in two with the slot containing the stairs. […]. But the plan is also rich in associative qualities […]. There is the suggestion of a sort of solar calendar […]. It is an observatory, a bastion, a tower for spiritual retreat […]. The forms of the Casa Rotonda have resulted from a thorough assimilation of Kahn, Rossi, Le Corbusier, the rural vernacular, and certain organisational principles from Palladio. The past is present in them in a way that makes the "Modern versus Post-Modern" affair seem quite beside the point.

William Curtis,
Principle and pastiche,
in "The Architectural Review",
August 1984, 1050, pp. 11-21.

FRANCESCO DAL CO

[…] Le costruzioni di Botta sono "preda di una vibrazione luminescente che esalta e al tempo stesso mortifica lo sguardo". […] L'iterazione dei segni e le metamorfosi, pur minime in certi casi, che questi subiscono trasferendosi da uno spartito compositivo all'altro, possono produrre uno stato di assuefazione solo per occhi pigri, incapaci di graffiare le superfici delle apparenze. La luce è il primo abitante dell'architettura del progettista ticinese. […] Vi è una componente tattile nella luce, che Botta riesce a cogliere ed utilizzare progettando innanzitutto i movimenti della vista, al fine di sollecitarne la capacità di percezione superficiale. […] Nella vista, infatti, si manifesta l'*ordine* dell'opera architettonica […] che la luce riscatta, rendendolo "dicibile". Il disegno individua le procedure che aprono la via all'incontro con l'intreccio che schiude all'occhio la mutazione della superficie nella forma dettagliata dal chiaroscuro. […] Disegnare è un modo di vedere – di scrutare le situazioni per predisporre le cose all'incontro con la luce […]. Lo schizzo è già un momento del costruire. […] Lungi dal denunciare una inclinazione naturalistica o un intimismo localistico […] il suggerimento implicito è di spostare l'attenzione prioritariamente sull'uso, nel senso più restrittivo del termine, che il progettista tende a fare della natura, assumendola come occasione di commento per i propri spazi e, soprattutto, trattando l'ambiente in termini estensivo-qualitativi, quale diaframma, […], atto a garantire la visione da lontano […]. Se il rapporto con la natura si dimostra strumentale piuttosto che supinamente fraterno, la stessa considerazione si può applicare alle frequentazioni che Botta vuole intrattenere con "il passato amico". […] non emergono quasi mai dal lavoro di Botta inclinazioni alla stilistica storicistica. Ma il problema della storicità dell'operare e il peso del rapporto con la tradizione sono ben presenti nella sua ricerca. […].

Francesco Dal Co,
La pazienza delle cose,
in Francesco Dal Co (a cura di), *Mario Botta. Architettura 1960-1985*,
Electa, Milano 1985, pp. 7-45.

TADAO ANDO

My meetings with Mario Botta have nearly always been unexpected […]. He is always so friendly, so full of vitality and always accompanies what he is saying with such a variety of gestures that, even though neither of us speaks the other's language, we seem to have a certain something in common which allows us, with the aid of sketches, to understand what the other wants to express. It would seem, in fact, as if his work emanates from his character, for he produces forms which are so open-hearted and passionate. And regardless of its symmetry and monumentality, his work exudes a rich humanitarian feeling. This may be because, just as he says, he has rejected simple historical references per se and, rather than borrowing here and there, he has developed his own individual set of naturally derived references. First he places a box-like form on the ground, and then he cuts various openings out of it to facilitate a rapport with nature. The box itself becomes an object and he arranges the form so that it is pregnant with connections to the surrounding natural landscape and the orientation which the chosen location has […]. There is within his work, an attempt to restore the links between form and location which disappeared from Modern Architecture […]. The simple, closed squares, circles and other geometric forms which Botta employs, may be seen as a reaction to Modern Architecture which had no use for centrality. Likewise, his choice of such forms is a rejection of characterless and limitless universal space and is perhaps an expression of his opposition to a historical movement toward homogeneity […]. His architecture seems to take shape out of a contrast between natural organic forms and man-made ones […].

Tadao Ando,
'Poetic Geometry',
in 'Mario Botta', edited by
Toshio Nakamura, in *a+u
Architecture
and Urbanism*,
1986, 9, pp. 262-263.

STUART WREDE

[…] In all his work the context is an important point of departure, whether by context is meant landscape, urban fabric, local building tradition, or past and present culture. And for him that context includes the modernist tradition in architecture. But Botta's modernism is not utopian[…] is part of a movement away from the technological and functional determinism of the 1920s which came to be known as the International Style, toward a man-centered modernism that sought fundamentals within a more humanist framework, using as points of departure archaic, primitive, and vernacular sources […] this modernist tradition similarly sought to strip architecture of its layers of style and ornamentation on search of the timeless […]. Botta's generation is struggling to overcome the resultant loss of a sense of center and place that today pervades the architecture and urbanism of the industrial mass democracies […]. Botta has, it would appear, almost by instinct, moved toward reintroducing axiality and a sense of center to a modern architectural tradition that formerly proscribed it […]. What remains unique to Botta, however, is that there is an internal consistency and logic to his evolution. He remains true to his modernist vocabulary. […]. Mario Botta developed as an architect immersed in the modern movement, but like others of his generation, he also became highly critical of how its ideals had been debased and exploited by commercial interests. Even more important, he has been able to approach critically the evolving ideology and theory of the modern movement itself. Unlike many of his colleagues, whose critiques of modernism have led them to abandon it altogether, Botta has continued to work within its context, transforming and revitalizing it in the process. The willingness to experiment, to push for new solutions and syntheses, not blindly but critically, characterizes Botta's work and is part of the legacy of the modernist tradition.

Stuart Wrede,
*Mario Botta and the Modernist
Tradition*, exhibition catalogue,
The Museum of Modern Art,
New York 1986, pp. 8-21.

JOSEPH RYKWERT

[…] He is recognized internationally as a star in the constellation of architects whose works are a touchstone for building all over the world. But he is very much of the Ticino, which has always been architects' country. […]. But Botta is definitely not tied to his region. […]. His early initiation into building and his contact with the great masters have meant that he does not see either the local or the cosmopolitan side of his heritage as a burden. The tradition of modernity […]. Secure as he is in this tradition, he is also very much its critic, and is all too conscious of that "erotic poverty" […] in much modern building. […]. Botta therefore objects most strongly to the excessive dependence of buildings on outside help. […]. Botta also insists on the weight and depth of the wall, on the materiality of its presence. The texture and color of the brick and stone have become increasingly important to him. […]. There are contradictions to be reconciled. Botta distrusts symmetry and is always trying to get away from it, yet it returns insistently in his designs. More recently he has noted that his façades seem to compose themselves into explicit faces […]. The facial reference is perhaps most explicit in his houses, […]. And since the house pins the sky to the earth by the primal act of dwelling, the raised skylight […] must make a gesture in response to the sky and provide an entry for the light he allows to filter through the building, guiding the visitor to that orienting axis whose absence Botta so deplores in much modern architecture. […] the site of the building also preoccupies Botta greatly. The place is observed, disassembled, an recomposed in the project. The site may dictate surprising solutions […]. Of all this Botta speaks with clarity and fluency, yet he rejects the role of theorist, preferring to see his work as a kind of craftsmanship. (…). The antiquity of the constantly new, the antiquity of cyclic renewal, is what fascinates him most […].

Joseph Rykwert,
'Design dialogue: Mario Botta.
Views of Modernist', in *AD
Architectural Digest*, January 1988,
pp. 54-64.

PAOLO FUMAGALLI

Wir glauben, dass Mario Botta mit der Banca del Gottardo seine […] architektonische Experimentierphase beschliesst und den Eintritt in die Klassik markiert: Klassik, verstanden als Bestätigung in seiner Art zu denken und zu projektieren, die Konsolidierung die ihm eigenen archetypischen Formen. Klassisch, weil er hier Typologien und architektonische Formen einsetzt, die er früher schon – in Form von Experimenten – an anderen Gebäuden anwandte. […]. Und tatsächlich finden wir "wie in einem Lehrbuch", in den Volumen und der Organisation des neuen Gebäudes die Elemente wieder, die schon die vorangegangen Werke charakterisiert haben. Eine "Rückkehr zu den Anfängen". Beim Gebäude der Banca del Gottardo finden wir die serielle Addition in Baukörpern wieder, […] das Thema des Verhältnisses eines architektonischen Körpers zum Baugrund […] die exakte Geometrie der Baukörper […] den Stein als Verkleidungsmaterial […] die horizontale Zeichnung mit abwechselnd hellen und dunkeln Streifen […] den Willen […], die Fassade mit dem subtilen, filigranen Beziehungsspiel von Licht und Schatten zu gestalten. […] Endlich […] räumliche Qualitäten […], wo das Licht in den riesigen Leerräumen eine entscheidende Rolle spielt […]. Das Gebäude der Banca del Gottardo ist vielleicht "alt" […], es ist aber auch "neu" hinsichtlich der spezifischen Antwort, die das Gebäude auf den Ort in der Stadt gibt. […]. Der Verzicht auf ein monolithisches Ganzes zugunsten eines mannigfaltig artikulierten Baukörpers drückt den Willen aus, kein isoliertes Objekt zu erstellen, sondern ein Stück Stadt […]. Hier […] besteht die Absicht, eine Form zu erschaffen, die man als episodenhaft definieren könnte, deren einzelne Teile notwendig sind, um ein Stück Stadt zu konstruieren. In Gegensatz zu anderen Eingriffen will die Architektur hier keinen Ort charakterisieren, sondern einen neuen erschaffen […].

Paolo Fumagalli,
'Vier Türme für eine Stadt',
in *Werk, Bauen+Wohnen*,
1988, 11, S. 4-11.

VITTORIO FAGONE

Esistono opere che – per un determinato autore, sito o periodo – assumono, senza sforzo, un valore esemplare ed emblematico. La casa a Breganzona […] ha, a mio avviso, un tale carattere […]. è, senza dubbio, costruita secondo un modello avvitante e suggestivo nella circolare varietà e profondità di punti di vista che propone; però è anche, nell'articolato movimento della pianta tra una zona fortemente luminosa e aperta e una zona densamente coperta e interna, una rielaborazione intelligente della calibrata casa di pietra e di legno caratteristica delle valli della Maggia. […]. Se dell'opera di Botta colpisce sempre il chiaro equilibrio interno di ogni elemento costitutivo nel dichiarato assetto spaziale complessivo, bisogna però dire che questo rigore non si rivela mai meramente formale, astratto. Botta sa che una architettura, oltre che costruita, è finita solo quando viene verificata da funzioni e abitudini sociali di vita. […] Paradigmatica la casa di Breganzona può risultare di una dimensione domestica della vita familiare, qui sollecitata a una partecipazione quotidiana al mutare di stagioni e paesaggi, ma anche a segnalare la propria presenza con un elemento costruito, individuale e riconoscibile […]. Esemplare, […] mi sembra anche di una capacità di stare senza disagio sulla linea più avanzata dell'architettura contemporanea, al di là di chiuse compiacenze vernacolari e di estetizzanti stilemi, senza tuttavia perdere la forza di una memoria larga, consapevole e colta, fondamentale per ogni innovazione costruttiva. È in questo modo che l'architettura di Botta azzarda un percorso creativo come metafora e segno di un mondo che può vivere senza ansie, ma non acriticamente, le proprie mutazioni.

Vittorio Fagone,
'In forma di freccia.
Il disegno e l'architettura
della casa a Breganzona',
in Francesco Dal Co
(a cura di), *Mario Botta.
Una casa*, Electa, Milano 1989,
pp. 7-10.

PAUL GOLDBERGER

Outflanked and outclassed in the last decade by the explosive growth of museums in Los Angeles, San Francisco on Tuesday had its first look at a bold design for a museum building that will serve as the centrepiece for a new downtown cultural district that public officials and arts executives hope will energize the city's cultural scene. The building is a new home for the city's 55-year-old Museum of Modern Art, and it is to be the first building in the United States by Mario Botta, the 47-year-old architect from Lugano, Switzerland, whose crisp, brooding structures in masonry have brought him international attention. […]. The Botta design looks as if it could be an unusually distinguished, even a remarkable, work of architecture. The building appears to be at once powerful and restrained, capable of holding its own as a monumental presence amid the taller buildings nearby (and two other skyscrapers that will eventually be built right next door to it), yet understated enough to be referential to the art that will be shown within its galleries. Like of all Mr. Botta's other work, the museum will be modernist in style, but without the sense of lightness and sleekness that so much modern architecture possesses. Indeed, like the work of his great mentor, Louis I. Kahn, Mr. Botta's buildings tend to merge modernism with a kind of classical formality – though they eschew classical ornamentation and decoration, they are classical in spirit, and occasionally almost medieval in their sense of tight, controlled solemnity […].

Paul Goldberger,
'For San Francisco, a New
Museum With Its Own
Signature',
in *The New York Times*,
September 13, 1990.

HARALD SZEEMANN

RUDOLF ARNHEIM

Mario Botta hat auf Castel Grande ein Wunder vollbracht. Seine „Tenda" hat in der Tat die trutzige Festung invadiert und ins Mittelalter eine Dimension eingebracht, die wohltuend von alla „Son et lumière" –Versuchen sich abhebt, weil für einmal die Vergangenheit nicht passiv über Ausstrahlung verherrlicht, sondern durch einen Körper herausgefordert wird. [...] eine weisse in der Sonne, silbergraue bei trübem Wetter, wimpelbewehrte Brust, [...] die [...] in einer Rüstung gepresst sich [...] freimacht, und hier aus der zinnenbewehrten, drohenden Umgebung von Mauern und Türmen, aus eckiger Architektur und Felsen sich erhebt und trotz Einpassung dem linearen, düsteren Wehrdenken die Verführung des Verletzlichen, des Fraglichen einfügt und entgegensetzt. [...] Das „Zelt" wie es stets genannt wird, ist ein genialer Wurf, da es ausser der klaren Eigenschaft als Zentralbau sonst alle Typologien von Architekturform und Struktur in die Einheit eingehen lässt. [...] das virtuelle Zentrum ist über das Zelt hinaus eine Kuppel. [...] Dieses Novum einer Kuppel, die auch ein Zelt, und eines Zeltes, das auch eine Kuppel ist, greift für ihre „chymische" Hochzeit auf das Stützenkonstruktionsmodell der Gotik zurück. [...] Nomadenzelt, Kuppel, gotisches Strebewerk, krönende Laterne, Offenlegung der Elemente und Kräfte, diese Verbindung verdankt sich nicht nur der Aesthetik und Invention, sondern ebenso sehr dem genialen Zusammenspiel der Teile im Prozess der Errichtung. Die Fotografien zeigen deutlich wie alle Einzelelemente auf dieses Unikat hin entwickelt und fabriziert wurden [...]. Aber das Wichtigste und Schönste ist doch der naiv-gläubige Nerv, der durch das Ganze vibriert, die in jeder Form sichtbare, unverbrauchte Freude am Gelingen des Werkes [...].

All works of art worth their name are symbolic, and works of architecture are no exception. By symbolism I mean that these works [...] convey through their visible appearance the spiritual and philosophical meaning of their functions. [...] To do its job, the symbolism of a building has to be spontaneously apparent to the viewers' eyes through the various aspects of visual form, such as size, shape and spatial relation. The elements of this visual vocabulary are the geometrical shapes, by which a work speaks to us. [...] The project designs a new church for the mountain village of Mogno [...]. His composition amounts to a modern synthesis of the traditional alternative between circle and ellipse by confronting the two in a contrapuntal relation. Philosophically and theologically, this is a confrontation of the more worldly ellipse and the rectangular space it controls with the more sacred realm of the circular roof. It will be evident that when buildings go beyond the closed symbols associated with their conventional function and rely instead on open symbols drawn from the spontaneous expression of visual shapes, their meaning also will be seen primarily in the human vision and attitude they express, rather than in their practical application. In the case of church architecture, this means that the designer as his or her mind on the basic human qualities emerging from the particular ritual – in the case of the Mogno church that of a Roman Catholicism. [...] this means that a good designer like Mario Botta gave up most of the literal applications of tradition, not to ignore them but to probe once again the deeper core of human feeling and thought.

Harald Szeemann,
'Das Wunder von Castelgrande', in Tita Carloni, Jacques Pilet
und Harald Szeemann, *Das Zelt-La Tente-La Tenda*, mit *Postscriptum* von Mario Botta, Edizioni Casagrande-Verlag für Architektur, Bellinzona 1991, S. 56-60.

Rudolf Arnheim,
'Notes on religious architecture',
in *Languages of Design*, 1993, 8, vol. I, pp. 247-251.

JEAN PETIT

[…] Si tu te risques à créer des formes inconnues, extraordinaires, massives et compactes auxquelles tu accroches d'autres formes plus aériennes, tu sais toujours réagir à l'environnement. Confrontant au lieu d'intégrer, ce n'est pas sur le site que tu construis, c'est le site que tu construis. Tout en créant des espaces où l'homme va pouvoir vivre et s'épanouir, tout en faisant ton métier avec l'habilité d'un artisan, tu réagis à la banalisation du "moderne" sachant qu'une meilleure qualité de la vie va de pair avec celle de l'espace […]. De même, tu sais ordonner, recomposer et magnifier les lieux amorçant de nouveaux tissus urbaines dans une continuité historique. Alors, tes architectures deviennent prise de possession et renouvellement…A la fois complice et soucieux de convaincre, d'être compris, tu aimes voir les gens parler, les écouter, faire partager l'émotion, l'émerveillement… Ton langage direct et concret sait faire partager ta vision de l'architecture, une architecture qui t'aide à mieux voir, à mieux comprendre. Et ta bouillante imagination, jointe à une grande intuition, te conduit toujours et encore à innover. Esprit curieux et investigateur, mais non dénué de sens critique, tu sais mettre la vérité en évidence. Clairvoyant et lucide, tu es aussi bien capable d'opinions courageuses que de provocations… Ton travail est ta vie […]. Ce métier d'architecte, tu l'exerces comme un artisan avec une perfection professionnelle acquise par la pratique depuis ta seizième année. En fait, ta plus grand habilité, c'est ton honnêteté, c'est elle qui te pousse à ne jamais rien entreprendre avec le doute, mais au contraire avec confiance […]. Avec toi qui pratiques l'architecture comme un engagement, comme un sacerdoce, la grâce est bien présente dans tes batailles quotidiennes. Ta paix, c'est dans le travail que tu la trouves… […].

Jean Petit, 'Salut l'artiste',
in *Traces d'architecture-Botta*,
Fidia Edizioni d'Arte, Lugano
et Bibliothèque des Arts,
Paris 1994, pp. 6-9.

ALLAN TEMKO

[…] Mario Botta's SFMOMA is not only one of the best museum buildings of our time […] but a new kind of symbolic monument altogether […]. The building has an undeniable spiritual grandeur. There is even a certain mystery as it is approached. […] the museum come into view by stages, rather like a cathedral above the roofs of a medieval town. […]. It is an Italian space. […]. Mario Botta is an authentic star of modernism in a confused architectural era […]. Botta is too serious an architect to succumb to such buffoonery. If anything, his severe art – the art that created the clifflike, forbidding façades of SFMOMA – may be too exacting, too tough for those who want "warm" buildings that reach out to ordinary people. Instead people are required to live up to his architecture. He came to such architecture almost by birthright. His native canton of Ticino […] has been a nurturing ground of renowned architects since the Renaissance. […] Botta's buildings have weight. They possess a gravity, a solemnity, that was apparent even in the hillside dwellings that made his international reputation in the early 1980s. These houses are invested with primordial strength. On lofty, isolated sites, they appear like castles of minor lords, thick-walled, impervious. They eye the valley below through colossal apertures, especially the huge Cyclopean "eye" of a house he designed in Massagno, near Lugano, that was the first forerunner of the giant eye of SFMOMA. […] Gradually, as he explored the same set of formal themes, these elements of his architecture came together with a new power in the mid eighties. The pivotal building of the period was the small stone church at Mogno, in the Ticino, a perfect cylinder raked back sharply in perhaps the most inspired of his skylights. From Mogno, the road leads directly to San Francisco […]. Botta has resorted to open historicism. Unlike the postmodernists, however, he has respected history without mimicking the past. […].

Allan Temko, 'Art and Soul',
in *San Francisco Focus*,
1995, 1, pp. 42-49.

FULVIO IRACE

Botta immagina Dio come il grande Architetto della tradizione sacra, il Costruttore di quel Grande Mondo i cui frammenti costituiscono il tema dell'architettura degli uomini. Identificando l'essenza del dettato religioso con la natura religiosa del suo lavoro, ne accetta le scommesse come l'atto di un dono: come un monito dunque e un richiamo alla funzione simbolica dell'architettura, alla sua volontà e al suo bisogno di testimoniare l'esigenza di una trascendenza che giustifichi la presenza dell'umano nel grande mistero della natura. […]. Dall'emozione dei luoghi e dalla violenza della storia nascono i progetti delle due cappelle dove si celebra il mistero drammatico della fragilità e della tenacia, della modernità e delle origini, della possanza e della trasparenza, del limite e della sua forzatura. Non a caso un singolare filo umano congiunge gli sforzi dei due sacrari *en plein air*: il mattino del 23 aprile 1986 lenta e inesorabile una slavina cala sul paesino di Mogno […]: vittima sacrificale, la Chiesa di San Giovanni rimane al suolo. […]. Devozione popolare e devozione progettuale trovano un significativo incontro nell'immagine di una geometria che pare quasi elementare, come un totem […]. Fondata sulla geometria, la chiesa ne torce la solida chiarezza facendone vibrare le superfici di contenimento dal rettangolo all'ellisse, al cerchio finale. Ne descrive insomma la metamorfosi della materia, mentre allude all'incombere del pericolo, della rovina, fermata in quel gesto di un tetto trasparente, di uno spazio eternamente scoperchiato. […]. Tra *memorial* e luogo di culto prende corpo l'immagine di Santa Maria degli Angeli come un viadotto che crea la sommità del monte […]. L'esperienza del sacro apre una finestra sull'intorno per permettere al viandante di leggere nelle profondità del suo interno: si cementa nella struttura di un percorso, di un asse, di una discesa, di una risalita, di un esterno che si ribalta nella rotonda piattaforma della cappella, facendosi arco, ponte, galleria, piazza sospesa…

Fulvio Irace,
'Due chiese in Canton Ticino',
in *Abitare*, 1996, 347,
pp. 84-91.

CESARE DE SETA

[…] Botta è nato in una terra dove il romanico ha radici ben solide e profonde, essendo essa una propaggine di una più ampia patria lombarda dove il romanico spuntò, facendo germogliare una nuova civiltà architettonica. Nella sua architettura c'è una sorta di primitivismo barbarico che riconduce a questo humus: la sua vocazione alle forme elementari non va confusa con il semplicismo di un abaco […]. Espressione della sua creatività, le chiese sono molto diverse tra loro ma tutte nate da una logica imperturbabilmente coerente a un'idea di architettura che si riconosce di primo acchito. […] Si diceva della coerenza di Botta, della sua fermezza nel perseguire un fine primario che è quello di definire uno spazio e di costruirlo come se fosse tratto dal ventre più profondo della *Mater Tellus* cantata da Lucrezio. […] Dicendo del primitivismo barbaro di Botta proprio a questo bisogno primario ho pensato: non per negare religiosità ai suoi spazi sacri, che ne sono intimamente pervasi, ma per ricondurli a una condizione più profonda e astorica. Quella appunto che ci suggerisce la sua forma del sacro, che è legata al luogo, all'immanenza della terra, alla sua immutabile e pur cangiante essenza. […] Botta, in sostanza, in dieci anni ha costruito non solo delle chiese, ma una tipologia meticolosamente strutturata secondo un frasario che non è mai uniforme. […] Questa attitudine dell'architetto ha la sua più convincente espressione nella cappella sul Monte Tamaro […]. Qui l'architettura è interno ed esterno, non c'è discontinuità tra la squamata corteccia del monte e questo "altro" che sembra essere sortito dalle viscere della terra e ne conserva l'asprezza. […] Quella del Monte Tamaro è una architettura nata per star lì e la montagna la riconosce come una sua figlia, perché essa è nata nel suo ventre.

Cesare de Seta, *Mater Tellus*,
in *Mario Botta. Emozioni
di pietra*, con testi di
Benedetto Gravagnuolo,
Werner Oechslin, Gabriele
Cappellato, Mario Botta,
Skira Editore, Milano 1997,
pp. 17-21.

WERNER OECHSLIN

[…] Architecture is neither virtual nor ephemeral. It has never lost its desire to endure, nor has it ever ceased to aspire to the eternal. How else can we explain the success of Mario Botta, who apparently always uses the same geometry, if not the same materials? It is hard to imagine that he could ever succumb to the fashions of the moment. The keystones of his architecture are constancy and perseverance achieved through patient research. […] So how are we to explain Mario Botta's success? For one thing, his architecture does not seem to suffer from the influence of currents in architectural fashions. In Botta's work there is no place for the *non-sequiturs* of the exclusive, avant-garde modern movement […] Current attitudes and fashions hold no interest for Mario Botta, who consistently refers to his works only to the permanent, ongoing requirements of architecture, which are so far removed from academic influences and temporary, passing fashions. […] Botta's architecture rightly aims for a validity that endures over time – far beyond the fleeting moment. This is why he will always create real, genuine testimonials of 'memories' and this also explains how he is able to work so easily and naturally with themes as 'difficult' as those of the monument and the sacred building. […] All this sounds very much in tune with the architecture of Mario Botta, who works in the best traditions of a modern movement in which the unity of the image constitutes either a formal purpose or a major cultural objective. And yet anyone who expects to see only formal constants in Botta's work does not understand that for Botta, just as for other great architects of our century, the real question is not the repetition of external form, but the constant striving to express oneself in a coherent language. The artist's strength is demonstrated when he is able, under variety of complex circumstances, to recreate the unique synthesis required for architectonic unity.[…]

Werner Oechslin, "*Considérations morales sur la destination des ouvrages de l'art – Q. de Quincy*" – *Mario Botta's Vocation for the Sacred and the Monumental*, in *Mario Botta-Public Buildings 1990-1998*, with texts by Benedetto Gravagnuolo, Cesare De Seta, Werner Oechslin, Gabriele Cappellato, Mario Botta, Thames and Hudson, London 1998, pp. 26-30.

BENEDIKT LODERER

Botta baut. Das ist die Zusammenfassung. […] Botta baut International. […] Botta leuchtet […] Botta stellt sich. […] Botta bewegt. […] Botta polarisiert. […] Denn Botta bleibt Tessiner. Obwohl er international geworden ist, bleibt er zu Hause. Er gehört zur Lombardei, zum Mittelmeer, zum Katholizismus,. Er gehört nicht zu den berechnenden Protestanten, nie ist er modern im industrialisierten Sinn. Englisch, die Lingua franca des Geldes und der Moden, spricht er nicht. Venedig, nicht Chicago; Mailand, nicht London; Lugano, nicht Zürich. Verkürzt gesagt: Form, nicht Zweck. Botta bleibt Künstler. […] Botta ist allgemeinverständlich. […] Sein Formenvokabular hat nur sieben Worte: Mauer, Körper, Höhle, Schlitz, Symmetrie, Ornament und Licht. Mit diesen sieben Worten macht er ganze Sätze und erzählt einleuchtende Geschichten. […] Denn Botta ist archaisch. Zwar ging er bei den modernen in die Lehre […], aber je deutlicher sich sein Formenvokabular herausbildete, desto archaischer wurde er. Seine Bauten haben Masse und Geschichte. Sie sind alle älter als ihr Jahrgang. Selbstverständlich sind es zeitgenössische Bauten, doch in ihnen steckt mehrfach verwandelt, die mediterrane Tradition. […] Botta gelingt es, mit modernen Formen römisch zu bauen. Botta hält ewig. […] Botta ist massiv. […] Botta unterwirft sich. Den geometrischen Regeln des Sichtsteins nämlich. […] Botta hat Gestalt. Seine Baukörper haben immer einen klaren Umriss. […] Botta zieht Grenzen. Dass innen und aussen dasselbe sind, hat Botta nie geglaubt. […] Botta kontrolliert. Er macht keine Fenster, er schneidet Lichtstreifen in die Wände. Er will nicht hinausschauen, er will die Aussicht kontrollieren. […] Botta ist symmetrisch. […] Botta spielt. […] Die Spielfreude ist zwar offensichtlich, aber auch das Einhalten der Spielregeln. Damit ist viel von Botta's Arbeitsweise beschrieben. Spiel und Regel, Erfindung und Disziplin. […] Botta baut Lichtfülle. […] Botta ? Einer der Grossen.

Benedikt Loderer, 'Mit modernen Formen römisch', in *Mario Botta Gesamtwerk Band 3, 1990-1997*, Birkhäuser Verlag für Architektur, Basel-Boston-Berlin 1998, pp. 6-7.

GIOVANNI POZZI

Quando Mario Botta mi illustrò il progetto della cappella di Mogno. […] Dapprima pensai al Colosseo come idea generatrice, non del progetto architettonico in sé, ma dell'idea così singolare di costruire una chiesa che evocasse una rovina; poi al simbolismo legato a quelle forme geometriche inconsuete. […] progettando un edificio, per giunta sacro, che porta in sé l'impronta d'una sopravvivenza al disastro, tanto evidente nel declinare della parete e nella voragine che l'invaso crea e il tetto vitreo non copre, Botta vuol proporci sostituendo al sottratto l'aggiunto, al negativo il positivo, un'architettura non dissimile da quella che il Colosseo mostra ora ai nostri occhi per disfacimento. Se la forma violata del Colosseo deriva da una sottrazione lenta alla sua integrità monumentale, la chiesetta dall'aspetto in rovina sarà il risultato di una costruzione. Costruire evocando un'imperfezione significa annettere in modo perentorio a quella falla un significato. Perciò, mediante un richiamo così augusto l'umile cappelletta testimonierà la resistenza della coscienza storica alla violenza delle forze che sovrastano l'uomo […]. L'altro pensiero cadutomi in mente riguarda il simbolismo delle forme geometriche lì messe in atto: un'ellisse che si trasforma in cerchio; un ovale che l'occhio vede in prospettiva confrontato con un cerchio che gli si para di fronte; un'ellisse posata sulla terra e un circolo elevato verso il cielo. L'ellisse è una figura sconcertante. Avendo due centri o fuochi, è un circolo distorto; la sua circonferenza allungata comporta l'intrusione del moto rettilineo nel perfetto moto circolare. […]. L'ellisse che termina in circolo verrebbe quindi a evocare uno sconcerto che si risolve in armonia; o, che è quasi lo stesso, l'imperfezione dell'opera terrena, tale anche quando è sacra, che si trasforma in perfezione quando si alza al cielo […].

Giovanni Pozzi,
'Evocando uno sconcerto',
in *Mario Botta. La chiesa di San Giovanni Battista a Mogno*, Associazione Ricostruzione chiesa di Mogno - Skira Editore, Milano 1999, pp. 131-132.

STANISLAUS VON MOOS

[…] Naturalmente non si può definire monumento nazionale la ricostruzione, su una piattaforma sul lago di Lugano, di una metà dello spazio interno della chiesa di San Carlo alle Quattro Fontane di Roma […]. Comunque sia abbiamo a che fare con uno straordinario intreccio di temi e di interessi: una passione, forse pericolosa, per l'esplorazione delle possibilità e dei limiti della monumentalità nell'architettura di oggi, unita all'idea di spostare l'urbanistica sull'acqua […] la rappresentazione in scala 1:1 di Botta ignora intenzioni illusionistiche. La struttura delle tavole di legno impilate le une sulle altre non lascia alcuno spazio a tale inganno. […] L'originale, riprodotto tridimensionalmente, viene così riproposto come concetto astratto e si sottrae a ogni naturalismo pittoresco. Il risultato comunque non è una "copia" bensì una ricreazione didattica in scala 1:1. In quanto tale, essa rappresenta lo spazio interno del Borromini, mentre offre verso l'esterno la stereometria di un oggetto scultoreo di oggi. Nello stesso tempo la collocazione sull'acqua di questo cubo chiuso su tre lati, che si pare a ovest come una nicchia, segue una logica urbanistica decisamente latina, rappresentando la continuazione dell'estremità orientale del centro cittadino e sottolineando così il limite tra "città" e sobborgo. […] Botta stesso […] insiste sul carattere del progetto come "costruzione scenografica", che trova la propria ragione d'essere in se stesso e non in un'illusione. Una costruzione che non ha altro fine se non quello di coincidere "con il suo essere architettura e con il suo modo proprio di organizzare lo spazio". In altre parole, un monumento che, mentre celebra Borromini, dà anche una lezione su come Botta vede l'architettura […].

Stanislaus von Moos,
Urbanistica virtuale. Due quasi-monumenti di Mario Botta, in *Borromini sul lago*, a cura di Gabriele Cappelleto [con testi di E. Sanguineti, M. Botta, C. Bertelli, G. Panza di Biumo, A. Cantafora, N. Emery, G. Abou-Jaoudé], Università della Svizzera Italiana, Accademia di architettura di Mendrisio, Skira Editore, Milano 1999, pp. 33-38.

IRENA SAKELLARIDOU

[…] Mario Botta has indeed given form to space, and meaning to form. Both in his homeland and abroad, and all over the world, his buildings assert their powerful configuration. Their clarity of outline defines a figure immediately perceived and understood, its meaning lying in the longing for the spiritual and the ethical. […] His forms search for the eternal and not the ephemeral, for the long-lasting and not the transient. While the density of their meaning carries the memory of the archaic, his architecture is nevertheless modern. […] Mario Botta's narrative is structured, with content and form in close relation. His text is controlled, measured and weighted. And yet, syntactic order does not limit, but liberates; does not confine, but enriches with its potential. It does not remain silent; it speaks about the adventures of space, it tells the story of form. What gives Mario Botta's architecture its strong identity is an internal logic that guides and underlies formal expression. His first buildings have already introduced his themes. These themes combine, interweave, and influence all aspects of the building, they set architectural rules that order the formation of the volume, the elevations and the plan, define the way the building will be looked at from afar and will face the world. All this defines his logic of form. Rules in interrelation create an *intensive compositional structure*, by virtue of which everything relates to the other and everything obeys the overall order. It is a structure that is stable and yet in a continuous state of oscillation between the creative search for the new and the transformation of what has already been explored…

Irena Sakellaridou,
"Logic of Form, Richness of Meaning", in *Mario Botta, Architectural Poetics*, Rizzoli, New York, 2000, pp. 6-11.

PAOLO PORTOGHESI

[…] Degli architetti che appartengono allo "star system" decretato dalla pubblicità internazionale è il più coerente. Fin dal suo esordio, agli inizi degli anni '70, la sua opera si presenta come sperimentazione ininterrotta di un tema prediletto: lo spazio scavato all'interno del volume "per via di levare", con una tecnica che proviene dalla scultura ma è completamente riscattata da ogni velleità "scultorea" attraverso il filtro di una geometria rigorosa […]. Botta, con rare eccezioni, parte da volumi enunciati nella loro purezza geometrica, per ritrovare in essi lo spazio della vita. Incidere, scavare è il modo con cui Botta recupera il metodo "moderno" della scomposizione […] senza però sacrificare la purezza dei volumi. Ciò che viene scomposto e ricomposto è infatti lo spazio interno, che l'architetto immagina spesso come pacchetto di cellule individuabili e sottraibili […]. Lo spazio scolpito, sottratto a una materia cosiffatta conquista trasparenza e leggerezza e consente di ricavare un rapporto originalissimo con il paesaggio recuperando il tema del "belvedere" e delle logge tipico dell'architettura italiana […]. Un filo sottile lega il giardino di Gerusalemme alla sistemazione di Piazza della Pilotta ed è il filo della memoria. A Gerusalemme la memoria mitica dell'Arca rivive nel sogno infantile e si dispiega nella scelta di una tecnologia come quella muraria, arcaica […]. A Parma la memoria si esprime nel rispetto dell'esistente, nella capacità di riproporne una immagine nuova attraverso lievi modifiche della superficie del terreno e degli itinerari di lettura; ma si esprime anzitutto nella felice rievocazione della antica chiesa di San Pietro Martire, attraverso una grande vasca e due file di alberi che, rispecchiandosi in essa, "scavano" nel terreno uno spazio analogo, uno spazio mnemonico ma "vivente" perché plasmato da elementi come l'acqua e le piante che continuamente si trasformano.

Paolo Portoghesi,
Scolpire lo spazio. Due architetture di Mario Botta/ Carving out space Two architectures by Mario Botta, in *Abitare la Terra*, 2003, 5, pp. 20-25.

COLLABORATORS

1970-2013

Maria Della Casa Botta

Agazzi Gianfranco (1972/1985-87)
Albinolo Andrea (2009-11)
Albreiki Waleed (2010)
Anchora Donato (2001)
Andreani Nicola (2010-11)
Andreolli Giulio (1987)
Andrey Sabine (2004-07)
Annaloro Antonino (2000-04)
Bächler Jean-Michel (1978-79)
Bachmann Jonas (2007)
Bachry Hélène (1984-85)
Bamberg Thomas (1988-91)
Bandiera Francesco (1988)
Battistini Appien (2000-01)
Begolli Kujtim (2001-02)
Bellini Fermo (since 1990)
Bellorini Andreina (1985-86)
Beres Platane (1986)
Beretta Marino (1986-88)
Bernasconi Giorgio (1972-73)
Bernegger Emilio (1972-73)
Bertoni Riccardo (1981)
Beusch Gabrielle (1986-87)
Bianchi Silvana (1975/1978)
Bicho Duarte Vaz Pinto João (2013-14)
Biondi Alessandro (2003-05)
Blouin Francis (1994-97)
Blumer Riccardo (1984-88)
Bonderer Sara (1998-99)
Bonini Marco (1987-97)
Borgye Xavier (since 2011)
Borri Silvio (1992-93)
Bösch Martin (1975-80)
Boschetti Lorenza (1990-94)
Boschetti Patrick (1988-89)
Bösch-Hutter Elisabeth (1976-81)
Botta Giuditta (since 1996)
Botta Guido (since 1989)
Botta Tobia (since 1998)
Botta Tommaso since 1998)
Bottinelli Alessandro (1974)
Brackrock Tim (1995-96)
Brauen Ueli (1985-86)
Bressan Emanuele (since 2010)
Brunstein Sophia (2013-14)
Bütti Andrea (1973-74)
Büttiker Urs (1983-84)
Caldelari Giuliano (1980-85)
Camenisch Giancarlo (1970-71)
Campisano Mara Belen (2004-06)
Campopiano Juan Manuel (2009-10)
Cantoni Sandro (1971-72)
Caramaschi Andrea (1990-96)
Castagnetta Botta Eleonora (since 2005)
Catella Gianni (1987-88/1994-95)
Cazzaniga Raimondo (1982-84)
Chartiel Jean-Michel (2000)

Cho Dana (1996)
Coletti Ezequiel (1999)
Colombo Claudia (1982)
Cortat Sabine (1990-92)
Crivelli Roberto (1973)
Crivelli-Looser Marianne (1971)
Croci-Gerosa Patrizia (1991-98)
Daneshgar Moghaddam Golrang (2002-03)
D'Azzo Marco (1984-85)
De Filippi Filippo (1993-95)
Della Casa Paolo (1993-98)
De Prà David (2008-12)
Di Bernardo Elisiana (since 2005)
Duci Roberto (2006-07)
Duda Emilia Maria (2004)
Eisenhut Daniele (1984-10)
Falconi Carlo (since 1992)
Felicioni Andrea (1990-91)
Fenaroli Antonella (1992-93)
Ferrari Pietro (1987-88)
Ferrari Marta (1985-86)
Ferrario Luca (since 2013)
Ferrier Marcel (1980)
Filippini Sonja (1989)
Floriani Filippo Paolo (since 2009)
Flückiger Urs-Peter (1991-95)
Fontana Luigi (1985)
Früh Ugo (1985-2000)
Furuya Nobuaki (1986-87)
Gaggini Isabella (1986)
Galli Valerio (1973)
Gehring Daniel Pierre (1979-80)
Geller Alice (1997-98)
Gellera Fabrizio (1978)
Gemin Mario (1990-93)
Gilardi Mauro (1971)
Giovannini Piero (2012-13)
Gonthier Alain (1978-79)
Goy Michael (2002)
Grassi-Maffi Monica (since 1983)
Groh Claude Michel (1982-86)
Han Man Won (1990-94)
Hegi Thomas (1987-91)
Heras Carlos Maria (1985-88)
Höhn Thierry (1978-79)
Hunziker Rudy (1972-79)
Kaczura Wojciech (1989)
Kappeler Sinue (2011-12)
Kaun Anne (1989)
Keller Bruno (1974)
Koch Julia Maria (1999-2001)
Konrad Christine (1985)
Koyoshi Yasuhiko (1991-92)
Kress Laurie Mae (1987-88)
Külling Urs (1981-86)
Lazzati Mirko (1998-00)
Lazzareschi Sergiusti Giovanni (2012-13)
Leuzinger Remo (1977-79)
Liegeois-Dorthu Mariette (1990-94)

Lo Riso Claudio (1979-89)
Lorenz-Meyer Ferrari Juliane (1989-92)
Liu Chang (2013)
Macocchi Athos (1970-72)
Macullo Davide (1990-09)
Maggiolini Niccolò Carlo Maria (2011-12)
Marinzoli Alessandra (1992-95)
Margraf Stephanie (2011-12)
Marzullo Giancarlo (2002-04)
Mazzola Lorenza (1987-93)
Medri Guido (1996-97)
Melegoni Adolfo (1993-98)
Mensa Alessandro (1985-87)
Melzi Federico (2009-10)
Meozzi Vanni (2005-06)
Meroni Francesco (since 2011)
Merzaghi Paolo (1984-96)
Meshale Anna (since 1987)
Meyer Indra (2006-07)
Mina Daniela (1981-82)
Molteni Francesca (2009-10)
Monnier Sandrine (1989)
Moreni Massimo (1985-2010)
Moretti Valentina (2003)
Mornata Marco (since 2011)
Moscardi Alice (2007-08)
Müller Küffer Ursula (1991-92)
Nasincein Maria Carla (1988-90)
Negrini Claudio (1973)
Orsi Claudio (2005-13)
Orsini Giorgio (1983)
Ostinelli Elio (1973-74)
Ottolenghi Roberta (1991-95)
Pachoud Daniel (1994-98)
Palavisini Laura (2001-02)
Pecora Viviana (2006-07)
Pelis Marco (since 2007)
Pellandini Paola (since 1988)
Pelle Oliver (1997)
Pelli Maurizio (1979-2013)
Pelli Olivia (1998)
Perea Ana Alicia (1999-2000)
Perret Jacques (1982-83)
Petraglio Etienne (2010)
Pfister Nicola (1988-2000)
Piattini Ira (1992-93)
Pico Estrada Bernabe (2003-04)
Pietrini Guido (1994-95)
Pina-Blouin Paola (1996-05)
Plummer Robert (1994-95)
Pochon Jean-Pierre (1978)
Poliac Raluca (2001-02)
Porta Alain (1981-82)
Pozzi Daniele Pietro (2009-10)
Pozzi Paolo (1992-95)
Qehajaj Adhurim (2000-01)
Ranieri Drew (1979-80)
Realini Juliana (2011-2012)
Redaelli Ivo (1997-09)

Robbiani Ferruccio (1973-85)
Rosselli Luigi (1979-80)
Rossinelli Silvia (since 1992)
Rovelli Ida (1971)
Rucigaj-Vehovar Mateja (1982-83)
Ruffieux Jean-Marc (1979-81)
Rusconi Letizia (2003-09)
Ryser Eric (1980-81)
Sakurai Taro (2005-06)
Sakurai Yoshio (1993)
Salvadé Nicola (since 1997)
Salvadé Simone (1988-01)
Sangiorgio Marco (1991-92)
Sano Mitsunori (1999-00)
Sassi Valeria (1999)
Saurwein Emanuele (2002-02)
Scala Antonello (since 1989)
Schiavio Andrea (2011-12)
Schmid Moreno (1976)
Schönbächler Daniela (1990-92)
Schranz Caroline (1989-1991)
Schwitter Carlo (1987-94)
Sepiurka Mariana (1999)
Serena Riccardo (1971-72)
Sestranetz Raphaelle (1991-92)
Sganzini-Nerfin Dominique (1987-91)
Shah Snehal (1984-85)
Sieber Adrian (1979)
Sokolov Alexandre (1999-2004)
Soldini Danilo (1990-2001)
Soldini Nicola (1979/80/81)
Spada Chiara (1992-93)
Spring David (2002-03)
Staub Peter (1998-99)
Steger Monica (1990-96)
Stömer Michaela (1989)
Strozzi Marco (1998-2012)
Tami Luca (1974-76)
Tarchini Fabio (1977)
Tavelli Natalie (1993-94)
Tejedor-Linares Mercedes (1987-88)
Teodori Costantino (2006-07)
Thomke Sybille (1992)
Toletti Tiziano (2013-14)
Torriani Anna (1975)
Trebeljahr Cathrin (1986-87)
Trevisiol Emilio Antonio (2013-14)
Trifan Constantin (2003-04)
Tüscher Anne (1995-95)
Urfer Thomas (1977-82/1983-84)
Varnier Tiziano (1990-92)
Verda Gianmaria (1981)
Vidoni Pier Luigi (1982)
Villa Maximilian (2012-13)
Viscardi Ares (1989-1991)
Vivarelli Veronica (2007-08)
Von Allmen-Bosco Monique (1988-90)
Weckerle Thomas (1988)
Zecchino Renato (1998)

Mario Botta with students
of the Architecture academy
in Mendrisio

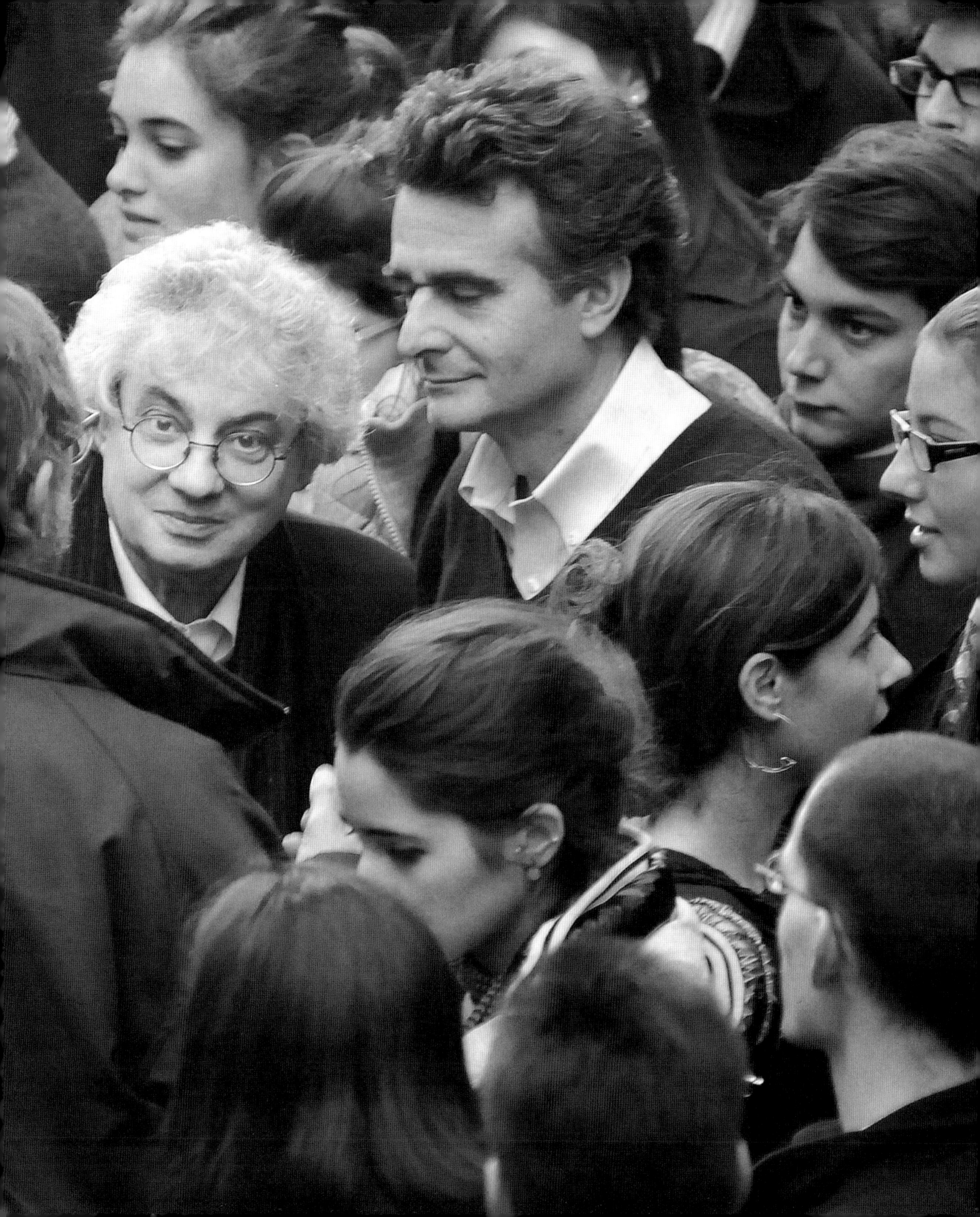

BIOGRAPHIES OF THE AUTHORS

CARLO BERTELLI

Born in Rome in 1930, he was an administrator at the Central Institute of Restoration, where he dealt with exceptional monuments such as high-medieval icons, Saint Sophia in Constantinople, Piero della Francesca. He was Director of the National Photographic Cabinet and then of the National Chalcography Institute; since 1978 he has lived in Milan, where he was Director of the Brera Art Gallery. From 1985 to 1995 he taught at the University of Lausanne, from 1996 to 2001 at the Academy of Architecture in Mendrisio. He has been visiting professor at Berkeley, at the Centre for Advanced Study in the Visual Arts and Dumbarton Oaks, in Berlin, Geneva and in Venice at the IUAV. He has written several essays and monographs on the Medieval and Renaissance, as well as on the history of photography and incision. He was often a consultant in musical projects for institutions in Siena, Paris (the Louvre), Geneva, Chambéry, Patrasso, among others, and is the author of a successful text on art history for high schools.

JOHN BOYER

John Boyer is president of the Andreas H. Bechtler Arts Foundation. Prior to joining the Foundation in February 2008, John was the president and CEO of the Franklin and Eleanor Roosevelt Institute. He previously served as the Executive Director of the Mark Twain House and Museum in Hartford. John taught art history, architectural history and the history of photography at Trinity College, art history at the University of Hartford and has lectured at Columbia University, the University of Illinois at Chicago and Brown University. He is a graduate of University of California, Santa Barbara with a degree in art history, and of Princeton University with a degree in art and architecture with special emphasis in the 19th and 20th centuries.

ALDO COLONETTI

Born in Bergamo in 1945, he is a philosopher, historian and theorist of art, design and architecture as well as journalist and teacher. He graduated in philosophy with Gillo Dorfles and Enzo Paci, and since the 70's has been involved in the research into the esthetic and semantic problems in communication, graphics and design. He was a lecturer of aesthetics at the State University of Milan (1972-75); he is scientific director of the IED Group - Istituto Europeo di Design. Besides collaborating with the Italian daily newspaper *Corriere della Sera* he is the author of several articles and essays on the problems of aesthetics and the philosophy of language; he has taken part in many cultural initiatives and has helped organize exhibitions dedicated to graphics and design all over the world.
From 2002 to 2006 he was a member of the scientific committee of the Triennale of Milan; since 1991 he has been director of the magazine *Ottagono*. In 2001 he was awarded with the title of "Member of the British Empire" by Her Majesty, Elizabeth 11 for cultural merits. Since 2009 he has been a member of the Italian Council of Design, under the Ministries of Cultural Assets, Foreign Affairs and Productive Activities.

GILLO DORFLES

Born in Trieste in 1910 he is an art critic, painter, university lecturer and author of several essays on aesthetics. He enrolled in the Faculty of Medicine in Milan and completed his university studies in Rome, with the aim of specializing in neuropsychiatry. From the thirties onwards, during his intense activity as art critic and essayist, he has collaborated with the magazines and journals *La Rassegna d'Italia*, *Le Arti Plastiche*, *La Fiera Letteraria*, *Il Mondo*, *Domus* (where he was also vice-director), *Aut Aut* (of which he was editor-in-chief), *The Studio*, *The Journal of Aesthetics*. Between the 50's and 60's he increased his work as a critic and at the same time devoted himself to university teaching, as a qualified lecturer and then as professor of aesthetics at the Universities of Milan, Trieste and Cagliari. Alongside these activities he was visiting professor in different foreign institutions and conference lecturer at important congresses and conventions in Italy and abroad. In 1948 he was one of the founders of the MAC - Movimento Arte Concreta, with Bruno Munari, Atanasio Soldati and Gianni Monnet and in 1956 he had a hand in the setting up of the ADI - Association for Industrial

Design. In 1954 he was a member of an Italian section of Espace; he has continued with his painting and exhibition activities throughout his entire career. His activity as a journalist with the Italian daily *Corriere della Sera* is of considerable importance, as is the corpus of his critical, essay and monographic activities. He has won many prizes and awards, is honorary professor of Brera, a member of the Academia del Diseño di Città del Messico, fellow of the World Academy of Arts and Sciences, Doctor *honoris causa* of the Polytechnic in Milan and of the Universidad Autonoma in Mexico City, honorary citizen of Paestum.

JACQUES GUBLER

He was born in Nyon, Switzerland in 1940 and graduated in History of Art in 1965 from the University of Lausanne, where he earned his doctorate in 1975. In 1983-84 he was a lecturer at the New Jersey Institute of Technology, Newark, and at the Institute of Theory and History of Architecture (ITHA), in Lausanne. From 1984 to 1999 he was professor of History of Modern Architecture at the Polytechnic in Lausanne and then at the Academy of Architecture in Mendrisio (1999-2006). He has written several essays and research studies on the topics of modern architecture; since 2007 he has been working freelance in Basel.

ROMAN HOLLENSTEIN

He was born in 1953 and graduated in History of Art and Architecture at the University of Berne; he started work as a scientific assistant for the collections of the Prince of Liechtenstein in Vaduz and Vienna. He then collaborated with the Kunstmuseum in Basel as assistant for exhibitions and at the same time taught at the University of Berne and at the Zurich University of the Arts. In his function as member of the governing board at the Swiss Institute for Art Research in Zurich he was head of the department of History of Art from 1987 to 1990. Since 1990 he has been a journalist on the editorial staff for culture at the *Neue Zürcher Zeitung*, where he is responsible for the sections of architecture and design. As well as his activities in journalism he has written texts concerning art around 1800, international artistic expressions, contemporary artistic and architectural production in Switzerland, the architecture of museums and synagogues and architecture in Israel.

LIONELLO PUPPI

He was born in Belluno in 1931 and graduated in 1958 from the Arts Faculty at the University of Padua, where he was assistant lecturer in the History of Medieval Art from then to 1966. In 1964 he earned his Doctorate in the History of Medieval and Modern Art and was lecturer of the History of Architecture and Town Planning, then lecturer of the historical subjects of art. He was director of the Scuola di specializzazione in History of Art (1972-73) and then at the Institute of History of Art (1974-78); from 1974 to 1990 he was lecturer of History of Architecture and Town Planning. In 1990 he was appointed to the staff of the University of Ca' Foscari in Venice, where he had various functions; among those he was full-time professor of History of Contemporary and Modern Art, president of the degree course in Conservation of Cultural Property, director of the Department of History of Arts and professor of Methodology of History of Art. In 2005 he was appointed emeritus professor in Methodology of History of Art. He was also a lecturer at several foreign universities and member and consultant of important international bodies as well as of Italian and foreign institutions. He carried out periods of research as fellow at Harvard University, Villa Tatti in Florence and at Dumbarton Oaks in Washington, then as visiting scholar in Princeton and in Japan. He was curator of important art exhibitions and coordinator of international study conventions; he was on the editorial staff of scientific journals and published articles in major international magazines. His works of research have appeared in over one thousand publications, concentrating on Venetian civilization from the 14th to the 20th centuries, art collection, editions of historiographical sources, on town planning, landscape, gardens and the topics of architectural culture in Verona, Padua, Vicenza and Venice and also in Buenos Aires, Montevideo, Brasilia. He was Senator of the Italian Republic from 1985 to 1987 and is a member of the Cultural Commission of the Association of ex-Parliamentarians.

CREDITS

Photographs of works of art reproduced in this book have been provided in most cases by the owners of the works or their representatives. The individual works appearing herein may be protected by copyright in the United States of America or elsewhere and thus may not be reproduced in any form without the permission of the copyright owners. The following copyrights and/or other photograph credits appear at the request of the artist's representatives and/or the owners of the individual works. Additional credits are listed alphabetically below, followed by the number of the page on which the illustration appears. The publishers have sought, as far as possible, permission to reproduce each illustration, and gratefully acknowledge the cooperation of all those who gave their kind permission to reproduce the listed material. Pictures with no particular reference are property of Mario Botta Archive

PHOTO CREDITS
Archivio Mario Botta
Alinari Archivi Italia 78
Archivio Mario Botta-Ticino Turismo 101 (9)
Archivio Mario Botta –Dim associati Firenze 105 (22, 23)
Archivio Mario Botta-Arch-Unisi Mendrisio 115 (19), 116 (21), 183
Archivio Mario Botta- Fanzun AG 106 (24)
Archivio Max Frisch 66
Ballo, Aldo 33 (19)
Beretta, Stefania 34-35
Bleyl, Marcus 225 (8)
Bon, Elena 266-267
Caleca, Santi-Serafino Zani 33 (18)
Cameraphoto Venezia 39 (3-4)
Cano, Enrico 13 (3), 16 (9,10) 18 (13), 19 (14) 23 (5), 28 (13), 29 (14), 40 (6), 44, 53, 80, 84-85, 96-97, 101 (12), 105 (21),114 (13,14), 122-123, 131-132, 133 (model), 141 (model), 145 (model),
149 (model), 151 (model), 153 (model), 155 (model), 157, 161 (model), 163 (model), 167 (model), 171 (model), 173 (model), 174-175, 177 (model), 179 (model), 180-181, 182-183, 190-191, 207 (12),
206 (16), 209, 210 (21), 211 (24), 212 (26), 214, 215 (34), 216, 217 (38,39), 218 (4), 225 (9,10)
Canfield, Robert 144
Carpi, Arno 99 (5)
Carrieri, Mario 33 (17)
Carron, Cav. Angelo, Treviso 22 (2)
Cassina, Mauro 100 (7-8)
Chea Park, Young 23 (6)
Chemollo Alessandra 210 (22), 224 (7)
D'Anna, Marco 83, 147(model), 169 (model)
Doisneau, Robert 59
Eccher, Nicola 143 (model)
Flammer, Alberto 171, 172, 205 (5,6)
FLC/ADAGP 49
Frank, Robert 58
Fu Xing 136-137, 219 (42)
Hofmann, Rainer 213(30)
Homberger, Urs 215 (33)
Lassiter, Joël 154-155
Mangani, Simone 114 (15)
Mulas, Mario / Piccolo Teatro di Milano-Teatro d'Europa 65
Musi, Pino 23 (3-4), 25 (8-9), 26 (10), 29 (15), 31 (16), 101 (11), 104 (20), 108-109,
110, 111, 116 (20), 117 (22-23), 128-129, 134-135, 140-141, 142-144, 145, 146-147, 148-149, 150-151, 158-159, 160-161, 162-163, 166-167, 168-169, 170-171, 174, 176-177, 178-179, 182-183, 205 (7), 206, 207 (11,13), 208 (14,15), 210 (20), 211 (25), 212 (27), 213 (29), 224 (6)
Pedroli, Paolo 85 (7), 204 (1)
Pelli, Maurizio 43, 103 (16)
Ramsey, David 48 (small), 71(small),
Reiser, Micheline 118
Richter, Ralph 132-133
Reduzzi, Alberto 70
Riva Mobili 1920 S.p.A. 218 (41)
Rosselli, Paolo 211 (23)
Savorelli, Pietro 152-153
Scala Archivi Firenze 74,75
Schwiertz, Suzanne 198-199
Spiluttini, Margherita 103 (17)
Seung-Hoon, Yum 217 (37)
Sieburg-Baker, JoAnn 46 (small), 50 (small), 70 (small), 72 (small), 73 (small), 76 (small),
Swiss Confederation - Vincenzo Vela Museo 113 (12)
Toselli, Mario 38 (2)
Uluhogian, Haig 88 (5)
Vitali, Sara 20-21
Wehrli, Claude 212 (28)
Werner, Berthold 79
Williams Paul 15 (8)
Zaghi Alchide, Mantelli Silvia Maria 22 (1)
Zanetta, Alo 24 (7), 28 (12), 42, 101 (10), 102 (13), 126, 204 (2,3), 205 (4),
Zeni, Mauro Lugano 113 (11)

COPYRIGHT INFORMATION
© 2014 Calder Foundation, New York / Artists Rights Society (ARS), New York
© 2014 Artists Rights Society (ARS), New York / ADAGP, Paris / F.L.C.
© 2014 Niki Charitable Art Foundation. All rights reserved / ARS, NY / ADAGP, Paris
© 2014 Alberto Giacometti Estate/Licensed by VAGA and ARS, New York, NY
© 2014 Artists Rights Society (ARS), New York
© The Henry Moore Foundation
© 2014 Artists Rights Society (ARS), New York / SIAE, Rome
© 2014 Artists Rights Society (ARS), New York / SIAE, Rome
© 2014 Artists Rights Society (ARS), New York / SABAM, Brussels
© 2014 Estate of Pablo Picasso / Artists Rights Society (ARS), New York
© 2014 Artists Rights Society (ARS), New York / SIAE, Rome
© 2014 Artists Rights Society (ARS), New York / ADAGP, Paris
© 2014 Frank Lloyd Wright Foundation, Scottsdale, AZ / Artists Rights Society

© 2011/2014 Mondrian/Holtzman Trust c/o HCR International Virginia USA
© 2011/2014 Jabbeke, Belgium, PMCP- Museum Constant Permeke
© 2014 Mario Botta, Mendrisio
© 2014 CDN Centre Dürrenmatt Neuchâtel
© 2014 Max Frisch Archive, Zurich
© 2014 Fondazione Matasci, Tenero
© 2014 Swiss Confederation, Museo Vincenzo Vela, Ligornetto
© *Gonzato, Mostra di Guido Gonzato,* catalogue, Circolo di Cultura Mendrisio –Galleria Nord—Sud di Lugano, Ginnasio Cantonale di Mendrisio arti grafiche A. Salvioni+Co. SA, Bellinzona 1965.
© 2014 Mart Museo d'Arte moderna e contemporanea di Trento e Rovereto
© 2014 Mart, Rovereto - Augusto and Francesca Giovanardi Collection
© 2014 Centro di documentazione "Arturo Benedetti Michelangeli", Brescia
© 2014 Carlo Scarpa, Restauro e allestimento del Museo di Castelvecchio (Restoration and Outfitting of the Castelvecchio Museum) *Statua di Cangrande. Sezione trasversale dell'area di esposizione della Statua di Cangrande in corrispondenza della passerella obliqua,* 1961-64, inv. 31585 r. Verona, Museo di Castelvecchio, Archivio Carlo Scarpa
© 2014 Gabinetto Scientifico Letterario G.P. Vieusseux, Florence
© 2011/2014 Mario Mulas / Piccolo Teatro di Milano-Teatro d'Europa
© 2014 Tullio Pericoli
© 2014 Louis I. Kahn–The Architectural Archives- University of Pennsylvania
© 2014 Courtesy of Western Pennsylvania Conservancy (Frank Lloyd Wright)
© 2014 The Frank Lloyd Wright Foundation, AZ/Art Resource, NY/Scala, Florence
© *Obra Publica* n°7-8 –El Diseno en Ingenierie Civil, Barcelona 1987.

Every effort has been made to contact copyright holders and to ensure that all the information presented is correct. Some of the facts in this volume may be subject to debate or dispute.
If proper copyright acknowledgment has not been made, or for clarifications and corrections, please contact the publishers and we will correct the information in future reprintings, if any.

Silvana Editoriale

Direction
Dario Cimorelli

Art Director
Giacomo Merli

Copy Editor
Clelia Valentina Palmese

Layout
Donatella Ascorti

Production Coordinator
Michela Bramati

Editorial Assistant
Emma Altomare

Iconographic office
Alessandra Olivari, Silvia Sala

Press office
Lidia Masolini, press@silvanaeditoriale.it

All works and text reproduced in this catalogue are protected by copyright owners. No reproduction, transcription, extracts and copies even in digital form are authorized without any previous written permission of the authors and copyright owners.

© 20013 Silvana Editoriale Spa
Cinisello Balsamo, Milano
© Mario Botta, Mendrisio, Switzerland 2013
© Bechtler Museum of Modern Art, Charlotte, NC 2013
© all authors for their texts and photographs

ISBN
978-0-9842896-1-5

Silvana Editoriale Spa

via Margherita De Vizzi, 86
20092 Cinisello Balsamo, Milano
tel. 02 61 83 63 37
fax 02 61 72 464
www.silvanaeditoriale.it

Reproductions, printing by
Arti Grafiche Amilcare Pizzi Spa
Cinisello Balsamo, Milan

Printed
December 2013

Print and Book binding
Print on paper GardaPat 13 KIARA – 135g/m²